Bettina Al-Sadik-Lowinski
Women in Top Management

Bettina Al-Sadik-Lowinski

Women in Top Management

Role Models From Around the Globe Share Their Paths to Success

DE GRUYTER

German edition: Der Aufstieg der Topmanagerinnen – Weibliche Rollenvorbilder aus fünf Wirtschaftsnationen über Erfolgswege zu Spitzenpositionen

Edited by Ian Lawrance, Australia

ISBN 978-3-11-071503-3
e-ISBN (PDF) 978-3-11-071513-2
e-ISBN (EPUB) 978-3-11-071519-4

Library of Congress Control Number: 2020945759

Bibliographic information published by the Deutsche Nationalbibliothek
The Deutsche Nationalbibliothek lists this publication in the Deutsche Nationalbibliografie; detailed bibliographic data are available on the Internet at http://dnb.dnb.de.

© 2021 Walter de Gruyter GmbH, Berlin/Boston
Printing and binding: CPI books GmbH, Leck

www.degruyter.com

For all the female top managers from France, Russia, Japan, China and Germany who have shared their experiences with us.

Contents

1   Forging careers around the world – role models for women in top management from five leading economies —— 1

2   Chinese women: Strong through flexibility and global mindsets —— 17

3   Chinese women in Europe: The conflict between fitting in and meeting their own performance targets —— 81

4   The French women: Intellectual warriors against role conflict —— 96

5   Japanese female executives: Beating the system —— 142

6   German women: Shaping strategists in the middle of men's clubs and motherhood stereotypes —— 171

7   Russian women: Succeeding through intuition and forging opportunities —— 214

8   The ideal female executive: A résumé based on the global analysis —— 246

9   Recommendations for the next generation of female executives —— 253

Annex

Acknowledgments —— 259

Author's note —— 260

Methodology at a glance: The Global Women Career Lab —— 261

Bibliography —— 267

1 Forging careers around the world – role models for women in top management from five leading economies

The subject of women in senior management positions is one which is discussed the world over. There are vocal calls for greater numbers of women in top management positions who can act as female role models. Despite the fact that these days women in many countries have better educational qualifications and are an integral part of the global economy, their low participation at the top of the executive ladder is still a reality. Although the proportion of women in middle management positions has increased worldwide, equality between men and women in senior management has yet to be achieved. A variety of different analyses and views exist as to the causes. The continued dearth of female role models is well-recognized and the number of women in senior corporate positions is still low.

And yet they do exist: women who have managed to work their way to the top of companies all over the world! They are everywhere; fascinating women who, with their extensive knowledge and experience, have the potential to serve as role models for other women and so support them in their careers. Role models like these can also provide an important source of information for other corporate managers as to which factors their companies should consider if they wish to attract qualified women to their senior management ranks. This book is devoted to addressing the following questions: How do women get into top corporate positions in a globalized economy? Which talents and characteristics make them stand out? What steps have they taken to develop themselves? And which recipes for success have worked for top female managers in different countries over the course of their careers and when dealing with the challenges that, typically, only women face? This book will take you on a journey to meet women in top management positions in Russia, China, Japan, France and Germany.

Having more women in management positions delivers greater benefits for companies and more economic power for countries

Why should women around the world continue the struggle to escape middle management? And why is it important for companies to promote qualified women to senior management? A simple Google search on the benefits of gender balance in top corporate positions yields nearly 18 million results. A number of these illustrate key findings for companies aiming to do better at having both women and men in their top positions. A Peterson Institute for International Economics survey of 21,980 listed companies in 91 countries found that a higher proportion of female managers in a company equates to higher profitability. Research by McKinsey and Women Matter

(2012), Catalyst (2016) and Noland at the Petersen Institute (2016) shows that higher proportions of women on company boards delivers higher profits and better overall company performance. These examples alone highlight what other research around the world confirms. Pioneering companies everywhere already have greater numbers of women in top management positions and are convinced that the presence of all genders increases corporate success.

> Women are the world's least used natural resource (CARE)

So having the right mix of women and men in top management positions brings measurable advantages for companies because the strengths of males and females can in this way be blended and targeted to achieve corporate goals. Companies that support women obtain the best managers globally for their top jobs and benefit from the best mix between the experience of male managers and those of successful women. The promotion of talented women signals to employees and customers alike that women are treated equally and provides role models for young female talent. Ultimately, the promotion of qualified women guarantees that all levels of the corporate hierarchy are filled by the best people. The benefits to both national and international companies of promoting female managers effectively is obvious, considering the worldwide shortage of skilled personnel. In the global battle over the coming decades as to who gets the best managers, women will become increasingly important. It makes little sense to neglect half of the world's leadership potential. Women already have enormous economic power as consumers and control a substantial chunk of consumer spending around the world. In many industrial sectors, such as the automotive, tourism and housing markets, it is women who make the main purchasing decisions. Women are thus the largest segment worldwide. There is also ample scientific evidence that companies with an equitable proportion of women in top positions are more competitive and achieve better results. Although these findings have been widely communicated, especially in recent years, there is still a lack of parity between women and men in top management positions worldwide. This means that all over the world companies continue to underutilize the potential for success which comes from mixed gender management teams. There is still no country in the world where women have achieved real equality and the barriers that women have to overcome in management are real. A first step towards more parity might be to identify and better understand the particular barriers to women attaining top positions and to develop strategies for successfully overcoming them. There are various possible approaches to achieving greater numbers of women in top management positions. In addition to the necessary political and legislative measures, an important step would be to assist companies worldwide in their efforts to promote more women.

The other key step would be to support talented women in developing and strengthening their own leadership capabilities with an eye on international job opportunities. Women who want to move up the career ladder and companies that want to promote women need a greater wealth of insight from female role models in order to be able to draw on their experiences and learn from them. This book, with its international research into female top management role models in five leading economies, is intended to help contribute to this goal.

Proportions of women in management positions differ around the world

According to a global study by Grant Thornton (2017, 2018) which has been underway for several years, the average proportion of women in senior management positions worldwide was 25 percent in 2017 and has changed only marginally since 2014. The study focuses on so-called C-suite functions, which comprise the senior management levels. Researchers have observed a worldwide increase in the proportion of women in management and the American researcher Eagly (2007) even goes so far as to say that the proportion of women has skyrocketed in recent years. This, however, only relates to the lower and middle management levels, where the participation of women has increased in most countries. Women remain under-represented at the top of the corporate hierarchy around the world. In many places, "pioneering female CEOs" continue to be celebrated and this highlights the growing stagnation. Even in the second management tier, i.e. corporate executive teams, there are big differences between individual countries when it comes to the presence of women in management and some are more advanced, going by the statistics, than others. The economies considered in this book – China, Russia, Japan, France and Germany – represent the upper, middle and lower portions of the global rankings for numbers of women in managerial positions. According to the data presented in the following chapters, Russia and China are at the top of this ranking, France occupies the upper middle ground and Germany and Japan are at the lower end of the scale of female participation in senior management among leading economies. A glance at the world map shows that not many of the leading industrial nations are frontrunners, but that smaller countries such as Poland, Lithuania and Georgia, and also some Asian countries such as the Philippines, are particularly strong in this area. Nevertheless, statistics are just numbers which, depending on the initial conditions and the interpretation given, can be presented in different ways. But one thing seems certain. Progress in lower and middle management has been remarkable when one considers that historically women have only been involved in management roles since the mid-twentieth century. In the top echelons, companies around the world continue to fare badly. Or is it that women themselves in the various countries give up their careers? This book covers that aspect too.

Various political measures, such as quotas for supervisory boards in Germany and France, are hotly debated but have shown promising results, especially recently. At the Global World Women Forum in Paris in 2019, the success of quotas was publicized and their approval was sought from all the women present. Women in France and Germany prefer not to get their jobs because of quotas, but to be at the top through their own achievements. Women who have already made it, in particular, often refuse to accept quotas as a means to an end. In China and Russia there are no quotas for women in companies, but there are other measures that tend to increase female participation. And in Japan, the response to the continuing logjam has been for the government to make clear statements of intent, combined with the setting of targets. It is also interesting to note in this context that greater female representation in top political posts does not automatically lead to more women in top business roles. An example of this is Germany, where, despite having a female Chancellor, little has improved at the industrial helm over the past 15 years.

Companies and women themselves would benefit from more research into role models of women in international management

Looking at the available research on women in senior management, it is striking that career research in the field of management has for a long time focused exclusively on the experiences of men. One reason for this is surely the fact that the numbers of women in top management worldwide have historically been limited. Management and career research that focuses exclusively on women has only been around for a few years. Well into the 1990s, studies on women in management positions were, according to Powell (2011), still based on a male perspective. To this day, academics continue to debate whether specific theories and concepts are needed for examining women's careers against the backdrop of their own experiences and challenges, or whether the concepts developed on the basis of male patterns of experience should continue to be applied to women. More and more international researchers, such as O'Neil (2013) and Lepine (1992), are developing women-specific approaches because they believe that women's careers follow different patterns than those of men. Other researchers argue that women are already exhibiting career patterns reflecting changes that will occur in the labor market in the near future. The researcher Rump (2017) describes how growing globalization, changes brought about by the digitalization of entire industrial sectors, artificial intelligence, the aging of entire populations and ecological issues, will all influence and continue to change, if not completely reshape, corporate careers. Global crises such as the COVID-19 pandemic show how fragile traditional work patterns can be. Even if conventional, hierarchically structured careers still predominate in many companies around the world today, career patterns other than the purely traditional ones can already be observed among women. This is reflected in the career paths of the high-flying women surveyed here. International research on women in top management positions is rare compared to within-country studies. While several researchers have compared the situations of women in management between, for example, two countries, multinational observations are rare, partly due to the complexities of data collection.

The Global Women Career Lab: A research-based analysis of female role models in five leading economies

For the research-based, empirical study on which the book is based, over 110 top female executives from five countries were interviewed in qualitative, in-depth interviews. What is distinctive about the findings in this book is that we hear from the top women managers themselves. Original quotes provide very personal insights into their experiences, approaches and mindsets. The women in China, Japan, Russia were interviewed and quoted in English. Quotes from the women interviewed in Germany and France have been translated into English, as needed. When signing up for the research, the women interviewed were aware that the primary goal was to support other women.

All of the women interviewed here are employed as executives in leading positions in mainly international companies and were selected through a process based on theoretical sampling. The data collected forms the cornerstone of one of the most extensive research projects in the world involving women in senior management positions, the Global Women Career Lab. Evaluation and analysis of the empirical data was carried out using a scientific approach with the help of qualitative content analysis and parts of the project formed a dissertation supervised by the University of Burgundy in France. So why China, Russia, Japan, France and Germany? The aim was to survey successful women in leading economies. The selection was also influenced by the fact that in those countries the author had access to women suitable for the study and, with the exception of Russia, had lived and worked in all the countries herself.

Women's careers exist in the area of tension between society's view of what roles women should play, the opportunities for women in companies and the goals and constraints of the women themselves. A variety of contextual factors influence the progression of a female manager's career. Researchers face the challenge of doing justice to the complexity of women's careers while taking these various influences into account. The analysis in the Global Women Career Lab is based on a framework called the FemCareer-Model (Al-Sadik 2017, see also annex) in which important determinants of women's careers are encapsulated. The focus is on external influences on women's careers and the individual factors that the female managers describe, in other words, the career profiles and paths of the women is affected by the various determinants. The context of the home countries and cultures is central to all areas of the model described in this book. The model is based on, and supported by, current international research which has been used to place the interviewed women's experiences into perspective. The model was the guiding principle for the interviews with the top female managers as well as for the evaluation and analysis, and serves as a sort of road map for the book. All 110 women were interviewed using a set of guidelines based on the model, in other words, the interpretation and results pertaining to the careers of women in China, Russia, Japan, France and Germany were viewed through the lens of the model parameters.

The country chapters: Information and learnings from the experiences of women in top management across different cultures

Within the country chapters the insights gained from the interviews, which were conducted according to the FemCareer-Model as described, are organized into sections as follows:
- Socio-cultural and political conditions in the country and the proportion of women in senior management positions
- Characterization of the female senior managers interviewed
- Career strategies of the women in the given country
- Particular preconditions which women in the given country need if they are to reach a top management position
- Factors promoting the careers of women in senior management
- Factors which hold back the careers of senior women managers and how they handled them
- Any outstanding questions

This overview section provides a brief chapter-spanning summary of what the research findings tell us so far about these factors. Readers can switch between chapters or read the book in sequence. At the beginning of each chapter there is a depiction of the varying socio-cultural and political contexts in which the women executives find themselves. The focus varies from country to country so as to highlight the differences and this provides the basis for subsequent analysis. For China and Russia, for example, the restructuring of the economic system and its effects on women's careers are presented. Germany's cultural heritage and the partition and reunification of the country provide a unique framework for the development of women's participation at senior management level. France is often praised for its leading, vanguard status concerning gender equality in Europe. And the difficulties faced by women in Japan are described as they attempt to operate within the country's traditional employment model.

The senior women managers' own assessments of the perceived degree of gender equality in their country are recorded on a ten-point scale and this serves to illustrate their experiences in the context of the sometimes contradictory figures published in their respective countries. The executive women were asked, from their individual experience and perspective, how they assess the gender situation in their country when it comes to a management career. The book thus serves as a comparison with the published data on the participation of women in management positions, albeit qualitative. It is interesting to note that in some circumstances, even in Japan – the country with the lowest proportion of women in senior management positions – high ranking female managers give top scores. Contrary to the high scores reported in numerous publications, Russia falls short of expectations. And Germany and France are not as drastically dissimilar in their scores as one might assume if looking at them from a German perspective.

> L. General Manager, France: I would probably put France on five. To be honest, I think there is gender equality up to middle management, so I think middle management is probably eight. The top management falls to three or now you could say two. I think the average is five.

Senior women executives operate in very diverse labor markets, some of which have undergone major upheavals in the course of their careers, which average 25–30 years. Examples given here are the opening up of China to the world market with the many opportunities that offered women, the transformation of the former Soviet Union, which women describe as resulting in a U-shaped curve with regard to opportunities for women in senior management, and the question of whether it is only in German culture that the role of the mother is so deeply rooted and the image of the uncaring mother so prevalent. The quotations cited offer interesting insights into the working worlds of women in these countries.

> I., Country Manager, Russia: It is very ambivalent. On the one hand, a deeply rooted genetic memory in our country, which puts men first. I know women who are the big boss and when they come home, they only set the table. On the other hand, if we are looking for suitable candidates, we will not find a single man who is good enough. Yes, we have a lot of women in senior positions because we do better. If a woman really wants it, she can achieve anything.

The chapter on "Career Strategies" provides insights into the career profiles and trajectories of top women managers in the given countries and their main approaches to advancement. The exact paths taken by the women provide information as to their starting positions, promotions, future career ambitions and decisions to change jobs. Concealed behind these are issues such as work–life balance and geographical mobility, which represent a challenge for many women. Both external and personal factors have an impact on career decisions and career strategies. They both affect the career paths of women from different countries to a greater or lesser extent. A substantial part of the book is devoted to the question of "what criteria women in top management positions fulfil". In this model, these are the factors which are unique to the study participants, and they are rooted in their own individual characteristics and personality traits.

Individual career prerequisites are also defined here as the family of origin, educational background, management capabilities and personality traits that are of relevance to a senior female management career. A further significant influencing factor is a woman's particular ability to lead, along with her associated management style.

A number of research studies, for example those of Bourdieu (1982), show that family background can have an impact on a senior manager's later career path. The professions of the parents and especially of the mother appear to influence women in their later careers. European and purely German language research by Hartmann (2002) also shows a connection between social class and career. The women's families of origin and formative familial role models point to fundamental differences between women across the five cultures. While in China full-time work has been the norm down several generations of mothers and grandmothers, in France, Japan and Germany it is the exception. In those countries, women have used strong fathers as their role models. In the individual country chapters, women describe their upbringing and how their family backgrounds influenced their later corporate careers.

> M.M., President, China: I was born in Beijing and my parents were members of the government, but all of this was razed during the Cultural Revolution, so we children had to go to the country side immediately. I was sent far north and was there for ten years... yes, that was difficult. Of all those sent to the country, the parents were in a higher position. We were a total of twelve girls, someone cried every day. I knew by nature that crying doesn't help and you have to watch what you can do instead. After less than a year I was the head of the group.

> A., Director, China: My father is an accountant and my mother was the head of a company. Very active. She used to be a factory manager or company manager. She is always active as a female manager. She is very active. My father is not that ambitious.

Previous scientific studies by Tharenou (1994) and Judge (2004) have examined what direct share of career success can be ascribed purely to education. If we look at management studies, it is noticeable that men still seem to benefit more from a high level of education than women do, and this is directly reflected in their salaries. It is indisputable that graduation from a prestigious university, length and level of study, and semesters abroad, all positively affect subsequent career opportunities. In many of the countries, women are currently overtaking men in terms of university qualifications and marks attained. However, there are areas – in the so-called STEM subjects – in which women are still under-represented. The analysis shows that a proportion of Chinese, German and Russian women in particular do have a technical qualification, but the majority of the women surveyed have a language training background with additional management qualifications. In France, attendance at one of the elite national universities, the Grandes écoles, plays a major role.

The analysis of women's management skills was based on criteria collated by the German researcher Regnet (2017) using the findings of the IBM Global Human Capital Study 2008 of 400 companies worldwide. The resulting profile of prerequisites for executives includes the following factors: ability to motivate, willingness to learn and employability, teamwork, diversification management, communication skills and conflict management, change management, systematic and holistic thinking, health and the ability to work under stress, ability to communicate a vision, intercultural leadership skills.

All the executive women interviewed for this book meet these prerequisites in large measures, but their descriptions of themselves tend to vary in terms of which skills are foremost. For example, there is one country in particular where the women give priority to their intercultural skills. In two other countries, health and the ability to work under stress tend to be somewhat more important. And there is one area where almost all women in the various countries say that they have some catching up to do, compared to their male colleagues – the capacity of being visionary.

> M., President, Japan: We are exceptions. Do you understand? Most women in Japan don't even think that they could become managers. I even mean the lower and middle levels. It is not yet available as a possibility in their worldview. The framework conditions for equality? Of course, we have them in Japan. It depends on how our working world is organized. That makes it much more difficult for women. But I have never seen any limits for myself.

In addition to education and management skills, personality is of major importance for executives when it comes to the traditional corporate career. The scientific studies in this area are manifold. In general, scientists understand personality in this context as having to do with certain characteristics, attitudes and values related to the professional environment. Career direction and underlying motivations among other things are, according to Mayrhofer (2005), central aspects of a successful career in management. Individual values, motives and concrete goals with regard to one's career are what determine career direction. Put simply, it is a question of whether, and to what extent, a woman aspires to leadership responsibility in the first place and to what extent there are cultural differences when it comes to how strong their desire is to move up into top management. The question of whether they have "the desire to pursue a career up to senior management level" is central here. The answer to this, as is evident from the numerous interviews with highly committed women around the world, is of particular relevance to their resulting career strategy and ultimate goals given the different role expectations that are placed specifically on women. Without this, women run the risk of satisfying all the role expectations but failing to find the right balance in their own lives.

> K., Board Member, Germany: Men tend to think more about what they want. Women often don't dare. You have to "hunt them to hunt".

> E., General Manager, France: Equality is a big issue. We are quite good, but we are still far from reaching our goal. We still have a lot of encrusted traditions, men's clubs. And women often see themselves in competition with each other. I think it's a lot about the individual woman. And how much she really wants to make a career. Do not get me wrong. Every woman can make her choices. But you cannot have it all. Men neither. It depends on what you want and how much you want it.

Researchers typically discuss to what extent the career motivations of women and men differ, but research on cultural differences between women regarding career motivation barely exists. According to most studies, the importance and value of work dominate for women just as much as they do for men. Motivations for pursuing a career have also been considered from a cultural perspective. For example, one might ask whether a German top female manager would describe a different motivation for her career than a Russian or Japanese counterpart. The best known concepts for describing management-relevant aspects of personality are the so-called "Big Five" from Cartell, "Leadership motive pattern" (LMP) from McClellands (1982) and Miners' (1991) "Role motivation" theories. In the German-speaking world, Hossiep's (2003) "Business Focused Inventory of Personality" (BIP) is based on a definition of personality that considers the behavioral traits, motivational factors and values of a person. Nine of the dimensions considered in the BIP contribute directly to an executive's career success. In the interview analysis, the women's self-descriptions were grouped and categorized according to the relevant BIP dimensions, using special codes for each country, and analyzed to identify any differences between the women. It was apparent the women's professional focus was differentiated by performance and leadership motivation, along with the motivation to influence and shape processes. Performance motivation describes how pronounced a manager's own need for superior performance is. Women who are highly motivated to shape their own work have a strong desire to intervene and, for example, to remedy grievances and implement their own ideas. Women who are highly motivated to lead have a strong desire to take on leadership responsibilities, persuade employees in an effective manner and have a motivating and inspiring effect on others. In terms of professional conduct, factors such as flexibility, conscientiousness, i.e. a degree of perfectionism, and a focus on action, i.e. goal orientation and a readiness to make decisions, are particularly important for advancement to a higher management position. Flexibility here refers to whether a female executive can adjust well to new situations, cope with uncertainty and rapidly adapt methods and procedures to changing conditions.

Management responsibility in international companies brings with it particular physical demands on women. Long hours, the need to work across different time zones and international business trips are just a few of the demands that accompany leadership responsibility. In addition, women often face greater challenges than men because of the demands of their other roles outside of work. Women perform – and this too has been scientifically studied on many occasions – a higher proportion of the parenting and household duties in addition to their professional roles. Emotional stability, resilience and self-confidence are the factors that characterize the psychological make-up of female executives. Managers' social competency is a particularly widely aired issue and a central theme in many management seminars. It is frequently asserted that female managers have particular strengths in this area. They are team-oriented, sensitive to the needs of others, sociable and assertive. Is there such a thing as a global female leadership style? Or is it the case, as with men, that context determines leadership style? The scientific literature from Eagly

(2007), Rosner (1990) and Powell (2011), for example, distinguishes between employee-oriented and goal-oriented leadership, or between transformational and transactional leadership. Transactional leadership assigns clear roles to employees and applies its power of authority, combining reward and punishment to achieve goals. In the literature, women are attributed with a tendency towards transformational leadership, which uses motivation, personal relationships and inspiration to spur employees on to higher performance. Women also more often choose a democratic leadership style where employees are involved in decision making. Ayman and Korabik (2010) report that where women display a more purely goal-oriented and transactional, authoritarian leadership, this more often leads to a negative evaluation of their abilities. The woman's cultural environment determines whether an authoritarian or democratic approach is more likely to be accepted within the company. Russian and Chinese women, for example, report that they try to use the best of each style. Women working in multinational companies in particular have a very good mastery of the range of options and say, with a wink, that they can do both. In Germany, on the other hand, there are hardly any references in the narratives to authoritarian leadership. Many of the Russian women describe finding a leadership style as their greatest challenge, not least against the backdrop of the sometimes-ambivalent expectations towards women in the wider environment.

> N., CEO, Russia: I think I'm very nice, but I'm very hard. I understand the business from both sides from the front office and back office and very often people from the front office can fool their colleagues from the back office. Therefore, I can allow myself to get harder because I understand all business processes in sales. I also have very, very good technical training. I believe that the main quality of a good CEO is making decisions and taking responsibility, and I know I can. I can also inspire the team and this is also the main quality for the CEO.

The career-furthering factors and inhibiting influences on the careers of women vary from country to country. Particularly important for learning from the experiences of these role models is not only what factors predominate in the particular country, but above all how the senior women managers surveyed deal with them. Additionally, the effects of some of the factors are uncertain, since they cannot be clearly identified within the groups surveyed as being positive or negative in terms of their impact on professional success.

The following important determinants were examined for each country:
- The role of the husband
- The influence of motherhood
- Support in the form of mentoring, networking and coaching
- The existence of a glass ceiling
- The image of career women in the local culture
- Discrimination against women

Global research findings concerning these determinants are many and varied, and will only be outlined here.

In relation to family circumstances, this book explores the effect of the partners on the careers that the women describe. Are the women in dual-career relationships, are the partners taking a back seat or is it the case, even, that the traditional role models are reversed? Insufficient or non-existent support from the partner is described in the research of Halpern (2008) as being one of the greatest challenges with regard to women's careers. This includes the equal distribution of childcare and household tasks, but also the emotional attitude of spouses towards their wives' careers. So what do women have to say about their partners' roles? Are there fundamental differences between Paris, Moscow, Tokyo, Berlin and Shanghai in terms of support or lack of it? One might be tempted by the accounts to issue recommendations to young women as to how to choose a partner, and the women managers interviewed here in fact do so quite openly. This important topic is examined in more detail in the subsections.

> M., President, Japan: He is really a supporter. I think he's a unique Japanese man. He wanted me to work. He doesn't like a housewife. He always said that housewives stay at home and always complain, and his mother was also a working woman, so he wanted me to work, and it may be very important to him that I work, which, I think, is quite unique. He doesn't do most of the housework. He doesn't do anything when I'm home, but he's really good at taking care of my children. He doesn't actually prepare food. He doesn't do a lot of the housework, but he likes to look after my children. If forced, he can do housework at the minimum level.

The influence of motherhood on a woman's career has been studied extensively and the term "motherhood penalty" can be found in many international scientific publications like in the work of Budig (2012). The term refers to the fact that mothers suffer a loss of salary and are in many societies regarded as less qualified. The overall anticipation that a woman will become a mother is a barrier to recruitment and promotion. Companies fear financial losses due to maternity leave and prefer male applicants. So mothers do seem to have a harder time building a career in management than both men and non-mothers, and need special strategies if they are to successfully negotiate the balancing act between career and child. Do other perspectives exist in other cultures? In Germany in particular, female managers often forego having children, and the proportion of childless female executives is, according to Holst (2013), over 74 percent. In China, the picture is diametrically opposite, possibly due to the fact that mothers who are successful in their careers conform to the ideal image of womanhood. This is the picture that emerges from a major survey of more than 2,000 respondents conducted by *China Daily* in 2001. The majority of the women researched for this book have children and have successfully negotiated the balancing act between childrearing and career, sometimes with as many as three or four children in countries such as France. The German researcher Regnet (2017) finds that it takes a man's involvement in childcare and daily housework for the woman to become more involved in her career. Are there any perspectives from the women in the countries we have studied? The experiences of the study participants offer women a variety of ways of thinking about the question of children and careers.

> M., Chairman of the Supervisory Board, Germany: Child and career? Still a tightrope walk. I once had an employee with me who cried when she told me that she was now pregnant. I will never forget that. It is a real brake in many companies. In my generation it was still a total exception for women with children to reach the top. I don't think it really works – career and children...
>
> R., Member of the executive board, China: These four years I separated from my husband, my husband was in Hong Kong, flew around the world, my son was in New York. My parents are in Shanghai. When we left my daughter was so young, only seven years old. I did it because I believe in diversity. Bettina, you have to mention that, I am a strong promoter of diversity. I hired my sister and her husband to help me in Germany. With the child and with driving. That was a huge financial burden. I was firmly convinced that I was a role model and gave up my pleasant life in Shanghai. There you have a driver, you have a nanny 24 hours a day. And then go to Germany without all that.

Mentoring, networking and executive coaching for women are three more important aspects of relevance to companies wishing to further the promotion of qualified women. Ragins (1997) and Burke (1990) describe that if mentoring is important in a man's career, in a woman's it would appear to be essential. Since the barriers to women in senior management are many and varied, they benefit from mentoring by more experienced executives when seeking to overcome them. The illustrations in this book depict the strategies that women develop with regard to their mentors and to what extent they do so actively or passively. Chinese women, for example, actively develop "mutually beneficial alliances" in which mentor and mentee both benefit from each other. In some cases, the mentoring relationships that develop are so strong that a woman's career path becomes intertwined with that of the mentor. Russian women talk about the difficulties associated with mentoring, which differs from that of men because of concerns about bullying and its so-called "bad reputation" often set limits on the extent to which mentoring is used. In conjunction with this, the topic of sponsorship will be discussed, which in contrast to mentoring is more about career advancement and less about building up expertise. German women in particular report very positive experiences of executive coaching at various stages in their careers and when dealing with various challenges. Special coaching for women managers makes sense because as mentioned above, their situation is more complex than that of men. In fact, coaching for women in management should be as natural as going to the hairdresser, according to one of the women interviewed.

> I., General Manager, France: Women have not always understood the importance of networking and networks. Ask them if they are on networks or networks. And insist because women don't understand the importance of grouping. We also have to insist that women stand together to help each other, just like men. Sometimes women compete with each other, and that's a shame. So these are issues that should be addressed with women so that they understand the interest of a network that is mutual help and not to compete with each other. I do a lot

of things. I organize events with women that I invite at home. There are years when I have three dinners with twenty people at home in the summer. I am very involved in associations.

Men are known to support each other through strong networks. In the literature one can read about so-called "old boys' networks" such as in Rastetter's (2012) work, for example. Among women, networks are still relatively new and are mostly limited to exchange of information and knowledge gain. However, it can be observed, especially among French women – where there are reportedly over 500 women's networks nationwide – as well as among German women, that women's networks are springing up everywhere. Women are striving to build up structures like those of their male colleagues, where the focus is on mutual career support. What these networks lack are sufficient role models in high corporate positions, as well as the art of targeted give and take. French women report observing men in their country deliberately using private and professional networks to achieve their goals. And they are now learning from them. In China, networking does not really come up in the interviews, because it reaches deep into the culture of the country and is thus woven into everyday life. But where different cultures collide, in multinational companies, it takes on a new relevance. Despite these women's networks, the barriers women experience are those between themselves. The lack of solidarity among women is an area currently being vigorously debated in France, and one that is particularly evident in the French interviews. At issue here is the idea that women in higher positions erect career barriers for other women. In the American research literature this phenomenon is termed "Queen Bee Syndrome". At an event in Paris on International Women's Day, a plea was made for a greater sense of understanding for these women, who have had to fight hard to be pioneers in a male domain. The many reports by women from all five countries of the female colleagues they have supported, and reports from strong women's networks – such as GenCEO in Germany – stand in direct contrast to this.

> M., President, Japan: It is everywhere in the hiring and promotion system because all of these systems are operated by current managers who are men. Glass ceiling exists in the male mind. I don't think they recognize it as a bias, but there is an invisible bias in their mind. They don't know a female manager. At the entry level, there are already some cases in which female students do better in the interview and have better academic results. At the entry level, I think women have no trouble now.

The existence of a glass ceiling can prove to be a career obstacle for women. Career paths can be smooth for female managers or they can terminate at barriers that only women face. The phenomenon of the "glass ceiling", much-discussed in the scientific arena, attempts to answer the question of why women are represented worldwide in lower and middle management, but only a few rise to the absolute top. An invisible ceiling is used as a way of explaining why women, more so than men, find their paths blocked. According to this notion, one of the reasons is that women are excluded from the circles of power. Stereotypical behavioral expectations, informal organizational structures that exclude women, male-only networks and informal rites are further aspects that characterize the glass ceiling and which have been investigated by various researchers. According to Ragins (1997), the existence of a glass ceiling is confirmed by around 92 percent of executive women in the USA. Ganrose (2007) concludes from her research on Chinese women in Singapore that a glass ceiling does not exist in a general way for all women, but is a function of the type of organization. In Germany, Funken (2015) interviewed successful career women who, despite a high level of commitment to their work and foregoing having children, do not get beyond middle management. These women report being undervalued, bullied and being excluded from promotion. What do the women interviewed as part of the Global Women Career Labs think about the glass ceiling in their countries? Women in China are skeptical whether it still exists in the country's economic metropolises. Women in France and Germany are certain that it exists and that it is located somewhere below the top of the corporate hierarchy. In Japan, on the other hand, it starts much lower.

> A., CEO, France: It still exists. And I don't know what to do to make it explode because we've been talking about it for decades. There is always a glass ceiling. There is always a moment when young women have children, so they adopt a different rhythm. The explanation of the men for the glass ceiling is that women then dedicate themselves to their children. But on the other hand, I know women who are top managers and had 4 children, and that didn't stop them. So the apology with the kids doesn't work for me. It is the will for career that counts. I think that men don't strive to promote women, that's for sure. And on the other hand, women do not manage to break through, they do not give themselves the opportunity to break through.

> K., Head of HR, Japan: Man, I thought, I could lead this team or organization better, why is he doing it that way, I don't think it's good, we should do it differently. I looked at my boss and thought I could do it better, I could run the department better. Money is secondary to me.

The image of the female executive arises in relation to the question of the general social acceptance of women in higher management. Cultural stereotypes are often cited as the reason why women are still under-represented in senior management compared to men. Probably the best known studies on the image of the female executive are those published by Schein. She researched the existence of what she called the "Think manager – think male" phenomenon across different countries since 1970. Early research pointed to gender stereotyping as one of the reasons for the under-representation of women in high management positions. As a consequence, men considered women in the corporate environment to be generally less qualified and therefore rarely promoted them. The characteristics necessary for success in management were those attributed to men. The women interviewed here were asked to describe how they would assess their image as top managers in their countries. The descriptions are striking and range from "highly respected" to "bitch". The chapters which follow will examine which image predominates in which country.

> N., CEO, Russia: I already told you that women in Russia have to be the best – in the household, with raising children and, of course, with the Beauty Queens. And we have these stereotypes – if we look good, we're too stupid for upper management. If she's ugly, it also does not work. Well.

Executive presence and the importance of a female executive's appearance were topics in many of the interviews and were especially prominent in those of many of the French and Russian women. The literature describes, for example, how Russian women seek to develop their feminine identity as women leaders, blending feminine looks and attractiveness with their roles as leaders. In France, too, women like to emphasize femininity as part of their professional leadership role and speak animatedly on this point. The French women describe country-specific codes, which to a large extent are reflected in external appearance, including language, posture and manners. Chinese women do not have a homogeneous view on the subject, but they do attach a different importance to it. German women tend to be rather pragmatic in their approach to the subject and aim primarily at a professional effect which is then only occasionally – and deliberately – enhanced in a controlled way.

Does the ideal female top manager exist?

The factors influencing the career paths of the 110 top female managers outlined here will be analyzed by country, illustrated with numerous quotations from the journey around the five nations. Differences between women in a cultural group are highlighted. The book closes with the question of the ideal typical top manager. What commonalities can all women from the five countries depict as knowledge gain for other women and interested men?

The experiences of the women in the Global Women Career Labs offer interested readers a wealth of knowledge about female careers and leadership in various cultural contexts. This book is primarily aimed at women with an interest in the subject. Interested men will also gain an array of insights that they can then put to use in their roles as leaders of female employees to help them advance their careers. In addition, experts from companies that want to blend male and female skills in order to solve future business challenges can benefit from the accounts given here. In view of the global shifts in labor markets and the need to work together to shape the future, the time has come to listen to female role models.

2 Chinese women: Strong through flexibility and global mindsets

Chinese top managers are the largest group of women interviewed in this international research. Their career experiences provide insights into the career paths of successful Chinese female executives who pursue their goals with high flexibility, are opportunity-oriented and with a deep intercultural ability. The career experiences of these fascinating role models are analyzed against the background of cultural norms, external influences and the leadership skills of women themselves.

Framework towards equal opportunities

Two main aspects of the situation faced by women in China can be found in current literature. The country is culturally very rich and multi-layered and the socio-cultural framework for women and their careers fluctuates between very opposing influences. For example, the women of the Mosuo ethnic group, one of the world's rare quasi-matriarchal cultures, are just as much part of the cultural influence as Confucian traditions. The Confucian traditions, which make up a large part of China's cultural background, are reported far more frequently in scientific literature in connection with the role of women. This is in contrast to a policy aimed at promoting equality in many areas.

Chinese women between traditions and political equality

The well-known feminist and gender studies scholar Li (2000) describes the May Fourth Movement, which emerged from protests against China's political and economic system in the period from 1910 to 1920, as the country's first feminist movement. It has been possible to observe specific positive effects on equality of opportunity in China since the founding of the People's Republic of China in 1949. The state played, according to Cooke (2012), a leading part in establishing greater equality by dismantling the feudal system that it is generally agreed oppressed women. Various steps were taken to achieve this goal, involving legislative, administrative and economic mechanisms. Mao Zedong's speech with the much-quoted phrase *"Women can hold half the sky"* became the expression of a new equality movement, and is characteristic of the determination with which the government proclaimed this goal.

At the legislative level, the state introduced Article 6, which established the basis for improving women's status: *"Women shall enjoy equal rights with men in political, economic, educational and social life."* The two most important laws were passed in 1950: The Land Reform Law and the New Marriage Law, which inter alia gave women the right to divorce. This was part of a plan intended to bring more women into employment. Subsequently, the employment rate of Chinese women rose sharply. The state continued to introduce regulations and laws that established new rights for women or protected existing ones, with the aim of creating equality of opportunities. The media also disseminated the idea of equal opportunities. Examples of measures that were introduced include maternity leave, quotas for women's jobs and state planning of posts for female workers near their husbands during the period from the 1950s to the 1970s. The number of nurseries and crèches in rural regions multiplied during this time. A high, almost equal proportion of women in employment was achieved, and this was maintained even during the chaotic years of the Cultural Revolution from 1966 until 1976. According to feminist theorists, women's issues were masculinized during the period of the Cultural Revolution, and women were treated as identical to men despite often having different life circumstances. This masculinization went against their actual interests. The slogan *"Whatever men can do, women can do too"* and uniform clothing for men and women were, according to Wang Zheng (1997), an expression of the views that prevailed at that time. For today's China, one can say that the double employment model is a socially accepted norm. The high proportion of women in employment, which far outstrips other industrialized nations in the West and the global average, can be seen as the result of the last 50 years of action by the state. Today, the model of dual employment, where both partners work, is the socially accepted norm in China. The researchers Korabik (1994) and Ayman (2010) discuss to what extent laws and regulations are applied in practice. Authors like Stockman (1995) see more equality of opportunity in China than in Western nations and describe a continuous decrease in inequality since the establishment of the current Communist government in the mid-1980s: *"Chinese institutions are seen to have a higher level of gender equality than Japan, the UK and the USA, with permanent full-time work being the norm for all adults and a high degree of egalitarianism in family roles."* Opposing positions point to the underrepresentation of women in senior government roles and conclude, inter alia, that women in China still do not have as much power as men.

> "Gender equality is an important part of corporate social responsibility and we count on organizations to take the lead and give talented female staff the support and career opportunities they deserve",

remarked Xu Feng, chair of the Shanghai Women's Federation, at the Shanghai International Forum for Women's Development in October 2014. Accordingly, gender equality remains an ongoing concern for China, just as it does for the rest of the world.

China's opening to the world market: Women's careers between two economic systems

The interviewed women's careers in management took place against the background of China's economic development, making it a central external determinant. In the following, an outline is presented of the key changes that provided the framework for the interviewees' career development over time. The history of China's economy is unique, transforming from a socialist planned economy to a market system under the leadership of the Communist Party. The transformation of China's economy into a social market economy and the ensuing liberalization have restricted the state's influence on issues of equality. The unemployment rate rose with the transition from a planned to a social market economy. Women were especially disadvantaged, since proportionally many of them lost their employment and they found it harder to find new jobs. The success of such a transformation and hence also economic development depend, inter alia, on how ready executives are for the challenge posed by these changes. In general, it can be said that China's reforms and liberalization have accelerated economic growth and created many jobs and career opportunities for women. Until the start of the reform movements in the late 1970s, the Chinese economy was in effect completely isolated from the global economy. For thirty years, the state had given the Ministry of Foreign Trade a monopoly on foreign trade and foreign currency, preventing Chinese businesses and consumers from having direct contact with the global market.

The labor market reforms began by targeting the so-called "iron rice bowl" system (*tie fanwan*), in which jobs were guaranteed for life. The system had been enacted in the 1950s to protect agricultural workers, but was soon extended to all urban workers too. Until 1998, the state assigned employees to state-owned or collectively owned enterprises, SOEs or COEs, by quota. Working life in China had been structured around work unit systems known as *danweis*. Workers were employed for life, and their unit was responsible for providing social security services. One peculiarity in China was that jobs could be inherited (*dingti*). The members of the *danweis* enjoyed job security and various benefits such as guaranteed housing, health cover and childcare. It was almost impossible to switch units, and only with the approval of one's superiors. The *danwei* that a worker was assigned to was responsible for the *hukou* household registration system, which was introduced in 1958 to regulate and prevent migration within China. The aim was to ensure social order. A person needed official permission for a change of residence. In the 1980s and 1990s, a series of regulations and measures was introduced that helped to create a labor market.

The year 1978 represents a historic turning point in China's economic history. It marked the start of a radical new direction for economic policy and the gradual integration of the country into the global economy. The three core principles of the new strategic direction are a socialist market economy, opening-up to the outside world and continued leadership by the Communist Party. The goals of the reforms have gradually expanded in scope over the course of time. What started out as an attempt to repair defective areas of the previously dominant planned economy led to market-based reform elements being incorporated into the creation of a planned commodity economy and eventually, in 1992, to the decision to develop a new market system: the socialist market economy. In the early 1990s, the Chinese were given the right to choose their own jobs for the first time. To do so, they had to reach an agreement with their employer to terminate their existing contract, though to begin with not all employers were willing to do this. Where previously seniority and political loyalty had been the things that really counted on the labor market, from this point forward qualifications and motivation also became competitive factors. Women in particular took advantage of the transformation in the labor market and actively moved from secure, state-run jobs to the new, yet unknown world of multinational companies.

China's policy of opening up to the world formally culminated in 2001, when the People's Republic of China joined the WTO. As a condition of membership, the government agreed to a compulsory program of further economic liberalization measures. Since then, China has been one of the world's leading recipients of foreign direct investment, taking over the top spot from the USA for the first time in 2002. China has developed into one of the leading economies in the world and continues to expand its economy in cooperation with other countries. Women play an important role in various areas.

Proportion of women in senior management roles in China

Studies on the proportion of women in management often contain contradictory data and interpretations. Different data sources show different proportions of women in senior management, both globally and in China. This is due to different definitions of what is meant by "management role" or "senior management".

The various figures show that in international comparison, China has a very high proportion of women in senior management. According to Catalyst (2016) in 2014, 64 percent of women were in the Chinese labor force compared to 78 percent of the men. Although the number has gone down since 2010, when it stood at 74 percent, in worldwide comparison Chinese women still have a very high employment rate. The World Economic Forum reported in 2010 that over 50 percent of all professional entry level positions in China are held by women. In studies on the proportion of women in senior management roles, on the other hand, China is one of the world leaders. Thornton calculates a proportion of 39 percent for 2013, which places China at the top of the world rankings for that year alongside Russia and certain Baltic states. The study shows an average 38 percent proportion of women in senior management roles at companies over the last eight years. This picture is confirmed by a study carried out by Hays (1998) in 2015, according to which the proportion of women in senior management roles in China is 36 percent, compared with an Asian average of 29 percent. A study by McKinsey in 2012 shows a proportion of only 8 percent women on boards and 9 percent women on executive committees, which was below the figures for Europe and the USA. Other figures show a 21 percent proportion of women on Chinese boards compared with a global average of 19 percent. However, the proportion of women at the very highest executive level, CEOs, is like in all countries worldwide, lower compared to men. The high proportion of women in China is found in the second executive level directly below the CEO and in management team positions, which here include Chief Financial Officer with a proportion of 81 percent women, and Human Resource Directors being 61 percent women. The different data shows the following: China is amongst the leading countries concerning women's participation in senior management functions. However, the participation of women as CEO is significantly lower. The women in this book represent both, the highest corporate level and the other C-suite functions.

The Chinese female executives in this research

Chinese women in leadership positions are the largest group from the five countries examined in the international research of the Global Women Career Lab. This group covers a wide age range. It shows the career paths of women who started their careers before the opening up of the Chinese economy to the world market and had no experience with the mechanisms of careers in this new world. It also covers the career developments of the younger women who started work in a country where free choice of one's own career path has been in place for a long time. The majority of women started in the transition phase of the Chinese economy, which can be seen as an adjustment phase to the independent job search.

Most of the 35 women in the research were aged between 36 and 45 at the time of the interviews. Around 14 percent were aged between 46 and 50. The oldest participant was 63 years old and still active despite an average female retirement age of 55 in China. Only three of the women were under 36; the youngest participant was 32 years old.

Of the women interviewed, 77 percent started their careers in China and the rest abroad, for example, in Germany, the UK or Singapore. Two-thirds of the women who started their careers in China commenced while the country was under the old economic system, and worked in positions assigned by the state. The women come from various cities across China such as Wuhan, Xiandu, Guangzhou, Beijing and Nanjing. They were sometimes tied to the *"Hukou"* residence system at the beginning of their careers, regulating their movement. Almost all interviewees in government-assigned positions started as English teachers, translators or in a research institute. Only two started directly in roles in state-owned companies. The women who were able to choose freely at the start of their careers commenced as management assistants in the areas of sales, finance or administration. The positions held by interviewees at the time of the survey were predominantly management level 1, i.e. general management and CEO and minus 1. Except for one, they were part of an executive team with most in a role with a very high level of responsibility, with the titles of CEO, GM, Senior VP, VP, HRD, CFO and other positions at the C-level. In terms of numbers, there were many national HR directors amongst those surveyed. They made up the largest group of participants and reflect the high proportion of women, 61 percent, among HR directors in China. A third of women hold GM, president, or vice president positions, or have Asia-wide responsibilities. The majority of management women were working in Shanghai at the time of the survey. The career paths included cities like Wuhan, Chengdu, Guangzhou, Beijing and Nanjing. 74 percent of the women worked abroad and 34 percent studied abroad. The women were active across a wide range of industries, in both 'women-typical' sectors such as the luxury sector, the fashion, tourism, health and nutrition sectors, as well as in segments that are often more male-dominated, such as steel, electronics and material processing companies. The survey group therefore represents a good cross-section of very different sectors. The women came from German, American and French multinational companies at the time of the survey. Previous experience while working for private Chinese companies and state-owned entities was also included. Many interviewees were women participating in the author's work as an executive coach and management trainer in China. This, along with the snowball of recommendations that followed, resulted in the largest research group of Chinese women in management to date being identified.

Assessment of equal opportunities in China against the background of tradition and present

In almost all publications on the career of Chinese women in senior management, reference is made to the historical cultural imprint of society and thereby to Confucianism. This cultural imprint is in contrast to the equality measures of the Communist Party and women's organizations in the country.

Confucian values and their importance for Chinese women's careers

Almost all published studies, including those by Frank (2001), Li (2000) and Korabik (1994), on the situation of women in China make reference to the influence of history and culture on Chinese society. This includes studies that are general in nature and those that specifically concern the careers of women in management. Confucius' teachings are most closely related to Chinese culture and the situation of women being reported in numerous publications. Almost all Western gender studies research, as well as studies originating in China, interpret this tradition as having a mainly negative influence on women in general, and conclude on this basis that it impacts negatively on the situation of Chinese women in management. The researchers argue that cultural values derived from Confucian teachings continue to have a directly negative or inhibiting effect on women's careers. However, the efforts of politicians, which have manifested the equality of men and women in various legislation since 1949 and which have been implemented through various measures, are diametrically opposed. There are different perspectives when it comes to evaluating the extent to which one can actually speak of equal opportunities in Chinese management in recent times. A large number of authors point to continuing inequalities. Only a few authors like Blanchard (2010) paint a more positive picture regarding Confucian values or emphasize the importance of traditional values for present-day Chinese management practices independently of the gender debate. Aside from gender-based perspectives, various authors such as Arthur, Hall (1996, 2001) and Yuan (2013) have published works concentrating on the relevance of Confucius for present-day management practices and values, without specifically addressing women's issues. The main focus is on a more modern interpretation of the relationship constellations, which are a core component of the teaching, and their positive expression in the leadership style.

When asked about the influence of Confucian values on their career development, a large majority of the female managers interviewed were in agreement: they do not see any direct connection between their own careers and Confucian values, and do not believe these values have had any negative influence on their personal career development. *"Not relevant for my career"* was the most frequent spontaneous response to this question. The women argue that the portion of the old traditions relating to the role of women has been superseded by recent political developments in the country towards equal treatment of women. The Cultural Revolution is seen as a break with these traditions. According to this view, the image of women has fundamentally changed since then, with the massive scale of action in the period of the Cultural Revolution resulting in rapid changes in how women are seen. These changes are unanimously seen as positive. Responses such as *"China, the most liberated country in the world"* provide a clear counter to the more pessimistic assessment found in the literature regarding the situation in China for women in general and female managers in particular.

> M.: This is a very, very small portion of the social structure which came from very early China. But obviously, due to the Cultural Revolution, China is the most liberated country in the world, maybe the cultural revolution was bad, but one good thing it has done is to liberate the ladies' minds. They basically destroyed all the old culture including the old Confucian stuff about gender. So I never had anything in my mind about this.
>
> S.: During the period of President Mao we had the revolution. The cultural revolution. In fact, all the theories of Confucius have been considered as bad during that period. So all those people, my parents' generation had been brainwashed already. I think that in their head it is not any more like that. The men shouldn't be higher than a woman. In some way the revolution helped to balance more the power of men and women.
>
> H.: I think it coexists. Deep down, the fundamental society links to the Confucius, the Chinese traditions. That's still very male dominated. But I think the ironic thing is the communist influence on the culture is that the communism has broad perfect gender equality. It encourages

women in the revolution to be as active as men. I think that's the influence from the communists.

The women are hence in agreement with the accounts from the literature that describe the advances in equality between men and women that have been achieved as a result of policies diametrically opposed to Confucian traditions that have been enacted in China since 1949. They see these policies as having more influence on their careers than the subset of Confucian traditions that are claimed to have resulted in Chinese women historically having a lower status. However, when giving their personal assessments of the influence of Confucian values on careers, the women mentioned regional differences within China. In the view of the interviewed women, old and discriminatory interpretations of Confucius are no longer relevant in big cities, especially Shanghai, but they may still be influential in the north of the country and in rural regions.

> S.: Confucius is not special for gender. He is a philosopher of behavior. Maybe he will say that women should do things more inside of house. Men should do things outside the house. But for our generation we don't think so anymore. Not that kind of difference for men or women for a management career. Maybe there's still a connection. Because traditional philosophy can still have an influence in rural areas, but I would say not in big cities- Shanghai, Beijing, Guangzhou. But for the North regions in smaller cities there could be more influence from old traditions.

> Q.: I think that in the original Confucius idea there is some misunderstanding; because some phrases say that the female is in an inferior position. And I think that the government had played a deliberate role in removing these old values and concepts and said that it's wrong. Female and male are equal. Female should also work and be independent. So the government was kind of eliminating this idea of inferiority. But for sure not completely. I think it's gone in the big city. But on the countryside, in the agricultural environment there are definitely still lot of issues for putting female inferior. But I think in the city it's quite gone.

The interviewees believe that the core of Confucian traditions is made up of different, very positive values that apply to men and women in equal measure. They take these positive values as points of reference for their own lives and management styles. A particular emphasis is placed on balance, striving for harmony, respect for older people and superiors, and hard work. These women interpret Confucian values as generally positive and as unconnected to any debate about gender. For them, the values are about achieving balance, harmony and respect. They believe that both men and women strive equally to uphold these values, and view them positively as a guiding model.

> C.: These old traditions do not mainly focus on the position of women, but they mainly impact general societal values like being humble, respect authority, work hard. It's cultural traditions from thousands of years that influences our thinking. More general. Not specifically related to females.

The explanatory approach offered by the women has parallels in the literature. The authors Arthur, Hall (1996) and Rousseau (2001) show the connection between Chinese business values and cultural Confucian values. Three core values occupy a central place: obligation-based relationships, continuous learning and a focus on practical worldly existence. A capacity and a willingness to learn, the cultivation of relationships with people, the development of moral maturity and a general caring orientation are regarded as positive aspects of Confucian values. In this connection, the women also reflected on the strengths and potential disadvantages that emerge from these core values, for example the striving for harmony and respect for "keeping face". It became clear that the women see Confucian traditions as being more relevant to general management practices and less so to the specific context of gender.

> J.: One of the most important things is to have harmony. This we learned also from our government. We would like to have a harmonize society where everybody is the same and which not too sharp. Then this of course will have a huge influence. For example, on why we are not really brave enough to say what we want. If you want something else then another person then there is no harmony. The other thing is that the majority of Chinese, not only women, men are the same, are not really brave enough or not willing to face the conflict directly if there is an issue. Whatever you are doing I don't agree. But I can't say that to you because then it would create conflict then I will talk to you but I don't really say the problem, but I try to build kind of relation. Can we go to dinner? Have a chat? We were thinking hopefully we can build a little bit private relationship then you give me face, I give you face. Then I can sort the conflict. They don't really go directly to confront this kind of thing.

The women believe that the subjugation of women to men is either an aspect of Confucian traditions that is no longer applicable today or that it only pertains to achieving harmony within the family, and hence has no observable discriminatory effect in the management context. They assign Confucian values to the family sphere and believe that these values strengthen women's role within the family. The women in this research do not believe that Confucian traditions have any discriminatory or negative effects on their careers nowadays, though regional differences are ascribed to northern China. The traditions are seen as relevant to management practices, since they influence Chinese management styles in a gender-neutral way. According to some of the women, at multinational companies these practices need to be adapted to Western practices on a case-by-case basis depending on the respective context.

How the Chinese women assess the equality of opportunity in their country

The best-known gender researcher of China, Liu, states to the question of equality in China:

> The saying "Women are half the sky" acknowledges two things – the importance and contribution of women for the Chinese society and their position in the modern China. If you ask me if women can carry half of the sky, my answer is yes. If you ask me if women in China should carry more than half the sky, I doubt. The Chinese women already carry more than half the sky – this has to be said. We are now coming to a point to discuss more actual questions related to the consequences of this development on women's lives and the society in general.
> (authorized citation, German Consulate, Salon Yongfu Lu, Shanghai 2014)

Like all other participants of this international research, the women were asked to verbally rate equality of opportunity for women in management in China on a scale from zero to ten, where ten means that opportunities for men and women in senior management are completely equal and zero means there is no equality of opportunity at all. Chinese women who are pursuing their careers in China at the time of the interviews rate China in terms of equal opportunities with 8.5 out of a total of 27 responses, 13 women were awarded a maximum of ten. Nine other women awarded values of around eight. The Chinese women thus award the highest ratings for their environment in comparison to all other women surveyed from the countries considered here. The women, who gave eight points, explain the gap to the highest value with regional differences in the huge country and point out that in the north or in more rural regions, equality has not yet been achieved to this extent. The high values then refer to industrial metropolises such as Shanghai or Beijing and other mega cities. Most women feel absolutely equal to men and some said that as women they even have advantages over men. Above all, the factor of trust would be a considerable advantage for women in multinational companies, since the foreign executives in the company headquarters trusted women more than men.

> M.: There is no single answer. In big cities it is quite equal. In rural areas less equality. In multinational companies no preference of male or female.
>
> J.: In some case the female has more equality. In big cities it is quite equal.
>
> A.: I think it is equal, also the pay. In China women do not stay at home like in other countries.
>
> C.: Today women are more powerful than men in China. Also, girls today are already much better from school onwards.

In addition to the mostly positive assessments for China, the smaller proportion of women also mentioned limiting factors that lead to few evaluations of six or seven points on the 10-point scale. Alongside the predominantly positive assessment of equality of opportunity, some isolated remarks were more critical and led to lower ratings on the scale. At the forefront they see CEO or GM roles are primarily reserved for foreigners. In addition, a woman argues that women often prefer a middle management position to meet the needs of their various roles. Another opinion relates to the career delays that can be observed as a result of motherhood.

C.: It is quite equal. But the fact of getting pregnant and the four months' maternity leave might be an issue that lead to preference of male.

C.: Gender is no issue. Same as in the US. It really depends if a woman has children and gets support for raising them. I don't think that culturally people are biased toward women being inferior to men. I really don't think that kind of mentality exists in the US or here. But it's the expectation the family have on you. The very practical issues that you have to balance.

Unlike most studies and publications, some of the study participants thought women have better opportunities for senior executive roles than men. However, it was disputed whether Chinese women have equal opportunities with regard to CEO and GM roles, which are usually held by men from overseas. This is also reflected in the figures in the literature, which show that in China, just like in the rest of the world, it continues to be uncommon for CEO positions to be held by women. The interviewees reported that motherhood and the special demands it places on women have a limiting effect on their careers. Again, this matches the literature. Overall, the women in this study group presented a more positive picture of equal opportunities for women in management than would be expected on the basis of the published literature.

Career strategies of female Chinese executives

The Chinese women's career strategies reveal the following approaches, which are interwoven:
1. Long-term career planning
2. Developing expertise and lifelong learning at a high level
3. Internationalization of career and/or mobility within China
4. Making use of local potential
5. Strategic choice of industry, company and field
6. Putting work before personal life
7. Considering factors such as happiness and backwards steps
8. Seeking exposure and allies

Most of the women planned their careers with a focus on the desired end point taking a long-term perspective.

Long-term career planning

Some women claim to having strategically pursued their career from the start, while others dealt with long-term planning only in the first years of work. The goal was clear for all women: to achieve a high level of function and responsibility.

In their descriptions, the women used terms such as *I chose to, planned to, asked for, raised my hand, applied for, initiated, voiced out* or *was determined to*, which suggest very active career planning and an autonomous approach. Several interviewees explained their motivations for their planned career steps. Answers such as *"wanting to rise up higher"*, *"expanding my responsibility"* and *"striving for a position with more influence"* were very common in this group.

All the interviewed women knew from early on that they wanted to rise higher in their careers, take on a lot of responsibility and reach a high level in the hierarchical system. Hence, the women's goals were already clear in the early stages of their careers.

Developing expertise and lifelong learning at a high level

The second strategy that all the women have pursued is to be the best in their field. This includes planning learning and training and precisely selecting positions that allow them to build up specific expertise. All the women have strived to maximize their level of qualification in order to stand out, including making plans for lifelong learning. The oldest participant only completed her MBA at a late stage in her career, when she was already a CEO. The women in the study who went to university abroad said that they planned this step very precisely; since they believed a qualification from abroad and experience in a foreign culture would enhance their future career prospects. Some of them chose very well-known universities such as Harvard, INSEAD or Stanford specifically in order to increase their chances of landing a management role in future. The women who studied in China attempted to get into the best Chinese universities. For some of them, choosing a top university was more important than which subject they studied.

> Mi.: I realized it maybe when I was six or seven. I do a lot of planning already, I showed my notebook to everybody, they were shocked, they did not think this came from a little girl who write this kind of mature stuff, but I was kind of pre-mature when I was young.
>
> L: Planned in my case means that I was thinking about where I wanted to be today. I was quite aggressive compared with others my age. Not a very clear timeline but at that time I told myself when I will be 35, 36 or 40 I want to be the head. I wanted to be really number one owner of sort of area. Maybe OD number one in China or HR head but I didn't have a very clear concept about power. I didn't care basically. But I wanted to really become competitive with a sort of competency in the same industry compared with my peers or compared with my friends. This was clear. But a no time I planned to join some big company. It was very clear for me that I did not want to join big company. Even today or the past few years when any huge company approaches me I always say no.
>
> Mo.: I think everything is planned or not planned to be honest. I think the result is not planned but the things I want to achieve very much are planned. For example, when I wanted to get into (Company name) actually at the beginning I knew nothing about the company. I knew nothing about it because there was limited information at that time. When we started to learn, know about the careers progress and how we need to perform in the company basically I started to plan or to know what I want to do in the company. I wanted to do financial analysis. I wanted to do a better job. I wanted to learn more and get promoted. Eventually I never set a target that I

want to get promoted in two years or three years. That was not planned. Every promotion is not planned. But I will plan that I want to do this job. I want to grow into this level. Eventually it will come, it will be good.

The women continuously built up their expertise from the start of their careers. One interviewee gave the following representative description. Positions and companies were selected accordingly. Especially at the start of the career, reasons for changing were always related to the desire to develop quickly and not to stagnate. When choosing a new position, the development of one's own expertise was closely linked to the increase in market value. In addition, prestige and interpersonal relationships were the most common reasons for choosing a position.

> An.: Actually, it's a kind of funny to say. So when I move, I'm thinking and say, ok if I look at my skill set as pie. I will see which areas I still lack of. I'm more like how I can build my resume internally or externally... This is how I choose the position.

> L.: I was not looking for balance. I was looking for some stretch and challenge. I wanted to really step from a supporting role, nice role to a very business impact role. Impact again. This is my first role in (company name). It's an HR business partner role when I joined in 2012. My key work was really about redesign the company and support the company to do the change management, also the layoff. All the tough things. Then I was promoted to be the China HR head in 2013. At that time, I started to own everything including operation, strategic at partner level to today.

Internationalization of career and/or mobility within China

A core competence of Chinese women is their interculturality combined with great mobility. A total of 74 percent of the women surveyed stated that they had gained experience abroad during their career. The list of the 10 countries mentioned ranges from France and Switzerland via Sweden to South Africa, the USA and many countries more. The experience abroad took place in relatively early phases of the career and helped the women to expand their strategic advantage in the foreign companies in China.

> S.: This is interesting. I worked for an amazing company for several years. Multinational company for several years. And I'm original from Shanghai, right? I think I needed to find some life experience and go abroad. To see the Western style. To understand the culture deeply. Even for the food. Just have some different experience. At that time also I just have to plan it. I needed to obtain my Master Degree. The Master Degree I just applied to Sydney University. They are located in Sydney and that's why I choose Australia.

All the women who studied abroad or worked there at the start of their careers did so with the deliberate intention to return to China for further career progression in future. When asked about their planned career steps, several of the women replied *"I wanted to pursue a career in China"*. One participant who studied in Germany reported that she specifically looked for companies that had joint ventures in China. She then attempted to get internships at these companies so she could write her dissertation about one of them. Hence, her strategic plan was to prepare for career progression in China from an early stage. One of the older women in the study described how she specifically looked for an executive job in a less desirable part of China after her experience in Germany because she only began her ascent up the career ladder at the age of almost 40. She described her plan as follows: *"I wanted to go somewhere where they definitely needed me."*

> J.: Yes, I started with a basic training and an expert training with company XY (German) and build a relationship to them and I saw the advertising at our mechanical engineering department at University, they were looking. And I started researching and saw that they had started the first joint venture with China just recently. In the 90s many had started there. That is the reason why I started goal oriented with company XY during my thesis with the topic 'Construction of a joint venture in China'. We had already a joint venture there but wanted to install an assembly plant. I planned the whole concept taking into account the country specifics. We had worldwide high automation, without automation, little automation, so I worked on specific assembly concepts for Shanghai. Of course, I got the chance later to implement them and be responsible.

The women can be divided into subgroups with respect to mobility within China. One subgroup, which started out with Shanghai *hukous*, has generally worked continuously in Shanghai with intermittent assignments in other cities; the main examples given of these assignments were times when the multinational companies opened new factories, making it necessary for the women to relocate for longer or shorter periods of time. The other subgroup, which started out with non-Shanghai *hukous*, has a high level of geographic mobility within China. Some of the women reported that they specifically attempted to obtain certain state-assigned jobs so they could get *hukou* for a particular city. Hence, the women who came from the country had to make plans to move to a big city in the initial phases of their careers. Accordingly, *hukou* was the most important decision criterion for the women at this stage. The women in this group mentioned working at the following cities in the course of their careers: Wuhan, Yunnan, Nanjing, Xiandu, Szechuan, Beijing (multiple mentions), Shenzhen, Tianjin, Guangzhou. Several of the women reported moves between Shanghai and Beijing. For the sake of their careers, the women accepted relocations that in some cases meant having to travel long distances between work and family each weekend sometimes for periods of up to two years. In this context, the dimensions of the country must be taken into account. Around 75 percent of the Chinese women in the Global Women Career Lab have high or very high geographic mobility.

Going to where the chances are: Strategic choice of industry, company and field

It is characteristic of the Chinese women's career strategies that they primarily seek opportunities and go where they think the opportunities are in order to achieve their ascent-oriented goals. When pursuing opportunities for themselves, most of the women interviewed consciously opted for the newness and uncertainty offered by the multinational companies at a time when the country is still characterized by assigned, lifelong careers. Moving from the secure government agencies environment, which up to a certain time window also represented the social norm, into a multinational company signals a high degree of flexibility for these women with regard to the achievement of their goals.

All women reported on their curiosity to get to know foreigners, their working methods and the associated foreign cultures. The women hoped to gain more knowledge and skills from working for the foreigners. Initially, the aspects of learning and interest in foreign cultures were the focus of choosing a multinational company. The knowledge of another culture and their way of working, combined with detailed knowledge of the local ways of working, subsequently brought great personal advantage in the career. This will be covered in more detail later.

Another strategy mentioned by several women in the group was to observe economic and market trends and plan their careers accordingly. Examples included China's early economic development at the start of the reforms. One woman described how she specifically followed the growth in foreign investment across different regions from Shenzhen to Shanghai, and chose positions accordingly. Another described development in her industry and how she deliberately looked for an executive role in the growing sector with the assistance of head-hunters. Targeted choice of industries, companies and fields was another key focal point of planning. Examples given included selecting companies based on their size or country of origin or deliberately choosing to work on the service provider side. For all the women, the decision to work at a multinational company rather than another type of company was the result of deliberate planning. The majority of women have worked in four or five different companies. The decision for a company is often made according to the company's nationality of origin, as well as the level of awareness of the company. An analysis of the industries chosen by the women shows that only 17 percent of the women have pursued their careers exclusively in one industry. The vast majority have changed industries at least once, and many of them have switched multiple times. Forty-five percent of the women have pursued careers in a single department type. These women have remained true to their chosen fields and worked their way up to the highest ranks. The other women, by contrast, have consistently switched between different roles and obtained qualifications that cut across different departments. Thirty-one percent of the women can be categorized as "lateral movers". As well as working in the corporate world, they have worked at agencies, service providers, consultancies or institutes, or been self-employed.

Ag1: And then I felt my value and I used my English. It can be a commercial. After I find a job, I talk to my school leaders and they say "no you cannot". No. You have to come back. But at that time, I think the government in the country just started to allow that you can resign from a state-owned company and I feel I was the first person in my area, the first person resigned. It actually made a lot of noise. In my education system people thought "how can she?" First of all, nobody resigned at that time because teacher is still dream job for many people. You can teach and it's a state-owned company. You are guaranteed rights and decent jobs. Then you resign and you work in a remote city you do not know and it's called a capitalist. We were educated that capitalist always exploit the people... My parents at that time my mother was very worried. She says really you want to put yourself in the risk. I was struggling for about 1 month and I consult people and ask because in that company there are a lot of young people from different parts of the country. People like me have educated. Most of them resigned so I consult them but nobody gives me the answer this is the right one. Nobody can guarantee. For me I say it's a risk taking but it's worth it to try. I write a resignation letter. In the end they have no way to prove. Then from there I just started take care of myself. Not the country. Take care of myself. That was in 1990. That's my second start my career.

K.: Then I had this opportunity actually it was my first offer, that's by an executive search firm. Its US based and at the time it was rated number five globally. I was very excited looking at the profiles of all the colleagues, the consultant. It's a very high profile and it's really a great group if I could join. It all looks like an elite in this market and I want to join in this group. So that's how I joined that company. Started to do executive search. At the time, it's really very early. I think it's a very new concept in China market for executive search. Nobody actually knows what it means. It may just translate as head-hunter, but head-hunter is very new concept in China market. I ever encounter to make a call to that person, that's showing him or her that I have a great opportunity and whether this person will be considering any external opportunities, or go forward and explore. The answer was usually "I need to talk to my boss first." That's how it works. That's really interesting. I think that also its kind of luck we need to make some further progress to educate the market to hook up the client company and the potential talent in the market. That was the fun part. I explored a lot of different industries and even back to 2000, that was the .com years so the millionaires came up. Although there is a lot of bubble in the market, we also tried to dig out all of the potential talents.

Putting work before personal life

Many of the descriptions show that most of the Chinese female executives in this group have prioritized their careers over their personal lives in their decision-making. This once again confirms the findings in the section on the comparative importance of professional and private success. Examples of the women prioritizing their careers included moving to places far away from where their families lived. Several women mentioned doing this; one described her decision to accept a more senior position in Beijing while her family stayed behind in Shanghai as something *"which was totally against my family planning"*. Unlike in Western research, according to which women evaluate each action in the light of the impact a decision might have on their relationships, the Chinese women in this study are not swayed by personal factors when they make decisions about their career development. The high importance of careers for Chinese women is expressed in their clear career orientation and high career motivation. Both aspects are discussed in depth in the section on career meaning.

> E.: After that there came a time that I requested by myself, to the holding CFO, that I need a change. I want to do something new. We discussed the different positions and finally also this was a hard decision to take over this real estate position, because it was never on my agenda list. And it was in Beijing again, which was totally against my family planning. Because at that time I already had family here in Shanghai. But we finally decided on a certain working model. And I took over that position. At that time, it was in Beijing, later on came back to Shanghai.

Considering factors such as happiness and backwards steps

Another factor that became apparent in the women's descriptions of their planned career steps is how self-reliant they are in planning their careers. Although they attribute a role to factors such as chance and opportunity or being in the right place at the right time in determining the paths their careers have taken, what predominates in the women's descriptions is their own proactive action, initiative and planning: spotting opportunities and then seizing them. These descriptions suggest a more internal career locus, defined by O'Neil as the belief that one is responsible for one's own career and in charge of managing it. There are some descriptions in the group that point towards a more external career locus, in which a career occurs as a result of chance or other external interventions from which the career opportunities emanate, but when the accounts are analyzed as a whole such descriptions are always subordinated to the women's own goal-focused career planning and desire for career advancement.

> E.: I don't really say planned, in early ages you have certain desires and career steps and you want to plan it. There is definitely some luck being in the right place at the right time. My first assignment to Hongkong it just happened, me standing there with my Asia face, at the time there was nobody there and they suddenly see me and say, Oh, she is doing the training and she knows it, maybe we should consider. A lot of people say this is luck, but if you really look back, but you also have to bring your own value.

> Q.: It's difficult to say planned. Because it comes both ways. That means this new opportunity comes to the table and of course I took it. So in a way the opportunity, but also my choice. If you say planned, the only think I can say planned is yeah, I planned to progress more in terms of going to higher responsibilities and expand both the scope and both in terms of job and geography. So, in a way that was the plan, but in a way the opportunities were always kind of given. I was approached always by head-hunter or referred by a friend. I was approached even this moved within LVH group from Shanghai to Singapore was offered by the company. And I took it. Probably because I have expanded my scope beyond marketing it be involved in distribution, the overall brand management, and also having more experience in international organization. So it's clear for me that I want to have a bigger scope and have higher responsibility. And in terms of geography it's also, after seeing people being mobile across the market, then I realized it's also a possibility for me.

Seeking exposure and allies

The final factor mentioned in connection with career planning relates to exposure and looking for allies. The women specifically looked for and accepted positions that promised a high level of exposure in their companies. According to the women, exposure increases their chances of advancing further. Here once again, the women took the initiative and planned how they could maximize their visibility in their companies.

However, visibility and self-expression differ among the Chinese. They report that there is a need to catch up with the Western style of self-expression. The Chinese are looking for their "stage" on the important projects that they are actively pursuing. They also involved key decision-makers in their career plans and continuously worked to win and retain their support. This point will be discussed in the section on mentoring. What is relevant here is the women's individual planning and the ways in which they exerted influence on these connections. The women develop mutual mentor relationships, in which the mentor also benefits greatly and catapult themselves into very high positions through trusting relationships with decision-makers who depend on them. These factors also speak for self-determined career planning and support the attribution of an internal career locus.

> T.: I think a lot of things were planned. Planned in a sense when I started with my company, I have a vision of working cross functions and then I always told my boss and maybe, the HR department and also my peers and also other functions had, that brought exposure. Also in the American company you have to talk a lot about your career. You have to get people engaged and also connected of your career plan and then they could be able to provide me something. Maybe not the things I want but at least a door, more doors were opened. So the opportunities I had with (name of company unit) as well as the States I think I reach out to some senior people to get it and fortunately at that time, they want also to open my horizon and also get more exposure for me.

Individual career requirements of the Chinese female top executives

Analysis shows the individual factors that supported the rise of Chinese women in management. This includes family factors, as well as education, their management capabilities and parts of their personality which are related to rising in hierarchy and their leadership style.

Influence of the family of origin on the Chinese women's careers

The majority of the women came from Shanghai. Only a small portion came from other cities in China such as Beijing, Guangzhou, Hunan and Xian. The following overall picture emerges from the study participants' accounts of their families of origin: most of the women grew up in families where both parents worked. Both highly educated professions and laborers are represented among mothers and fathers alike. Some of the women grew up in larger families, since the one-child policy did not yet exist at the time of their childhoods. Grandparents, aunts and cousins were mentioned alongside parents as other close figures. Many women were often separated from their parents for a long time in their youth, which was the norm in society. Looking at the parents' occupations overall, it is striking that they include both academic, medical, political and entrepreneurial occupations on the one hand and factory and agricultural workers on the other. However, occupations that require a higher level of education predominate. Hence, the majority of the women come from highly educated families, but there are also women from families with very simple backgrounds.

The Chinese women have mothers and grandmothers as role models who were employed and professionally successful and in highly qualified occupations that earned them a lot of respect and acceptance in their social environment. Fathers were often absent and are only mentioned as role models in individual cases. The mothers imparted values such as hard work and discipline to their daughters. The Western model of housewife plays no role in the socialization of Chinese women. Women grow up in situations where they had to take responsibility quickly and grew up early. In doing so, they learned to overcome inconveniences early and to assert themselves. Several of the women interviewed described their mothers as very strong personalities who had a profound influence on them, given the mothers' leadership qualities and achievement motivation. According to the women's accounts, the mothers repeatedly pointed out that it is only possible to achieve a better life through hard work, education and lots of discipline. These values were imparted to the daughters from an early age. Chinese women do not have the image of mothers as housewives, which predominates in parts of the West.

The women described how they learned certain traits and capacities, such as discipline, industriousness, assertiveness and how to handle power or money, in their families of origin. In the women's view, being separated from their parents at an early age either intermittently or for an extended period, which is described as typical for China in other studies, led to them acquiring additional traits at an early age, such as a sense of responsibility, independence and perseverance. In this study group, the described characteristics and skills predominate, which resulted from the living environment of the parents and also from separation situations these women experienced. The women see these skills as relevant for their career success.

> Ag1: My father is accountant and my mother is a leader of a company. Very active. She was used to be the head of factory or a company. She's always active as women leader. She's very active. My father is not that ambitious.

> L.: Although my mother she was not very well educated, she actually is very aggressive on the target, on the result. What I mean she wants to achieve the best. No matter on herself or on her kids, she will not be satisfied. She will say "Next time you need to get number one". Something

like that. She always gave me a stretch target. She always inspired me to move out of this island because she already spend her half-life in the island.

J.: I was living with my family in the courtyard. There were a lot of neighbors there. Basically, my mom was the one with the highest title. They always call her in a nice way, Professor Wu. It's a little bit like joking because normally in Chinese culture you don't call somebody with the title but they did it in a good way. I felt really good about it. I also felt benefit from my mom's background, she is professor, she always has a lot of students in the same age like us. I call them big sister, big brother...my mom always understood how the young people are thinking. It's not really like normal parents who say you have to do this or that. Her students somehow like us.

M.M.: Yes, in the countryside. I was born in Beijing and my parents belonged to the government, the Central Government, but during the Cultural Revolution it was made equal to the ground and we kid had to go on the countryside. I was sent far in the north and had to stay there for ten years. In the beginning I needed to work as a farmer, a normal farmer. Most of us girls were in middle school and had been send to the countryside. We were many girls together. I was 15 years old and worked around ten years on the farm. One was hurt sometimes and I grew into the situation and became strong. Yes, it was difficult. All who worked on the farm had parents in higher previous government functions. All girls. We were twelve girls all together, each day some girl cried. My nature is that I knew that crying will not help. Instead one has to see how to survive. My parents were sent to prison during these times. After one year I was the boss of that group of girls.

Me: I think my parents just motivate us to be self-motivated. Self-manage our studies. Told us, that they don't have much money. But they can ensure us that we will have enough tuition as long as we can continue our study. So we manage our self. If we don't study harder then I will we farmer. We will be farmer. This is their own way to educate us. They told us; you do not need to worry about money. You do not need to worry about tuition. You just worry about your study. This is your task. Our task is making money for you. Your task is to manage you own study. My parents work two times harder than other farmers at their age because there are so many kids to feed. And so many kids to go to school. It's unusual. It's unusual so many kids in one family go to school. Normally one only sends the son to school. Because my father is very open. He thinks son and daughter are the same so he treated us the same.

C.: When I was very young, I had to take up my family myself... Because my father actually he works, he came home very late because the place he worked is very far away. He used to take buses. Long time buses from where he worked. He still came back home every day but he very late. And my mother was sick in hospital for quite a long time. So it's just only me and my brother. I, as a bigger sister, had to take care of my younger brother and also cook for the family, do laundry for the family. I think compared to people my age; I took the role to take care of a family much earlier.

Education and degrees of the Chinese top women managers

The women of the Shanghai Women's Career Lab are highly educated and motivated to learn. Many of them have acquired additional qualifications in the course of their careers. Most of the women have a BA as their first degree. As well as language degrees in English and French, there was a broad range of BA degrees in subjects such as electronics, computer science, biology, chemistry and law.

But only 22 percent of the group reported that their highest, and only, university degree is a bachelor degree. Twenty-seven of the research participants hold a masters or equivalent qualification; 19 of them have a Master of Business Administration and four have MAs in science, law, history or physics. Four of the women hold a German MBA equivalent, including *Diplomkauffrau*, *Diplomökonomin* and *Diplom in Maschinenbau*.

The MBA schools that the women mentioned attending include world-famous institutions such as Harvard, ESSEC, Stanford and the Shanghai-based business school CEIBS. Five of the women have two or even three MA qualifications. There have been various studies on the connection between the prestige and reputation of the university that someone attends and their subsequent career success. Several studies measured the connection by reference to impact on salary development. Although participants in the present study were not asked about this connection, it can be noted that the women hold some highly respected qualifications and attended many highly prestigious universities.

> C.: I think that it is Harvard just to be honest. I think that HBS had a stronger brand globally. INSEAD may have a very good brand in Europe but then globally HBS has a better brand, so I go with the better brand.

A third of the Chinese women surveyed studied abroad. One woman even studied in two countries outside China and obtained qualifications in both. Germany was the most popular choice of location to study abroad, ahead of the UK, France and Singapore. Seven percent of the women chose to study in the USA, Hong Kong or Australia.

Language skills are very important for executives at multinational companies in China. All the interviewed women speak English to a high standard and use it on a daily basis in their working environments. Many of them studied English for their BA degree and are completely fluent in both written and spoken English. Fifteen of the women do not speak any foreign languages besides English. Another fifteen are proficient in a second language, and five women in a third. The second most common language in this group is German followed by French. Seven of the women have passive knowledge of Japanese as a third language. Italian, Korean and Spanish were also mentioned. Due to the women's high level of English, the interviews could be conducted in English without any comprehension problems. Four of the participants preferred to carry out the interviews in German, which attests to their strong proficiency. It is striking that most of the women who work at German or French multinationals are proficient in the language of the head office. Only one of the nine women who work for a German company does not speak any German. Four of the nine women who work for French companies are fluent in French. According to the interviewees, particularly at the time of China's economic reforms, language skills were an enormous advantage for potential executives, since they made up for the fact that most foreign executives could not speak any Chinese. The women's proficiency in multiple languages gives them an advantage over foreign executives. Purely by virtue of being able to speak other languages, they are able to carve out greater scope for decision-making and make use of the power vacuum resulting from the foreigners' linguistic dependency. The women believe that this advantage was greater at the start of their careers, when proportionally fewer applicants spoke English or other languages and almost no foreigners were proficient enough to conduct negotiations in Chinese.

Competencies and skills of the Chinese women: Global mindsets

One noteworthy feature of the women's answers is that they were very readily able to state their own strengths, skills and competencies. They reported extensively on this point, with descriptions coming thick and fast. None of the women appeared reserved, modest or shy when they were asked about their own strengths. It was not unusual for them to use superlatives in their descriptions.

> VP-HR: "I am the best HRD in China."

The Chinese women use understanding of the system, i.e. understanding the different interest groups in the company and global structures, as a career component. This also includes the correct selection of employees and successors to secure their own internal network. They emphasize their deep expertise in China business combined with global expert knowledge as a competitive advantage over other colleagues. This is closely linked to the ability and the will for lifelong learning. They have a communication style that they can adapt to the environment – be it in a Chinese or global context. The strongest and most outstanding competence of Chinese women in senior management, which can be derived from this analysis, is their global mindset and the associated intercultural competence, as defined by Black (2014) and Tucker (2014).

The women share a very open-minded, positive and curious attitude towards other cultures as well as the desire to learn about and understand them in depth. They are open to adapt and integrate the foreign cultures depending on the context. "*My initial idea of working with foreigners was the idea of freedom*" was how one participant described her original expectations of the values of multinational companies. All the women started out with great curiosity mixed with very positive assumptions and expectations regarding foreigners in general and their ways of working and management styles in particular. The participants frequently formulated goals involving working with foreigners. The most frequently mentioned goals were to be able to work well with people of different nationalities and to be able to lead them effectively. Another goal that was mentioned was the desire to learn from people from other countries by focusing on their strengths. In the view of the interviewed women, "*being a Chinese woman among foreigners*" is one of the biggest advantages they have when it comes to advancing in their careers at multinational companies in China. This refers to a capacity to not just understand but adapt to the culture of the head office or foreign decision-makers at their companies that goes far beyond simply understanding the language and being able to communicate in multiple languages at company management level. All women have the ability to adapt to the different cultures of their superiors or colleagues abroad, and/or the culture of the international head office. The descriptions suggest the women possess strong empathy for cultural peculiarities. They also have a strong understanding of their own market and are able to build bridges with people from other countries. However, ultimately it is the adaptation of the women in this group that constitutes their particular strength: their ability to adapt to different cultures as and when necessary. Most important for the career path is the ability to "move" and act between cultures and to use this advantage strategically. In this context, the literature indicates *"moving easily between cultures"*. It is a special ability of intercultural flexibility, which runs through all members of the women interviewed and emerges prominently from the descriptions. The Chinese demonstrated they possess this competence to a higher degree than the other four country groups involved in this research. They have what the scientist Black (2014) means when he defines global mindsets at the different levels – intercultural business expertise, character, perspective and positive curiosity. The Chinese women possess savvy in the form of strong knowledge of not just their local market but also of international business and on an organizational level. They also possess inquisitiveness about, meaning extremely high curiosity, and interest in foreign cultures, international business and foreign leadership styles.

> Ag2: You need to unlock the culture of origin in a multinational, understand it...
>
> V.: My capability is to know where the business is going, to anticipate it, link my actions to the same direction...smelling the changes coming.
>
> M.M.: OK, after five years I knew how much I did, but also that I can do more. And then I presented my idea to the company. We also produced paper on the country side, but also in Germany. Why shouldn't we sell paper from Germany in Asia? And I proposed to have an office in Hong Kong, which I would lead beside the joint venture. So that not only our Chinese products but also German products would sell in Asia.
>
> Mi.: Innovation is not really an important thing, but at least visionary is important. People need to have a bigger picture, envisioning what your next five or ten years are supposed to be. Not only on your career path but other things you do your daily job. In the company, not stick to the small area.

The women described the many and varied cultural differences that they have experienced and learned about during their careers. Their detailed observations about the culturally specific working styles, communication and values of different nationalities are presented. These precise observations were made possible by the women's high level of cultural sensitivity and keen perception. The observations involve management and work styles, communication and personal values. The answers are, of course, subjective, but are based on many years of lived experience and observations. The women reflected on their own management styles and similarities and differences compared with another nationality; many of the women made comparisons with multiple nationalities. They described skills and ways of thinking that represent particular strengths of people from other countries compared with their own culture, and reflected on strengths and weaknesses of Chinese culture. The consistently positive and also humorous way in which the women describe cultural peculiarities is worthy of note.

> M.: Chinese say 70, German say 100, US say 120 – for 100...

Hence, their greatest skill, and something they take pleasure in, is to be able to "move" between the worlds of Chinese and foreign cultures and to make use of the positive strengths of the other cultures. This explains what Rosinski (2003) means by leveraging differences. It is a proactive attitude, looking for gems in your culture and mining for treasures in other cultures. Trust was repeatedly mentioned in this context, especially among women who work at German companies. Specifically, some participants observed that German executives are more likely to trust Germans, especially when it comes to CEO appointments. Hence, their own nationality is a competitive disadvantage with respect to trust. However, this disadvantage is more pronounced for men and probably only affects women at CEO level. In their experience, as women they have clear advantages. The women are not merely able to recognize and accept fine-grained intercultural differences, but also view such differences in a very positive light and find it fulfilling to work in a professional environment characterized by cultural diversity. They possess the ability to switch between different worlds. The findings suggest that the Chinese female top managers have the ability to understand, connect and integrate different culture. In other words, the Chinese women have global mindsets.

High significance of careers for the interviewees

Career success is a central dimension for describing careers. The significance of careers for the Chinese women is also essentially connected to their understanding of success and how satisfied they are with their achievements. When asked about their personal definition of success, the Chinese women mentioned objective and subjective components in equal measure. Objective components of success that can be clearly measured from an external perspective were described using terms such as good results, efficiency and achieving high targets. Terms that can be categorized as relating to subjective career success included fulfilment, being happy, enjoyment, a sense of achievement and doing a job that you love. Supporting and standing up for other people were the third most common terms mentioned in the women's definitions of success. Single women in particular also mentioned giving something back to society. These answers were followed by far less frequent ones such as work-life balance and a good family life. Hence, with respect to the four central concepts of career success – effectiveness, happiness, utility and satisfaction – the women's definitions of career success placed just as much emphasis on factors that could be categorized under the heading of effectiveness as on the more subjective concepts of satisfaction and happiness.

The group was evenly divided between women who clearly prioritize professional success and ones who strive for a balance between professional and private success. The portion of the women who regard professional success as more important described their attitude as follows: *"home is no option, want to work, chose work always first, important for independence"*. These interviewees tend to measure success in purely professional terms. Work is viewed as a crucial factor behind satisfaction and happiness. With the exception of one interviewee who did not become a mother herself and regrets this, none of the women in the study regard it as sufficient to have lives that revolve solely around children. The interviewees' self-worth is closely tied up with their career success. Answers in this connection included *"work is more important than they would like"* and *"I tasted blood"*. The mothers rate family as a slightly more important factor for happiness and satisfaction than the single women in the group, but all the women in the study tend to attribute considerable importance to their careers, regarding them as an essential component of self-worth. Many of the women who favor balance described how they focused exclusively on professional success in the early stages of their careers. According to these women, it was only as they got older and rose up the ranks that they became aware that private success also mattered to them.

> C.: I think for me it's more professional success rather than private. My private life is very simple. I don't have a family of my own. I have my mother and my brother and so I don't spend a lot of time worrying about them although sometimes. I have a very simple family and my private life I think you can call it my church life and my surface those are also relatively simple and I try to have the balance but because that side is relatively simple, so I will more think of the professional success.

> X.: To be honest in the past 20 years, I wanted be very professional manager in multinational company to have skills, different kind of skills…. Just more recently I said I want to have good family. I started balance the work and my family. And think about should I go to UK or US?

> Z.: Because the main target is work and the main target of my life is work. I have a 'road map' in my head and it makes me happy to conquer it day by day. I do not have so many private targets. I do not have many private hobbies either. Besides making sports and travelling I have no private stories.

> Ag1: I enjoy my career very much. Really, very much. That's why I still feel I'm very energetic everyday coming here to work. I also enjoy my personal life a lot. Without my personal life I probably would not have the energy. This is more and more important. One day I remember I was in a leadership training and the Indian master of meditation asked all of us a question. Can you think about five years, ten years later how your office look like? Interesting I found when I deep think about five minutes later, in the past my office in XY (company name), I almost

had no family photos. All XY different Olympic photos, XY trophies, XY things, it's all XY souvenirs everywhere. They were right. Now when I move from XY (Company name) today you will see more and more family photos. Small big family photos. My sons' small notes sometimes and also my different peers in global write small notes to me. And my training partners send Christmas card and I keep each one. These are the thing I keep more and more in my office. I still have one or two XY trophy, XY trophy that reminds me of my career. This is part of my blood but it's not all company things.

Ca.: I think that is the problem for most Chinese people, we just combine our professional and our personal life. I think I didn't have my definition of private success; I always think maybe career is what I can do more. But I think from last year, I did some change, small changes about myself, which make me feel more content with my private life. I picked up one hobby, the Chinese calligraphy. So that makes me feel better for me as a person, because I don't have a hobby before. Which I think is very strange for foreigners. Because the way we are raised, parents just ask you to focus on your studies. So a very small step, but a big meaning for myself, that I have something to identify myself. So, for private life, I think I will think about it further and define what success means to me. First, I think just separated professional and private, now I think about it.

This is interesting given that most of the Chinese female top managers who have not previously lived abroad became mothers at a relatively young age by modern Western standards, 23–25 on average. Hence, becoming a mother at a young age did not change the women's attitudes to their careers. Many of the interviewees displayed attitudes that are more common in men. The women focused on their careers for much of their lives independent from the fact of becoming mothers and only came to accord a greater status to their private lives at a later stage. The answers are in line with a study cited by Ganrose (2007) on values and social status involving 1,550 Chinese women from Taipei, Hong Kong and Shanghai that was published in *Reader's Digest* in 2001. Here, 81 percent of the women from Shanghai in that study described careers as very important, ahead of women from Taipei and Hong Kong. However, family is a very important and undisputed value for all the women in the present research. It is women with two children who said that they strive to achieve a balance between professional and private success equate private success with the amount of time they can spend with their children. *"You cannot have it all"* was how one woman described the conflict between spending time with children and being committed to one's work. It is striking that reflections on the role of mothers and what constitutes successful mothering brought up dilemmas of conscience more frequently for women in the study who had previously lived in Germany for extended periods or have a foreign partner.

J.: Privately I would describe myself not as so successful, because I do not have enough time for my child. I try to spend as much time as possible for my parents, they are both over seventy. I take them to vacations. I have bought an apartment for them. I always take them with us, we have been together to Hawaii. I pay all of the holidays for them. I try to make it possible as much as I can. My son calls me still a successful mother. Because I do not go in the office on week-ends and I do not bring my laptop home. I try to spend as much time as I can with him. A typical Chinese mother does not allow so much freedom. I am discussing topics with him, because he already has his own ideas with his seven years.

H.: Private success I think for me is very easy. For me is to be there for my kids. Again, I have very strong minds about not delegate even my kids now. I coach their homework. I don't hire tutors to do that. For me if you miss out on that you miss out.

Mo.: I think professional success is according to the work. Did you deliver the result? Did you motivate people? People work here, work hard and also work happy because sometimes if you do not work happy there is no meaning. It's all meaningless. I want to work hard and work happy. As long as you get result you enjoy the process. Sometimes the process is painful once you get the result you feel happy. I feel that professional result you get your salary. You get your pay so you can contribute back to the family. For the family success I feel first of all its the entire family's happiness. Including the husband, the kids, even the parents in law. We enjoy live together. Especially I would say most of the time I feel my happiness come from my kids instead of myself. When I see they are happy than I am happy. And also, I try to understand what they need and try to get what they need.

Another aspect that came up again and again, though here it was not the most frequent answer, was recognition from others. Some of the women's personal definitions of career success make direct reference to respect from employees and superiors. When asked how they rate their satisfaction with their career success, the interviewees sounded a positive, grateful note with respect to their achievements. They placed their satisfaction in the 80–100 percent range. Barring a few exceptions, overall, they are satisfied with what they have achieved. However, many of them wish to achieve even more. They gave examples such as *"getting to the next step up the ladder, learning even more, pushing through improvements at their companies or generating higher sales"*. One woman reflected that she wants to do the things she has not yet managed to implement. More than half of the Chinese women who have already achieved high positions named another hierarchical promotion goal for the future, combined with clear positional wishes such as GM, VP, board member or a hierarchically high role in the company headquarters overseas, which in turn illustrates the high career orientation.

C.: If you call it, I'm very grateful for what I have done and I think that I am also very lucky and I'm very grateful. From that perspective I'm very satisfied yes but I'm also from the perspective that ok if I want to do more, I want to do more and contribute in bigger ways.

S.: Private I think is you have happy family. Have family members that rely on you. You feel ok you have a responsibility I think is good. Professional life I think is maybe the position. You get higher position. You can show your success. Second is that you are you really recognize by the many people. Even you are not in the higher position but you are well accepted and well respected by the boss by the top management. By the peers. By the people. I think that will be success.

Leadership motivation and the need for handling of power and competition

The Chinese women's answers show a need and desire to serve a role model function at their companies and in the market. In addition, they are motivated to influence and support others in equal measure. The women's descriptions of leadership motivation primarily center on the desire to be a role model, on the willingness to assume responsibility, and on influencing other people. The women frequently described achieving a respected role model function as their main motivation.

> S.: I think I want to be a person that my colleagues see as very professional, that I can support them, they can learn from me to be successful. This kind of recognition is not just achievement. You are the person that can really help them to be successful and very professional.

Strong and genuine interest in their employees also plays an important part here. The women see themselves as responsible for motivating employees and supporting them so they can develop. Chen et al. (1997) describe traditional Chinese leadership principles that might underlie these descriptions of their motivations. According to their research, *"Chinese leaders establish themselves by promoting the success of their followers and enrich these followers by extending to them opportunities to develop their careers"*. This matches the descriptions of the women, who want to support others. In order to achieve this goal, the women delegate tasks, issue clear instructions or provide coaching, according to the specific situation. The answers regarding the women's own relationship with power and the role this relationship has played in their careers reveal that the women engage with the issue in a nuanced manner. Many of the women believe that female executives in China are very good at exercising power, and better than their male counterparts. Once again, they trace their strong, positive relationship to power back to their own upbringing and early experiences. According to these accounts, parents in positions of power teach their children from a very young age how to exercise power in later life. These accounts suggest that it is important not to be afraid of power.

> M.M.: That comes from the Cultural Revolution. My parents came from the government, my father had power and my mother had power. I have always seen how powerful they were...I always saw people in high position and heard that these are normal people. I had no fear of the big boss, because I was used from early on being around them. All are the same for me. Sometimes it disturbs people in big meetings that I say what I think...most important, no fear. My company says, this woman has no fear, she is too courageous...no fear. I have no fear.

In this connection, the Chinese women emphasized the responsibility that goes with power. Some of them said they believe they have less power than outsiders and company employees assume by virtue of their position, since the corporate system and its rules generally limits the exercise of power within the system. On the other hand, examples such as the power to dismiss or hire staff demonstrate the great power wielded by HRDs, CEOs or similar. The women said their personal goal is to use power with sensitivity, rather than exploiting it. They think that power should be used fairly and transparently. The Chinese executives distinguished between hierarchical power by virtue of position and power arising from communication skills and assertiveness. They use hierarchical power, which they described as more straightforward, but would not want to use it as their main tool. Rather, they use it when quick decisions are needed. Many of them only like to use hierarchical power very rarely, *"only when there's no longer any other alternative"*. Excessive use of hierarchical power was equated with *"immature leadership"*.

Business-Focused Inventory of Personality (BIP) developed by Hossiep (2003) is the leading method used to categorize personalities in the German-speaking business world. "Personality" refers here to the structure of all of a person's behavioral dispositions, including motivational structures and values. In the analysis of the transcripts of the interviews most of the condensed self-descriptions of the Chinese women could be assigned to the areas of performance motivation, leadership motivation, flexibility and team orientation. In terms of frequency, most of the women's descriptions could be assigned to the category of achievement motivation, which studies very clearly show is associated with progressing further in management. Achievement motivation refers to a willingness to measure oneself against a high benchmark, to constantly measure one's own achievements, to compare oneself with others and if necessary, to improve one's own performance. The Chinese female top managers described themselves as ambitious. They set themselves high personal goals and benchmarks, and are very focused on success. One woman summarized this high goal motivation as follows:

> J.: Ambition. I should say I'm a very ambitious person. I want to be somebody because in (company name) I worked with many smart people. I want to be my boss. That's always what I think. I want to be my boss at the end of the day.

The goals *"be the best"* and *"be outstanding"* were frequently mentioned as career drivers. The women believe this originated in their childhoods and upbringing. The women were raised with the goal of being top of the class at school. They were identified as exceptionally gifted, and their teachers and parents gave them further encouragement to excel.

> Ag1: That's very interesting. When I was young, I think I was always a top good student in the teacher's eye. ... Always on the top. Maybe in my teachers eyes I should be in this way. I don't know. Everything I did should be outstanding. That's maybe in the beginning, in childhood. Feels like I should be a role model. Probably that's kind of influencing me- in everything I do I should be role model.

> Mi.: Yes, I remember very well when I was eight, I told everybody I wanted to be like Marie Curie, I think it was like the lady who won the Nobel Prize for Physics, the lady who was in the quantum Physics together with her husband. I really wanted to be a scientist, I wanted to be a physicist to make a lot of research, find out the rules of the universe. That or be a professor one day,

that was my original dream, and I was very good in abstract thinking, so I read a lot of physics study, like Einstein, when I was young.

J.: "First, I always wanted to do something special. The reason why I wanted to go to Germany was my fear to foresee with at the age of 20 the routine of my next 20 years of life. Like my parents – school, study job. A relaxed job, high reputation, not well paid, not so that we had to suffer from hunger, but enough to live. This is not what I wanted. I wanted to do something valuable, something different.

Most of the interviewees reported that they see competition as a motivating factor for their careers. It is notable that competition is generally regarded very positively. The women described competition as a source of inspiration, strength and learning. Many used the phrase *"excited about a fair game"* or interpreted competition as competition with themselves with the goal of improving. They described competition as making them stronger, more assertive and tougher.

V.: Competition? Sometimes competition can make you stronger.... the competitor maybe somehow has some strength which you don't have. You should very frankly observe yourself and him and what things he does better and you should learn from him. I think the only way to face the competition is to make you stronger. So, competition for me I think it's okay. If you are stronger, really stronger, you should take the higher position.

They once again traced their positive handling of competition back to their socialization, and presented examples from school and university. Even back then, the women already wanted to be *"number one"*. They see winning as something very positive and valuable. Many of them described how they could not bear to lose children's games such as card games or table tennis, or mentioned dreams such as *"wanting to become world table tennis champion"*. For many of the women, their parents (alongside factors such as school and other groups of children) had a strong impact on their positive attitude towards competition. A desire for success and the goal of becoming more influential were mentioned as motivations for competing. Another motivation is the feeling of happiness that they experience when they win. The interviewees reject unfair competition. According to the women, winners or stronger performers deserve respect and their advancement is not resented. Less than 25 percent of the interviewed women view competition with others unfavorably. Typical explanations for this were that they find it unpleasant or that their company does not have a competitive culture. This more reticent attitude towards competition in a minority of the group could be due to cultural background factors that, according to Hofstede (1998), derive from China's collectivist orientation. According to this theory, the desire to compete runs counter to this traditional group-focused orientation.

Cl.: This is funny story but it helps explain my competitive side. As children we would play a card game. If I felt I am not going to win in this game I would quit. I would not join in. I would find reasons to say that I'm sick today. I'm tired. I felt like if I am going to win a game, I am very active in participating.... Later on, in work I always wanted to be the best. I always wanted to have the highest score. Be the best to get recognized. That also was part of problem when I became a leader. I probably was not able to appreciate the people who are different from me. I would encourage people to take on challenges and to be aggressive. I probably was not able to appreciate in full those more introverted styles. Later on, of course I learned about that. By nature, I'm actually competitive.... Later on, I learned to better manage that side of me. I actually feel excited when I have a chance to compete. But I have to use that in a good way.

H.: What drives me is that I am a very competitive person. Perhaps it's also linked to the way I was brought up. My parents' expectation in me. I wanted to succeed. I wanted to have more influence. I wanted to apply my knowledge whatever capabilities.

X.: ... for men, I believe, they are more afraid to lose face so you have to be more careful because they are men. But for women, for some Regional Manager's, my observation is they are tough. They are aggressive. Otherwise they will not in that position. They are very competitive. Very, very competitive. They don't realize they are very competitive. They are not afraid to lose face because they are so competitive and so aggressive. They fight back and the want to win. They want to win always. If one is woman and the man in the same position normally the woman is 3x's stronger than the man. This is the comment from my boss 10 years ago. When I look at this female, managing in my team now, I will remind them they are so competitive and their peers may not be so comfortable to deal with that. I will remind them.

Mi.: But when I grow older, I didn't feel the competition is that obvious any more. You don't compete with anybody for any specific thing. So I am more focusing on myself. In other words, I am competing with myself every day, whether I can be better than before.... It is also the maturity of age. Seriously, you don't compete with anybody. That is why my first question was to compete with whom?

Q.: For me it is more about source of inspiration because I always thought that I learn things from those type of situations. I think then it depends on how the game is played. Most of the time I feel excited, if it's a fair play that the person is playing.... if not then I will feel kind of, I may lose my interest. Feel a bit frustrated if it's not the same way I expected. Like for example if I argue with reason and the other person is rather more emotional then I lose interest.

Financial motivation of the Chinese women: Independence

The women also mentioned extrinsic career motivations. In this connection, several interviews touched on the financial incentive of rising to senior positions. This factor was very openly described as one of their key motivating factors, especially at the start of their careers. The women noted their strong negotiating skills and financially focused goals. According to the women's descriptions, financial motivations for careers appear to be socially accepted. All the women addressed the topic openly and directly. Key goals that the women aim to achieve by advancing to a position with a higher salary at their company included providing support and security for their families, becoming financially independent (especially from their husbands) and strengthening their own position within their families. In line with China's rapid economic growth from the 1990s to the present day, the women reported rapid increases in their incomes compared with the low starting salaries when China's economic reforms were just beginning. Some women reported a 16-fold increase over their starting salary; others reported ten – and then five-fold increases in their salary within a short period of time. They described how China's 1970s generation, which most of the women belong to, was not affluent, and that consequently women needed to earn an income in order to start families and safeguard or improve living standards. In their view, the 1990s generation has a different relationship to money and generally has higher expectations. They also observed that the 1970s generation did not have to fight much for more money, pay increases came about pretty much as a matter of course, provided their performance was good. In general, the women described their generation as being motivated both by achievement and money. However, they said that the financial motivation becomes less important the further up the hierarchy one rises, and is replaced by other intrinsic factors.

> Ju.: If I look at all the steps I had in the past, I think from intuition point of view there is something in my body that I really like money, I should say that. Because why I say that is if you look at all the things, I've done I'm always very self-independent. I didn't ask my mother or my parents for any financial support. I also want earn my little penny to support myself. Why I say that? Because when I was in the university, I had plenty of two part time jobs. One is to be a teacher for a small child. That earn me in that sense I can earn some money to support myself. I wanted to be financially free."

> L.: I think freedom. What I mean is the control of my life. It's also a motivation for me. I'm talking about money. Actually, my earning is much higher than my husband. And my husband his earning can almost manage my family livings. So basically, my money earned money doesn't have any use for my family unless we want to invest in something. But we are not really plan so well the investment. I have a freedom to manage my money. I enjoy this kind of situation that nobody controls me. When I was very small my parents let me go, let me free, whatever you do, you just do what you want to so I enjoy this kind of thing. For family or myself I don't want anyone control me. That's my work motivation number 1. I earn the money. I earn the freedom for myself.

> M. M.: They said..." Yes, what do you want, what we pay you is enough for a Chinese" ... I said "Yes, but the company earns a lot of money because of this position. The position is paid, no matter woman or man, German or Chinese...". At the end they agreed. I negotiated a fixed salary plus a bonus. If the result gets better, I get more bonus, if not it goes down. This has to do with performance. At the end I renounced a bit as the result was so good, we had not thought that.

> Jo.: Both quantitatively and qualitatively I would say in terms of salary package, which XY (company name) had higher, and benefits as well. Secondly recognition is very important to me, I think. I'm one of those persons who believes if I spend enough effort and contribution, I will deserve what I need to deserve.

> St: Respect. Also, money. Because you have senior position, you earn a lot. You earn more than others. Now, my motivation is self-satisfaction.

Only a small portion of the group reported that money is not particularly important to them. However, this answer was relativized by reference to the fact that they have already risen to a high level and are financially comfortable. Two women reported deliberately taking pay cuts for the sake of career moves that they knew would mean a lower salary. For the interviewees, status primarily represents success and recognition from their families. The women said that, for them, status means their parents and children being proud of their success. Another definition of status in this group concerns being recognized as an expert in their companies, in their networks and among their colleagues. Many of them equate status with a good reputation in the market. They also regard working at a company with a good reputation as an aspect of status, as this in turn increases the recognition from their family. Accordingly, women described how, for them, status means working at a Top 500 company that attracts admiration in their social environment. The women only demand externally visible status symbols from their companies if this is justified by the company's success and is in keeping with the company culture. In this connection, they described their own titles as a means of getting things done more easily at their companies. The female executives furnish their offices in simple style, with no recognizable status symbols. The offices of CEOs and vice-presidents differ from those of directors only in terms of size. All the interviewed women have a personal assistant and an office with a window, but none of them have a traditional anteroom. The women's assistants are based in open-plan offices near their bosses' offices, and their role is not immediately identifiable to visitors. An assistant was only involved in preparations for one of the interviews. Hence, for the women in this group status primarily means social recognition and recognition within the company. There was no sign of external status symbols.

> M. M.: That was important to me, I would say. But only through my hard work. Company XY asked me if I wanted a bigger office. I said no, first we have to earn money, then we will make that bigger. At the first joint venture I got a Mercedes as bonus, but at the beginning I had an old car. I do not need it, but if the company earns well than I want it. If we build a swimming pool for the staff than I want one for myself.

> Ma.: I was very proud when I leaved XY (company name) my north Asia president asked my boss to offer a farewell party for me and a very precise gift. It's a crystal something and very expensive. About 3000rmb as a gift for me. And our greater China HR department went to Hangzhou and stayed in five-star hotel for my party. That's a special award the north Asia president offer for my farewell. That's really amazing. I got a lot of recognition.

Working behaviour of the Chinese female executives – determined and flexible

In the Big Five theory of Cattell (1986) and Judge (2004), flexibility is classed as "openness to experience". In relation to career development, the aspect of flexibility that concerns openness to changes in one's professional life is of interest. This involves the capacity to adapt flexibly to frequent changes in working conditions. High acceptance of change and openness to new perspectives and methods fall under this category. For women in particular, it has been shown that there is a link between flexibility, understood as a tool for independent career development, and the executive level that they reach. The descriptions provided by the Chinese women that could be assigned to the category of flexibility are highly varied. They repeatedly described themselves as flexible and as welcoming change. Some of them described how they are constantly looking for new challenges and variety. Boredom triggered by overly monotonous work and professional environments is one of the main demotivators for these women. The most common phrases that occurred in their descriptions of their career paths, which will be considered in greater depth in a later chapter, included "to be exposed to many industries, experience different businesses, see different ways of managing, experience different roles in different departments". This suggests a high degree of flexibility concerning different types of work. The women's descriptions of their career paths reveal that the women in this group are very flexible not just with regard to their work, roles and experiences, but also with regard to geographical mobility, both intra-organizationally and when switching companies. Examples of this included relocating, living away from their families and commuting.

> Ke.: I think that was for me key challenge is to getting to know the different market of other countries. I don't know I was put on the spot I remember to Malaysia. At that time, we do not have an HR. the whole team was gone before I took it over. That was very challenging because that period exactly is our budgeting period. I had no idea how the salary is calculated. What is the package we are talking about? What are the benefits? Package that we need to include in this budget? I had totally no idea and what are the government compliance regulatory and monetary requirement. I totally had no idea but I need to do this in 3 days. I really slept like 3 hours maximum per day. I went there and spend my whole weekend in the hotel. I searched the website of their government policies. Studied one by one. And consulted my external HR consultant in Malaysia and asked her to provide me guidance suggestions. I gave her call during weekend, I apologized but I have to until I come up with a very accurate budgeting plan on my own."

> C.: I think at that point I did not know which industry or which particular company would be interesting. I interviewed with XY Company and the consultant role sounded very challenging, very interesting to me so I joined XY. I think it was come to think of it; it was good thing because I got to be exposed to a lot of different industries. A lot of different business issues.
> I think it was different of course and you got to work in one company, work in one industry instead of different industries. I think one good thing about YZ (Company name) is we have multiple business units with more than 1. It still gives me a little bit of different sectors to look into. So, it is not that boring and so that was good. The fact that YZ has given me different roles and keep me challenged I think that was also good...

> L.: I wanted to join a relatively small company but I wanted to join a consumer or rented company. I told him very clearly my background and my personality. I talked to head-hunter and luckily, they got this opportunity. I'm not looking for balance. I'm looking for some stretch and challenge. I want to really step from supporting role, nice role to a very business impact role. Impact again. This is my first role in YZ (Company name). It's an HR business partner role. Its (inaudible) builder so when I joined in 2012 it's an individual contributor. It's an HR partner. My key work is really about redesign the company and support the company to do the change management, the layoff. All the tough things.

The women accept frequently being away from their family and, if necessary, having to travel between family and work, sometimes over thousands of kilometers. Examples that were given of this flexibility were linked to the expansion of multinational companies: for instance, opening new factories or offices in China, or acquiring new sales regions. Many of the women's career development phase coincided with the period of Chinese expansion following the economic reforms. The women offered a number of accounts of how they took the chances that were available. This required acceptance of change, both mental and geographical, and the flexibility to reorganize their families in the face of the new challenges. A number of examples demonstrated a high degree of flexibility in order to meet companies' requirements and develop their careers even in difficult personal situations such as a partner falling sick or needing to arrange childcare for two young children in their home city.

> Ca.: I always chose work first. That's why I think in. 2007, I worked in Shanghai for about ten months. I travel back every week to Beijing because my son and my husband were still in Beijing. Just I came here just to temporarily replace a colleague who had to be off for eight or nine months. So, I took her job and kept my job as well. Two jobs and then travel every week to Beijing.

The women described themselves as being more courageous and more willing to take risks than other colleagues. In this connection, they also frequently mentioned the courage to take decisions, noting that it was important that they are not afraid of certain risks. Qualities described in this context included optimism, a capacity for enthusiasm and a positive attitude to change.

> M. M.: I have always worked as an executive in China, I knew that getting recognition would be difficult in Germany, but I thought, it will come one day. The third company was a company in Rheinland-Pfalz (part of Germany) that started a joint venture in Yunnan province. The newspaper 'Welt' had made an article about my career, you can have that. They wanted a joint venture but Yunnan was not cultivated, but a poor place to be. This company was small, they needed someone. For a joint venture a strong Chinese partner is important.

> B.: Yes, it is my strengths – I am target oriented and have no fear of obstacles. And I am not afraid of the change and I look for the change. I want to learn new things and I believe it is also my strengths that I can see the whole picture.

For these Chinese top managers, the search for new challenges and variety is in the focus of their professional decisions. Boredom, triggered by too much consistency in the field of work and professional environment, is a clear de-motivator. The women described seeking out challenges, developing themselves and avoiding boredom as the main motivations behind flexibility. The big majority of the women seek out and welcome change.

Chinese women, the ability to handle conflicts and assertiveness

The ability to deal with conflict is closely related to assertiveness in the job. Most of the women described their attitudes and responses to conflict against the background of their socialization and upbringing, which primarily focused on avoiding conflict. In Chinese culture, a high value is placed on respect and friendliness.

This corresponds to the studies by Chin et al. (2001), who found that *he (harmony)* is central to classical Chinese management. The key traditional values of Chinese managers are maintaining good personal relationships and *keeping face* even in cases of conflict. According to one woman, bosses from other countries sometimes fail to respect these values out of ignorance, which can often have drastic consequences – even to the extent of Chinese managers quitting.

> J.: I think my strengths is communication, empathy. In a joint venture communication is essential. It is not like company XY has the say in all, it is all about persuasion of your partner, I think I have an advantage with my language skills and my convincing skills. It is not working like you just say 'it is like this and you must accept it', but convincing is important.

> M. M.: ...difficult to say. As a female I can communicate, convince well. I am not good at logical talk, but I can convince with some good examples. The disadvantage is that they did not take women seriously (compared to German men). In the board meetings for example, when I had ideas, at the beginning they do not take it seriously. This is crazy as many innovative ideas are difficult to accept in the beginning. I had to prepare better. But here in China I am always accepted right from the beginning.

> Cl.: I'm not really good at that. For example, if I have an argument, I never really have an experience of having an argument with a male people. At XY (Company name) especially no because we are too gentle with each other. We don't argue a lot with each other. But at YZ (company name) yes, I had a really bad experience. Someone came from US and we had an argument and he made me like a fool in front of a group of people. I didn't handle it very. I was silent here. And I hide my emotions although I was very hurt here inside. That's one of the things I decided to leave. There's no longer a place for me.......Like my subordinated? Here I don't think they're fighting in front me. They don't do that. But if they do, I would not take sides. I would not say who's right who wrong. I would not say that even if I think one part is right and one apart is wrong. But I would do that. Make sure no one lose face here.

However, some of the women welcome conflict and believe this means they are closer to the directly confrontational American style. From their descriptions, it does not appear that these women adopted this more direct response to conflict as a way of overcoming intercultural challenges; rather, they present it as part of their personalities. Many of them described how they deliberately bring conflict to the surface so they can look for solutions. In this connection, the women often used the terms *"aggressive"* and *"hard"*. The women described themselves as capable of making unpleasant decisions. A number of women gave the example of dismissing staff. Several women explicitly mentioned their own strength at dealing with conflict. The term *"tenacity"* also occurred very frequently: the ability to keep going when times are tough and to take difficult decisions. Many of the women pay great attention to the emotional aspects of conflict. According to the women, the first step in dealing with conflict is to bring emotions under control; feelings need to be brought out into the open and calmed down. When conflicts arise among their staff, the women want to be authentic, like a friend. The most commonly mentioned values in this context were kindness and honesty. The women expressed a desire to coach their employees, find out what the problem is and listen to both sides impartially. Other women described a more rational approach towards finding solutions. In cases of conflict, they like to stick to the facts and concentrate on the concrete issues. These women frequently spoke of *"not getting too excited"*.

> M. M.: This came with age. At the beginning with the joint venture I was young and I fought until the bitter end and achieved it all. Now I am better, more compromising. Little things I will let go, peanuts. With small things, peanuts, I am easy now, but with important things I fight until the end. No matter, fought all the way up to the CEO, everywhere I will go. They say I am assertive.

> C.: I think that I try to get the emotions out of the topic first. Because the conflicts for example we had a recent so-called conflict. I think that first of all do not get overwhelmed by the emotions and because the emotions may burn you and make you so you first of all understand that the emotions are there but do not let those emotions burden you or consume you. You take them aside and look at the issue. The issue you will find you usually have to accept it or you can do something about it. If you need to accept it you will just have to accept it. You will have to help yourself and help your team to accept it. And if there is something you can do differently about it whether to change it or do something then you can work on it. If you let the emotions consume you and you argue not over the facts but over the emotions that's probably not very meaningful, I found. Sometimes we argue over emotions. There is no right or wrong over emotions. Something happened and how I feel about is very different from how you feel about it. There's no point in arguing if your emotions are correct or not. There is no right or working. I have different emotions, you have different emotions, somebody else has different emotions. So there's no point to argue over emotions. If you take that aside and only look at the issue sometimes, I also accept that things are not going to be always to my liking. It's not going to work out. Every time not going to work out the way that I want them to work out every single time and if they don't work out like the way I want them to work out either I can still do something about it or I have to accept it and I if have to accept it then I will not.

> M.: Conflicts normally come when you have different opinions to certain things. And on a job, you normally always have conflicts. How do I handle them? I am usually a very rational person. I state a lot of facts, I stick to the facts either until the other people convince me, then I give in or I still stick to it. But I don't normally get too excited. Even when I get excited, I try to calm down a little bit, for example when I write an email, I don't send an email right away, I just hold it for some days until I take out all those emotions. And then send the things out. I am not so good in front of a person, when you start a very hot discussion, then it may be appearing on my face, then my emotion is a little bit less controlled. Then I start to get a little bit hot. This is still something I need to work on in general.

> Z.: You have to watch the other person first and find out what each of you controls. How the person reacts to you. I mean to observe the opponent very carefully. This is very, very important. There is a clear strategy that fits for each person. Number 1, observe the opponent, what is important for him, what not. And when it is very important for him, try to not tough that point, but go around. But some cases compete aggressively, they want to win all. That you must know. In that case I say, ok, I give you this and I get that, find a compromise. But there are persons, once you made a compromise, who always want you to give in. With such persons you need to stay tough. Perhaps not always, but for the important things, stay firm and strong.

The older women in particular described gradually learning to not only fight for their own solutions but also to avoid taking conflicts too personally and to put themselves in other people's shoes. They described their ideal strategy as making a case based on solid facts and remaining rational and calm. Other interviewees made clear that competing and fighting for their own solutions generally remains their primary strategy in cases of conflict. The strategies for dealing with conflict include the whole spectrum, from constant competition to more compromises and cooperation.

Dealing with criticism and mistakes against the backdrop of cultural norms

The way the Chinese women in management deal with mistakes and criticism must also be viewed against the background of cultural values. Traditionally, direct criticism was seen as damaging to relationships and hence avoided. Overall, the women are very ambivalent about this whole area, including the way they deal with criticism and mistakes themselves.

> S.: I don't feel lose face if I make a mistake. Because if I made a mistake I will say "Oh I'm sorry. This is my mistake. I need to correct it." If I communicate my work failure, I will say ok. "What is the reason?" But I will not blame the team. If they have done wrong then I will ask few questions, let them think if this way and that way. For example, the sales revenue goes down and then in the sales meeting I have to let them think what we can be improved.

Taking a rational view, the women try to see criticism positively as an opportunity for improvement. Emotionally, criticism is rejected as shameful and unpleasant. This can be assessed against the cultural background of *"saving face"*, which led to Chinese managers traditionally taking a more indirect communication style that preferred to avoid conflict. This management style, derives from Confucian tradition. However, according to the interviewees, losing face, something that is universally feared in China, is easier for women to bear than men, since they can count on more empathy when they are criticized, especially from foreign bosses. The women described one of their strengths as the ability to take criticism more calmly than men. On the other hand, they also noted that women are more critical, since they think everything through more than men. The women frequently said that they have learned to accept criticism, though not personal or subjectively baseless criticisms, which they said could quickly trigger aggressive responses. They claimed that men are more afraid of losing face and react to mistakes in a very hostile and arrogant manner, whereas women find it easier to deal with mistakes since they have greater perseverance and, as one participant put it, are *"able to get back on their feet again more quickly"* after being criticized. According to the interviewees, it is easier for women than for men to relieve their feelings of tension when they make mistakes, for example by crying. Afterwards, they are quickly able to deal with the situation again.

> St.: First of all, there's no big mistake in my career because I am very careful. Each time when I make a decision or make a judgment, I do a lot of research. Of course, I have little mistake. I just confess. I'm sorry.
>
> T.: Woman and failure. Well. I think for woman, women are very persistent and also in fact I saw a woman stronger than men in times of failure. So when woman fail, they come back and they

do it again and they fail and they do it again and again. And then for men if they fail it may take longer time for them to reenergize. For woman it may take one day to reenergize. Typical example will be when, when, when my female colleague broke up with a male friend. I mean broke up with boyfriend they recover so soon but for male it's difficult.... and then women are not afraid of failure I think men are more arrogant and also men see failure losing face. But woman sees failure as a natural so something like that and then they come back.

Cl.: I guess being viewed as a failure is really hard. It's really hard for me. And that would give me a lot of pressure. I would try to work very hard to avoid that……Avoid being perceived as a failure. Later on, I learned to accept failures more and more but when I was younger it was very bad.... In my case not really. In general people would not care so much. But I think if there is a career failure it is easier for women to accept it than men in our culture. But personal life, no. It's still bad for both sexes.

Chinese women's leadership style: Democratic, transformational and if needed autocratic

Most of the Chinese top women managers spontaneously described their own leadership style as democratic, and distanced themselves from hierarchical styles. By democratic leadership styles, they mean ones that are open, encouraging and involve everyone. The aim of a democratic style is to be approachable to employees, minimize hierarchy and give staff autonomy. By contrast, just under a quarter of the women described themselves as having leadership styles closer to ones referred to in the literature as autocratic. The participants said that they lead teams in a way that maximizes performance, and once again mentioned the democratic style described earlier. *"Team performance is my performance"* said one participant, who described seeing herself as part of a group. The women described building up trust as one of the highest values for their careers. They want to develop honest and trustworthy relationships, and want other people who work with them to see them as a person with these qualities. They frequently mentioned supporting other people and contributing to their success as personal strengths and intrinsic motivations, and described themselves as team players with a high people orientation. Empathy and caring for others were repeatedly emphasized as social competencies. At the same time, receiving recognition from others is an important aspect of collaboration. Recognition from the team is very important for all the women; they want to be seen as role models.

So.: Before a problem I think we should discuss. Perhaps my manager has her solution and I have mine we should put all together on the table and discuss to find the better solution. I don't like the hierarchy. I think everyone is equal and someone is more competent than the other with more experience or something like that. But everyone should really take down his or her own opinion then we decided together.

M. M.: My leadership style. I am a strong character. Most people say dominant. It shows quickly that I am a dominant character. I became like this through my work. I am not like this naturally.

> I am positive and open. I like to sing, to dance and make sports. I laugh a lot with others. I like to sew and I am good at designing. Making many beautiful things, that is my nature. Originally, I wanted to be an artist. But with the culture revolution we had no choice. I came to Germany and then saw that there is a chance with that job in Yunnan as nobody wanted to go there. So I went. The people in the factory have to be led strongly. This was my leadership style.
>
> S.: I think I want to be a person that my colleagues see as very professional, can support them, they can learn from to be successful. This kind of recognition does not just come through achievement. You are seen as the person that can help them to be successful and very professional.

One focal point of the Chinese women's descriptions was staff development. This category could be understood in terms of the "individualized consideration" element of the transformational style, which concerns development and mentoring of followers and attention to their specific needs. Many of the women mentioned delegation and employee coaching as personal strengths in conjunction with a style that recognizes, motivates and supports others. They described this style using terms such as engaging, empowering and encouraging, with a focus on employee motivation and a desire to minimize the sense of hierarchy. Approachability and developing trust are regarded as especially important. Being approachable, involving others and listening were other frequent descriptions. Accordingly, the main aim of their leadership is to develop and support other people.

Three of the interviewees used the metaphor *"like parent and child"* and a comparison with the metaphor of *"the dominant Chinese mother"* to describe their leadership style. By this they meant, first, being 100 percent behind employees and giving them their full support, and, second, combining everyone's goals and giving employees flexibility in how to implement these goals. The aim is to give them the freedom to make their own decisions while setting clear targets. Staff development is particularly important to the women. As executives, they see themselves as having a role model function. The term "caring" occurred frequently, relating both to employees' feelings and enabling work-life balance. There were slightly fewer descriptions that could be categorized according to the "intellectual stimulation" component of a transformational leadership style. The women said that they are exceptionally able to *"bring up the big topics"*. They described themselves as inspiring, motivating and a source of ideas. At several points, they specifically noted that they are willing to subordinate their own views to better ideas that come from employees and that they view it as their primary task to create a climate in which everyone can contribute. However, some of them feel that their staff are too inexperienced and so need clear instructions. Some women described their style as a mixture of Western and Chinese leadership cultures. They noted that they share their emotions with their employees and develop high levels of trust and respect. They classify this as part of the more Chinese-influenced aspect of their leadership style.

> Jo.: I think I have a natural advantage, which is being educated and lived in the UK. I think I learned how to managing people in the Westernized way. And being Chinese myself I think I do share the emotions with Chinese colleagues and friends. I guess I combine the two, which

made me quite smoothly in terms of managing people. I do give them the autonomy to do what they think they can achieve. I have a very result driven style. Two of my mangers, very senior said to me when I just join the company, we are very experienced manager within the industry. I don't need someone to be the mommy. I said fully understood. I am very result driven as well. As long as you deliver, I will not interfere with the way you manage. As long as you are not coming out of the standards frame. They were very clear if they don't reach the results, I expected I would interfere for sure. So far it has worked well.

Ja: Maybe this is from my female part. Currently I'm leading a team of five persons. Three in China, one in Malaysia, one in Korea. A Korean guy. So I'm leading multicultural people. I think they will say quite good boss. Why good? They will say I try to understand. I try to talk to them. I think I take care of their feelings in the work. I spend little time with my family but I make sure they spend time with their family. Although some travel in weekend I say is it necessary. Please don't worry if you fly out on Monday and spend one night more or later. I try to reduce them to spend private time for the business. If they have some issue at home, I say go there.

Table 1: Results on female Chinese leadership in comparison with current research.

Western female leadership *	Chinese female leadership **
Transformational	Transformational
Democratic decision making	Democratic but also autocratic
Visionary	Acting as role model
Facilitation of communication	Ask for collective wisdom
Involvement of employees in team building	Team development and team performance
Reward power	Developing others, care, consider emotions
Inspiring and motivating	Inspiring and motivating
Fostering mutual trust and respect	Mutual trust and respect

* Based on Stanford, J.H. et al. (1995), Eagly, A.H. et al. (2007), Powell, G.N. (2011).
** Based on research by the author.

The peculiarities of the Chinese leadership style lie in the high importance of the role model function that shapes the style and the situational use of authoritarian leadership. The respondents believe that women's leadership styles are more empathetic and sensitive than men's and that they care more for their staff overall. They also think that women are better listeners and communicators, and that women are in principle not able to act the same way as men. The respondents think that women are sometimes judged differently for the same behavior and that there is a general social expectation that women should be nicer than men. Hence, they believe that women in leadership positions should focus on their strengths rather than attempting to copy men. In their view, women's strengths lie in interpersonal relationships, including caring for employees. Only one participant generally considers women to be less sensitive towards employees.

Career-enhancing factors

When the Chinese women are asked why they were selected for a managerial role, the answers reflect a mixture of different components. In addition to a good education and good language skills, women spontaneously mention various skills and abilities, their own personality traits and the aspect of mentoring as well as having a supportive spouse. In addition to external influences, it is therefore of interest to consider individual factors that have promoted the ascent. *"Being Chinese"* and *"local market knowledge"* are factors that run through the entire survey and have been repeatedly mentioned in connection with the factor *"being a woman"* as an advantage for a career in a multinational company in Shanghai.

Active relationships with mentors and culturally shaped networking

When asked about the influence of mentoring on their own careers, the Chinese women described different types of persons: sometimes, they described mentors who were formally appointed by their companies, while in other cases they described informal mentors. Formal mentoring programs are special programs, often aimed specifically at women that are being established at an increasing number of companies. However, only a minority in the study group mentioned formal mentoring relationships and with a critical view on the effect on their success and career.

> T.: Our company encouraged the culture of mentorship. So I told them is better to have a mentor from overseas because I need some global connection and also global mentoring. And then the HR assigned this person to me because they see it very relevant so I connected with this person. We have been working together for about a year and it was good and he recently left the company and started his own business.

Twenty-four of the Chinese women mentioned informal mentoring relationships that came about without any formal programs. Some of these mentors were working at the same companies as the women, while others were based externally. Eleven of the women spontaneously described multiple individuals who had acted as mentors to them. These women had actively and deliberately initiated the mentoring relationships. Personal chemistry, the potential mentor's comparative expertise and hierarchical considerations were key criteria when it came to choosing a mentor. The women all agree that informal mentoring relationships have had more benefits for their careers. "Support", "understanding" and "encouragement" are the main factors that were spontaneously mentioned when the women were asked about the benefits of mentoring. They reported how mentoring had helped them to cope with very difficult times at their companies or to persevere in positions that they did not particularly enjoy and then nonetheless advance in their careers. Other perceived benefits of mentoring included trying out new approaches or stepping out of their comfort zone. The interviewees also regard mentors as playing a key role in teaching about cultural differences, for example, the art of debating at French companies. The interviewees repeatedly emphasized how mentors help to explain other ways of communicating. Another important contribution made by the mentors was helping the executives to understand the corporate system. This is regarded as particularly helpful at early career stages. The women regard mentors who act as career coaches and supervise the women for a long period of time, even after switching companies, as highly beneficial. There were reports of specific support that resulted in career advancement, such as rising to a GM role. Several of the interviewed women thought it important to emphasize that mentoring is equally beneficial for men and women. The point that mentoring can benefit all staff at a company, not just women, was made on multiple occasions.

> H.: Informal. I have a few people that I have from the past companies that I stayed friends with and sometimes when I would discuss with them o things or things I'm not sure about or even when I'm thinking of new job opportunity I would talk to them but it is not a formal mentorship. I think generally if you have people like that. It could be your friends. It could be your previous colleagues I think it is great to have just a few people. And my husband is a great person. I think it's nice to have a few people you have in your life that can do that.

> Ag2: I think one thing is clear in my mind is I need to have a mentor. A mentor, who is in Paris. A person that would know there is a China A. (her name) and everybody says good things about her. I decided to have a female coach because currently my boss is a female. I wanted to look for the opportunities for woman because I'm a woman. Sometimes we have different language, how we think. I think they help me out a lot.

> V.: I think they can give you very important advice to let you avoid unnecessary concerns or worries. If you will be with something that is not important, they can tell you what is really important. And also, when you in big pressure with challenges, mentoring encourages since they can look much further away from your view, they can say "It's not a big deal...you can conquer that" or "You will deal much better and become stronger."

> K.: Always when you look back you will find those "wow moments" from them. From your conversation with them and from the information they share with me. From when I do the reflections with them.... and I mention what I did and what is such challenge and how I come up with it. They also share with me their similar experiences and we come up with learning from each other from all these different experiences.

Several of the Chinese see a great benefit of mentoring in career coaching even beyond their recent company. One possible risk ascribed to mentoring is that mentees become dependent on their mentors' reputation at the company. A few women reported being disadvantaged by their mentor relationships when their mentor's position at the company weakened.

> Ja.: I was his assistant. When he was away, I was the GM of the whole factory, looked after purchasing department, operational, even selling.

The group most frequently mentioned in connection with mentoring is the women's bosses. The Chinese women developed "mutually beneficial alliance relationships" in which both mentor and mentee benefit. They act as an extended arm of the CEOs into the Chinese market and into the company. The women supported the mentors with local market knowledge and acted as their spoke person inside and outside the company. In return the mentors supported the women in earlier career stages with advice on Western management skills and sponsored their careers. The boss therefore plays a central role in the career development of the women interviewed and his or her success is often closely related to the own success. Trust is central to the women's relationships with their bosses. Chinese women are shown more trust than men by foreign or female bosses. As a result, they are given high levels of discretion and responsibility, even at early stages of their careers. The interviewees' decisions to switch companies were also often closely linked to their bosses. In this connection, the women described how their bosses had the female executives follow when they switched companies themselves and specifically enticed them away. What is striking among Chinese women compared to all other women surveyed in the other countries is the large number of female role models, in the form of female superiors, who also became mentors. In terms of sponsoring, which, unlike mentoring, involves being represented by a higher manager for promotion opportunities, the Chinese managers describe the hurdle of finding a sponsor from the company's headquarters, which is far away. This is only possible from a certain hierarchy level or for activities that require frequent travel to the headquarters. Here, too, the women show an active examination of the question of how to attract suitable sponsors.

> K.: She was Chinese. That was my first Chinese boss. She was my first Chinese boss. Previously all my bosses were foreigners. She said don't regret just go. Don't hesitate just go. After two months I got a notice that she resigned. She had proposed to our headquarter. I was successor candidate. So became her successor. She is also top ten global. Of the most influential women leaders in the world. I think she sees a lot of opportunities. And she's the one that is taking actions very quickly. And she's also empathetic towards the local situations. She's very brave. She has the guts to make tough decisions.
>
> Ag2: The boss, she was a French lady. Very, very smeary. She brought the brand to China in 1994. Very, very successful, during the Olympic games. I would say I back than grew the company. Recruit people. Build organization. Build HR function and brought company to be top employer of China market…When we talk about the leaders of this generation in the market, these people all remember me and they are all very, very successful. They are all company manager levels. CEO levels. And I feel that's really rewarding. They are all the key players in the market now.
>
> Ag1: The reason I left actually is again my boss. I worked for her for nine years. She is a real respected leader with me. Very smart. Then she resigned first. (Company name) is her baby, however this is not her company, so her dream was to create something of her own…. They invited my boss to be the chairman of that big project. It was very exciting. Then my boss talked to me and said: A., are you interested to join that company?
>
> X.: I started at XY (company name) and I have to be honest I was very lucky because I had a good manager. My first sales manager was a lady. She was a very good coach and taught me a lot of things like selling skills, how to become a good sales person. I became the top sales person in XY (company name) after 2 years for 3 products.

Mo.: I had a very good role model who was previous, previous CFO for XY (Company name) in Greater China. She is from Singapore. A very tiny, tiny lady. I know her now from my Hong Kong time. More than ten years. She is now the YZ (Company name) CFO for Greater China. She was a pretty good role model for me. She said: "You do not really need to be stronger in whatever than men. You really can use different strategies to be still powerful."

Very supportive husbands, à la "Shanghai men"

The Chinese female executives are lucky to have very supportive husbands. A large majority of the study participants said that their husbands are very supportive of their careers. The term *"encourages me"* was mentioned in many of the answers. For many couples, the roles are reversed and for the majority it cannot be spoken of as a dual-career partnership. A part of the men slip into a classic support role with a "normal job", but this is also secured by other people. Two different types of husbands were described: ones who are strongly career-oriented themselves and ones who are family-focused rather than ambitious about their careers. The latter are in the majority in this study. Most men have regular working hours, are freelancers or stay at home. The husbands who are not career-oriented take on a portion of household organization, often with the support of housekeepers and in the best case with four grandparents. The less ambitious partners take a particularly strong role in their children's upbringing. The women describe these husbands as helpful in the household, family-centered, and active in raising and caring for children. They correspond to the stereotype of the "Shanghai men", which in China stands for a husband who cooks, shops, cleans and holds his spouse's handbag on her shopping tours. There were no indications that the women specifically sought out partners who are not career-oriented. When asked about this, the women said that they were more or less on equal footing to begin with and the role distribution came later. The wives with husbands who are not career-oriented expressed regret at their husbands' lack of career ambitions. They described how it was only in the course of their marriages, and in particular after giving birth, that they also saw advantages in this distribution of roles. Common descriptions of husbands in this regard included *"no ambition"*, *"lazy"* or *"I need to push him"*. The female executives themselves appear to have stereotypical ideas and hopes regarding their husbands' careers.

> Ag3: He actually encourages me to work. It's not like in some other cases; some husbands will say I need you to have full attention to the family, to the kids. He really thinks I need to get more connected. We have more common language. I would discuss with him some of the challenges I have and he would give advices. That's very helpful. We have more issues to talk about.

> Ag1: Actually, my husband is very supportive. He's not the career ambitious person actually. He likes more freestyle. He works as like a finance consultant. Takes care of children. He did not like have my job full-time. He had a lot of free time. I think he does more than me. Before we had an Ayi. Five years ago, my sister left us, then I have Ayi but a few months ago she left. And we de-

cided not immediately backfill. My husband does the cooking, buys vegetable, shopping and a lot. He drives. It's easier for him. He does a lot of house things. He's very supportive to my career -always when I talk to him, should I go to Hong Kong, should I go global. Basic decision of course we discuss but he's always supportive.

J.: I have talked to my husband (laughing). And he stayed much longer at home than me. Yes, he has stayed three years at home. (Laughing) Yes. When I had the offer from company XY we discussed this, because one had to stay home for the child. In China it would be common to bring the child to the grandparents, but his parents are dead. My parents take care of my nice already. And I did not want to bring our son to my parents and hire another Ayi (housekeeper). Therefore, I said "One of us must do it."

L.: He is a person who never thinks about future. He thinks about today. Even today is not planned. He's a very peaceful person. Not aggressive. His job is very normal. What I mean he is an operational personal. He manages the plant. Do the productions. All the things actually have been scheduled. He starts work at 8:30. Arrive home at 5:30 every day. Almost same unless he has some trip.

Ju.: My husband is just opposite but I pushed him. I say "see I don't want you to be so successful but you have to be the same as what I'm doing. We have to be equal".

The men with their own careers take on parental duties that are more associated with men, such as supervising sporting activities. Most of them do not do any of the housework, since that is taken care of by the *Ayis* or grandparents or coordinated by their wives. It is striking that there were no negative reports of husbands who are critical of or obstruct their partners' careers. Only in two cases were there repeated mentions of conflicts about the distribution of responsibilities for their children's upbringing. The husbands in question work as CEOs or senior executives themselves. Their wives described them as less family-oriented, less involved in their children's upbringing and household management. Conflict generally arises over travel, which frequently takes the interviewees away from home. But here, too, the women's accounts suggest their husbands have a high tolerance threshold, given the frequency of the absences described. Two factors are associated with increased pressure on the Chinese female executives if they occur together. First, having more than one child; and second, having conceptions of childcare that differ from the traditional Chinese system and assign more familial responsibilities to women. Such conceptions exist among women who previously lived abroad in the West or are married to a foreign spouse.

Ag3: That's something I've been struggling to be honest. He has busy job and he travels a lot. It's hard for him to get more attention to the kids although in a weekend I think there was something to do with Chinese men and their role in the family. In a weekend sometimes he would play golf, again half day is gone. Kids already are used to calling mom whenever something happens and I am not happy with that. I'm trying to doing adjustments but he will discuss with me the weekend arrangements etc... I would try to keep him at home or to go to kids' activities.

H.: That's an interesting question. I think the decision to go part time he pushed me definitely. I think if not for him, I don't know if I would come to the decision so quickly. I think I always had some thoughts about it, but he was understandable very concerned that my workload was very heavy. But I think we got a line on this very quickly. I don't think he pushed me into something I didn't want. But I think he probably pushed me to make the decision faster.

M: You can get men to cook for you in this country. You don't get that very often in Germany.

Dealing with challenges on the career path

The challenges outlined regarding the career paths of these female Chinese top managers result directly from the career strategies they have chosen. Many spontaneously say that mistakes were necessary to really grow and become successful as an executive. An area of focus in their reports is interculturality, which is at the same time the real strength of the Chinese top women managers.

With regard to the cultural challenges, adjustment problems with foreign workplace postings are described. Most examples in this area relate to communication problems when using another language, different ways of working and the management of international employees abroad. Women who have worked abroad particularly report on intercultural problems. Women who worked in China in an international environment did not describe this challenge. One explanation could be that the ability to move between worlds, which is highly advantageous for the executive women in China, was largely or completely irrelevant in the positions they held abroad. There, it was less important to be able to move between Chinese and foreign cultures than it was to be able to adapt to the local culture alone. These descriptions reflect challenges that are also faced by many expats of other nationalities when they work abroad. For example, two women who returned to China from abroad, from Germany and France, found that their overseas experience did not bring about promotions but, on the contrary, led to them having lower positions than before they went abroad. In retrospect, the women questioned viewed it as an insight that did not lead to a standstill. Cultural challenges were not just limited to differences between foreign cultures; there were also reports of such challenges arising from differences between corporate cultures within China. The issue of compliance was mentioned repeatedly. The main challenge in this regard was dealing with differences in values between companies when switching to a new employer. One woman described how, when it came to compliance, her superiors had values opposed to her own. Other examples of challenges arising from different business cultures included changing from a service provider role as an external consultant to an in-house corporate position or switching to a different consumer market. The women cope with the necessary adaptations to the changed environment and other ways of working and mindset.

Je. (about time in Germany): That was actually another challenge because although we brought XY (Company name), there no AB (own company name) people wanted to move there from one town in Germany to around 500 km away. There were less than 20 people from our company who moved there and there were 5000 XY (company name) colleagues. I moved from one German town to another one. So I needed to find my way to survive in Berlin. I did interview to find a new job there basically. I still worked in the global controlling department but I changed a little bit their direction. I had started with the working capital management and added together integration with XY. I moved to XY. Basically, they had everybody denied in this position but I am the one wanting to move. Not every German wants to move. So, I changed the department to be controlling excellence. I moved from one German town to another one.

Ca. (about working in France): First I think the working, the way of working. The way of working is different. The understanding of collaboration is different as well. At very beginning I think the most difficult thing for me is, every week, we had weekly meetings to oversee all our training courses and evaluations of (inaudible). Every training courses. For some colleagues, when there is some problem, they think it's your problem. They don't want to work for your problem. They just want to work for themselves. "This is my course. Don't touch my course." So when I arrived, I asked them to work together. To put everything on a big bulletin and to share information together.

Je. (About returning from Germany): Very unhappy. I shouted to my bosses, say how come. One of the reasons I came back to China was because of the family. My parents this year are 75 already. I want to move back to Beijing to be closer to them and take care more of them. This is also the difference Chinese and Western people. We are more family oriented. I'm moving back to China but not to Beijing. I also felt treated unfair because the other lady doesn't want to move to Shanghai too. I have to. The boss said "You don't want to move to Shanghai, you can come back to Beijing." What position? He says "I can give you projects". But it's not what I wanted. I wanted some real thing. Although I'm really unhappy I talk with my previous bosses, the German guys because we are really good friends. They are like my mentors. I decided, ok I move to Shanghai. I take the better job. That's the reason why I'm now in Shanghai and my old parents in Beijing.

Ca. (about return from France): It was planned for two years. Two or three years. And in China almost at the end of the two years my old China boss told me there's vacancy for staffing director. Every time when he came to Paris for meetings, I always said "Boss don't forget me. I'm always willing to work with you. So if there's any vacancy, don't hesitate to tell me. Let me know." Because my husband doesn't speak English, neither French. He loves the living in Paris but it's the communication language problem. You can never really enjoy the time. After two years I decided to come back to the new role.

Ag3: XY (Company name) had actually had a very tough environment. The business environment was tough. XY's own business is tough. It's at a time of reforming. Because of lack of headcount I was asked to pick up some compliance job as well. It was really a good experience for me to know, to deal with people. Difficult people in their job to make difficult decisions. I covered employment law. I covered HR. For a short period of time I covered companies. Just to give an example we had a case that had potential FCPA. Do you know FCPA? Foreign Corrupt Practices Act. FCPA issues. So, we had to make difficult decisions, to terminate a few of the employees. We received strong resistance from the bases and at the end we still managed to do that. It was difficult.

H.: I didn't have a very large team. I don't remember. I think I had five or six people. It was quite a challenge because I joined as the leader for the consumer practice. I quickly realized consumer is not for me. I think the challenge is the people on my team are really into consumer type of work. I think the challenging part is my heart is not on consumer. So, I didn't, but then I quickly moved, they moved me to corporate practice and I felt the fit was better.

Several women mentioned leadership challenges. One executive who works in sales found asserting herself to be a particular challenge, for example when she had to manage older men in the sales department. Other women reported that they sometimes found it difficult to win their teams' trust and to learn how much to delegate. They regarded dismissals of team members as personal defeats. Examples were also given of managing multicultural teams abroad, which was seen as a particular challenge.

It is striking that only few of the women reported on the challenge of combining a career at a large corporation, and the mobility this necessitates, with their duties as mothers. Some of them accepted living far away from their families for work and having to commute long distances to see their children. Other women described the challenge of combining their workload and working hours with their role as the mothers of two children. They reported dealing with emails at night for long periods of time. Once again, having two children appears to represent a particular challenge for the women in this study.

> X.: I think it was very challenging because in 2000 we were total eleven branch-sales manager. The average their age was ten years older than me. There are only two ladies. And I was one of them. I was very young and a woman, so people looked at me very different. Some of them were very experienced and ten years older than me, but because the two company merge some people left. Half were existing colleagues but the rest was new hiring because some left the company. With the guys who just joined us it was much easier because we were able to find people who have same values. But for me it was very challenging to manage the direct reports, ten years older than me. Also, my peers were ten years older than me so it is challenging

> H.: I think the down side again is you cannot be perfect on both fronts. What I tell myself is on the home front; sometimes I am definitely not as perfect as the other moms who can go to the schools. Cannot be on the school activities. Not go on school outings with them. I would love to be on that but I cannot. I cannot be as perfect as they are. At work I cannot compete with someone like- imagine there is something equally capable as I am but he or she can put in 50 percent more time to travel to network. I cannot do that and they deserve more opportunities than I am to get the next promotion. I am okay with that. I think that here are downsides on both fronts but for me this is the best outcome for me. The total outcome and I am very happy with that.

Some of the women reported stress and pressure, and being worried about their health. According to these women, having a very high workload for many years can have consequences for one's health. There was a particular emphasis on the strain placed on them by frequent business trips. One woman remarked that men can pursue their careers aggressively for many years to come, while this tends not to be possible for women. This remark was made in connection with the strains that careers can place on women's health. Other challenges that were described included the loneliness that goes with being in an executive position and the issue of how to deal with no longer being universally liked. Some women describe that companies function according to their own rules and how they were put in jobs that they did not like. Enduring certain unpopular phases in the company is described as a challenge that was necessary for career development. The interviewees gained knowledge that a long career in the same group made these phases unavoidable and that one had to persevere or adjust the strategy. The incompatibility of the new corporate culture with one's own personality is described as a challenge when changing companies. Women who switch back and forth between American, German and French companies in particular experience this aspect. The country cultures of the head offices and the associated different business styles between US, European and French companies were mentioned as an example. Women implement adaptation as a solution. However, some women reached their limits here and then switched to a different company with the culture they preferred.

Restructurings during the Asian financial crisis were mentioned as another challenge. In particular, HRDs reported having to implement large waves of layoffs themselves. The conflict between, on the one hand, their own values and their fundamental desire to support employees and foster their development and, on the other, the necessity of reducing staff numbers was difficult for several of the women. They said that although they successfully mastered the challenge, the situation placed a great strain on them. Other factors mentioned in this connection included the pressure arising from the fast pace and constant changes and the difficulty of persevering with jobs they did not enjoy. The Chinese women see themselves as faced with the challenge of remaining constantly up to date and keeping pace with rapidly changing markets. Persevering with certain less enjoyable phases at their companies was described as a challenge that was necessary for their career development. According to the Chinese female executives, they have learned that such phases are inevitable if one spends a long time at the same company. As described at the beginning, the women in the Chinese group, like the Russians, have experienced major upheavals in the country. These upheavals have been particularly dynamic in China, occurring at a rapid pace. Responsibility for yourself, your own health and satisfaction as decision parameters are described here as coping mechanisms.

> Ag1: I feel sometimes there's some voices, concern is you would take more responsibility. Keep too much pressure for yourself. Just things like my health, maybe life. All these are things. Energy. I don't want to disappoint people but I don't want to over commit over myself. I just say I want to do something I can reasonably control. People sometimes have a middle age crisis. They don't know what's the next one. There is no ending. So, I asked myself if is this global, Asia Pacific role can bring me a lot of joy? Probably a little bit but no. It's not truly what I really wanted.

> C.: I guess that of course you know with the role comes the stress and you just have to find ways to deal with the stress and sometimes of course you feel a little bit lonely because you ask me, I'm the most senior person here. My boss is miles away and you also do not want to cry to your boss or complain to your boss although sometimes I do. You don't want to do that all the time or your boss will feel like you are just complaining. You have to do that. I think that you just have to handle stress. You just have to at least come across as professional especially the people who are younger and who are more junior. You do not want to come across as panicking or weak or don't know what to do. Because if you don't know what to do, how can they. I think that is really perhaps if you call it the downside. You just have to find a way to handle it.

Ambivalences concerning influences on women's careers in China

Is there a glass ceiling for women in management in China? And how does motherhood affect management careers of women in the country of one-child politics? The Chinese female executives were ambivalent about these and some other factors.

Ethnic ceiling instead of glass ceiling for Chinese women in management

One-third of the interviewees deny the existence of a glass ceiling for women in top management at all three types of company – state-owned, private and multinational – though their opinions on how difficult it is to attain a GM post in the different types of company differ. Having high career ambitions and a well-organized family life were mentioned as preconditions for reaching the top position at a company. Another third of the women defined the concept of a glass ceiling as not being restricted to women, but as applying to all Chinese at multinational companies regardless of gender. They noted that CEO and GM positions are still reserved for people of other nationalities and are not filled by Chinese. Hence, the glass ceiling phenomenon is understood in cultural terms rather than as depending on gender. The interviewees do not believe this culturally defined glass ceiling exists at Chinese private companies or state-owned enterprises. Half of the Chinese women believe there is a glass ceiling for women in China, but in their view, it is only to be found directly beneath the CEO role, that is to say the highest position in a company. The majority of interviewees do not believe there is a glass ceiling in China for any other hierarchical level, such as other C-level functions, management team, director or vice-president roles.

> Ja.: The glass Ceiling does not exist. Even though there are always discussions about female being emotional and having family duties, in my experience I do not see a glass ceiling. Most female CEO perform better. And they give up their families.
>
> Z.: I do not believe in a glass ceiling- everything is possible- for men and women.
>
> Ag1: The glass ceiling is still highly linked with the risk-taking spirit and your career aspiration. I don't think there's a glass ceiling. It depends on how much aspiration a woman has. In multinational companies it is more difficult compared to local Chinese companies. For the level below CEO there is no glass ceiling.
>
> Jo.: I do not think it exists. It depends on if the women really want to go to a top level and how she organizes her family life. I know some CEO women in the government backed companies. There it is easier than in the multinationals or private companies.
>
> Ca.: The glass ceiling is for Chinese- not male and female. In state owned and private companies it does not exist.

> Ki.: It is there for Chinese people in multinational companies. The percentage of Chinese people that have been send to Europe is still small compared to the number of foreigners coming into China. Chinese people are more introvert and foreigners like to present themselves. Intercultural pre-judgements are also one reason for the glass ceiling for Chinese.
>
> T.: In our company we talk a lot about the glass ceiling. Here women are many on the level below CEO. There are in general not enough role models at CEO level. So women decide to be comfortable on the second level.
>
> M. M.: Yes, it exists in all companies. The problem is only for CEO level. Most women do not want it. And some do not have the required skills- like strategic planning. Some women like to be in a lower function because they can give responsibility away.
>
> Mo.: I had no experience with that but I think it is existing starting from GM level. Perhaps there is a psychological difference in male and female when it comes to obtaining GM levels.

The women identified four main reasons for the existence of a glass ceiling. First, the family-related challenges faced by mothers are incompatible with the requirements of a CEO or GM role. The main example given of this difficulty was the travel that such roles inevitably involve. Mothers thus rule out the possibility of being able to meet the requirements of this role from the outset. A second reason that was mentioned is women's lack of ambition compared with men. According to the interviewees, many women feel comfortable at the second executive level and do not strive to become CEOs. This reason is again seen as related to the challenge women face in balancing their professional and private lives. A third factor mentioned by one participant is the different retirement ages for men and women. She remarked that since women retire five years earlier on average, they have less time to dedicate to reaching the highest level in a company. Another factor behind the glass ceiling that was also only mentioned by one woman is prejudices about female leadership styles. According to this interviewee, women are stereotyped as being overly focused on small details and more emotional, which has a negative influence on perceptions of their suitability to be CEOs.

> Ju.: Traditional family burden are the main reasons why there is a glass ceiling for the CEO level for women in China. It is not because people have a bias, it is because naturally men and women are different.
>
> Ma.: I think female in many cases do not want to go up there but male want it. I do not want to deal with all the hurdles and have no time for my family.
>
> Zi.: I think it exists. Men have bigger ambitions. And it is more difficult for women to balance their private life.
>
> An.: The glass ceiling exists in multinational companies because women do not want to move further up-they feel good on the second level.

In summary, although a majority of the group believe there is a glass ceiling in China, only half of participants think it relates specifically to women. In the view of the interviewees, the glass ceiling primarily applies to all Chinese at multinational companies, and is exclusively restricted to CEO roles rather than to the second executive level that is generally also classified as senior management. The interviewees believe that in their environment, all other senior executive level roles are just as accessible for Chinese women as for men.

Temporary delays due to motherhood – especially with two children

Most of the women in the group are married (83 percent), live with their partner and have children (74 percent). Nineteen of the women have one child and seven have two children. This means the proportion of mothers in this group of executives is higher than in other studies from the West. For around 70 percent of the women with children, the women's parents or parents-in-law live in the same household or in the immediate vicinity. Twenty-six percent of the study group are childless. At 11 percent, the proportion of single women in this study is lower than that described in many international studies of women in executive roles.

The Chinese women mainly said that they regard work as their core task, and do not have to constantly be there for their children. As a result of their socialization and political influences, for the Chinese female executives it is the norm for women to work, pursue careers and primarily identify with their occupation. It is also the norm for these women to frequently spend time away from home, including for extended periods. According to the women, in Chinese family's childcare is not just the mother's responsibility; especially in the classic one-child family, childcare is the collective duty of the family system. Society recognizes work and careers as having a high value that benefits the entire family system, which is more extended than in the West. According to the women's accounts, there is no expectation that mothers have to primarily take care of the household and childcare themselves. While they work, the family support system comes into play, backed up by external helpers.

> L.: I like to work rather than take care of everything at home. And I am also aware that my kid is not just my kid. It belongs to the whole a family. Everybody owns her and she belong to everybody. It's not my asset. So I started to empower my family. I start to not take care of things at home and let my family handle it. Slowly, slowly until today basically I don't need to take care of things at home. My parents in law take care of almost everything for my daughter, on her daily life. Even school.
>
> An.: Yea and I am traveling a lot. I'm not the person that can be at home every day on time. And accompany my daughter to study. It's not my life. But if I look at work life balance, I think I'm balanced. I don't feel unbalance. But I don't spend like every day 4 hours with my kids. But I think I'm balanced in my kid, also view, she understands. I think I m a good example for her because if I work. I work very hard and dedicated. So she actually is a pretty self-independent study. I feel good on that as well. She never complains, never complains that I'm not spending time with her. She is happy with this as well. Of course, my husband helps her on the academic

> side because he is better than me on that. And my mom helps on the logistics. So like eating and all this. I think I'm lucky to have the family support. It's like everybody have their own job at the family. I never feel I do not have work-life balance.
>
> Ki.: I think for myself I'm not like traditional or those big population of Chinese moms. I'm more independent and I want to be that. Some of them combine their kid's success with them. I definitely expect my son to be the most excellent one but on the other side if he cannot do it, I will not regard it as my failure. Myself is myself. My son is my son. My success is my success. My son's success I expect that but I will not pin too much hope. Some Chinese parents think if their son is not excellent, their whole life is not worth. I don't think that.
>
> Mo.: I think it is more or less the same. Not too much change. I feel kids were never a barrier for me to do stuff.

According to the Chinese women in management, motherhood often delay career progression for defined periods of time. The women pointed out that as a mother and career woman you yourself are responsible for achieving your own individual balance between the two areas. In their view, this necessarily involves sacrifices or trade-offs, since it is impossible to strike a perfect balance that accommodates everything. Many of the Chinese women focused on career development in their own careers, and accepted the trade-off that they were often away from home. Some of the women reflected on the consequences that their strong career orientation has had on their relationships with their children. Some of the children have developed stronger relationships with their grandparents or fathers. Other women described positive effects of motherhood, such as the personal growth resulting from the experience. According to the women, their experiences as mothers helped them to cultivate positive strengths such as patience, empathy and the ability to deal with conflict. Cultivating these strengths has had a positive effect on the women's leadership styles.

> Ki.: My husband actually spends more time with my son. Because I needed to be away two weeks per moths, that's why my son had to sleep next to my Ayi. He got more used to the Ayi before he was three because I could not guarantee every night that I will be home. Frankly speaking, my husband, because of the nature of his job, spend more time with my son. My son is closer to my husband.
>
> Z.: It has not changed my career actually. It changed my personality. When I had the baby, I got the feedback from my peers and colleagues who told me that I became very much patient than before. Changed me a lot. And also, when you have a baby it becomes one of your priorities. You take less part to other things like people conflict, like something that makes you unhappy.

The Chinese women reported that in organizations mothers receive a very positive response and lots of respect for their dual roles, and that they are supported by their colleagues. This does not correspond to the picture that emerges from the literature, according to which mothers are regarded as less competent and receive less support. Most of the interviewed Chinese female executives described motherhood as slowing their career progression. The interviewees spontaneously reported that it is easier for single women to pursue careers, since they are more flexible, can travel frequently and are able to move around the world without shirking childcare responsibilities. This suggests that the phenomenon known as the "motherhood penalty" also occurs in this group. However, in these women's experience, the impact that this penalty has on women's careers has a clearly limited duration. The Chinese women certainly did not describe it as a career stopper. They spoke of career "delays" that were subsequently followed by further career development. The family support network plays a key role. If women receive strong support from their families, especially with respect to caring for young children, this reduces the supposed disadvantages, since the women are quickly able to concentrate fully on their careers again. Another strategy for women is to limit maternity leave. In China, women are entitled to four months of maternity leave, followed by six months of parental leave. There is a legally protected breastfeeding period of one year. The women reported that it would be a significant hindrance to a woman's career to take a whole year off after giving birth. None of the interviewed women reported that they had taken the full leave they were entitled to.

> H.: Like on the highway, I put my foot on the break, little slower, but now I am back.

> Ca.: It will slow a little bit down. Cannot say affect, because, I always like to observe other people, I think a lot of successful women have a very good family and take care of their children and I believe, that at some stage of their career they will slow down, because they are giving birth to one child or to the second child. So, I am pretty comfortable with this slowing down part.

> L.: That's because I had a very great company and great boss. She supported me. She said family first. This is the most time you need family. But in most cases, the boss just treats people like workforce. If you take long maternity leave, they will give them lots of pressure and when they come back, they might lose their position.

Isolated comments such as *"I could have progressed further without children"* were made by the women with two children. Raising two children was described as an additional stress factor that has an impact on career development. In one case, a woman chose to temporarily go part-time after giving birth to her second child. By contrast, one of the interviewed executives who already had a young child was promoted to an even more senior executive role while pregnant. Although most of the Chinese top managers who were interviewed have children and rose up the career ladder as mothers, pregnancy is generally viewed as a disadvantage for women at multinational companies.

> Mo.: It was a difficult decision to be honest. I spent 13 years with that company. I felt very happy working in that company. All my friends. Even my company worked in that company before. I enjoyed my life in Tianjin before. When this came to us actually, we were seeking do we want to keep the baby or not. Because even the beginning both parents in law and my parents didn't support that decision. They feel you don't have to have a second baby. And you have such good job. Such good career in that company. Why do you want to give up? So, I talk with my husband. Sometimes we want to keep sometime we want to give up. But my husband and I come to a consensus that we want to keep the baby because that's a life. It's a given. We didn't plan but since it's given. It's a life, it's something for us, so we decided to keep the baby.

> Then I talk with my boss and share with my family members that we want to keep the baby. Then they tell me the parents since we made the decision already, we cannot change it. We help you anyway. If you decide we help you.
>
> Actually, after I deliver the baby after one or two-months rest, I talk back to my old boss because actually we were kind of keep contact for a while and he said, yes, come back I have a job for you. I said actually because of family reason I want to stay in Shanghai. I delivered baby in Shanghai. Then he said okay let me find a Shanghai job for you and eventually he did find one for me in Shanghai and I was about to go back to the old company and we made an appointment with my boss and say tomorrow I'm going to come back, meet him. So we met in a restaurant and unfortunately, he was very sad. Sorry, I have bad news for you, I cannot take you back. I talk to HR and legal and they didn't support this. They still feel there is a risk for the company even after the delivery of the baby. I was shocked. Oh. Because even I made the decision before, I left the company I feel I had support because my boss says he want to get me back. I was pretty uncomfortable.

In summary, the Chinese women in top management functions, with only a few exceptions, believe that motherhood slows down women's career progression. Some of them believe that this factor was less critical before the opening up of China, and less critical in the state-owned companies.

Childcare in China as a task for the family system

According to the women, when career women are successful in China this is regarded as a success for the whole family. Families hence support women's career orientation and make sure they are able to concentrate fully on their careers.

> Ag1: Female have more equality than male- especially at home.

Different cultures have different approaches towards the balancing act of combining multiple roles. In China, grandparents play a key role in looking after children. Given the high women's employment rate in China combined with the absence of part-time working models, grandparents are the most important link in the childcare chain. According to Chen et al. (2011), this reflects not just the strong bonds between parents and children but also a strong cultural focus that values the family over the individual. Childcare by the grandparents can be interpreted as a familial adaptation strategy that aims to bolster the well-being of the whole family by reducing the burden on the mother, who then in turn supports the family financially. Grandparents either live at the home of the working parents or close by. This support is based on the grandparents being financially dependent on their grown-up children and on their taking up a key role in the support system. One result of China's "floating population", who move from the country to the cities for work, is that grandparents are often temporarily the main guardians for their grandchildren, since parents leave their children behind with the grandparents. A 2004 study from Liang (2004) found that 45 percent of grandparents live in a single household with their grandchildren. This phenomenon also demonstrates the social acceptance of working mothers who live apart from their children for extended periods of time. Unlike in the past, it is no longer just the parents of the husband who play a key role in caring for young children. Rapid socioeconomic changes have transformed cultural traditions. According to several authors, maternal grandparents can be just as involved as paternal ones. All the women reported that they have a full-time housekeeper, *ayi which means aunty*, to help with their household. The *ayis* do the housework, cooking and shopping, and provide support to the grandparents. The women's parents and parents-in-law assume full responsibility for looking after young children and oversee the *ayis'* housekeeping tasks. There are special night *ayis* who look after the babies of working mothers from the evening to the early morning so that the mothers can sleep. Some of the women also reported childcare facilities at former employers in the state sector, which were fully tailored to the women's working hours. Tutoring schools, all-day schools and the offer of boarding schools with overnight accommodation are the third important area that enables mothers to work full-time in China. Some women reflect on the childcare facilities of former state employers, which were completely tailored to the working hours of women. These systems are now completely adopted by the family system in the women surveyed.

> L.: She's 58. She's very diligent woman. She takes care of me, my husband and my kid. She can organize everything. Sometimes I feel that I need to do something so I will buy something which maybe they don't have time. They never ask me for anything.

> Mi.: I don't do big things in my family. I just come back to home and I'm playing or discussing or reading with my son. I do nothing for the home. If I want, I have a lot of freedom, I have a full-time nanny, and I have one cleaning lady. And I have my mom on a daily basis, and you know the Chinese grandmas, they are just unbelievable. They just stick to the baby. My partner, generally speaking, he is a nice man, so on the weekends I like to read books and drink coffee, so if we are together, he is playing with the baby, so I drink my coffee and read my books. So theoretically speaking, if I want I can completely free myself from the whole thing, but I do not want. The reason I have my baby is I want to give my love to him. When I come home from work, I like everyone to go, so I can take care of the baby by myself, changing diapers, feeding him, put him ' to sleep, I insist he sleeps in my room, rather than by the nanny. I am emotionally attached to him, so I am willing to do this, but if I want, I am free. For the job I need to travel, yes.

It is striking that culturally mixed married couples and Chinese parents who have lived abroad for extended periods make less use of external assistance, and that women in such couples take on a lot of household chores and childcare duties themselves. It might be speculated that in these cases the role models for mothers' responsibilities have been changed by other cultural influences.

Balance not as a goal, but as a result

When asked how satisfied they have been with their work-life balance over the course of their careers, the answers tended to be very similar. All the Chinese women concentrated almost exclusively on their work at the start of their careers and invested many hours in their careers. Today, many of the interviewees see their lives as more balanced, with more space given to their personal lives. Many of the Chinese women have a high level of travel activity, which, depending on the phase of their career, spans days or even whole weeks and work regularly at night, due to different time zones, and on weekends. The women have a positive attitude towards work-intensive phases that place great demands on their time and see themselves as responsible for restoring a work-life balance after such periods. Examples of phases where they have to work long hours include changes of position or field or special processes such as restructurings. They regard regularly recurring periods of intense work when they have very little free time, such as the end of the accounting year, as normal. It is mainly Chinese mothers with two children who often do not want to delegate most of the educational work, often against the backdrop of mixed national marriages, who describe that they actually live in a race against time.

> T.: In the first ten years I would say a lot of the time because I know what I want to get and I know I have to invest extra so I would say 90 percent of my time is on the job. Particularly when I moved to Shanghai, I have no friends, I have nothing to do to start with so I invest a lot of the time even Saturday and Sunday too to work. And this is almost like my leisure time and I like because I also like it. Like, most of the entrepreneur like yourself. we work long hours but we like it. And I really enjoyed it. but in the last maybe I would say in the last ten years so it's the second half of my company career, I had a very different perspective so I want to reach out to more people from my church and also from my personal connection and also I learn some more new skills like playing the piano or like nutrition etc. So I think after ten years with the company I know how to survive. I may not be reaching out to the division president's job but I know I will not be fired so I'm more comfortable to do something on top of the career so I have my habits, I have my religion. I think my life is a lot well more balanced over the last ten years and I'm happier with my job and other interests.

> Mi.: In my case it didn't change much in terms of my own choice, but it rather depends on whether there are things to do, there are some busy periods, there are sometimes not busy periods. But overall, I am a person crazy at work when I have work to do, I wouldn't be able to put it down. But I also need entertainment, I always need a strong balance at both ends. I mentioned the period of time when I was taking three jobs together – in Germany, here and also study, that was a very exhausting period, because I slept two or three mornings, then I also get up on the weekends and I still do a lot of partying meeting friends. Now because the company is relatively in a stable stage and my position, I have been here already quite a long time, the challenging thing is becoming less. Then you could say I don't work as much as in the past, it's the normal working hour. But if anything comes and requires me to work as much as in the past as I used to do, it depends on the need.

> Ag2: Of course, there cannot always be work-life-balance. There's always peak and low season. Especially first years. The first-year work life balance is not good but the family will understand because you just choose a new job. But in the second year I know I need to go to work life bal-

ance. So in the first year I make sure I achieve several things. One, I build a good team so that team can later on be empowered to do things. Two, I build all of the trust with my boss and peers. So they can trust me to do a lot of things they will not ask a lot of things and I have to prepare answers for them. Three is I understand business as quickly as possible so in future whatever small area happen something, I know what is the course. Lastly the fourth thing is I view the relationship with Paris and Asia pacific. They know China is doing the right track so they do not question us and appreciate us. Actually, I'm more and more our client balance. I have regularly meeting to make sure my team is alright. I have regular meeting with my boss to make sure one on one update with him. Things are on track. I also have time to actually go out of my regular work. Sometimes I go to a seminar to share what works in China best practice. And I designed some best practice for Asia pacific. All of the other Asia 15 countries learn a lot from China best practice to implement their country, which is highly appreciated by Paris as well.

H.: I think it's very stressful. I cannot say that I feel peaceful and balanced every day. I think it's very difficult to balance. I'm a very practical person so I look at every day. If I go through every day and being able to still do my job and still be there for my kids. I think that's success already. I don't have the illusion that there is a balance. I think depends on how you define balance. For me you cannot have that perfect balance. It's just not possible. If you have a big job and you have two kids and you don't want to delegate your kids, you're going to have to have a very stressful life. What I would rather work on is how can I build energy for myself. I pay attention to what I eat. I exercise a lot. I have to have the energy it requires for me to do all that.

Ja.: My work hours are really long. I leave 7:30am my home and arrive home 8pm or 8:30 and I travel about 25 percent of my time outside. If you are talking about work life balance and the time I spend, I spend more time in the work. This is definitely not balance. But I tell my friends I am looking more about the qualities. How I keep the relationship with my family members although I do not stay at home as long as the other moms. We try to enjoy something together on the weekend or summer holiday or winter holiday. I make the time I spend with my family very good.

In summary, most of the Chinese female executives take a positive view of their current work-life balance. All the women described having a very high workload during the career progression phase, with long hours and frequent business travel. Mothers with two children tend to be the exceptions: they see themselves as constantly having to balance their time between their careers and their children's needs.

Strong self-confidence, need to catch up in self-confidence and the advantage of not being beautiful

Self-confidence refers to independence from the judgments of others and a high level of confidence in one's own abilities and performance. A high level of self-confidence is associated with high self-efficacy. The Chinese female top managers generally regard themselves as self-confident or very self-confident. They all consider a high level of self-confidence to be a critical career determinant. They regard it as a significant advantage to be self-confident, especially in relation to being assertive towards colleagues and superiors. Self-confidence was often equated with courage. When asked how self-confidence manifests itself, the women said it could be seen in a person's bearing, eyes and way of talking. Many of the women believe it is an ability people are born with. They reported that even as children they had leading roles: for example, they would speak in front of groups. Key phrases included *"natural leader"* and *"from early on"*. According to one participant, her high level of self-confidence derives from her strengths as a woman: *good intuition, persuasive communication style and the ability to sense things that other people cannot yet see.* The participants said that self-confidence and assertiveness are key characteristics of Chinese women, especially women in Shanghai. They reported that all their female colleagues are very self-confident.

> M. M.: Good question. They said, we already have a chief representative. I was General Manager at that time, I can lead big topics, I know both markets, I speak both languages. I do not need a boss here in China. No chance. When I go, I will be chief representative. The CEO said, that will be difficult. The board has to decide, I cannot decide alone. So I said, you do not need I go to the board. Two months later they had a board meeting and called me in. I flew to Germany. At the meeting during lunch I talked to all decision makers. They said Ms. Ming is no engineer, she is Chinese, she is a woman. This company has 80.000 people and 80 percent engineers with a technical background. This woman has none of this, why should we take her. I convinced them as follows: you have so many engineers, you do not need more, you need people with other skills. To sell your technology. A woman and so many men, that means the woman makes it extra good. Where I work now all others are men and I am the only boss, as female. And I make it better and I can do it better for you. And Chinese? And what? You want to do business in China and for seven years your boss has been from Austria.... Self-confidence from my good feeling as a female. I think I have a good intuition. This convinced in many situations, there for I know this is my strengths. Many people cannot see something while I already feel it.... I also learn easier and quicker (laughing). Every new environment, new topic, I gather it quickly. I believe this makes me a bit stronger.

The interviewees' most common response regarding their self-presentation was *"I am not good at it"*. This perception of themselves was justified by reference to cultural differences between them and people from other countries at their companies. According to the women, marketing oneself is not part of Chinese culture, which instead requires people to be *"humble"*. Shyness was given as the reason why, in their own view, some Chinese women do not use strategies for marketing themselves. Other women described how they go beyond what is asked of them at work and trust that this will lead to them being perceived positively by those around them. They think that other people's good opinion of them ought to be based on the strength of their performance and conduct, and that this is more important than strategic self-presentation. Even the women who regard themselves as having strong self-presentation skills said that self-marketing should be preceded by exceptional performance that they could talk about. Women who see themselves strong in self-presentation use conferences strategically to market themselves effectively to the outside world. A few women also remarked that they constantly and consciously try to talk about good results they have achieved so as to make other people aware of them.

Cl.: By nature, I'm still quite humble. That sounds weird. From time to time I'm still quite confused and I think that self-confidence piece still got shattered from time to time and I don't know if I'm making the right impact or not. Self-marketing? I guess as a Chinese we usually would not say a lot of good about ourselves.

G.: Well, I have to say I'm doing "natural marketing". I say what I believe and I do what I say. And I always want to be true to people and want to be true to myself. So that is the marketing, the self-marketing that I want to build. I hope I'm walking my talk. So that's generally my self-marketing. I didn't purposely do a lot of making-ups, show-off things. Not a lot.

When asked what initial impression they think they make on others and how they are spontaneously perceived by others, the Chinese female executives gave very thoughtful answers. The responses indicate they are very conscious of the impression they make on other people and how this affects their image as an executive. They talked very openly about the ways in which initial impressions can help or hinder them in their role. The descriptions they gave of the impressions they make on others can be classified into four main categories: assertiveness, loyalty, accessibility and competence. Women who think they are primarily perceived as assertive described themselves as tough, strong, determined, target-oriented and demanding. They also described themselves as coming across as less tolerant, strict and distant on first impression. The women are well aware that these impressions are not entirely positive, but do not regard this as a problem. Some of them described themselves as making a dominant and aggressive impression. They regard this image as positive and helpful for their career success.

Ju.: I recall one of my male university classmates. I used to be the monitor in the University for my class. He told me, my dean, sent him to my group because I was a leader, to lead those in the university who had to go to manufacturing plants to do the kind of real working practice. So I was the small leader of organizing these kinds of activity. This young gentleman was in my group and he had a very open discussion with me. ...That was the reflection of what is my image to others. He told me that I was really very demanding and what word did he use.... He made me think that I'm a little bit a kind of monarch... that every time I want to try to use my power. This is what he described. Then I always remember this because I don't want to give this kind of image. But in XY (company name) you have to because you have to show your own confidence. You have to show you are a decision maker and very decisive or otherwise you cannot win. I'm a naturally this kind of person. That's the reason I can be hired by XY. Their hiring philosophy is they want to hire people with similar values. Mindset and values otherwise XY don't think this person can survive in the company culture.

Mi.: What my impression on other people is, as I told you already, I look very dominant, determined, strong lady. Very tough.... Less tolerance, not so patient because, I talk normally very fast.

The Chinese female executives were unanimous about the importance of appearance and presentation for careers in senior management. In their view, Chinese women at executive level should look professional but not beautiful. Or, as one woman put it, *"pretty is good, but not too much, because people will feel distant"*. Younger women see both advantages and limitations to beauty and good looks for their careers. They think a little is an advantage, but being too attractive is a disadvantage for rising up the career ladder. According to the women, it creates distance, causes women to be misjudged and engenders reactions such as *"not very professional"*. They do not think beauty is important for leadership roles in China. The group was unanimous on this point.

> V.: I saw some quite not good-looking women leader they take very senior level.... very smart, very sharp and also very political.

This distinguishes the Chinese from the Russian and French female executives, who want to harmonize their femininity with their leadership role. Unlike Russia and France, there are no social requirements for Chinese female leaders to look very good. It is striking that several of the Chinese describe themselves as not being beautiful in the sense of common beauty features when answering the question, and are very self-confident about the advantages this fact brings for them.

> Q.: I mean I was never told I am pretty. I think I give overall people the impression of being smart and rather friendly. So that helps a bit. I say if I combine everything together, I say I'm average. And physically I'm quite small and quite petite so that is not so helpful in creating the presence. Because physically I do not have such a big presence.

Older women formulated matters in more drastic terms, and see good looks as having clear drawbacks for women's careers. They regard good looks as irrelevant. According to the women, a female Chinese executive should ideally look professional, capable, confident and smart. All the women consider professional appearance important, as emphasized by their deliberate choice of clothing. They all identified formal clothing and a smart, presentable look as important for being seen as an executive. In the view of the interviewer, all the women in the Chinese group share the following features. They wear markedly little make-up, no or only colorless lipstick and not much jewelry. Their clothing style is less formal than in countries such as Germany. They do not wear trouser suits and only a few wear blazers. The style could be described as business casual and in a few exceptional cases as feminine formal. Nothing about their clothing style indicates their position at their companies. The topic of age was mainly raised by the younger women. They said that "grey hair", referring to ages 45+, is a plus for senior management roles. In certain industries, for example, the fashion industry, a youthful look is, by contrast, considered an advantage. The younger women reflected on the issue of age and careers. Some of them have reached senior management positions while still in their early to mid-30s. They think that their youthful appearance can detract from their image as an executive. In particular, male German bosses were given as examples to illustrate this concern; some of the bosses have even expressed these reservations explicitly.

The image of Chinese women in top management: High flying professionals and also mothers

The women's answers regarding the image of female executives in China suggest that there are a lot of positive views and not many critical ones in their environments. The positive views can be understood against the background of strong family systems in which women's career success is regarded as a positive value since it helps to strengthen the entire family. There also appears to be a tendency in the group to rate female executives more positively than male ones.

There are a variety of findings on China in the literature with regard to these issues; these findings span the full range of possibilities and include some contradictory results. Educated women do not see themselves as being De Mente's *"moon reflecting the sunlight"*, that is to say, as serving a supportive role for men, but rather as being *"half the sky"*, that is to say, as having an equal and contributing role. The fact that women continue to be less represented in senior management than men is often ascribed to cultural stereotypes. The connection between Confucian traditions and associated values is also repeatedly mentioned in the literature in relation to the image of female executives. A saying by a Confucian master, *"It is a virtue if a woman doesn't have ability"*, is frequently cited in this connection. Research on Chinese women by Korabik (1994), Du (2016), Schein (1996) and Eagly (2007) analyzed the image of women in higher management functions in China. Some research concluded that Chinese women have a subliminal feeling of inferiority, they tend to be less accepted as they move up the management hierarchy and women preferred male superiors. Chinese males perceived women in middle management more negatively than men did in other nations. On the other side, there is the new image of the ideal women in China. According to a survey of 940 men and women from Shanghai, Beijing and Guangzhou published in *China Daily* in 2001, the new, current conception of the ideal woman in China is that of the "high-flying professional" who is simultaneously a successful family mother. In the survey, approval for women who were both mothers and competent employees was three times as high as for pure career women.

The social environment in China views and regards career women mainly as positive. The women have positive experiences of their image as senior executives. This image is associated with success, high incomes and dedication. According to the women, a successful, senior role brings social respect and acceptance, as well as a strong position in the family. In the eyes of society, if a woman achieves success in her career this represents a success for the entire family. The interviewees believe this image is rooted in China's history of universal female employment. Women's socialization is geared towards employment until retirement age, and hence aligned towards potential careers. The housewife role has previously been exceptional in Chinese society. According to the interviewees, discussions about the role of housewives are a new trend in China, one that only began recently in response to questions about how to raise children properly and the role of grandparents as primary caregivers.

An.: In the past it was a shame not to work. Not to work is like being a parasite, and women will be inferior if they do not work, you will be only an accessory of a men rather than an independent person.

The terms *"positive"* and *"commonly accepted"* were mentioned multiple times in relation to the image of female executives. In the view of the Chinese women with senior management functions, women actually enjoy a better image than men in the working environment. This image is based on qualities such as hard work, assertiveness and good organizational skills. Mothers are also admired for being so organized and dealing with two sets of demands, which brings additional social recognition. Interviewees described how mothers in particular receive a high degree of solidarity and support from colleagues and families. However, there were also a few reports of skepticism concerning career mothers' dedication to their children, resulting in a more ambivalent assessment of their image. More critical observations regarding the image of career women in China were less common in the research group than in some of the other countries. Those that there were related to factors such as the jealousy and insecurity triggered by women in top positions. The *"nu qiang ren"*, dragon-lady-phenomenon comprises the fear of strong women and associated value judgments: for example, that such women are *"difficult to deal with"*. The term "leftover women" describes single career women who are past marrying age. Since only a few single women participated in the study, these descriptions, which were made by only one single woman, remain exceptions. This aspect was also picked up again in the evaluations *"has no life"* and *"makes sacrifices"*. From an external perspective, it is said that women who aspire to CEO roles will either choose not to have children for the sake of their career or will be unable to spend much time with their children. Hence, it is believed that female CEOs are forced to make sacrifices in relation to motherhood. Only three of the women reported that they had experienced that employees prefer male bosses.

3 Chinese women in Europe: The conflict between fitting in and meeting their own performance targets

In the past, senior managers' international career paths usually took them in one direction only, from West to East. In such cases, multinational corporations sent more men than women to fill top positions. But for some years now, Chinese managers have also been relocating from China to Europe. Most of them are to be found in branches of large Chinese corporations. Chinese women in European senior management positions are still an exception when compared with men and even when compared to their female colleagues in China, who, as mentioned before, are often to be encountered at management level. For this book, Chinese women in senior management positions in Germany and France were recruited for the interviews. They are a distinct group in the book, as they are not top managers in their home countries. The remarks in the book have therefore been kept brief. The insights gained derive partly from comparisons of the different environments made by the Asian women. Chinese women in Europe cover the entire age range from just over 30 to mid-50s. They work predominantly for German or French companies; only two of them work for Chinese corporations. Based on the results of the analysis, foreign Chinese women in Europe can be divided into two groups:
1. Expatriate Chinese women who have been relocated from China to Europe by a multinational company in the context of a temporary overseas assignment
2. Long-term Chinese women who have lived and worked in Europe for a prolonged period of time, following their studies or because of their husbands

The two groups differ mainly in terms of length of stay and degree of assimilation to the new country, both are factors which affect their career direction and path in Germany or France. The women rate equal opportunities and in part, career opportunities for women, as being higher in China than in France or Germany. At the same time, the appraisals barely differ between the two countries. Only a few of the younger women, who have never worked in China, view their home country more critically in terms of equal opportunities and rate their adopted country more positively.

The female Chinese expatriate manager – a pioneer with role model prestige in China

Of the Chinese women interviewed in Europe, only a few occupy the standard expatriate role, i.e. they have been transferred to Europe from China by their company. In the research group there was only one woman transferred to Europe by a Chinese company. These women had already attained high positions in China and were keen to be transferred to Europe, mostly to company headquarters. The Chinese female senior managers who have been transferred abroad have pioneer status. Why? Because Chinese women transferred to Europe by companies in China are still rare. As a result, they soon become role models among the Chinese in both Europe and China and develop a high profile. As a rule, the aim of these women is to spend time gaining experience abroad and to establish themselves in the European headquarters before then returning to China.

> L. (Chinese woman in France): To be honest, going international as a Chinese had a lot to do with my ego. I have a big ego. I want to be successful. I want people to look up to me, to have respect, to be a little jealous too. That is very Chinese. But I don't want to be seen by others through a luxury life, but as a human role model, the way to help others to care for people. After retirement, I would also like to work for an NGO. That would make sense.

The Chinese women have undergone a number of career stages in China and Asia before coming to the company headquarters in Europe. Their education, skills and career aspirations are extremely high. What distinguishes them from the Chinese women in the group who were interviewed in China and who also have foreign experience is that they were transferred abroad at a later stage in their careers and to the upper echelons. Examples of positions held by relocated Chinese women are Global HR Senior VP, Global Chief Talent Officer and HR VP Global Procurement, all located at German or French headquarters. All of the women have worldwide responsibility in their own areas.

These women's motivations for moving from their already high positions in China to the company headquarters are in part due to the function they fulfil as role models for other Chinese men and women back home. They want to show that it is possible to play an important role as a Chinese woman in the headquarters of a multinational company. In addition, they want to implement changes to the company on a global basis, something that can only be achieved by moving to headquarters. They wish to drive through improvements that will benefit employees in the future and enhance the success of the company. A further motivation is the broadening of their own skills and expertise beyond Asia within positions of significant influence. This may also involve accepting a temporary retrograde step in terms of position in the corporate hierarchy, which is the norm for most executives when transferring between headquarters and local organizations. A third aspect is the desire to go beyond one's comfort zone. In multinational companies, advancement to the first management level is very often linked to experience in managing at headquarters. This step had been missing from these women's career planning when attempting to achieve CEO or GM positions in China. The move abroad gives the women a competitive advantage at home. It is also a risk because they give up a lot of what they have at home. This includes convenient family support organizations, everyday services and extremely strong networks. Chinese women are prepared to take risks even when they are already working at a senior level, and they show flexibility.

Financially, each of the women is already well off. The loss of quality of life they experience in Europe, especially in the service sector, is offset by good salaries during the assignment period. One advantage for the women in transferring to Europe is the possibility of enrolling their children in an international school. This is a key factor in women's decisions. During foreign postings they are prepared to accept temporary separations from their husbands and from older children in higher school grades, for whom changing schools is no longer an option.

> L. (in France): The main reason, there are a couple of them. I was 37 at the time and I wanted to do something new before 40, I was almost at the glass ceiling. I would have remained head of the Asia Pacific human resources department, but I saw no challenge, no jump. I would have stayed in the comfortable zone, also geographically. Of course, there was some risk involved, I could also fail (laughs). I could get fired and have to start over. I try to give myself the chance to try because I didn't want to regret anything later. I felt like I was carved into my comfort zone because I was in a nice, comfortable position in XY. Everyone knew me, appreciated me. I wanted to give myself the chance to try something new. I purposely didn't go to any other US company. I chose a company that has a purely French style and a completely different culture, landscape and challenge. I am willing to gamble to see how resilient the person I am is. I accepted this challenge. At XY, I lead a team of up to 100 employees. I had the feeling, "Wow, I never tried that." I appreciate that XY gave me this chance and I take it. This is a really international job for me, although I have had a lot of qualified experience in Asia Pacific and China before. I know it's complicated when it comes to staff regulation. I didn't have enough exposure. I really appreciate XY for giving me this chance to try. It is also a risk for them. It is also an opportunity for me to make myself known. My HR team has up to 100 employees. It's like an army. (laughs)

> R. (in Germany): These four years I separated from my husband, my husband is in Hong Kong, flies around the world, my son was first in New York, at New York University and now at the University of Southern California in LA. My parents were in Shanghai. When we left to Germany my daughter was so young, only seven years old. I did it because I believe in diversity. Bettina, you have to mention that, I am a strong promoter of diversity. Global leadership goes beyond "male-female". Global leadership means that a German company doesn't just have Germans as leaders. Because I want to be a role model not only for female managers, but for "glocal" managers. That is why I try to coach and support many young potential people who are waiting to take on the challenge internationally and globally. The world is now a connected world and only if we connect people around the world will we have many more sources of innovation and business trends. I hired my sister and her husband to help me in Germany. With the child and while driving. That was a huge financial burden. I was firmly convinced that I was a role model and gave up my pleasant life in Shanghai. There you have a driver, you have a nanny 24 hours a day. And, then you go to Germany without all that.

> B. (in Germany): I think there was a time when I had a little hard time with it, of course also on the ego level, because I was no longer a GM. But now, for a year now, I'm actually quite satisfied because I personally decided not to take the step because of the hierarchical ascent, but to expand my expertise further. And if I should have the opportunity to take further steps forward regarding personnel responsibility, I am completely open. In China I actually had a change every two years. Now I have a lot of changes every day, but not that I take on more hierarchical responsibility, so to speak. That's not it. But from all this professionalism, from what we create as a team, there are a lot of changes. I think that's where I draw my strength from saying that I'm okay, we're doing something really great for a company. We digitized an 11 billion Euro business. And we are the first.

At the end of their time abroad, Chinese female expatriates face the same hurdle as the male and female executives of other nationalities who accept a posting abroad, namely finding a suitable job at the next level. In addition, most women see their future as being in China and they plan to return to their local or APAC organization, which usually offers less choice of top management positions than the European headquarters. Sideways career moves are thus often the norm. Some women change companies when they return to China. The sole woman working in a Chinese company says she considers her future prospects in China to be high. This woman has had a long career in Europe and has so far worked in three different European countries. She is the only Chinese expat woman whose corporate headquarters is located in China. She is no different from the other women in terms of motivation, but has fewer challenges to contend with, as she has the advantage of "working in both realms at once".

> O. (in Germany): It's all about supply and demand. It's all about how much value you've added. There were expats in China or Germany who focused on enjoying life. According to the motto: "Oh, no. I'm not in my home country. I only take four or three years of vacation and really relax." Then there was not much value and not much to grow and learn. I always focus on the value that I have brought to Germany and the value that I have achieved for my growth and my learning. I also defined this together with my two partners in the company. We said, "What kind of footprint do we want to leave for three to five years? How do we want people to talk about it when we go?" That guided me in a way. I left the footprint and learned a lot at the same time. I thought I knew everything about the role. I'm such an experienced professional, but I've also found so many innovative things in Germany. Innovation in Germany, Europe, Berlin, Amsterdam and London. Expats who do not accept the international assignment as paid vacation create added value for themselves and for the company. As soon as you add value to the country, you also increase your value by learning, sharing and growing. When people see that you have value, they promote or hire you. If they don't see much value, who will pay you?

Chinese women in Europe long-term – between outright assimilation and the exploitation of homegrown success strategies

Of the Chinese women interviewed, the majority have been in Europe over a long period. The group is divided into women who have previously worked in China and come to Europe because of German or French husbands, and women who came to Europe to study and then stayed. The latter in turn can be differentiated in terms of their career path according to whether they have then chosen to marry German or French partners or are married to a Chinese man.

The Chinese women with Chinese husbands who have made the decision to settle in Europe long-term after their studies, seek to replicate with their partner the model they know from China of two full-time working parents. They are well educated and some have two degrees – one from China and one from their adopted country.

In both countries, Germany and France, a degree obtained in the country and a good command of the language are basic requirements that have enabled the women to start a career in management here. Chinese women tend to have their children relatively young and are very much supported in their careers by their Chinese husbands, whom they often met during their studies in Europe. These partners are usually more flexible in terms of time management. In the organizing of family life and childcare, one can observe that these women set Chinese standards and attempt to make up for the lack of help from grandparents in other ways. Outsourcing the childcare of infants is perceived as the norm.

> W. (in Germany): Yes, exactly, I commuted at the weekend and he played single father during the week. I would say unconditional support was very important for my career, and certainly easier for me too, as it were, to a large extent, that he was raising the child. In my eyes, it is easy to blame childcare on social responsibility or on politicians, which makes it easy for you. Certainly, more qualified care would help people, but I don't think that is the reason why no more women are making a career in Germany, I don't think so. For me, it is primarily your own will, which is decisive there and if the will is not strong enough, you can have even better environments and that still doesn't work.

In both France and Germany, Chinese women with foreign husbands try to assimilate as much as possible. In particular, women who have a German partner adapt to German social expectations of motherhood and try to integrate as much as they can. Their initially critical view of taking on the role purely of housewife changes with their decision to stay in Germany. The women adopt German values about motherhood and look for the positives in them. They are aware of the advantages that accrue to children if a mother has more time for them or devotes herself entirely to the task of raising them. It becomes part of normality for them to take long maternity leave or to work only part-time at some points in their life. Their German mothers-in-law are cited as being their new role models. The Chinese women who only came to Germany in their late 30s have made this decision consciously, as they do not envisage making much progress in their careers in Germany, mainly because of the language barrier. Many younger Chinese women postpone the decision to have children because they experience a misalignment in Germany between having a child and having a career. Others describe a feeling of conflict in deciding between their original career in China and their new German husband who wanted or had to move back to Germany. Family decisions are at the very heart of their professional thinking.

> M. (in Germany): I think being married to a German has had a big impact on my thinking. Because we communicate so much. He comes from a different environment and always thought differently than I did. So I always learned, thought, learned, thought. The decision to come to Germany was not my husband's decision. This is because I know that my husband is different from me. He comes from this background, so I wanted to delve deeper into this culture. I think my mother-in-law has shaped my thinking a lot. She is a housewife, she raised 4 children, she is very happy and charming. I came to the conclusion from her that it is also nice to be a housewife. In the end, she is happy and charming and makes a contribution to society as a whole. It's a good life.

Chinese women who are married to French husbands try to continue working full-time and here, too, attempt to conform to the prevailing social model. They struggle with the limited family support when compared to China. Unlike in China, they are more aware of the double burden that women in France have to bear in balancing work and family life. They too have fairly long spells in which they cannot pursue their careers seamlessly but have to take career breaks and/or circuitous routes because of children or language problems.

> S. (in France): I am very happy because I have a very good husband who has loved me for more than 38 years now. He is a really good husband and he cares a lot about my child and me. Thanks to my husband, too, I was able to take up an executive position because he supports me very much. When I gave birth to my child, I tried to find a job that was much more relaxed, with little travel. That's why I spend four years in a department store to avoid traveling because I think my child really needs my presence at home. I have been the CEO for two years. I travel to Asia a lot because we shop a lot in the Asian market. It's a very long trip every time.

> Y. (France): Maybe if I had a Chinese husband I would still be there. French man, that's serious business. It's my private life, time with my parents, what has changed? Now my parents have to come when the baby is there, to visit me in a country whose language they don't speak. If I were in Asia it could be a lot easier, I could be with my parents. My husband shares all family tasks, cleaning up, everything. He can't cook, but he's improving. The rest, with the child, we will share when it is born, I think. For example, we have to take the child to care later and pick it up at 6 p.m. Everyone makes a path – he picks them up. We'll share it like most French do what I've heard from my friends who have children.

The success of Chinese women settled long-term in Europe depends on whether they succeed in exploiting their advantage as a Chinese woman in Europe and in using it strategically. Not every woman succeeds on all fronts. They view their strength in the foreign country as lying in their ability to bring Chinese know-how to the company. This advantage becomes important when they take up positions in which Chinese expertise is relevant.

In those cases where they take on positions which are unconnected to China, the increase in skill levels is typically high, but only in isolated cases do they rise through the hierarchy. Here, Chinese women are in competition with local employees, who inevitably not only have language advantages, but also a better understanding of the local culture. It is when the women take up positions that have no connection to China, that particular challenges arise.

> X. (France): The advantage? Europe is so different. Although France is like a small province, it is so different from Germany or the UK. And I now know France well, the way I work, many companies from before. That is my advantage as a Chinese in a Chinese company.

> M. (Germany): I think we should know what advantage we have. I cannot compete with a German colleague on the same level. I am still Asian, I don't speak the language 100 percent and I have a different background. I never get to their level. I concentrate on my strengths and promote myself where I am better. That is the intercultural, my China knowledge and my languages. So it's my responsibility to be strategic.

W. (Germany): So according to the motto, I am something special, something exotic and then I get more recognition from society? I think a positive point is always when you are at such a big event that many people remember a Chinese woman more easily.

L. (Germany): I am a "strange thing", I am neither Chinese nor German and you can sometimes rate me on a double scale, depending on the situation, sometimes I hear, yes, for example, "how long are you taking parental leave?" I know that the Asians only stay at home for a very, very short time, hmm "... or else, yes," they speak German so well, they lived here for so long... they have to understand everything ", there you expect a German from me again (laugh).

H. (Germany): I think that with my engineering background and additional management experience and language, I am an ideal person. For Germany-China business, an international project, then someone like me, of course it's ideal. In theory, I could do anything. Yes, ideal mix.

Challenges faced by Chinese women in Germany

For expat Chinese women, the challenges lie in managing German employees and adapting their management style to large, change-resistant structures. In addition, they learn to adjust their management style to what they perceive as a lesser degree of flexibility and agility among the local employees, and to apply new communication styles.

> L.: My seven direct reports in Germany, they were on very senior levels and they've been 15, 20 years with the headquarters and love to finish everything by three o'clock and then go running in the forest or do barbecue in the garden. They do not like change because change means more work. I have to really over communicate why change and why we have to do things. Why we have to do business different from ten years ago, five years ago. I think in my first 18 months I spent most of my time doing communication. One on one, one to a small group, with a big team I think the first 18 months were extremely difficult. I got so many confrontations from my German team, challenge me, why I want change so much. They need more capacities, they need more resources. These things I found very challenging, exciting and successful in my three and a half years in Germany. I think I underestimate how important in a German company, the side-talks are, the people, the community, the desire of convenience, the German language, I underestimated that. Because I got some encouragements, people said to me, "Please speak English, bring some English to the headquarters. Please." This is first thing. Second thing is I think a lot of women only have functional competencies, they do not have technical business competency. I strongly believe that females from childhood could be scientist, be engineers, because the techie and the business side is pretty much dominated by males and woman are mostly in the functional role, finance, HR, whatever. If a woman, outstanding woman, speaks German and has very strong business experience, the sky for her in Germany is unlimited.
>
> W2: The biggest challenge at that time was – I was the bridge in between – I was in the European time zone, the project was in China and the technical inputs came from America. So we really worked around the clock, twelve hours because of these different time zones. When America is early in the morning, China is already done. A bit difficult.
>
> R. (in Germany): I think China is still a child, so open to change. There are common characteristics for Chinese. If we talk about my strengths, I think I'm a catalyst of change. I'm not a commander in control person, this is coming from Chinese culture, consensus, harmony, making

people understand why is so important. This is me, rather than a normal commander to control like some of the local leaders. Like I said I spent a lot of time to tell them why we should change. My strengths compared with a normal local manager is that I'm more leading than controlling. I'm focused on knowing why, other than knowing how, because I firmly believe with such a mature and confident team once they know why they will change, they will move. That's where I spend really maybe 60 percent on communication. One day, some of the early adopters said, "You are on such a high level, you can say: Just do it." That's where I realized, okay I'm too much aligning. Today if I have maybe 80 percent aligned I will say, "Guys do it, I want you to do it." Then it moves.

Discrimination in particular makes working life difficult for Chinese women. They have to learn, not only as women, but additionally as Asian women, to deal with male prejudice regarding their suitability for higher management tasks.

L. (in Germany): With the first child – that's one of the main reasons why I left XY(company name), in addition to the reason that I was looking for something new – I had a boss who was … a thoroughly … XY'ian, he did an apprenticeship, middle 50, had a child himself and he wrote me off, but really. I really did a lot of very good work before and was a top talent in the pool of XY with only a few selected people worldwide. I also have various management trainings and … and fireside chats. Then I had a child, when the end of the support and bullying started. My boss wanted me to change my job with a colleague who had just left the university two or three years ago, in the sense of "job rotation". They were just basic administrative tasks, that would have been too much for me. It was just when I thought it didn't make any sense to stay here anymore, I can't go on with this job. At this point I also have to say that I have three or four women, my friends, who I think are very professional, very committed, very competent, have similar experiences … Yes, I'm not an isolated case.

L.2 (in Germany): Yes I think so, before I started to work in Germany, I had very long and nice hair, and everyone loved my long black hair, but when I started working as a consultant I cut off my long black hair, yeah, and I also look younger than my real age, so when I worked as an auditor at 28, I was an auditor the whole career and I looked maybe only 24 years old. So when I worked with the German company, I worked with the leaders, with the general manager, most of them are white male and I couldn't ignore that they look at me not as a professional auditor but as a beautiful Asian woman. And sometimes they even make bad jokes and that was annoying. Sometimes about my beauty, one time it was a very old white male it was about sex – I don't think he would make this joke to any older woman or any other guy. As an Asian girl living in Germany, I have to face conflicts very often. Because Germans are sometimes not very nice to foreigners. I speak German, but I don't speak German fluently. I read and write better than I speak. Several years ago, when I didn't speak German very well, when I wanted to do something, my Master, to extend my visa or ask some questions related to my Master at some governmental department, they were usually very rude to me. And told me "this is Germany, you should speak German." And also, there are some, when I walk on the street, there are some old male German losers, they are drunk, and when I pass by, they try to attack me. It happened about three times in the past.

S. (in Germany): Nah, that's not discrimination, rather I see that Germany is a relatively closed society. When I speak to Germans privately, I think they're curious, willing to learn, that is, you're curious about the other culture. But when Germans are together, you immediately feel a wall. As a foreigner, you have to break this wall and then integrate it into this society. There is no way that the Germans will accept you so actively. You have to behave the way the Germans speak, you have to know all the topics that the Germans know well, then you can be with Germans. Because, here is a very individual culture. I also read an article, for example that in Australia, Canada, that it is really a mixed culture, the acceptance for foreign people is much greater than in Germany. But in Germany there is a long history behind it, and this history never ended. It just developed like that, that's why people have very firm mentalities. You, as a foreigner, can only proactively integrate yourself.

R. (in Germany): I think there's stereotypes to Chinese, to Indians, to many different nationalities. One of the top managers told me, "For the Asia Pacific role we cannot have a Chinese, we cannot have an Indian because Chinese will not listen to the Indian, the Indian will not listen to the Chinese." I said, "Come on." This is really stereotyping. There could be stereotypes on any nationality, just like Chinese who have stereotypes on German. However, it's really about personality. It's really about the person, the leadership style. When we select leaders, it's more important to focus on the personality, the leadership style. What's the benefit of this person, not that he is Chinese or Indian. Is the reality. Yes, there's stereotypes or discrimination to this serious degree. However, there are tons of Indian who are very successful global CEO for many organizations and there are also Chinese being successful, not as much as Indian but also– I think, yes, we have to manage the discrimination or stereotypes. The real question is how do you select the right people.

Perceptions of the gender situation in Germany

The long-term and expat Chinese women agree that the situation for women in Germany is challenging when it comes to careers in senior management. Some of the Chinese women speak quite frankly about it. In their opinion, it is not only the environment that is not very supportive, especially for mothers: the core problem is the traditional values surrounding motherhood and the way these remain internalized by the majority of women. Many German women lack the will to pursue a career, as the reconciling of a career with having children is seen as an insurmountable hurdle. Chinese women at top management levels in particular believe that in comparison, Chinese women are on average more ambitious. They see a lack of career focus as the main barrier for women in Germany.

Younger Chinese women especially, feel judged on two fronts – being a woman and being Chinese or Asian. Both are stereotypes that tend to count against a career in management. They overcome the barrier by using their cross-cultural advantages and by seeking out positions where these are of value.

> W.: I would say it is a matter of course in China and at least in my generation, and today's generation, if they want, they can too. In Germany there are fundamental social problems, i.e. As the saying goes, "Rabenmutter" (raven mother, or bad mother) this word is in German and there are also enough parents-in-law who say that if you have children you shouldn't go to work. That's why a working mother in Germany has a much poorer reputation. The social environment for career women in Germany is more difficult because the fact that a working mother is something normal does not exist in Germany and the second point is that women want to pursue less careers and the will of women is also not strong enough. That is my explanation. I have enough

young women with me, I would like to support them, they said, Mrs. C., please do not put me under pressure, I just want a normal life with children and part-time work.

L.: Well, Angela Merkel, she was once the pride of Germany that you had a female chancellor, but she was given a role, the "mother", she was called "mother". they had to change her role a bit so that a woman was legitimized to be at the top, that was my feeling and when I talk to people in the society, in a doctor's office or in the supermarket, when people hear that I "only" take 6 months of parental leave, then they always says, "oh so short, what do you do with your child, poor child, for so long in daycare?" that is always so subliminally accusing "how can you as a mother so career-oriented … and treat your child badly like that?".

M3: I think there is a strange management atmosphere in which a career woman is not normal or a negative stigma for mums. I find this gender-based discrimination maybe three times, maybe five times as big as in China. And this outer atmosphere of society and in the company goes deep into the mind of the woman, into her inner self. They limit their objectives, their thinking, they make themselves smaller. So that's the most negative part. The second is the supporting resources. In China, children go to school all day, whether in kindergarten, elementary or middle school, it's from eight a.m. to six p.m., it's normal. Here, you know that school is only half a day, or when you go to school, most are offered until three p.m. I don't know how many are open until five or six p.m. And then, here to find a nanny 24 hours a day, I didn't find one in my network of friends. It's normal in Shanghai, Beijing.

R.: I think my German colleagues, they would not understand why I'm separating location-wise with my husband. This for them is totally not understandable, not even acceptable. Hiring my sister, it's a financial investment. I think for this one, they're also surprised. That surprised them, the separation from my husband. I would think maybe Asian women are a bit more career-driven when a chance comes. They're more courageous to take the chance other than going back to the family and say, "Well, I'm not willing to live in another location than my husband." I think for this one, I see the culture difference. Quite a few Asian women I know, they chose to live in another country than the husband which is still fine, not for ten years or eight, five years, maybe three or four years. Asian women are willing to focus on the quality of the relationship and to get the chance other than to give up the chance and being together and hanging together on a day-to-day basis.

F.: I don't feel any inequality in China. At least in my own experience, I was brought up just like my brothers in our family. Also, after I started working, I saw no less opportunities for women there. Many successful women, not only from my classmates, but also at work. In general, when I came to Germany, I was quite surprised that it is much more traditional in many ways. I was quite surprised.

S.: I believe that there are fewer opportunities here than in China. Then of course you think that the difficulty of getting into German management as a Chinese woman becomes even more difficult. Then of course you have a bit of reservations yourself, prejudices.

L.: I notice that with my daughter, when I take her to music school or take her to ballet dancing, all the mums are waiting in the waiting area with their children and it was so difficult to talk to them! Everyone has such a position, please don't look at me, please don't speak to me, I don't know why. I would say that it already started in kindergarten education, I don't know why, but the German girls are driven to always see each other as competitors, to always focus on trifles, to always start to bitch, and this continues into professional life.

Challenges faced by Chinese women in France

The Chinese female executives describe cultural differences in interpersonal relations and issues of feminine solidarity. The added value they bring to France as Asian managers does not give them any real advantage here. They say that it is difficult to achieve a leadership position as an Asian because they experience a kind of ethnic glass ceiling. In their experience, senior management positions are mainly reserved for French people. In addition, just as in Germany, they describe the need to adapt to local customs in terms of communication and decision-making. Differences in working methods exist between their own action- or process-oriented working style and the local style, which is described as being more time-consuming and communication oriented. The Chinese women achieve this cultural transition after a phase of adaptation and navigate the cultural barriers very successfully, as far as it is possible for them to do so as foreigners in France. An important aspect of the descriptions is the women's awareness of their effect on their French colleagues. They encounter insecurity or even fear towards themselves among their French counterparts. After having considered the matter, they start to consciously use communication to break down this threshold of insecurity among French colleagues. Another feature is a perception of envy. It seems to be a new experience in this milieu that top positions in French headquarters are given to Asian women. Here, too, the Chinese women deal forthrightly with the phenomenon and try to overcome prejudices. It is easier for Chinese women who are expats than for Chinese women who have never really worked in China, because being expats they can draw on the expertise, leadership experience and self-confidence they have acquired in their home country. They have the advantage that they have been able to hone their business expertise and intercultural skills in the safe haven of a multinational company in China.

> L.: If you talk about how French look at me being a Chinese successful woman living in France, well, first of all, by looking in their eyes, I see a lot of surprise. They make me feel like wow, full of surprise. Like yesterday, I was in another city, Grenoble. People in the Grenoble city, they don't think so international. People came to me saying, "You like cheese, and I thought Chinese never eat cheese," and I said, " I don't like all the cheese, but I like some of the cheese." People are surprised to see me as a successful Chinese woman standing in front of them. The second thing I want to say, I cannot say judge, but they scan me a lot, they scan like the X-ray, (laughs) like, "What do you have? What brings you here? What is the difference you have compared to us to position you in this the senior position?" I didn't know if I like it so much, at the first year I felt like I was scanned, I was judged by the people. You can easily tell from their body language, it makes you feel sometimes uncomfortable. (laughs) I would say suspicion or maybe judgment, that's the second reaction from the French team. It just depends on how you going to do it. Then the last two and a half years, I really change myself so much.

> X.: XY is very tough in terms of culture, publicly recognized tough. You hear comments from even French people, it's a tough company. Another level of harshness applies to foreigners, especially Chinese or Asians who come from a completely different culture. So, there are two sides. One side is at company XY in terms of culture. I have to say that this is notorious in France, everything is known. The second side is the beauty industry. People are very subjective, constantly

changing everything and we are Asians, we are better organized, we are less spontaneous than the people of the South. I have to say, I don't think French people care about advantage that we think we have. Although we have a very obvious advantage, but they don't care. They don't care that you speak better English, they don't care you speak Mandarin, they don't care you came from another world. On the paper, yes, we're all objectively, we have some advantage, but if you don't speak French, you don't understand, so who cares? The good management job anyway is reserved for French.

J.: I think the one thing, even for me now, sometimes I need to always remind myself is firstly you need to listen more because, in Chinese culture, we're very action-driven, we want to do the things fast, normally we want to go to solution. We don't spend the time into debating forever but I think in French in all the meeting everyone will say "No" first. They will give you all the difficulties. For me, this means you need to balance the goals. If you want to come close to the people you need to understand where they do not feel comfortable. In China, maybe you don't need to do it because you can say, "Okay, I'm the boss," or "it is given by corporate". "Why are you asking? You should do it." French will think that Chinese people, we're a bit too much solution oriented and process driven rather than the people driven.

H.: XY drives diversity and Inclusion, inclusive KPI and they set the KPI for every ExCo. We have index to measure, now improved. When I moved 2016, I'm almost the only one Chinese at a certain level above or is intern or new young ladies or assistant. Chinese faces but they all speak French. I could not. I am one day in front of the copy machine and I say tot wo French assistants, "I want to copy in color but I cannot do it" and both French ladies say, "We cannot help you." Then I asked the assistant, "Would you please help me and teach me?" She says, "Helena, I think you need to take French lessons." I say, "I need to work right now, I need your help now." She says, "I can teach you but you should learn French first." This happened all the time to me. From some business leaders, some assistant. Not nice, not helpful.

X: They have an assumption perception. A manager in XY used to tell me "you are the first Asian that we've recruited at headquarters at this level". They said I will have my base at headquarters on the seventh floor. It's the famous floor. First of all, they're afraid, because they're afraid of something they don't know and they are not familiar with. Second, I guess beyond that is that they think you are so, so different. Kind of mysterious. One side is you are so different, so they do not know how to cope with you. Along with this comes fear, uncertainty, whatever.

So far there is very little scientific evidence concerning the experiences of Chinese expat women in Chinese companies. This study's isolated case of a Chinese woman in a Chinese company illustrates the fact that in this first wave of European postings, domestic Chinese managers are preferred for key positions. This creates an opportunity for women in China who want to go overseas. Once abroad, they move between the two worlds, and become intermediaries between the European and domestic headquarters in China. What is special about this is that they are participating as managers abroad in the rapid growth of Chinese companies and are playing a pioneering role here, too.

A.: I think it's vice-versa. It's also something not difficult to understand because the owners want to control the key roles and trust is very important. They only trust the people that understand them. If you're coming from a totally different background, a totally different mindset, how could they trust you? If they don't trust you, how could they believe they could control you easily in the future? I think it's very easy to understand.

Perceptions of the gender situation in France

The assessments made by Chinese women in France regarding their host country as compared to their home country are extremely varied. Women who have had a long career in China place France in the middle range with a five to six point rating on a scale of ten when it comes to equal opportunities in management. By contrast, they give China a high score: eight out of ten. They attribute the superior equal opportunities there to the way women are brought up in China and to the way successful women are recognized by society. Furthermore, the way in which Chinese women are socialized to focus on their careers is perceived as being greater than that for French women. Only one member of the study group, a woman who worked for a Chinese company in Europe for some time, rates the two countries almost equally positively, but nevertheless sees France as being one point above China, the reasons given being the high level of childcare provision and the state-subsidized maternity leave in France. In her opinion this stops companies in France from discriminating against women because of the risk they will become pregnant. Some of the women who have lived in France for a long time are more critical of their home country. The under-representation of women in politics is given as the main reason for this, as well as the fact that they are disadvantaged in the race for the best jobs because of the expectation that they will be absent from work due to pregnancy, even if only for a short time.

> L.: In my opinion, China is very close to eight. I'm starting to discover France more. I used to think that gender equality should be much better in Western countries than in developing countries, which is not really the case. I will probably give five, especially in France.
>
> X1: I think there are certainly differences between cities in China. The support system in China is more mature for women to move forward or pursue careers. For example, babysitters can be hired relatively cheaply. Childcare support and social support is better. People in Shanghai have more choices with childcare. Second, it's about taxes. If both work in France, the tax is very high. Of course, China is very high at 45 percent. I believe that it is economically less economical in France if both parents work. I think that the mentality of women in France is not that the only to be professionally successful. They are proud to live a very chic life, to travel, to dance, to do yoga, no matter what profession they are, other areas. They have more arenas for their skills than a Chinese. I think it's a variety of areas where they can live out.
>
> Y.: I really don't know the details, but I heard that men and women in France are not paid the same. In terms of management, I think that even with a large company like XY, there are many middle management women, while senior management starting with C still has a lot of men. For me I give France a six. I really don't know in China. I have never worked in China, I cannot say.

X2: I give France six and China four or five. Why? In France there is great respect for women, there are not so many senior executives but there are many salaried women and middle managers, and women are also in politics in France.

A. (Chinese Company): First of all, when you look at society facilities, in France they have much better facilities for women with kids. No matter from pregnancy to giving birth, the creche and the kindergartens. They have end-to-end solution to support women to be independent. In China, you can only have your freedom after the kids are three years old, unless you have someone to take care of the kids for you full time. Also, the notion. People's notion. In China, when they recruit people, normally they discriminate against ladies who are at a certain age but without kids. That was when China had a one child policy. If you already around 30 years old, but you still don't have a kid, that means in several years that you are risking of having maternity leave for a long time. Normally, they would choose a man over this lady. Even if this lady is much more qualified. In France, I don't see that. I also recruited people in France market. We never look at this one because people said, "Don't need to worry about this one. First of all, we have this system. If they want, they could always spend time to get back to work after four months of giving birth. Even if they choose to stay at home after the maternity leave, then it's the society, it's the government who pays the salary, not us. No worries." In China, it's always the company who must pay, yes.

M.: I see female managers more in China than in France. In France all of my bosses were men. In China, on the other hand, I met women in the same company. There is a cultural reason for it. In fact, I've heard from several Chinese bosses why they choose a woman to run their accounting department because they think women are more loyal. Indeed, they know that the chief financial officer manages the core of the company and the Chinese bosses always want to trust someone, especially in this type of position. They trust that women are more loyal and reliable. This is because I see a lot of women in China who hold high positions in the financial function.

L.: If I talk about eight in China woman can easily approach those senior jobs. Leadership role, there's no clear bias because you can say whatever you want. I think most opportunity in my career path was promoted because I'm very vocal. I always speak on behalf of others. I don't like your kind of follower. I don't want to hide in my opinion. I think this kind of vocal brave straight forward really positions myself in the different company and I was given the opportunity. Compensation wise you see very equal. No, even sometimes I know my pay is even higher than my male colleagues. That's because I'm the HR, I can access all those kinds of information. When you just facilitate some events being the woman sometimes you even can use your power or charming to get more impact. That's not me, I feel so comfortable in China. Being a woman, you have so much privilege to do the things that you can. I never have very clear comparison for the gender equality because in China I get used to it. I was always treated very fairly. Moving to France, it's totally different. I still see the female engineer doing the same job as male or buyer in the procurement organization. Their pay is 30 percent less than their male colleague. If you look at these leadership roles, I think most of them, higher percent of them are male. And really wake me up, I felt like, "Wow that's different landscape in terms of the awareness and the motivation."

X2.: If I consider equality more broadly as a career in the economy – I would give China less than France, in France it is possible for women to become CEO, no glass ceiling, I am optimistic, it is difficult in China in state and private companies. Multinationals are only one part of the reality.

S.: They did not learn how to be lady and that's why they just grew up in the fight of the power. They did not learn how to be a real lady real women role and that's why they are very dominant in family life and in the company life. Then I am the generation of the children of this lady generation in China now who are 30 years old, 40 years old or even 50 years old. We are just the children of this older women generation and we just took the example of our mom to show our power. Of course, we are more educated and we are educated to take our place at our home, to be a mom, to be a wife et cetera. There is something that we copied our mother generation unconsciously and that's why Chinese ladies express their power, they are willing to succeed in the professional life and sometimes they really dominate.

4 The French women: Intellectual warriors against role conflict

The female top executives in France give insights into their strong career orientation which they pursue against a backdrop of rights won and ongoing resistance. Challenges include the mastery of country-specific codes, the search for a French female identity as executives and maintaining solidarity amongst the women colleagues who accompany them during their pursuit of career success.

The socio-cultural framework of women's careers in France

This story of French women is marked by intense conflicts and battles. The socio-cultural character of the country is seriously impacted by powerful male spheres of influence, which men try to keep women out of.

French Women – fighters for equality

French women were not granted the right to vote until 1944, 26 years after German women. Yet French women were the first in Europe to demand their political rights through petitions, at meetings and on the barricades.

As early as the fourteenth–seventeenth centuries there were demands in France for equality and attempts at emancipation by individual women who published works such as Pizan's *The Female State* (1405) and de Gournay's *On Equality between Men and Women* (1622). They were seeking – at a very early stage in French history – to oppose the principle of male superiority. With the advent of the French Revolution, a new French women's movement developed during which, under the leadership of Olympe de Gouges, their "The Declaration of the Rights of Woman and the Female Citizen" was published. These early politically active women were publicly condemned as mannish and meetings forbidden. It was not until around 1840 that women's clubs and newspapers were re-established, demanding votes for women and equality in marriage. But these were also soon banned. Fraser (1992) pointed out that from the perspective of French feminists, the "déclaration des droits de l'homme" restricted universal human rights to men's rights only. The golden age of French feminism is considered to have been the period after 1880, when the suffragettes led the campaign for women's voting rights. From 1914, women's suffrage was put to the vote but rejected several times, centering on the motto that "women's hands are there to be kissed, not to vote". Several authors have discussed whether it was ultimately the participation of women in the Resistance during the Second World War that brought about a breakthrough in the French gender issue. Sanchez-Schmidt (2013) reports that in 1946 an equal opportunities law was introduced

https://doi.org/10.1515/9783110715132-004

in parallel with voting rights for women, and its implementation, which included laws such as equality in marriage, took until 1965. Only then did French women, according to Herve (1995), acquire the right to exercise a profession without official permission from their husbands. And only since this period have they acquired the right to make decisions about their own bodies, their bank accounts, their married lives and their choice of profession. Contraception became legal in France in 1967. The head of the family was no longer defined as male and "paternal" authority (*autorité paternelle*) was superseded by "parental" authority (*autorité parentale*).

Even in the 1960s and 1970s, women in France were still predominantly housewives. The decisive laws on employment equality date from 1982. In the last 40 years, there have been significant developments in public awareness in three specific areas and this is reflected in the growing degree of female self-determination and autonomy. Neubrand (2009) described that female employment is seen as normal and a matter of course. This has been helped by government family policies, which have extended the childcare system to enable women to work full-time. These days it is the norm for 99 percent of four-year-old French children to be in pre-school. In the 1990s, French feminists shifted the battleground to victims of discrimination and violence against women. Since then, the focus has been on ensuring that rape, marital violence and sexual harassment are taken seriously and properly punished. Benoîte Groult has reflected on a new phenomenon in French society: a sense of fear is developing among men, because in their eyes, equality for women means defeat for men. Every effort to improve the situation for women in society and to promote their rights is perceived as aggression, as an insult to masculinity. Men are defending themselves against this in both the social and the political arenas.

French politics – a male domain?

French women were among the last in Europe to gain the right to vote and politics in France was for a long time reserved for men. In 2019, Galetti has analyzed on behalf of the Adenauer Foundation the fact that, from an external perspective, the image largely prevails in France of a "lived equality" between women and men. The assumption that French women appear to be less disadvantaged in their professional lives than in other countries is based to a not inconsiderable extent on the French childcare system, rather than on equality in all social and political spheres. In politics in particular, parity seems to have been established in France since the 2000s – and not always without conflict. Patriarchal structures can still be seen today at the political level. The adoption of the law on gender parity was nothing short of revolutionary. In 1982, a women's quota failed due to a veto by the Constitutional Council of a law intended to establish a 25 percent quota for women in local elections. In 2000, France introduced political parity by law as a pioneer for many other countries. The law makes it compulsory for the parties to draw up gender-balanced electoral lists for the European, local and regional elections. However, it does not apply to parliamentary elections, for which only fines are imposed for non-compliance. Despite these new regulations, some French male politicians have found ways to circumvent gender equality. Galetti (2019) reported this was clearly evidenced in the 2007 parliamentary elections, where some political parties demonstrated open hostility towards women. To counteract this, penalties were imposed, but these were accepted by the parties in order to safeguard the men's pre-eminence and were offset by donations from male networking groups. The penalties have been increased in recent years and in 2014, a doubling of fines for political parties that fail to comply with the laws on equality in parliamentary elections was imposed. Discussions within the political parties on the issue of parity are growing increasingly heated. Most party statutes contain declarations of intent regarding parity, but the formation of the movement "La République en Marche" seems to have breathed new life into the debate. While still a candidate, Macron made the issue the focal point of the 2017 presidential and parliamentary elections. Despite this, most chairs of National Assembly standing committees were held by men. Even though "La République en Marche" complies with the law on parity in the National Assembly with its 47 percent proportion of women, it has been criticized on several occasions for awarding key posts such as Party Chair, National Assembly Chair, Chair of the Parliamentary Group and various committee chairs to men. Reports by political observers from media outlets such as Germanys' *FAZ* (2018) and *Spiegel* (2019) have described opposition to parity as being so pronounced that many posts were intentionally filled by young, inexperienced women who were then replaced shortly afterwards. Patriarchal structures and sexism – tolerated or at any rate ignored by society – are still firmly entrenched in some sections of French life, and it is not only in the context of the "me too" debate that they have moved up the agenda. Time and again, reports come out of the National Assembly of sexist verbal abuse of female members of parliament. Nevertheless, the measures are having an effect and the proportion of women in the French contingent of the European Parliament is, at 43 percent, far above the European average for the member states. However, in 2019, only 25 percent of the women on the candidate lists ended up in government, as the parity ratio only applies to the lists themselves. Up to the year 2000, the proportion of women in the National Assembly was below 10 percent. At that time, the proportion of women in the German Bundestag had reached around 30 percent. However, the new measures are now beginning to have tangible effects and the involvement of women in French politics is gaining ground.

French women in senior management roles

In companies, too, change came about only after the introduction of legally prescribed quotas. An important step was taken towards the greater involvement of women at the top of large French companies with the passing of the Copé Zimmermann Act of 2011. The law set a target for 2017 of 40 percent women on the supervisory and administrative boards of French companies having over 500 employees, as well as in the civil service. Companies with between 250 and 499 employees and a turnover of more than €50 million are required to meet this requirement from 2020. According to the consulting firm Ethics & Boards EWOB (2019), around 44 percent of the boards of directors of large companies in France are now female, propelled by this quota. A shift in attitude, prompted by the new legislation, is evident, since recruitment agencies throughout France are now looking for women who can fill these positions. There has been little in the way of change on boards of directors however, which in France have a female contingent of 18 percent. One example of an influential woman is Isabel Kocher, former executive board member of the energy company GDF, who in France is both celebrated as a role model and treated with hostility, in equal measure.

In France, the employment rate for women aged 25–49 more than doubled between 1960 and 2002, from 40 to over 80 percent according to Ambafrance. However, the total percentage of working women in France is only 66 percent, which is below that of Germany. Despite this, fewer French women work part-time, although this figure rose steadily from 13 percent in 1973 to around 31 percent in 2006. The global economic crisis has been cited as one reason for this, but the authors Sickinger (2005) and Wegener (2004) attribute it to the considerable double burden placed on French mothers who, by the time they have had two or three children, tend to opt more and more often for part-time work.

Women in France also earn less for the same work, on average they earn 18 percent less than men, and this figure is still 11 percent after adjusting for maternity leave. French women also often take up part-time work in order to be able to combine work with family life, which is not the case for men. French women are frequently still being denied really senior management positions, although there have been some successes in this area.

For all the countries considered in this book, the Grant Thornton (2016, 2018) global survey shows that in 2015, 33 percent of senior management positions in France were held by women; in 2017 this figure was 31 percent. All so-called C-level functions were included in the analysis in addition to the highest-level corporate positions. By way of comparison, the European average for the present study is only about 24–26 percent.

Reconciling work with family life in France

French women play a wide range of roles and seem to be successful in combining childrearing with professional activities. In France today, it is pretty much taken for granted and socially accepted for women to work, and this attitude remains widespread even after they become mothers. France has a high birth rate, which in 2018, according to World Bank data and data published by Ambafrance, was the highest in the EU. However, the more children a woman has, the more likely she is to give up full-time employment, even in France. Although 82 percent of French mothers with only one child work, just 35 to 43 percent of mothers with three or more children are in employment. There is a wide range of childcare options available in France, but they all have to be coordinated with the demands made on any top executive's time.

Considerable trust is placed by the French in the state childcare system. One reason for this could be the long tradition of pre-school education in France. The salles d'asile, precursors of today's pre-schools (école maternelles), were brought into the general education system as early as 1881. After the Second World War, their provision expanded considerably due to population growth and increased participation of women in the workforce. Today, almost all French children aged between three and six attend these facilities, which aim to foster their social, emotional and cognitive skills. In addition, children in the final year of the école maternelle have already started learning to read, write and do arithmetic. School children in France generally attend all-day schools, where there are accompanying childcare facilities, as school hours do not correspond fully with parents' working hours.

A majority of French women go back to work six months after giving birth, thanks to a well-established network of state-run crèches, which are supplemented by state-subsidized childminding schemes, because their opening hours differ from standard office hours for executive levels in France. However, the need for infant daycare is not fully met in France and, according to Les Echos, there are only sufficient places for one in eight infants. In the big cities in particular there is a shortage of childcare places, and parents have to resort to the comparatively expensive option of the childminder. The full-day care of small children by childminders or nannies is thus very common. Childminders and nannies are required to be registered, but do not have to undergo any formal training. The French have confidence in this system, and there is practically no public debate about whether it has any disadvantages for infants or mothers. The "baby leave" taboo is perceived by many French women as a burden. In recent years, various authors such as Reuter (2003) and Sickinger (2005) have noted an increased criticism by educational experts of the prevalence of outside infant care and a trend towards the private, subsidized care of young children. And there are more and more young women in France who are postponing the decision to have children until later in life or else do not want to have children at all. Some of them do not have a partner – a phenomenon that is becoming increasingly widespread in the Western world. But this lifestyle choice is still taboo in France. Part of it is to do with ambivalent attitudes to motherhood and the permanent state of exhaustion that mothers in France experience. For a long time, any discussion about the double burden faced by mothers who worked full-time was a no-go area, as was the notion of a woman not wanting children.

The country that once had the highest birth rate in Europe is now experiencing a decline. Only 767,000 births were recorded in France in 2017 – 17,000 fewer than in 2016 as reported by the German Journal *Die Zeit* (2018). In addition, French mothers are getting older and older. On average they do not have their first child until they are

30.6 years old. Nevertheless, the country has achieved much for working mothers over the last 50 years. And it is a social expectation that women should be capable of having a career and simultaneously raising children.

The French women in the survey – strong 55+ and with lots of children

The Global Women Career Labs interviews reveal fascinating French women who have made it to the top in France. At the time of the interview, they all occupied senior management positions, for the most part in large or medium-sized French companies. Only three of the women worked for foreign companies in Paris, two for US corporations and one for a Chinese company. The companies involved are active in the automotive, minerals, luxury fashion, food, banking, electronics and communications sectors. Examples of positions held by these French women include General Manager and CEO, Executive Board Member, Human Resources Director and Head of Communications. The women differ from the other survey groups in terms of age distribution. About half of the women are between 55 and 64 years, so compared to other countries, the French group is the oldest in the study. Our analysis reveals that the older French women are a relatively homogenous group in terms of their views on many topics, in contrast to the younger French women who want to be more independent from traditional company cultures.

All but four of the French women interviewed are married: one did not marry until her late 50s; two are divorced; one of these has recently remarried. They are the group with the highest number of children in the study, with between two and four children each. Only four of the women are childless, of whom three are older women.

The level of education of French female executives is high and ranges across fields such as law, engineering, finance, business studies, communication and philosophy. The universities attended are mostly French elite schools such as HEC, ESSEC, the Sorbonne, SKEMA and Dauphine. Only three of the women have studied abroad, and those that have, did so at top establishments, including Harvard. Over half of the women have MBAs or other masters' degrees. Two of women over 60 have not studied but started work immediately after graduating from high school. Apart from in France, there is only one other study participant, a woman from Germany who is also over 60, who has attained a senior position without having studied. All of the women give English as their second language and some mention up to four other languages in which they have a basic or more advanced level of proficiency. The interviews were mostly conducted in French, although four of the women chose to use English for the interview.

Gender equality in France – how the French female executives perceive their environment

The French women in this survey give France a subjective score of between four and seven, in a few cases eight, on a scale of zero to ten, where equality for women in management positions is concerned. Ten points would mean that women and men are completely equal with regards to careers in management. The group average is six points – a good mid-range score, one point higher than the German group but two points below the Chinese women, who rate their professional environment on average at eight points. The women's assessments of gender equality in France is equivocal and their answers do not focus only on management, but also assess various other aspects of gender equality.

The French are very well disposed towards, and proud of, the legislative progress made in France in the field of equal opportunities for women, family-friendly policies and childcare provision. The women emphasize that compared with the period between the 1960s and 1980s, when women in France were more likely to stay at home, enormous progress has been made towards a more equal opportunities environment. Reference is repeatedly made to the 40 percent quota for supervisory boards and the Copé Zimmermann Act. The French women are very proud of the advances that have been made in these areas. They describe how French legislation has been outstanding in securing equal rights for women, and how their country sets an example to many other countries where, in their view, no legal framework has yet been achieved for women. Again and again they mention the success of the quotas and of the political initiatives that have been successfully implemented. It is the social norm today for women to be in work, childcare outside of the family is socially accepted, and the range of childcare services available enables women with children to pursue their careers.

However, the respondents also soon highlight the problem of equal opportunities for French women in management. Equal rights are established in law as well as in the minds of the public, but not in real terms. It is noticeable that different arguments are cited by women over 55 versus younger women about the specific steps still needed.

For the women under 55 the debate is largely around the issue of maternity, the overall discrimination against mothers and unequal pay. They talk about the need for significant improvement in this area. In their view, mothers are placed at a disadvantage as a result of the wage differential. They have salary gaps during pregnancy and early childhood and are systematically excluded from pay increases. The reconciliation of maternity with career is, in effect, possible only for the upper middle class who can afford the high cost of round-the-clock care. For women in top management in France, as for men, being in the office well into the evening is more or less required. This makes it necessary for women in management positions to have a nanny who regularly looks after their children in their own home until late in the evening. For the lower salary brackets, it is difficult to combine children and a full-time job, as childcare services are associated with costs that make it uneconomic.

The descriptions of the problems arising from gender relations are very detailed. Old boys' networks that systematically exclude women remain a reality and discrimination against women and stereotypes in the minds of male decision-makers are cited by female research participants as being a major problem for women who want to move up. The topic is regularly discussed at numerous conferences in Paris, including on International Women's Day. It is noteworthy that some of the older female participants in the study regard the workplace as being fairly egalitarian and blame women themselves for their failure to propel themselves upwards. Older female participants said their main shortcomings are a lack of self-confidence, too little networking and too little career planning. The problem of coordinating career with children, expressed by the younger women, is denied by the older women. The issue of working hours is the main area of disagreement, however, between the generations 55 to 63 and 40 to 50. Women who are still bringing up children argue for working hours that dispense with the traditional expectation that they will work evenings. They want companies that take into account the concerns of mothers with management responsibilities. The older women, attuned to upper management according to men's rules, seem disappointed that younger women are not continuing with this struggle. They take the view that a woman in France who wants to move into the upper echelons must conform to the standards set by men.

> D.: I'm going to give France a six. I almost said five and then I thought to myself well, things have changed in France and we are moving in the direction of gender equality. But we haven't solved the problem of violence against women. A lot of women in France still die because of domestic violence. We haven't solved equal pay or the gender pay gap. We have 17 percent women on executive committees. We have all the same stereotypes as in every country. We haven't solved any of that. But, all the same, we do live in a society where women have a place, they can go out in public, they don't have to hide away, they can go to work. It's not like that in every country. But I think that given that France is supposed to be the country of Human Rights and Women's Rights, we really could do better.

> M.: Seven or eight for work, but only five for the social aspect. I think that we see them as intellectually equal in society, but not in reality. If you look at people's actual home lives it's not true. Everyone still has these clichés, I mean about women and men, men are still men and they have to be strong and in charge, and women are still the ones who take care of the house. Things are changing, but we haven't totally stopped thinking like that. I don't think France is too bad really. Because we do everything we can in France to enable women to work. What is still a problem in France is the status of men, many of them don't want that to change. They don't want society to change. Some men think women are taking away men's rightful place in the world. When we see what happens in politics when a woman comes into the National Assembly and talks about the sorts of things that really happen in a country like this, it's scary. I think an important cultural thing in France is the relationship between men and women. I mean on an intimate level. It makes men see women like prey. Men chase women as if they were prey.

> E.: France seven, America eight. I think that when women are hard workers and have good ideas and are good communicators, they communicate better than men, usually. If women use their competitive advantages in the right way, I think they pretty much get what they want. I'm not

giving ten because there are more men in the workforce, because there are men who are prejudiced. On the other hand, I also think that many women choose not to work. Then they say that they are discriminated against. I know of lots of women, including Harvard women, who really don't want to work, and they have successful husbands, and sometimes they say it's for this reason or that reason, but actually it's because they don't really want to or else they feel more useful taking care of the kids. I know a bit about Germany and I think that they put a lot of pressure on women to do certain things like breastfeeding. Basically, it's similar to Japan, society is very chauvinist, German society. They discriminate against women, it is very deep-rooted. It's the same in Japan. I see France in a quite positive light, although that's not altogether well-founded. But at least we aren't so discriminatory against women. You don't get this pressure from colleagues to breastfeed or to stop work. France has always been less macho than Germany.

S.: From a professional point of view, I'm aware that women on average get paid 25 percent less for the same job, and I've experienced this myself in my various jobs. I keep hearing comments from people like, "Well, she's a woman, she's gonna have kids." So, they're disadvantaged compared to men applying for the same job. I was really shocked and have fought against that. The situation isn't equitable because for women it always ends up being about family commitments, and they never ask men those questions, so I find that really unfair. France isn't that bad because there are so many policies aimed at changing things. There have also been quotas introduced, particularly in public companies, to force companies to have women on boards of directors, and it's better for the corporate image, from the point of view of the shareholders, if there are a few women in senior positions. It's part of the sustainable development agenda to demonstrate diversity. They are compelled to do so, in a way.

La.: So, the six I gave France. I think the situation has changed. There has been progress. We have come a long way if you think back to the period from the sixties to the eighties. We had this view of a society in which women really didn't work. I think things are changing as the younger generations come along. Basically, I see all the... I mean, in my own socio-professional category, most of the young fathers, the forty-somethings who are dads and forty-somethings who are moms, the women all work. Yes, these days they work. I see it with all my friends. I also know that this is not necessarily the case in other classes. Well, I'm in a... I am talking about my own socio-professional category. I know that in other environments it's not necessarily the case. I'm talking now about the middle classes and above. In the more disadvantaged social classes, I think there are still a lot of women who can't work and have children. They can't afford to pay a nanny to be there until eight in the evening. In more privileged circles, there are, I think, quite a few women, but not necessarily. Because there's less need to as well. And then in the underprivileged areas, it's complicated and you have to deal with the kids... I can afford to pay a nanny who works until 8 o'clock in the evening. Not everyone can do that. I don't know, I said the 60s, but maybe it was the 70s...

C: Because I think in France, we're fortunate to have a very strong legal arsenal when it comes to equality. We already have laws that are very strong and then it's just a question of enforcing them. But we do already have laws, for example the law on equal pay. For example, recently the Employment Minister, Muriel Pénicaud, set up a mechanism with sanctions for dealing with equal pay, because the equal pay law isn't enforced. There are laws and there are procedures for imposing sanctions. Which is good. Secondly, we were one of the first countries to implement a law on equal pay for work of equal value. We were one of the first countries to implement a law saying that forty percent of boards of directors have to be women, the Copé-Zimmermann law. So we're ahead of the game there too. And I would say we're also a country where women's rights have been a very powerful movement and these rights have been hard won, whether we're talking about reproductive rights or abortion. There are certain things France can be proud of in terms of the importance it has placed on women's rights. At the moment people are saying that equality is the most important issue of this presidential term. Which is good. So, there you go. But I wouldn't give France more than a seven, which is still a pretty high score, because I think there's still a lot of work to be done, because the numbers are still low, particularly at board of director level. And so, we aren't doing any better than other countries. Despite all the efforts that we've made, we are only making very slow progress. There are some fields, particularly science and biology, in which there are really big disparities when it comes to gender mix, whereas, and not just in France, in Europe in general, and in the US, whereas for example in China and the Middle East there are lots more women in science and biology. So that means that there's a mindset problem and also a problem with the basic education in France, and especially the problem that little girls are not being encouraged to go into certain careers, particularly the careers of the future, in science and technology. And I think I would say that in that area we aren't even at a seven. We are not ahead of the game yet and we are not treating these things as sufficiently important. The figures are staying where they are because we're only making slow progress, because I think there are a number of factors. There is also how willing women are to do these types of jobs. And when they're jobs where they're completely dominated by men, you can feel a bit trapped, you know. Because women don't always want to compete and be in that sort of environment, which is sometimes pretty tough and male dominated. And, as a result, it's true that they often just don't want to. And then there's the problem of self-confidence, I think. You know, they often haven't been brought up to be dominant or at least to take control or exercise leadership. And that's why we do a lot of leadership training for women, to build their confidence. And then, at some point, it's true that we just can't do it, and even if we're able to take less maternity leave, there are always those times when a woman will ask herself which is more important. Is it more important to have children, and it will always be the woman who has the children, even if we take as much parental leave as we can, and I do think we have to do better in that area. But there is still that period of time when, at a certain point, a woman might prefer to soft-pedal her career. And then suddenly she loses a bit of time because, inevitably, for a few years, that's what I did, for a few years we're not very productive. We don't want our lives to be overly complicated, put it that way. So later on, the ones who succeed are the ones who manage to do everything, and who are supported. Often, it's the relationship that makes it work.

Le.: I would probably put France at five. To be honest, I think there is gender equality and until middle management, so I think until middle management it's probably eight. Top management it drops to three or now you could say two. I think the average would be something around five. I think the US is a bit better. To some extent they're better with the workforce, they do at least raise the issue, where in France they honestly don't care, and it's a big difference. Having said that, when I was in the US and I saw women with very senior position, for me, one of the things, and it was almost 20 years ago now, but I remember thinking they behave like men, they dress like men. I think again, women will succeed only the day they can be themselves. Again, the value of having women and men, and I mean when we talk about diversity, it's not to be the same. It's to be complementary. Which is something clearly we haven't achieved, because we don't value the fact that we are complementary. Women are successful, in many ways, we are expected to be more like men. The problem is we will never be men. At some point it's like a lost battle.

M.C.: I'd say maybe six out of ten at this point in time. It's hard to give France a score because there are a lot of different issues. But compared to Germany for example, it's definitely better in France in that area. There are women in Germany who, well, the fact that there are no crèches and so on, there are a lot of issues that make it harder for women to work or, at least, to work in the sense of taking on certain jobs or being an entrepreneur, these are issues that we don't have in France. But in France, I look at the statistics. In fact, if you look at entrepreneurship, there are two statistics that come up constantly. You have one figure somewhere in the order of thirty percent and you have another one around ten percent. What does that mean? It means that if you take female entrepreneurs, I've written a lot about it, about female entrepreneurs, if you take all entrepreneurs, including the really small businesses, the self-employed, what it means is that a person can create their own job. If you take all those statistics – 30, 32, 33 percent... As soon as you start looking at companies with more than 10 employees, not big but with more than ten employees, if you start looking behind the scenes, if you look at start-ups, you look at how they raise money, you look at a whole host of other things, it's ten percent. So there are always two statistics. Those two numbers are important. So never forget, we're not at fifty percent. And, also, there's an OECD figure that's interesting as well, from 2016, but things can't have changed much since then, which said that France is number one in the world in terms of equality of access to healthcare and education. But on the other hand, it's sixty-fourth in terms of economic performance. Sixty-fourth.

D: – um, I'd say seven to... I'd say seven to eight. Because I think that on the plus side, there is genuine equality of rights ...and equality is theoretically possible ...and 2) there is a framework in place to help ensure that childcare, facilities, ...that are conducive to women working, I also think that culturally it's something that is accepted, ...on which ...that has been made possible, it's become part of our social model. So, the second thing I... my response is mixed, on the one hand my response is positive, because there are a few women who have been..., who are real role models, whether it's in politics like Simone Weil who has been an influential star, in history and in the collective imagination, or whether it's some of the big bosses, so on the one hand I would say... on the other hand, on the negative side, I have a gloomier point of view because women have less leeway to make mistakes, I think that that makes me lean more towards a 7 or lower (laughs) it's the fact that the day is coming, women today are getting onto boards of directors, but they have to be damn good to get there, the day when there will be just as many incompetent female board members, in management positions as there are men... then we'll have... today a high-up female politician or a woman running a company, she is possibly more subject to..., I mean, she has to be even more irreproachable perhaps than a man in that position does, I think there is probably still, this ... this requirement to be better. Okay, I have, this one small point, I don't know if it's part of the scope of... the study, I think that when it comes to the entrepreneur's image, we have to pay attention to the image that we present, our image when we are sitting around the table, where we have this ninety percent of men sitting there all wearing ties.

Al.: I would say seven, because I think we are above average in France, because when I was having meetings in Germany when I was founding XY in Germany, because women there told me "You know, I had to make a choice, either to have a career or to have children. I couldn't have both. I chose a career and I'm very happy." And I found it very sad to hear that men have the right to have both, but women don't. In France we don't have that at all. They can have a career and have children. But in France, it's the clichés that are annoying. You can have a career, but you won't make as much money if you' re a mother. When we find out we're still not being paid as much as men are, it doesn't feel great. Equal skills, equal work, less pay. For example, when I came back from maternity leave, I had twice as many objectives for the year. I achieved 200 percent of my objectives. I was absent in July, August, September and October. And I achieved my goals twice over. And so I explained to my bosses that if I had been there the whole time, I could have achieved maybe 250 percent in those four months. So, they were punishing me by a factor of 200 percent.

I.: I am almost inclined to think that gender equality is better in France than in the United States. I guess I might say that gender equality in France is seven out of ten. In France, the family policies have enabled the setting up of day nurseries and they have increased women's participation in the labor market to the same level as men's. The United States has created equality laws that France didn't have. But France has a very high proportion of women in work. I don't know whether the proportion of women in the United States is more or less than in France. I have the impression that in France most women do in fact work. But not ten out of ten, because we don't have equal pay for equal work, because there is only one CAC40 woman among the forty companies, because we still don't have parity in companies, because we are still contending with stereotypes. So we haven't yet got there – in terms of equality.

French women – career strategies

To analyze the career strategies of the French women, their career stages, their job changes and their descriptions of their important career decisions were evaluated. The French women's career strategies point to the following key factors:
1. Competitive advantage of the elite schools
2. International experience prior to career start
3. Early leadership responsibility
4. Preference for well-known companies
5. Searching out and generating opportunities
6. Daring to take risks
7. Promotions from one company or role to another

Education at a renowned university is very important for the French women, as networking among elite French school alumni is high and the reputation of the school enhances career prospects. In addition to renowned French elite universities, prominent US universities such as Harvard feature in some women's choices. Half of the French women interviewed have had experience abroad. With the exception of one woman, the time spent abroad has always occurred at the start of a career, mainly in the USA, and has followed a course of study. Only one of the interviewees is pursuing a career abroad in the conventional sense, involving several different posts, mainly in Asia. One further woman has two foreign jobs on her CV, in the USA and Belgium. So only for two of the women has an international career played a major role later in their careers when they returned to continue their work in France.

The women choose companies based on their reputation coupled with the opportunities on offer there. The opportunity to learn plays a role too. Another factor is that they seek out and take on leadership responsibility at an early age. Many of the women start out with very small teams early in their careers. In later career stages they make the decision to change jobs based on increased scope for decision-making combined with promotion. Around half of the women clearly give the goal of becoming GM or CEO as a reason to change jobs. One strategy that several women have pursued is the creation of a new opportunity within the same company, for example, the establishment of a new business unit or by taking on an additional role and so enlarging their existing authority or power. For some of the older women, a frequent career goal was Head of Communications in a large French company – a position with proximity to the CEO, and for some, this included international responsibilities. They then widened their area of responsibility in a targeted fashion to include other areas, such as Diversity Management. This is a role where, in line with their principles, a woman can put her pioneering role to good use benefiting other French women. The French banking sector is known for its opportunities for women. Two of the women, one from each generation age group, have used this strategy and pursued banking careers. Both represent women who have established new business areas within their banks, as start-ups, so to speak. The courage to take risks and to break out of familiar and often comfortable roles into new and more uncertain areas is part of the recipe for success. It is interesting to note that even in France, one of the women who does not have a degree has, like her German counterpart, risen to the highest levels of her company. Both of their careers have been forged in just one company and the women, both over 60 years old, stress that it would not have been possible for them to pursue their careers in the same way today as they no longer meet the selection criteria.

> L.: I don't know, but I know it was a very deliberate decision, so I studied math and physics in high school and then studied finance because, for me, the fact that it might be more male-dominated jobs, didn't mean I couldn't do it and I think I wanted to show that I could do it. It was actually easier for me than literature or marketing. I really wanted to go to Harvard, and in fact I applied, almost only to Harvard because I really wanted to go there. I wanted to have an experience in the United States. Study in the USA, work in the USA, really discover the world. I funded it and borrowed a lot of money to get to Harvard. I think it was a childhood dream. It was planned to some extent, although it is a bit of luck. After that I worked for AB because I could learn management there. Then it was important that I wanted to enter the consumer sector, from AB (US group) Technology and Finance to XY (French luxury company). I mean, they would never have hired me, never because it's an industry where we want people who have that background. If they had, they would have hired me for a job that wasn't interesting. I think I got into CD (US consulting firm) because I saw it as a learning experience and it was possible from there, that's right.

> M.C.: The management at the time wanted to create a private bank. That hadn't existed until that point. The idea was to establish a special private banking operation using existing networks. Basically, this led to me taking on the creation of this new division. The establishment of a company with a small team, we were five or six people at the beginning and we created this private banking business, which became the first private bank in France, which today generates €100 billion in assets. So, I was chosen for the job and I took it. And so we created a model which we then adapted to every country and culture and regulation, in Belgium, Italy, Luxembourg, Morocco, Poland, Turkey, the United States, in all the countries where the bank actually had a network. I spent about ten years on it. It was really fabulous. And then I was appointed director of the French network. This is a very important position in a bank, of course. That position put me on the board, and I was the first woman on it. And this position had previously always been held by men who were from ENA, polytechnics, they were always from the Grandes Écoles. Then I arrived, a woman with a high school diploma. So, it was very unusual. And so, I held this position for seven years, it was me without a doubt who held it the longest. I was chosen because I knew the entire company network really well, because I had the first part of my career in that network really, so I knew really well how it worked. I also knew the clients very well. On the other hand, I did not know much about the private banking profession. Of course, I also had

standing. And I accepted this position, which was a risk. It is very important when you're on a particular path to be convinced that there will be opportunities that you can take and at the same time to be prepared to accept risks. And so that' s how I did it. And it was great. It went extremely well. And once the French model had been developing well for a while, I exported it. So, I travelled with the team to 13 different countries. So, it is really a start-up that went international. And so, with the small team that I had, and without having any actual managerial authority, I went and visited all the private banks that we had created in those countries. It was all about the power of influence and conviction.

S.: There were probably two important steps that were significant. The first was when I was first appointed Marketing Director. That was in 2005. At that time, I was on the board of a very large company, with 7,000 employees, $7 billion in revenue, and I was the Group' s Strategic Marketing Manager. That was in 2015. And the other step was before that, when I was appointed Sales Director at XY. That was in 2001. I wanted much more autonomy and independence. I wanted to take more risks and to be more important – I mean, AB really was an excellent company right from the start because it was well structured with good procedures, expertise and management practices, but after a while I wanted to take more risks and make progress. In fact, I think getting on was easier outside of companies than inside them, for me. Part of the problem was that I was female, I was a woman. In XY, for example, that was a problem.

Ac.: Let's get started. Perhaps the first step in explaining my career is that very early on when I was in school, I knew I wanted to have a job that allowed me to go worldwide, globally. To be able to move. That's why I stopped working as a lawyer because I feared that law was not flexible enough to allow me to move throughout my life. When I came out of school, I tried to find a job in the US. I lived in the US for nearly eight years when I was a child and so I intended to go back in the end. Having not found one in the US that I was happy with, I applied to jobs in Asia and my first job was in Japan where I was in marketing for a luxury brand, I think that was almost the first step in me then moving to multiple countries and working in regional roles going forward.

E.: Being in the US and in finance were important because I learned a lot about finance, accounting and the financial markets and I have a good understanding of finance, which is less common among operational managers. I still use it every day. It was a great foundation. I had previously completed a two-year program as a financial analyst, and then they kept me there for five years, and I went to Hong Kong, then I went to business school. Then after business school I could have gone into finance, but I wanted to try something different. I got a lot of job offers at that time, and some of them were in marketing and consulting, and I also went there because it was friendly and there was more money involved. I wanted my intuitive skills to play a bigger role in my career, and I wanted to go into general management, and I did get offers in those areas, but I didn't think I knew enough. I took a temporary job, got a job with XY in Paris. I felt like I didn't know much about marketing, so I ought to take the finance job at XY, which would be a good bridge to the operational business and I could work in an area that I really knew how to do. That was a good decision and I did that for a year in Paris and worked on acquisitions. Then when there was an opening in a small subsidiary, they gave me this operational job and then I got an operational job at a higher level. I was Director of Business Development and was responsible for creating the brand in France and then in the other parts of Europe except England. That was also really important. Then I worked for XY (a French luxury brand) for ten years, which put me in an interesting French role. I didn't intend to, but it was there I stayed the longest (giggles). Then I wanted to try something more entrepreneurial, then I became CEO of this footwear brand. I really wanted to become the CEO of an expanding company. That's all of them. I worked for four companies in total.

Au.: I actually wrote a research paper for my MBA on retail technology. Mainly about marketing, about channels, how they work, how to connect things to the Internet that haven't yet been connected. Well, actually, to do behavioral analysis and so on. I came to realize that I didn't understand a lot about it. I thought that was a real shame, I was missing out on part of the story and it was also the most important part. That was five or six years ago. It was at the beginning in French technology. We were hearing a lot about technological trends and innovations and artificial intelligence and so on. There were lots of new opportunities thanks to technology. If I wanted to get involved in it, I needed to know more. That's why I chose IT, because I was very interested in it and wanted to ride the wave. Does that make sense?

K.: Yes. So, I started at XY in a European job. And then, after the French Communications position became available, I heard the president on the radio, and I found that really interesting. And so, I said I would love that job, so I ended up as an internal candidate for it. And then I met the president, and he chose me. It was so easy.

M.: In France it's quite complicated. In the Anglo-Saxon countries marketing has all the power. Every time. But in France, Communications is also important. For a very long time there were Directors of Corporate Communications who were extremely powerful. Today we are in a marketing boom. And when it was still the case that services also dominated, there were often clashes between the two. So, depending on the president's wishes, one or other of them was run separately. That was what it depended on. I used to come across headhunters, and one of them was on a mission for XY. I encountered one remarkable president, an extraordinary man who understood that he really needed Communications. Up until that point it hadn't been very well established. It was a no man's land. And they chose me to do it because of my personality compared to the other candidates.

D.: Eventually I got tired of that and I went to my senior boss and said: "Communication between the partners and the lawyers isn't working. I think we need to do something about it. We have to try to make it work more smoothly." I actually thought it was an Internal Communications task, but I ended up at HR with it. And he said, "Yeah, absolutely! You're right! I really like the fact that you've come to talk to me about it and that you've got the courage to tell me. We're going to resolve this. Let's deal with it together!"

Career Building Blocks for French female executives

What do French female executives report about their origins? What special management skills have they acquired? What personality traits are determining their success? The French are characterized by strong assertiveness, high motivation and a clear career orientation. They are, however, also conflict-riddled and competitive.

The French women's backgrounds: university-educated fathers, stay-at-home mothers

Equal numbers of the French women come from Paris and from various other regions of France, such as Lille, Besancon and Metz. All the fathers except one had university backgrounds. Their professions were all well-to-do and include doctors, lawyers, bankers, engineers, architects and entrepreneurs. Many of the fathers were away on business a lot and were often absent. The picture was different for the mothers, only three of whom had university degrees. Half of the mothers were housewives at the time their children were born while another group were working part-time. The handful of graduates were all teachers apart from one mother who was an entrepreneur. Two of the mothers had lived abroad during their childhoods. One of them spent 18 years in the USA and another in communist Romania, where she experienced equality between men and women at an early age. Most of the women describe fairly humble economic circumstances in which their parents had to work hard to achieve prosperity. More often than not it is the father who is cited as the role model; in exceptional cases it is the single mother. In other words, the majority of French women in this study did not have working mothers as role models.

> Ag.: My parents came from very modest backgrounds. They achieved everything on their own. They had a lot of ambition for their daughters. Because I'm the oldest, I was always looked at as if I was a boy. Because my father didn't have a son, I was viewed as being the son... I think it was more because of my upbringing, because politics was discussed a lot at home and there were always newspapers in the house so I got into the habit of reading newspapers. That was the thing. And I had this curiosity too, this curiosity to be up to date with what was going on. I was always being urged to do my best. I never had this idea that girls have to limit themselves to less important things. I had a lot of ambition.

> S.: Yes, so my childhood was spent in northeast France. I was brought up to believe in hard work and being perfect all the time. [laughs] Role models? Both parents. My father was somewhat of a role model because he had had a very difficult life and had started with almost nothing because his family had no money. Then he became a medic, a specialist. He's great. It was probably him who taught me the value of effort and hard work. Other role models, not so much. I think I've probably developed through my own inner energy and determination.

> L.: I think my parents made me responsible at a very young age and I think, somehow, they managed to convince me that I was responsible for my own life, and really, I was the only one who could make anything happen. They didn't pressure me into studying at all, so I would pressure myself. That I'm not sure why and how but I remember vividly. We lived in Paris. At six years old, I would go to school alone, a fifteen-minute walk to go to school. In Paris, you cross big streets. At six, it's very young but I think it's really, giving me the feeling that I should– I'm very autonomous and again, I think responsible is the right word.

> M.: I can't remember exactly when, but it was about 1975 or 76 that women in France were first allowed to have their own bank accounts. Before that, my mother, who had more money than my father, had to ask him for money. I didn't discover this until I was much older and I thought it was absolutely incredible. But the fact that I saw my mother as being a very independent, very independent woman, probably gave me the idea that women were independent. At the same time, this state of affairs and the very dominant position the father had at that time taught me that men were more important than girls. It really started in my generation. For me it was a real revolution. I'm the first generation to have had reproductive rights. The Pill was a revolution. I remember my male friends having to marry women because they got them pregnant. But I came from a generation where people didn't have to marry just because they were pregnant. And we were the only generation to experience real economic growth and to be able to find work easily. We could go out, spend a night with a man, say goodbye and the next day go on with our lives. Then AIDS came along. Then the economic crisis. But for us it was a fantastic time. I was lucky to be living then and I took the opportunity I was given to decide for myself how

to live my life. My mother didn't have choices. But my generation did. And all my friends are married, and I decided, I'm not gonna get married. I decided I was going to work. For me, working meant having an intellectual relationship with a job and not having to worry about diapers.

L.: I had lots of friends. And my relationship with my parents was excellent. I think I was pretty responsible. When I think back to the amount of independence I had, especially during my primary school years, compared to what my children here in Paris have, there's a big difference. I went to school on my own quite early on, maybe not in the first grade, but I think in the second or third grade and it took maybe fifteen minutes to walk to school from my house. And I walked home every lunchtime, I had lunch with my father, then I walked back. On Wednesdays my mother worked a lot, so I was home alone. I looked after my sister, who was four years younger than me. I always had a lot of responsibilities, I was independent from an early age. So, there was always a lot of trust between my parents and me, my parents trusted me. They knew that I'd come home on time, that I wouldn't get into a strange car, that I didn't smoke. I think I was a bit like an alien. I don't think there are many young people who've never smoked. I was very sporty, I did gymnastics, I played the organ, I trained a lot. I did six hours a week, which I think is really good.

M.: It was at school. I was in a school called C. Louise B. and I think the school was ranked third in the country. When we were about 13 or 14, there was a woman who came to talk to us about her career, she was Director of External Communications. And I had this image of a woman who had worked, who had worked with people, who had the opportunity to meet people. She was in this world full of interpersonal relationships, an elegant world, and that was the important thing. I remember that elegance really well, the elegance had an impact on me. She worked, she had interactions with other people. She also did a lot of different things. It was the era of public relations, as opposed to communications. And she got out a lot, she was out and about a lot in the outside world. And that encounter was formative for me. I didn't actually know that at the time. But I think it was that encounter that subconsciously was responsible for the fact that I ended up doing this kind of work.

M. C.: Women didn't work much back then. They didn't study. My mother got the equivalent of a Bac (A Levels). That wasn't that usual for women at the time. Her husband, my father, had a job at the time that meant he had to move out of the area. She didn't go with him. She continued working where she was. Then she was phoned up by the director of the company where my father worked and told: "Madam, you need to join your husband." And she said, "Absolutely not." So, I guess you could say she was a liberated woman. Liberated compared to how a married couple was traditionally thought of in those days.

Al.: I learned a lot from that because he worked in so many different industries that he broadened my mind so much from telling me the stories. I hang out with my dad a lot. I was having dinner with him every single night to hear the stories that he was traveling around the world with his staff. I loved the stories of his businesses and everything that was going on. That was pretty big. What else to tell you? To make it a little bit simple, I think I found that her life compared to my dad's was extremely boring in terms of experiences. I found that she had sacrificed herself. She many, many times told us that she had sacrificed herself for the family and that she could have done great marvels, and I'm sure she could because she was a pretty smart woman. She put it a little bit almost like complaining that fact that she hadn't been able to give in the opportunity she said to work and things like that, so I was determined never to do that. Yes, I think that I developed a crazy thing against housewives. (laughs)

French women – management skills

It is striking that when it comes to their individual skills, French women, unlike any of the other groups in the study, repeatedly cite general cultural understanding as one of the most important skills. In addition, according to their accounts the women have considerable expertise in their own particular area or market, such as specialist knowledge of the retail, financial, communications or digital media sectors. The French women also define themselves forcefully in terms of analytical ability and demonstrate a high level of understanding of facts as well as a strong methodological approach. As at various other points in the interviews with the French women, reference is made to the methodological approach taught at the elite universities. Their particular strength lies in their combination of various different skills. Intercultural experiences are described in connection with their periods abroad, which in this group include the USA, South America and Belgium. The feedback on experience highlights the fact that foreign posts are used to gain a competitive advantage. In contrast, the development of intercultural competencies as a career strategy, in the sense of a global mindset, is not apparent. International experience is considered a benefit in terms of developing business expertise and, in addition, is more likely to be related to geographical mobility.

> Ag.: Well, it's not just about knowing your job, you have to be interested in art, history, literature and so on. You need to be open-minded and know about the past in order to be able to envisage the future. For me, anything in the way of classical culture in quotation marks is important because it influences how you think. That's why Sciences Po is such a good school, because it gives you a broad general knowledge in lots of different areas. In terms of general culture. I don't want to brag, but I do write very well and I also enjoy it. I am curious. I like to discover new things. I am methodical.

> C.: Of course, you do have to know about today's media, today's social media. There are a whole range of techniques that you need to acquire. You also need political understanding and the ability to analyze and synthesize. I learned that when I did philosophy. And then, as I said, you have to be curious and energetic. I have a lot of energy. I think I was about 45 when I took up this position with XY France. So, there were people there who were much younger than me and each time it was always younger people I was with.

> E.: Well, I've lived in Asia and in the States. I'm genuinely international and it gives me the advantage of being able to make comparisons. I'm not even talking from the point of view of being a woman. It's definitely not perfect, but a lot better than average, because I'm very good at leading people. There's always room for improvement, but I'm at the end of my career. I'm good at evaluating situations and strategies and I have stamina, determination and good social skills.

> Ag.: I think I'm open-minded and adaptable, which is very important. In fact, my job is a bit like being a family practitioner, which means I need to be able to listen to people and write down what they say, understand their needs and support them and assist them when they are talking to different people so they can manage aspects of their lives. The dialogs they have will be with their portfolio manager, attorney, notary, accountant and so on. And in order to do that you have to love people, and I think that when we go to countries like that (Argentina), it's generally because we like people. And you also have to be adaptable, open-minded and curious, because

you need to be able to talk about almost anything to do with finance without necessarily being an expert. So, you have to bring a lot of curiosity to it.

There are many instances of the French women's capacity for innovation. The women are driven by a desire to improve and modernize aspects of the company, although their personal visionary abilities are only occasionally cited as a strength or equated with the capacity for innovation. This positions the French women alongside the majority of the women surveyed elsewhere.

> L.: Well I think I have the ability to see the direction we need to head in. With XY, for example, the path we had to take was very clear in my mind. The task then becomes: how do I get the teams to start down that road? Operationally, how do I achieve it? That's extremely important, because otherwise the whole thing is pointless. I think the vision of where we should be heading is extremely clear in my mind a lot of the time.

> Is.: Actually, I think I've been somewhat of a visionary about a lot of things. I could see the gender diversity problem before anyone else could, and the internet security problem as well. And I developed programs. And to be visionary is to be innovative. And I developed solutions. I achieved a lot of things within the company because I was a visionary and I was innovative. For me the two things have a similar character. When I was with the legal team, I won the Innovation Award because we were always doing innovative things. Early on I had the idea that we needed a program for gender equality or else we were going to hit a brick wall. And I also saw early on that we needed to introduce and implement a number of new types of industrial management contract. So, I think these are the two attributes I had that really shaped my career path.

> Al.: I don't know if I'd really say I'm a visionary ... Innovative? I don't know. Maybe I was kind of innovative at XY. It's just that I've worked with a lot of people. But maybe I am visionary because I always want to strive to improve things and go that bit further to make things better. I always want to participate in every project going. That's what it is, I always want to take part in the projects that are going to improve the everyday life of the individual, the daily life of our customers.

The French women's personality traits: highly career-oriented and motivated

The French women are very career oriented. The older women in particular are particularly so, with all other areas of life subordinate to their professional ambitions. The younger French women are more critical of this approach, in that they are not as willing to accept the double burden of career and childrearing. Their values have shifted slightly in favor of a better work-life balance. This does not in essence apply to their own ambition of rising up the career ladder but there is less willingness to submit indiscriminately to norms such as very long hours, for example. The younger French women are thus equivocal about the focus on career which the older women have. All of the women view careers and promotions as a way to support others, to achieve progress for co-workers and to be a role model for others.

When it comes to their own career motivations, the French women also mentioned the following:

- Being independent, having financial freedom
- Inner fulfilment
- Personal development, learning, discovery
- Having a positive influence on society, being useful
- Creating meaning for fellow employees, promoting employees' well-being, helping others
- Achieving recognition, leading a different life than that of a housewife and mother, satisfying one's own ego
- Excitement, having interesting experiences, the thrill of the fight

S: It's about personal fulfilment, I would say, the feeling that I have achieved something significant in my life and that I personally have made progress. That's what it is.

Al.: For me it's a very feminist thing. I was very angry at seeing women like my mother end up the way they did. They had no opportunities, as mothers they weren't recognized in society. I decided very early on that I would change that. I was eight years old when I made that decision. I remember it well. I was determined to work really, really hard and started trying to break through the "glass ceiling" as they called it. Another thing that I always thought was that if I wanted to change the world, the only way to do it was to get to the top. No one's gonna listen to a housewife who does nothing but people would listen to someone who was successful, like a CEO or something. If I wanted to change this problem to do with being female, the best thing would be to work my way up as high as possible, because up there I would be listened to more and then I could change things. It's almost like being an activist. I don't use that word very often, but for me it's been a lifelong thing, I just have to keep on trying. I want to at least be a kind of role model for every girl out there who asks "Is it possible? Well, it looks like someone out there made it.

L.: For a very long time I thought, in some ways I always thought, although I wouldn't admit to it, that I wanted to run a company. I think that's because I need to feel like I've made a positive contribution to the world. In the hope that if you run a business you can have a positive influence on the world, as opposed to a negative one, and I really believe you can. I think it's to do with how you behave as an employer, how you give your employees meaning through the work they do, how you create value, and by creating value you support the economy and you support the people who work for you. That was very important to me right from a very young age. Which industry it was, wasn't what mattered.

M.: Everything in my life revolves around the pursuit of independence. I got my driver's license so I could be independent and I have a car so I can go home whenever I feel like it. I earn money so that I'm independent, so I can tell a man I'm leaving him if I want to, because I'm independent. For a couple of years, I stopped working two jobs, and suffered intellectually but not financially. But in my head, I was dependent on the man I was living with then, and I just couldn't do it. So, it's about independence and secondly the desire to have my ideas recognized. Basically, what interested me in life was not power as such, but the ability to get my ideas heard. Because if I'd had the power but nobody had accepted my ideas, that would have been incredibly pointless.

E.: Motivation? Ego, and being appreciated beyond my own family, and money, but the ego thing is the most important. I call it ego, but you can call it fulfilment or whatever, but really it's all about ego. Other women can call it whatever they want, wanting to help others or something, but I categorize all that as ego.

L.: I think it's how do you give job, how do you give people a sense of purpose, how do you create value, and by creating value you actually help the economy and you help the employees that work for you. For me, that was something that was very strong from a very young age. The industry had zero importance whatsoever. I ended up in luxury, but honestly, I served at XY (US Company) because at the time, I thought it was one of the best companies in the world. One of the companies where I could learn, really, how to manage effectively.

The accounts the women give of their own strengths focus on certain key areas of the BIP dimensions developed by Hossiep (2003), which, as mentioned, were used as a framework for the personality dimensions; they are described in more detail in the Introduction section. The dimensions that stand out among the French women are a strong action orientation, a strong performance drive, sociability and a high degree of assertiveness. Resilience and emotional stability are also important. At various points, the women describe their readiness to take risks as particularly important for their careers. As with all the women surveyed, the other BIP dimensions also feature, but the areas mentioned stand out in particular among the French women.

M.C.: Well, first of all I've always been enthusiastic about everything I have done. I am a very determined person. I hate the expression "good luck." It's energy that you need, a lot of energy. You don't need luck or courage. We're not living in a country that's being bombed. So it doesn't take courage. I have lots of energy, lots of determination, lots of energy. I mean, of course I work hard. I have excellent health, so I'm able to work hard. I do maintain a balance though, so although I work hard, I'm also able to appreciate the moment, whether it's a moment of happiness or of pleasure or whatever. And also, I've always said to myself when I'd taken on a new challenge: It'll work out fine! I've always asked myself a lot of questions. I think it's healthy to ask questions and to have the humility to know what we don't know. But at the same time, when I am questioning something, I still think that there's no reason why I shouldn't be able to do it. See what I mean? I have an inner conversation with myself and think about all the things that need to be taken into account, but then I tell myself that it will work out fine, regardless.

C.: You have to have a certain openness, an open-mindedness, an adaptability, a willingness to take risks, these are the qualities that I think are you really have to have these days as a senior company manager, because the world is constantly changing and evolving very fast. It's essential for a manager to be able to adapt to each new reality that comes along and also to be able to anticipate it. And in actual fact we can only anticipate if we have the courage to overcome obstacles and ultimately to enjoy each new adventure, even if it's difficult at times.

L.: I think it's also important with that notion to embark teams. Another strength I believe I have, is creating an effective team and high performances. First, because I'm convinced that I'm as good as my teams. I want to have the best people working for me. If I were to have the best, I need to have them motivated. I need to make sure that they like what they do and they need to have some freedom and feel that they can come up with ideas, be innovative. I delegate very easily as long as I trust my team members. I give them a lot of room to grow and to develop themselves.

S.: When I went for this job, they told me that personality was the key thing. And because I'm a very determined person, I never abandon a task and I'm not afraid of obstacles or difficulties. That's why they hired me. I was in competition with other people who were already managers and had better skills and technical ability than me, they told me that. Previously I used to rely on my experience more. Having all these top companies on your CV is really reassuring for the people making the decision to hire you. I think that was what it was: lots of energy, enthusiasm, drive, vision and concern for other people, a sense of ethics.

D.: Perseverance, hope and willingness are the key elements, I would say, plus a really positive and supportive personal life, so no major health issues either personally or in the family and a husband who supports, helps and does his bit.

Ac.: I definitely think the international element is a big advantage. And on the skill side, I'm pretty motivated – driven. A bit of an entrepreneur. I'm quite good at coping with risk too. That usually goes down well when people want to expand or develop part of a business. They want people who aren't afraid to take risks. I'd probably say those are the main reasons, in terms of strengths. I think those are some of them anyway.

C.: I think it's a combination of things. A strong skillset, obviously, a lot of hard work, because they were both women who worked hard. Very capable. But also, they probably had energy and ambition. Katie Kot and Françoise Gri are very different sorts of women. Katie Kot spent her entire career in Human Resources and then became president. And then she returned to Human Resources with another company. Françoise Gri has had more of a commercial career. And then she became president at Manpower. I think they both had great empathy as well. And they're both charismatic. And I think maybe that's what makes the difference. There are charismatic men too of course. But when a woman reaches that level, she still has... It's not just ability. Ability is important, of course, but it's not enough. She has to have other qualities too, when you consider that in these sorts of very male dominated environments, there are women who also know how to dominate them, they're assertive and they know how to persuade. They have strong personalities.

It is the women who have worked overseas who speak most about their personal leadership styles. For these women, it is communication which forms the main focus. Their communication ability, employed in the art of persuasion, is their strong suit. Charismatic leaders are seen as orientation models. In addition, the leadership style of the French female executives is transformative, involving all employees whenever possible. Employee satisfaction, reflected through low termination rates, is their own benchmark.

Ac..: I champion collaborative leadership. I truly believe that we can only succeed if we work together. I have always aimed to build teams – the drop-out rates in my teams are always extremely low. In XY less than three percent of the people have gone elsewhere, and that's in teams which are very diverse. I consider myself lucky if I have good people and I do everything I can to hold onto them. At AB our churn rate was barely above zero. We kept the same people for years, which was incredible. I think that's had a lot to do with me as a leader. As I get older, I focus more and more on this aspect, on collaborative leadership. "

L.: I'm not sure whether I have charisma. I do admire it though because I think it's a good way to... I think it's important for a leader to have charisma. A key element in effectiveness is how you involve teams so that they'll follow you and perform well. I often observe people who've got charisma – I think it's linked to warm-heartedness and empathy, possibly. I'm really interested in people, but I know people don't really see me as charismatic when they meet me. It's something I need to work on.

French women – strong during conflict and competitive

French women describe themselves as resilient, unafraid of conflict and conflict-riddled. They approach conflict head on and describe the way in which they have gained in maturity through dealing with conflict resolution. Compromise as a way of solving conflicts is viewed in their opinion rather negatively in France. The primary approach is to assert oneself during a conflict and emerge as the winner. In conflict situations the French women executives tend to be combative and are not afraid to call a spade a spade. This is where French women's ability to assert themselves really comes into play, and it is rooted in their willingness to battle situations out. In this research, the pronounced willingness to fight is a differentiator from women in other countries.

> D.: I go at things head on, I go straight in, I'm like a Pitbull. I'm fearless and there's no filter between what I think and what I say… but maybe I have a tendency to go in too fast and not take enough time to listen and find compromises.

> Ag.: When I need to do battle over something, I get depressed, and any time I have had to fight, it's always been against men and not women. But that's because men want more territory, for them the company and their territory are part of the same thing. I never attempt to expand my own territory, but if you try to expand into mine, I really don't like it. And then I'll defend it, and I'm prepared to do anything… anything… I will always fight to maintain my territory.

> C.: Conflict? Well, you know, maturing as a person has allowed me to become much more confident in the face of conflict. It's true that I am consistently stubborn and very persistent and have sometimes been the cause of conflicts. Sometimes you need to "lance the boil" as they say in our country. So, it's useful to get things on the table and say: This is where we disagree. Why do we not agree? I don't see conflict as being negative. Sometimes it's unavoidable. But you also have to know how to deal with conflict. And always to come up with a way out of the conflict, even if it's a compromise. But that's what I've learned and that's what you are interested in knowing about. When the founder of XY (Chinese) came to France I was lucky enough to work with him and he always said, especially during an acquisition, that there has to be trust, trust and the ability to compromise. The term compromise is not see being as a very positive thing in French. But he said if we don't compromise, we don't move forward.

> L.: I don't have an issue with conflict per se, so I'm happy to disagree. I guess that's why I'm thinking it depends on what type of conflict. There are conflicts based on situations where we disagree on content facts and then it's a matter of exchanging convictions and sharing. Then there might be conflicts based more on politics and that I find much more difficult. I think that's one of my clear weakness, I don't think it's conflict, I think it's a political game. Which again, I think is inherent to any organization, but at some point, if you want to rise to the top, you have to understand and you have to learn to play it. I think you have to learn the rule of the game and if you don't play the rule of the game, then you'll never be in the game.

> M.: Then there is what I call your tolerance threshold. There is a level of tolerance for things which is different for you than for me. What is important is to understand your own threshold. I can be supportive of lots of things until that threshold is reached, but not beyond. So, you have to understand where that threshold is. Up to that point there can be compromise, but once you've reached that threshold, you have to react. There was this one day, I had a disagreement, an actual fight. I was on the board of XY. There were eight men there and I was introducing the

new advertising campaign. The team had worked really hard on it. And one of the guys suddenly decided to start talking about a particular problem. At first, I was irritated. The guy was telling me I'd done something I hadn't. And in the end, he told me I was a liar. In front of everyone, just like that, he said: You did this, you said that. I said no I didn't! I didn't know how to react. What I should have said was: This is not what we're discussing at the moment, we can talk about it later. Instead I carried on debating it with him until my threshold was reached. Then I left the room. And in the evening the president asked this man to come and apologize. So, I was lucky that the president thought I was in the right. But I shouldn't have reacted like I did. This situation really affected me. After that, I started learning how best to react. But at that particular moment I had reached my tolerance threshold. But I did ok because the person did come to apologize.

The majority of French senior female executives have a positive attitude towards competition. They prefer a fair competition and like to make use of competition against others in a way which has positive results for their teams. The French women show strengths in this area, which is one that they were taught about early in their school and university careers. It includes striving for high levels of achievement so as to be the best in a given environment. Success-oriented competition and attitudes towards conflict are intertwined. Women go on to use these skills in the professional context and respond to attacks by male colleagues in a combative manner. Some also allude to the subject of rivalry between women. Although they themselves object to this rivalry it was mentioned in 80 percent of the French interviews. The reader is referred to the descriptions later on in this book.

> Is.: I think I've always had a pretty competitive frame of mind. And I've always competed against myself in particular. When I passed my A-levels, I couldn't find my name on the list because I wasn't high enough up in the ranking. And when I got my Masters, in one of the best law schools in France, I thought: "I can't possibly have passed." But actually, I got an A. I have always competed against myself. So when I'm competing against other people in the industry, I'm actually pretty competitive on behalf of my team. Right now, there's a little bit of rivalry going on with some of my colleagues because they were here before me, so I'm in the process of marking out my territory. For the team. So, for example, every two years there's a management meeting in Switzerland. We were playing this game. We were on a boat on Lake Geneva and there were ten Montblanc pens to be won. So I said to the people on my table: "We're going to win. I am absolutely determined we're going to win." And we just went for it. I assigned all the team members tasks. I went to the captain of the boat while the others were asking questions. And we did win the pens. Because I was totally determined and I have a competitive streak. But it's not like I want to annihilate others. It's more the idea that I want the whole team to win. I like it when there's a challenge, I like taking on a challenge.

> C.: Yes, I like winning, I like being successful. It's not the same as winning, it's not like winning against somebody. I don't have a competitive spirit at all in that sense. I actually think of it as being a bad thing. In fact, what I really value is winning together. At the same time, I'm also successful. I like winning in that sense of the word, winning together.

Career-enhancing factors for French top women managers

Mastering French business codes is a prerequisite for success for the French women in top management. Although the codes are changing across the generations, their importance remains undisputed. Successful women connect the right networks and mentors to their careers and use executive coaching to overcome barriers.

Mastery of specifically French codes of business

The mastery of so-called codes in France, all of the women agree, is extremely important because these are so deeply rooted in French society. The codes operate on multiple planes and include language codes, educational codes, codes of behavior and dress codes. The mastery of these extremely country-specific codes is still essential in France today if one wishes to be promoted to senior positions. Where these codes were once well-defined, they are now more subtle, however, they are still very much present. Although there has been a shift away from purely male-dominated codes to ones allowing more freedom for French women in terms of choice of dress and management style, a conscious consideration of how to use codes to one's advantage is essential. The younger generations no longer follow the traditional codes so rigidly, and a new type of code is emerging. However, mastery of the traditional codes is still very important for career advancement in both management and politics. In France, these two areas are interconnected. An important aspect of the codes is language proficiency. Your linguistic skill level places you in a particular social grouping and a more educated style of language facilitates access to the upper circles of power. Good posture and an awareness of one's personal appearance are also important. As a result, especially during a first encounter, one will either be immediately identifiable as a potential senior executive – or not. For the French female executives, these codes take on a special relevance because nowadays they are concerned with differentiating themselves from male codes, although the latter still represent the social norm when it comes to the perception of power. French women consequently choose their clothing according to specific criteria and are judged first and foremost by their appearance and style of dress.

These codes are used to identify the individual as belonging to a particular social class. This categorization is independent of company and position. Codes continue to play a significant role in the higher social classes. Suitability for senior management positions is assumed to be closely linked to mastery of the codes, although this filtering process is becoming less rigid. The younger women in the survey talk less about this issue and in part differ significantly from women in their late 50s. A generational change would appear to be taking place among French women. However, the school codes, in other words, the assigning of people to elite groups, continues to hold sway in France's ruling circles. These descriptions reveal a clear difference in this respect between the French group and the other women surveyed.

M.: Well I think codes are very important in France. They are all the more important nowadays because they have evolved as society has evolved, and they are less visible and more subtle and so they are more difficult to analyze. So a woman who has power must have the clothes that go with that power. She will either choose a dress that is branded or shoes, or the bag will be branded. Not necessarily all three. She might buy something from Zara and something from Yves Saint Laurent. She's got to have something from Saint Laurent, though. Women who reach a certain level realize how important appearance is. Some realize it at 30, others don't realize it until they're 50. According to the press, some women say: I became CEO and I realized at that point that my clothes were important because now I was being scrutinized. If you read one of Marlene Sciappa's books, she's the Women's Rights Minister, she spends a whole chapter analyzing press articles talking about her earrings, her hair and her clothes. For me, Christine Lagarde is the archetypal French power woman, because she has attained a very high position and has managed to maintain her elegance. She wears jewelry and colorful clothes and dresses that accord with the place and the occasion. She likes doing that. At the World Women's Forum, Christine Lagarde wore a jacket and leather pants. But when she meets world leaders, she uses a tailor. She wears jewelry and makeup. For me, she is the archetypal Frenchwoman. Her appearance says: I'm in power and I like being in power, it's important to me. But the problem for women nowadays is to define their style. The style has to be right for the individual, it has to suit your body shape. You have to find the garment that suits you. And also find the garment that matches your profession. I think women are either shy and stick to the rules and wear a grey or black suit, or they do the opposite and wear something too sexy. But that devalues you. If you're too sexy, people think you're stupid. You have to strike a balance.

M.C.: Codes, well yes, I think there was the time when women in France – but not just in France – used male codes in order to be successful. They thought that to be successful you had to act like a man and be like a man. And so, they dressed like men, in grey and black or whatever. And there were behaviors that they associated with masculine behavior, being tough, in other words... They tried to adopt male codes and attitudes. I don't know, maybe that was the only way, back then. But I believe you should be yourself. So I always dress in bright colors and I wear something sparkly... Besides, I never had a problem because of being a woman. I'm very womanly, it's not an act. But I don't like using charm at all. I'm a woman in every sense of the word and I work on the basis that it's good to be a woman. And I've never tried to be like a man in how I behave. So, you see, the problem with the codes is that the first time you meet someone, you're evaluated, everything's evaluated: your stature, your general appearance, how you look, how you shake hands. It's only later that the real you comes out.

Is.: I have always been very keen not to gain weight. It's very important to me to keep in shape. I've always been very feminine. I wear lip gloss every day. I make sure I look chic. I don't want to look like Cinderella when I'm at work, you know. When I was on Wall Street, I wore pants every day. I wore suits and a shirt. I always take great care. I'm meant to be the face of the company. I like to have the right shoes in the right color with the right bag. In the summer, I have always painted my toenails. It's really important to me. I don't like looking masculine. My daughter has picked that up from me. So yes, in France, women in certain sorts of jobs should, as we say," tirée à 4 épingles " ("be dressed up to the nines"). If I go and see clients and I'm not excellently dressed, then I'm not excellent generally and then I think, damn, what have I gone and done? I think the image we project is really important. And at the same time, we are representing French society, where taste, fashion and chic still exist. That's always been important to me. And I think that's what counts for my daughter too, she's very feminine and uses jewelry to advantage, and I think that she projects that kind of image too. And I had a very elegant grandmother. My mother was older and didn't dress up as much as my two grandmothers. It was my grandmother's image that was my inspiration. I would recommend young women who are out and about in public and who play a representative role in society to be astute about these things. Especially in France, where fashion and taste are so important.

L.: There are the codes of the important French universities particularly, like the ENA, the National School of Administration, the Polytechnic, the various important universities. That's true even if the people who go there are from modest social backgrounds. I think there are language codes, educational codes and university codes. That's definitely true. But I think that in today's business world it is more the university code that matters rather than the coming-from-a-good-family code.

Mentoring, networking and coaching for career advancement in France

In view of the barriers faced by women in management, mentoring is considered an essential factor in career development, especially for women. Researchers who study the question of gender differences in mentoring highlight gender discrimination, male hierarchies and a lack of informal support networks for career women. The French women's descriptions of mentoring and networking are detailed. The women have had a variety of experiences with mentoring as well as of sponsors who have accompanied them on their journey. Mentors often come from the influential French universities and help with job searches, especially at the beginning of a career. Networking and mentoring come together here in a virtuous circle.

The effect of mentoring among French female executives tends to be in the area of concrete professional support, as opposed to psychological emotional support. Mentors provide access to networks or give advice when deciding on career moves. One challenge, which was also raised by Chinese women interviewed, is that one's boss might also end up being one's mentor, for example, when there is a change in personnel. If one's career path is too closely tied to that of a particular mentor, the close bond can become a disadvantage if the mentor changes companies.

> Ac..: Yes, I've had a mentor. He was an HEC alumnus. I was really, really happy when I came across him, about 17 years ago. I was ever so happy. He has always been there, I last saw him in Hong Kong a week ago, he has always been very invested in me. He gives me advise, he's found me work and he's connected me with people through his network. He always gives me great advice.
>
> Is.: If you could choose it would be good to have a much older mentor who'd be your sponsor and mentor and help you navigate things, so you'd have some kind of protection within the company. I never had that. I had to do everything on my own, but if I'd had someone to give me a bit of protection, I think that would have helped me a lot.
>
> D.: Mentors, whether men or women, work extremely well. It's one of the keys things when you're working in a company. There need to be more mentoring programs. They have a positive effect on the mentee, they help with your personal development. And they have a powerful inverse effect too. Most of our mentors are Comex mentors (Executive Team) and they are all over 50 years old and have never been confronted with female aptitudes or any other nationalities. A lot of them have had Damascus moments where they've said, "This is incredible! This is going to

change the way I see my career and my personal life..." They've really learned a lot from the mentees, so the reverse effect is very potent. It works fantastically when it's organized well.

M.: So, it turned out that the president I had been working for was retiring. In a lot of companies, the Director of Communications works very closely with the president. Then we got a new president. And all of the qualities that the first president had liked in me, the second president didn't. Oh, I've forgotten to tell you something that's important to the story. In addition to my position as Head of Global Communications, I took on an additional role at one point, which was Diversity. Ok, so what happened was that the previous president appreciated my work, appreciated my visibility and encouraged me to be visible and to talk about diversity when I was talking about the company. The new one didn't like that. We had had a leader and then we got an accountant. They didn't respond in the same way to things.

Ag.: Yes, I've had one mentor. He is an Alumni from SUC as well. I was very, very lucky to meet him about 17 years ago. I was very, very lucky. He has always been, I just saw him three weeks ago in Hong Kong, he's always been extremely invested in me. He's giving me advice, he's found me jobs, or through his network I was able to connect with people. He's always of extremely good advice. I haven't found the need for another one because this one really– He even found the school for my kids, he recommended. I'm so happy this is the best school in the world that I have here, and it's all because of him.

In France, networking in general is essential. If you come to France from abroad, you will soon find yourself being advised that in order to establish yourself professionally, you will need someone to introduce you to "the right networks". Access to specific networks and power circles is thus extremely important to a career in France. Networking, by definition, is about connecting with other relevant people both inside and outside an organization. It encompasses a variety of tactics of alliance and coalition building aimed at achieving personal goals. Women's career success in France is consequently linked to a willingness to invest time in this area – time that is already scarce. It is also contingent on the skillful use of networks and the contacts resulting from them. From the point of view of French women, networking events organized purely for this purpose are less effective than the established networks of the French elite universities, large corporations, private circles and other business connections. The mixing of private networks with professional interests is something that, up until now, French women have observed to exist to a greater extent among men, who apply this strategy very successfully. However, this means that certain networks are still only accessible to certain target groups and are difficult for outsiders to penetrate. French men use networking as a micro-political power tactic, by which they strategically and systematically seek to shape and use the network of relationships around them to further their own interests. By comparison, women in management positions have a lot of catching up to do. French women who have come to the realization that they need to invest a portion of their time in this area and give it priority are at a distinct advantage. The majority of the French female executives interviewed have established strong network structures and capitalize on them, especially when it comes to decisions to switch jobs. Irrespective of their own career planning, French women often get involved in networks that promote women. In France, there are about 500 such women networks, almost 300 of which are job-related.

E.: Women just don't have enough time here. They are always running after their children or their families. They skip things when they have children. So, then they get punished for that, they are at a disadvantage. I carry on despite the children. Women are okay at networking, not great, but okay. Women don't get much out of networking. When people are looking for board members, they hire their friends, good friends, and they have lots of those. Or else they go to a headhunter and he has lots of friends too. They don't even look at your CV. In France, the process isn't a very rational one. It's still about who you know, friends and the like. They're not going to go looking for new board members in some random women's network. Know what I mean?

S.: It all comes down to which University you were at. My husband was at HEC, that's the top business school in France. Their network is more effective than the ESSEC one, at ESSEC people look out for themselves, there's not much solidarity. I don't use my ESSEC network very much, to be honest. XY (US company) alumni have an excellent, close network, mainly because they all were trained using the same methods. My network is more the people I work with and meet at conferences and when I'm at other professional meetups.

M.: Well, not much really. I've always done a lot of international networking and had a lot of friends but I only realized very late on that personal networks like this are really important in your career. I hadn't wanted to mix the two, but men totally do. But I didn't get that. I had my home life, my friends and then the rest. I only made my personal network, so in other words my friends, available when I was asked to. But I didn't use my network very wisely for my own benefit. I should have got more involved as a network organizer too. And I should have been better organized. I did organize the directors' network, XY Board, and I was the first woman at the top after years of men. But by then I was already at least 45, quite late on. You're better off starting doing it when you're 20. These days, I tell women about how important networks are. I didn't work it out until it was too late.

Is.: Women don't always understand the importance of networks and networking. Ask them which networks they're involved in. And keep asking, because women don't understand the importance of being part of a group. We also need to insist that women stand together so they can help each other, just like men do. Sometimes women compete against each other, and that's a disgraceful state of affairs. These are the things we need to talk to women about so that they realize that the value of being in a network is about helping each other, not competing against each other. I do so many things. I organize events for women, I invite them to my house. Some summers I have as many as 3 dinners for 20 people at my house. I'm also very involved in organizations. I do a great deal to help the upcoming generation of women. I spend a lot of time working with management to expand the company's women's program. And I answer a lot of questions from young people who ask me things. I do a lot to help my daughter's generation. I give advice to my friends' children when they ask me about legal careers. I speak at lots of events. I spend a lot of time meeting people. And I'm in women's networks, contract management networks, and so on.

M. C.: There are these networks, men's networks, like you said. Except these days, the networks are becoming more mixed, in both directions. There were networks of very powerful men, very exclusively male. There are these women's networks that were created, and now there are lots of them. They started about fifteen years ago. These female networks are becoming receptive to being mixed gender, because it's important for them to be mixed. It's not about being a woman or being a man, the genders have to work together. But a woman's relationship with her network is important. Women are still not networking. Lack of time or wrong priorities.

In addition to mentoring and networking, several of the French women interviewed had had positive experiences using executive coaching to overcome hurdles and when making career decisions. Professional executive coaches are hired either temporarily or over longer periods of time in order to better utilize abilities or work on weaknesses. It is interesting to note that for French women in senior management functions, aspects of personal well-being and stress reduction are often the focal point of the coaching, as the women tend to benefit particularly from coaching in this area due to the constant double burden of work and homelife and their long working hours.

French women – career barriers

Barriers for women who want to rise in management also exist in France. The French women top managers report on the glass ceiling, rivalries among women and discrimination against men who see their supremacy threatened. And how they dealt with these barriers in their own career advancement.

The glass ceiling in France exists

In France, the glass ceiling is a reality. All of the women surveyed agree on this point. When asked where the glass ceiling starts, three different points of view are put forward. First, the glass ceiling exists because of motherhood – both the anticipation of possible motherhood and motherhood itself lead to negative consequences. Situations are described where pay increases did not materialize or where women were not considered for promotion because of concerns about motherhood. Second, the glass ceiling is located above middle management, in other words, in France it is located just below the top tier. The third area – identified by a smaller group of older women – is a glass ceiling created by women themselves. They argue that there is a lack of women who genuinely want to move up the career ladder. They perceive the number of women who are suitable for top management as being much smaller than the number of male candidates. They see this glass ceiling as being self-made by women who do not really aspire to rise to higher positions because it is harder for them to do so or because they lack self-confidence. According to this line of reasoning, the glass ceiling is the result of the fact that there are still very few women in France who really want to reach the top. The pipeline of women who qualify for top jobs is also limited by the fact that women do not opt for technical and IT training, despite the fact that these offer greater opportunities for advancement.

> E.: When women here in France talk about the glass ceiling, they ignore how many women choose not to work. The pool of men just is much bigger. There is a glass ceiling aspect to it,

but somehow, I don't see it as all that discriminatory. When I say there's a glass ceiling, it obviously is a form of discrimination, but that's why I gave France seven and not ten.

Ag.: I do think there's still a lot that needs doing when it comes to the glass ceiling. Progress has been made in promoting women to management committees, partly through quotas. But it's not enough. I think there's still an awful lot to be done to ensure equality between men and women. And then there's the inequality that stems from women censoring themselves, to an extent. So, it's not entirely the men's fault, it's also partly the fault of women who don't have the courage.

L.: For me, again, until middle management– let's say my direct reports, not an issue at all. Especially in my industry where there are more women than men. Top managements, executive committee level, there's a clear glass ceiling and then CEOs, I'm not even going to talk about it. I'm saying that in an industry where 70 percent of the staff are women, 80 percent of the clients are women, and when you look at the executive committee, there are no women left. When you look at CEOs, there are no women, very few women CEOs. I think there is a fundamental belief that men can manage business here and women cannot. Then because men are managing businesses, that's the other thing that I've noticed very recently, because until now I never felt it. For men it's just easier to be between themselves. Boys network.

D.: I think it is directly below top management. Even in companies with a large proportion of women, for example I can think of one company that specializes in children's clothing, out of ten directors, I only saw one woman. It is slowly getting better though.

Is.: In my generation it does exist. My daughter won't be affected by it nearly as much, but we're still very much influenced by stereotypes. It's still a man's world. For example, all the top professors of medicine are men.

Al.: Where in the hierarchy? Right at the top, I guess. I'll give you an example. I know a woman who was contacted by a shareholder of a large corporation. He asked her to undertake an entire project to set up a new unit. She took it on and really got into the work. After nine months, the shareholder said to her, "You know, I thought. ...maybe we could hire somebody to be the general manager. I'll give you his resume. Tell me what you think." She said to me, "Just imagine, I got the resume, and it was basically the same as mine. But he didn't say he wanted me to be GM. He wanted a man even though the man had the same resume as me." And then she said, "So I called him and said look, we need to meet up so you can explain. I don't understand why you didn't consider me for the job." So, he said, "Oh, I didn't think you'd be interested. I thought you'd want to spend time with your family. I didn't think you'd want to devote so much time to your work because it's going to be a very demanding job."

Ag.: Yes, it does still exist. And I really don't know what we can do to get rid of it, because we've been talking about it for decades. There's always been a glass ceiling. The moment always arrives when a young woman decides to have children and her life takes on a different rhythm. The explanation for the glass ceiling that men give is that women dedicate themselves to their children. But I know women who are top managers and have had four children, and it hasn't stopped them. So, the kids excuse doesn't wash with me. It's actually about having the will to do it. I don't think men are driven by the desire to promote women, that's pretty evident. And also, women don't succeed in breaking through, they don't give themselves the opportunity to break through.

M.C.: I think so yes, I think the famous glass ceiling does exist. There's no denying that. The main thing is to encourage cultural change. There is this temptation nowadays to think that the younger generation isn't going to have the same problems. I don't think it's that we need to carry on being on the alert, what we need is to keep sending out a powerful message, the networks, all these structures that enable us to spread the message... I'm talking about equal opportunities. It's about genuinely having the same ambitions. And if you have the same ambitions, then you should have the same opportunities to enable you to achieve them. And that means that networks have to be effective, management teams have to push things through. That's what we have to do when there's a high-level position vacant. Equality. Which means that we shouldn't simply accept it when people say the only people available are men and there is nothing they can do about it. There has to be another way, so let's find it. At the same time, we need to support women in overcoming their own mental blocks so they can be themselves and think "I want to do this", "I have the skills", "I have the abilities".

Rivalry between women in France

An important aspect of the French women's accounts, and one which was not mentioned in any of the other countries, is the question of female solidarity. The women talk about "sororité", or sisterhood, on the one hand, and rivalry and competition between women on the other. There is agreement between the younger and older women on this issue and the fact that it is important. Younger women aged around 40 describe how much they would like to receive support from older women, but they are denied this. The 55-plus generation, however, fought hard for their careers and expect the same fierce struggle and conformity to male norms from the women who come after them. Women aged around 40 want to build a career without having to submit unconditionally to male norms. One of these norms is the lack of family-friendly working hours, especially when it comes to evenings, which the executive women in France regard as an extremely widespread problem. Older women find themselves unable to accept the fact that the next generation of French female leaders wish to depart from these norms and so deny them their solidarity. This phenomenon is described in the literature as the Queen Bee Syndrome. "Queen Bee" is the term used to describe women who, in a male-dominated working environment, strive for individual success, distance themselves from certain other women and hinder the advancement of younger female employees. The syndrome comprises several aspects, such as emphasizing male characteristics, distancing oneself from other women and denying the existence of a glass ceiling and of the inequalities that only women, in this case with reference to senior management, experience. According to scientists, this syndrome results from the fact that when a woman belongs to a disadvantaged or minority group, she is likely not to view the qualities of that group as valuable or important. The stereotypical devaluing of, and discrimination against, women is perceived by the Queen Bee as a threat to her social identity. One of the potential coping strategies consists in distancing oneself from the disadvantaged group in order to seek acceptance within the higher group. In a male-dominated working environment, this is done by adopting male characteristics or value systems.

This issue was debated at the Women's Forum for the Economy and Society 2019 in Paris in front of an audience of over 2,000 participants. The discussion was aimed at promoting greater understanding for the older generation of women in France, who have struggled so hard to be accepted into the close-knit circles of male managers. The rivalry observed among women in France illustrates the intense struggle faced by French women in management and the strained relationship between genders.

> M.C.: I think the worst is behind us. But maybe I'm wrong. Women do help each other. I think it's getting to be commonplace these days. We also talk about sororité (sisterhood) these days, it's a new word that was invented especially to describe it. I think we've overcome that particular barrier now. But there were and still are places where women don't support each other and still see each other as competitors. So maybe that's still a problem. I personally have always been viewed as a woman who's helped a lot of other women. I've also always been surrounded by a lot of other women. The question is, what do we think when a new woman arrives on the executive team? Do we think, "Great, another woman", or do we think, " Oh no, maybe she'll outshine me"? It depends how you look at it.

> Al.: There's this syndrome among women in very high positions, I've met some of them in France, they say: "I got here because I fought for it and acted like a man and I don't see why I should help other women better themselves. Because I got to the top without any help at all. Here's an example of a situation where women don't want to help other women – situations in which there are women who don't want to help other women. There's this well-known journalist in a leading French newspaper who once told me: "In the editorial office, everyone gets in around eleven and leaves around nine. But I start at eight and leave at six thirty. When they had the Galette des Rois (Twelfth Night Cake), the party was shifted to later in the day. I had to stay and wait for the party to finally start. It was unbearable. Eventually the cake eating started, but all the mothers were penalized, because it didn't happen until seven in the evening. And all I could think was that I'd be late home and not see the children. So, there was a certain amount of tension in the air... There were about a dozen people there. And eventually one of the senior journalists exploded and said: "Do you think I would have been able to leave at six thirty in my day?" And my friend replied: "So what? Just because you didn't fight for your rights it doesn't mean it's ok for you to stop other people from trying to achieve a work-life balance! It's awful what you're doing." The senior journalist across the way started crying and said, "You're right. I really regret not having the courage to fight for more time with my children so I could spend those really important moments with them. And in a way I can't accept the fact that you do have the courage to and you don't get penalized for it. "

> L.: I think women are not supportive and not unified. Me, recently I've come to the conclusion that the main reason why women will not make it is because there is still that biological instinct to fight against the other woman, which men don't have. Men, they might fight if they're in competition for something, and that's normal but then if they're not, they're going to co-opt each other, they're going to help each other. Women, we say we do and then if you're in different companies, different industry, for sure we do. When it comes to same industry, same group I think women are worst enemies. I'm really sad to say that, I've experienced it a year ago when my former CEO offered me another position and he wanted me to replace somebody who was in the job, who decided to leave. She was a woman, she had been in the job for 18 years. She decided alone to leave the group. Honestly, nobody pushed her out. Now she left because she was so frustrated, because they had never offered her anything else, so she left being very bitter. He offered me that position. Everybody was aligned, the artistry director of that business, everybody was aligned. She found out I was offered the position, she went to see our shareholder and she told him, even though she was leaving the group, that I shouldn't get the job. I got along with her. I think she was just– She couldn't face the fact that I was getting something when she hadn't. For me, that day I realized, honestly– because if we had been in competition for the job, sure, that's part of life and men would do the same thing, but in that situation, you're

like, "Wow." It's so ingrained I think, for women that if they don't succeed, then another woman cannot. I think because it's so difficult, there's jealousy when women manage to do it. Why more between women? Again, because I tried to explain. Especially if we hadn't liked each other I would have understood, but it wasn't the case, because I respected her, I liked her, we got along. For me, it came as a big shock, the job was frustrating but the worst was really to understand how women sometimes can still be. Again, I fundamentally believe, if we don't all change that, we will never make it, never. Again, it comes from really ancient times where we were staying at home, raising the children, the men were going to hunt and fight, being together, between friends and we had to protect our nest against other women who would have stolen our money. I really do believe it's biological.

Is.: The three companies were all very male environments. They really were, and that's why I wanted to do something about it. The first was in the shipping industry and it was in the eighties and there were only men there. And in the law firm I was in, there was only one woman and she married one of the older partners and resigned from the practice and then I was alone there. Then I joined a very male dominated law firm and I was there for twelve years. And the fact that I was at XY, it's beginning to look like it was destiny. My destiny took me into a very male dominated world, perhaps in order to provoke a reaction in me to stand up for women. And it probably also had something to do with my upbringing, because my father used to say to me, "You'll do just as well as your brother." I was very girly. I love good taste and fashion. But at the same time, I'm also very committed to my career. And I've never had any doubts. And I've faced some very difficult situations, I really have. There have been some difficult moments. When you're the only French woman on Wall Street and it's the eighties and you don't speak very good English and all other women are protected by one of the men, who they happen to have married, you're clearly not playing the same game. And it was the same when I joined the law firm, there was only one woman but she got married and left after a year, and then I was the only woman again. I have always paved the way for other women. I really have, I have always cleared the path so that a woman can take my place after me and get all the benefits I've set up. So, I'm a sort of pioneer.

E.: That's a really interesting question. I have had a mentor, mentors are very important. Women aren't great mentors for other women though, generally speaking. I think that's a real problem. Women who give other women advice, there's a degree of competition and so on and so forth. If the woman's older than the mentee, then there's often envy, and that's not a great thing.

Discrimination – a career challenge for French women

Men's reactions to female top executives in France have often been described as discriminatory. Women report verbal discrimination, sexism and psychological bullying by men. These descriptions are consistent with the observations made at the beginning: for a lot of men, a strong woman in the workplace can feel threatening.

C.: You know, in 1991 the Human Resources Director at one particular company said to me, "Your husband's a senior executive and you have three small children, so why do you want to work? That was the day I became a feminist because that kind of thinking is completely unacceptable. That was in 1991, but it could still happen today. I decided against staying with that company. It gave me the impetus to move on to something else – the boomerang effect. And now I think if they had appointed me, I wouldn't have had the career I have, because I wouldn't have joined XY(company name). So, there's a lesson there: you need obstacles, that's what the Chinese say.

It's the opportunity principle. Something positive always comes out of something negative. I'm convinced of that.

D.: Never hesitate to articulate where the obstacles lie, because it's precisely these very real obstacles that hold women back. And sexism especially. We haven't talked much about that. Sexism, certain types of behavior, jokes round the coffee machine... All these things are still happening today, and companies are currently working to create a much more inclusive culture. I think that's really important. I do think we have more inclusivity these days.

Is.: It's not that level a playing field. So, it's difficult and pernicious. I've seen behavior and jokes and things sometimes that can really make it feel like a man's world. I've seen it all. Even jokes that are sexist. I don't think it's usually done on purpose. We tend to favor people who are like us. For example, men in dominant leadership positions tend to recruit men who come from the same university and have the same resume and they mentor younger men who resemble them. And it's still the case nowadays that men appoint men. And I've seen situations where young women have come back from maternity leave and have been given inferior jobs because people thought that when they came back from maternity leave, they wouldn't have the energy or the desire to travel any more. But in some families, it's the man who stops working. I think that stereotypes still exist that make young women vulnerable to indirect discrimination.

E.: Being fifty-five is a bigger problem than being female. I won't be having any more kids, but— (laughs) I won't be having any more kids, so they don't have to worry about that. I think when you get older, even though they need more experts, it's still age that's the hardest thing. Not the fact that you're a woman. There's more discrimination because of age than because of gender. I think that's going to be the next big issue – I feel seriously discriminated against here because I've stopped being CEO of XY and now I'm a consultant – "because you're not computer literate enough, you're not part of the digital generation", that's the latest way of saying you're old.

Ambivalent influences on careers through family

The reconciliation of career and private life becomes a question of generation among the French women. While the older women have found their solution to the role conflict, the younger women struggle with a life split between child and career, which is not easy for them.

Husbands and their role in the family

In France, in most cases both partners in a marriage are in full-time employment and both are pursuing a career. This distinguishes French couple relationships quite markedly from the German and Chinese groups, where the men take on more of a supporting role. There are no French husbands who are purely homemakers. The women executives give mixed descriptions of their French husbands. A proportion of the women express themselves mostly positively and feel emotionally supported by their husbands. The interviews yielded positive descriptions of husbands in about a quarter of cases. A few of the men take part in household and parenting duties when their work allows it, but most of the French women's husbands take on scarcely any housework or child-rearing tasks. Many of the women seem to have come to terms with this. Where relatively equal domestic responsibilities are reported, there are two prerequisites: the woman is paid the same as, or a higher salary than, her partner, and the partner's participation in household duties has been the subject of marital disputes, some of which have lasted for years. According to the descriptions, unequal roles are the norm in French couples. Inequality here refers specifically to the fact that women, although they work full-time like their partners, invest more time in housework and childcare. French women have to fight for equality in the relationship or in other words, they have to educate and shape their husbands over significant periods of time. Only two of the French women report that they are supported by their partners in their careers and that their partners have stood aside for them.

> D.: The final piece of the jigsaw... is finding a way to balance work and family life and to have a... good husband. I think I'm lucky to have a great husband who takes his share of the responsibility. He is a partner in an investment fund. We have grown and developed together. When we started living together, he came up and asked me what we were going to have for dinner. I said I have no idea (laughs) ... I think in a lot of couples, the woman plays a particular role, the imbalance often comes from both sides, on one side a man who doesn't do his bit, on the other side a woman who doesn't require him to or else does everything herself. When we were first married, I was studying and working at the same time. I made it crystal clear right from the start that I expected him to take an equal share. How we live isn't typical in France at all though.

> D.: It also depends on your partner. Two years ago, I had to travel all over the world for my company and last year I did five worldwide trips because I was running workshops in 27 countries. My husband accepts the fact that I do that, and he travels too. But someone has always stayed home, or if not, my mother has come to stay. You have to be very organized. But I felt able to do it because they were big by that time, about nine or ten. It's easier by that point because they are independent. And I think the second step is when they reach eighteen, when they go away to study, when they go to uni. If they don't do that it gets very complicated!

> D.: I told my CEO that we ought to set up a new position in America. Because we had just bought a company. And he said, "Good idea! But I don't want you to go!" Well, okay then, maybe an American should do the job. And then six months later they came back and said, "We'd like you to go." My husband and I had literally just bought a flat in Paris. I thought to myself, "The timing isn't right, because we've just got established here in Paris. We've got a baby... " But then my husband said," That doesn't have to stop us. We should go." I said, "Are you sure? We'd be going because of my work..." He said: "It's fine, I'll find something in Montreal". I have such a lovely husband. We'd always both done everything and that was great, so there was a lot of pressure on me because suddenly I was the main breadwinner. But we did decide to go to Montreal.

> Ac.: My husband had an opportunity to move to the Island of Guam for his work. I told him I would go only if I found a job. Over the years, I've had helped him understand my point of view. At the beginning, it was a bit difficult for him to understand, not difficult, but it was a bit of a new novel thing for him. Now, he's become a total feminist. He's actually set up a feminist club himself. The other day he came home and he had dinner with people and he said, "Oh my God, this guy is so old-fashioned. It's crazy". I think over the years hearing me and seeing me do things that maybe he didn't see other women do et cetera. It grew on him, and then he decided that, that was probably the right way to do it. We've been having a very good conversation

around having a dual career. Since we started, we said the most important is that we balance things out, and we know that careers don't always happen that way. I went to Guam with him. Which was, I decided to follow him in Guam. He then twice rejected job offers, very good job offers where he would have had a promotion because I was not ready to leave Hong Kong when I was an entrepreneur. He decided to stay where he was and not seize those opportunities. Then in Singapore, we just had a miracle. We had two jobs coming in the same day. I had a job in Singapore. He had a job in Singapore, which is a bit of a miracle et cetera. We dialogue a lot and we have an agreement that will do the best thing for the family. We'll do the best thing for our family and we'll try to balance it out over time so that I don't feel frustrated, he doesn't feel frustrated. That's kind of how we do it.

L.: He's a consultant and for about the last five or six years we've both earned the same. Before then he was the one who earned more. We both make the same amount. Exactly the same. He does a lot with the children. But he travels a lot and then I'm left doing everything.

S.: I would have progressed faster because – mainly because there were international opportunities I could have taken, because I did want to work abroad at some point, but it was a bit difficult to achieve that with two careers. At one point my husband had a good job opportunity, but I couldn't relocate, and then I had an opportunity when I had my job in London, but then he couldn't move. These days he earns more than me, a lot more. I think salary counts for a lot, it's an undeniable fact. Then there's the impact of traditional gender roles. I know couples where the man earns less than the woman, but the man still seems to have at least as much say in what he does with his career as the woman does. That's just not logical. Housework: My husband cooks sometimes and sometimes he takes the garbage out. But he only does stuff when I complain. Otherwise, he just assumes that everything's fine. I do a lot more around the house than he does.

E.: I had them very late on. I had my daughter when I was at XY, and then my sons just before I became CEO at the end of my time at AB. I had them very late on and had a lot of help, especially with the boys. I had someone there at night and during the day, two or three people who helped me. My husband helped a bit too. He cooks, not every day, but he is helpful. He's a macho man. He's not like one of those really helpful guys, but he's there when I need him, like when I travel for example.

L.: Yes. It's crazy, and I see all those men here– a big difference also is, I think all the men in senior position, most of them don't have a wife who works. When you think about it, all they have to do is think about themselves. Plus, they have somebody at home who thinks about themselves as well. Yes. It's crazy, and I see all those men here– a big difference also is, I think all the men in senior position, most of them don't have a wife who works. When you think about it, all they have to do is think about themselves. Plus, they have somebody at home who thinks about themselves as well. Around me, none of their wives are working. None. They are all at home dealing with the children, going with them to official parties when they have to, organizing vacation, organizing their life, making sure that dinner is served. Literally, that's what happens.

French women – career impacts of motherhood

The group of French top female managers surveyed has the highest number of children of any country in the research for this book. Of the women surveyed, only four are childless. Most of the women have two or three children, some even four. The French women recognize the advantages of the French childcare system, which is based on the widespread social acceptance of third-party care for children of all ages. The childcare options are many and varied and allow women in France to work full-time. All of the French women agree on this. However, the younger French women in particular feel guilty about the fact that they are quick to leave their babies in the care of others after birth. The interviews suggest that despite the social acceptance described earlier, women receive negative feedback from others around them when, because of the long working hours required of managers, they leave very young children to be looked after by others. Infants of female top managers are frequently looked after at home well into the evening by all-day nannies who have the flexibility to extend these hours if parents need to be away overnight or because of business trips. Negative views about having infants cared for by others tends to come from men in the women's professional environment. It is as if guilt feelings are being deliberately elicited within companies as a means of wielding power. Yet the subject is taboo. So does a "bad mother" syndrome exist in France as it does in some other places? There are subtle indications that it does, where the care of infants and toddlers up to three years of age is concerned. The reports given by the older women would seem to suggest the opposite, however. Either they have absolved themselves of guilt or else they genuinely did not experience it. However, new mothers in particular report a daily inner struggle that only subsides when the children start regular preschool at the age of three. But feelings of guilt do resurface among older mothers who regret having spent too little time with their children. This applies to about half of the French women surveyed. The rest of the women interviewed are very career-oriented and deliberately devote a lot of time to their careers and therefore less time to motherhood. They accept the culture of long working hours.

Older, childless women, especially, accuse mothers of not being able to separate their childcare responsibilities from their professional ones and regard it as unprofessional. Their starting position, however, is in fact the very attitude that makes long working hours necessary in management. A woman in France, they say, must be very clear in her own mind that if she wants a career in higher management, she is going to have very little time for her children. There is no middle ground. Here once again the "I had it tough, why should you have it easy?" syndrome evident among older women comes into play. Mothers are judged by whether they can delegate care of their children almost entirely – or whether they have problems doing so. The latter group of mothers is viewed harshly. These women, according to some of the older French women, do not want to have a career, they just want to complain. Fathers hardly feature in the accounts.

Another problem, mentioned several times, is discrimination against mothers when pay rises and promotions are due. The "motherhood penalty" thus also seems to exist in France. One indication of this, which appears several times in the accounts, is that the women's careers regain momentum once they are around 45 or 50 and their children are in high school or college. So, the French women's strategy seems to be to have children at a relatively young age so as to be in a position to fully participate in later career phases.

A challenge for mothers is that the French working culture seems to make very long working hours inevitable. Particularly in top jobs, they are long and extend well into the evening. The women surveyed start their day in the office between eight and nine, have long commutes and finish around eight or sometimes later. They thus have to come to terms with a culture of long working hours, especially as executives, and this seems even more pronounced than it is among the women from the other countries in this study. A work-life balance is thereby not to be expected.

French women and childcare – a balancing act

Although the French school system offers comprehensive childcare for small children and schools provide afternoon care, French top female managers by no means lead an easy life when it comes to combining children and career. This is due to time constraints within the childcare system and the lack of support at home. There are too few crèche places available, which makes finding a childcare place difficult in France. Schools are often closed for the whole of Wednesday, or at the least on Wednesday afternoons. Although there are programs available for children at these times, a lot of organizational talent and money for alternative childcare is demanded of the women. Good all-round childcare also costs a lot of money in France, as childcare facilities are by no means adapted to the working hours of women in high management positions. If children become ill or the nanny is unavailable, the carefully crafted childcare provision, made up of multiple components, simply falls apart. Some of the women describe how they go about coordinating contingency plans over the telephone at the same time as working, especially when it comes to dealing with the illnesses that regularly occur in younger children.

An essential aspect of the burden on French women seems to be that, as a rule, neither husbands nor grandparents can be included as a fixed, regular component in the care of young children. The working hours of women in leading management positions do not make it easy to achieve a good work-life balance in France. The women's accounts portray a daily balancing act or struggle from which they can only escape by almost entirely delegating the care of their children. In practice, this means that a French woman in a high management position normally does not see her small children between seven in the morning and eight in the evening, and the children's father has no time to look after them either. Although this model is accepted in society on a superficial level, many women report missing out on valuable time with their children or being absent.

> D.: When I had my first child, I was relieved of responsibility for the USA because I said I wanted to go home at seven. And I was told, "You aren't going to be in charge of the USA anymore because you have to be available in the evenings for that. We're giving you the Asia-Pacific region because with that you can make the phone calls in the morning". This was my first encounter with sexism and discrimination, I think. In other words, instead of trusting me and saying, "You have always been well organized, you'll handle it," I was told, "If you decide to go

home in the evenings to see your child, we'll take away your most exciting dossiers". Then I suggested we create a position in North America. First, I was told they were going to hire an American, and then I was told I could have the job. But after I got that overseas position, a week later I realized I was pregnant with my second child. ... Um... I was ashamed. I wasn't ashamed of being pregnant, I was ashamed because I was thinking, "I've signed a contract and now I'm pregnant, so I can't go…" Basically I was rattled." But then I was told, "No, no, it's not a problem! We're not going to change anything. You're coming to Montreal. " So, we went to Montreal... And now I'm going to tell you my second experience of discrimination. When I had the second baby, I took two and a half months' maternity leave again. Then I went back to work. Everything was fine until my annual appraisal, when I was told that I wasn't getting a raise because my performance hadn't been anything out of the ordinary because I had had a health issue.

E.: You know what? If you have kids and you're a middle manager and you go to work each day thinking, "So much of what I do is routine stuff, but they won't give me a new job", the reason it happens is because you know your job so well. You've reached a certain level. But you don't want to admit that you don't really want to rise any higher. Of course, women are under more pressure, so you have to be able to handle that pressure. It depends on how guilty you feel. In general, women feel more guilt. I always felt guilty, but I was very selfish, so I wanted to move up. I thought, "Okay, so I'll have to compromise where my kids are concerned," but a lot of women don't want to do that. There's no solution though – it's either or. If you have a big ego and you're selfish, you leave your children to be looked after by other people so as you can get out of the house. Women can't just say, "Oh, I'm not getting anywhere because they don't give women the good breaks." Because actually they really want to stay in middle management and spend more time with their kids.

S.: I had my first two children when I was at AB (Swiss company) and my third child when I was at XY (US company). When I was with AB, which is a good company, I heard some people saying things like "She's got a photo of her kids on her desk. She'll have less time for her work now." I was really shocked, especially because they were saying it behind my back... When I had my third child, I had been at XY (US company) for about 18 months and then I became pregnant. My boss, who was a woman, told me she wasn't happy about it. I was pretty shocked because she had children too.

Ag.: It depends on your personality. With some women children were never a problem. I never heard anything of them, everything was always fine. And with others, there's always something going on that really spoils the professionalism, because they can't do this or they can't do that, or they have to take the child to school or they have to be taken to the doctor. And that's a problem, it annoys me. To be perfectly frank, I don't like that kind of attitude. It all comes down to how organized you are. It's definitely about being organized. And it's also to do with your personality. Personality and priorities, how we conduct our careers. Or we can make it a priority not to be too ambitious and to give more time to our children. I understand that completely, it's not a problem. But what I don't like is when it interferes with the job too much.

L.: Yes, but because there are only men at the top, I only see women doing it. I think it's a big difference. It was recently 8:00 PM at the office and then I see three of the– CEO with two of his closest members together. I see them, they're in an office chatting, it's 8:00 PM and I really want to go and tell them, "Really? The only thing you have to do right now is to be here together, rather than go home and see your wife and children." Because again, you can work from home. I work from home. If I need to work at midnight, I will work at midnight. When I wake up at 6:00, I will check my emails and answer emails. I'm not at the office at 6:00 but it doesn't mean my job is not done. Now in their collective perception, because they can do it, it means you are not as committed as they are. So that is really for me– and I think that's less the case in the US, but here, that is really the culture, because it's a very French environment, you need the culture if you have to be physically here and show that you're there and tell everybody how hard you work and how late you stayed. For women, I think it's an added challenge, if you want to see your children. It should be a challenge for men, but they don't care.

M.C.: Nothing is easy. But just because it's complicated doesn't mean that it can't be done. It's a question of attitude. There are people who, no matter what the issue, find things difficult. That's why I hate it when people say "Good luck". Because if you say "Good luck", it means you think the opposite, it means everyone thinks "It's difficult, you have to have guts!", no matter what the situation. But that's not true. You don't need courage. You need energy. We have to be organized and find the wherewithal to be organized. In France it always depends on whether a couple actually work as together as a couple. And also on the financial resources. I interviewed a woman once who had nine children, and it makes me laugh just talking about it. She got asked the question "How did you manage it? She replied, "I managed it one at a time." No, but it's true, it's actually really that straightforward. It's a matter of conviction, whether you decide to put a lot of time into your family or not. Some women feel they need to invest a lot of time in the family. But every woman has to decide that for herself.

M.: So those are the reasons why we're so much further along in France than you are, and society doesn't make us feel guilty about working. Nobody here says you're a bad mother. I get the impression that you don't really have daycare in Germany and that the teaching hours are shorter and society tells women that they're bad mothers.

D.: If... I send my children away on holiday, I don't feel the need to call them, I don't need to talk to them on the phone. I don't feel the need because I've only just seen them, I think it's pointless. I don't feel the need to be constantly available when I'm not with them. I'm just happy to see them again afterwards.

Al.: In France it's taken for granted that women can work if they want to. It's not an issue. But if they have children people judge them on how much work they get done, and that's really tough. Even if you're confident that you're giving your child quality time. If I came home every evening at six thirty so that I could bath and feed her, I wouldn't be in a very good mood, I wouldn't be very happy. So, it's better if I come home an hour later and spend quality time with her and feel happy and fulfilled. And that's nobody's business but my own. People are very judgmental these days about whether you're doing what's best for your kids. I have never been so judged during my career and my studies as I am now that I'm a mother. When I was getting ready to come back from maternity leave, my bosses said, "No more talk about that". When I talked about salary increases and what I wanted to do in order to get them, my boss would say, "Oh, stop thinking about that! Think about your daughter. Money isn't everything." But I think that's awful... these days I work even harder than before because I've been so afraid, I was going to be hampered by having a baby. But now finally I've got into the swing of it. The weird thing is that everyone judges you. What I find really hard is the way people view the fact that you have a family. They say: "Oh you should be at home with your daughter" or "You leave her all day with someone else". People are very judgmental. Even the nanny, when I travel or have evening meetings, she says, "Say goodbye to Mom, you won't see her for two days. People don't know how much guilt it causes and I haven't been used to feeling guilty.

Is.: My boss was at the law firm in New York with me. I guess you could say he had a high opinion of me. He saw me as a talented young French woman. He has really empowered me. He gave me cases, he gave me the chance to really grow up, and when I left New York after three years, he said to me, "You would have been the first female partner here." It was really sad that I had to go back. After that I ended up in an extremely macho environment where women didn't even dare say if they got pregnant. I never announced it when I got pregnant. And after a bit it became very visible, but nobody noticed because we were working day and night. Our rights weren't protected. These days when I see someone's pregnant, I help them. I tell them to work one day a week from home. Take time to rest and all that. In my day it was different. So, we acted like guys. We did everything, we didn't ask questions.

Ac.: The first baby was a miracle, I would say because when I met the entrepreneurs, the Chinese guy in Hong Kong when I came back from Guam, I was five months pregnant. I was a bit concerned because I thought, who's going to hire me when I'm five months pregnant, but I went to the interview with a white shirt and nobody noticed anything. They hired me pretty much the next day. I was lucky. It was very fast. Then I went back to him and said, "Hey, Dennis, there's one thing I couldn't tell you yesterday is that I'm five months pregnant." Pregnancy was a breeze for me, so I told him, "Don't worry about that. It won't affect our business or anything." I was lucky enough because, in Hong Kong, he could have fired me on the spot, but he didn't. I had two more children while building the company.

Mixed emotions – the work-life balance

When asked about the disadvantages of a career as a woman, what emerges among French women in senior management is an ambivalence concerning the compatibility between career and private life. The women lack time for children, friends and partners. The older women look back and wonder whether they made the right choice. On the other hand, younger women who have invested more time in their private lives know that they are paying a price in terms of career development. French female executives also highlight the dilemma that affects women worldwide when it comes to their careers and the fact that, unless companies offer flexible working models, there is no ideal solution.

E.: It's not the most important thing, but because I was very focused on my career, I had a lot of problems with my husband because I married late. Perhaps there were men before him who would have suited me better, but I was too busy with my career. I was too selfish, I just wanted to work and work and work. I wanted to earn more. Sometimes I stayed in relationships that weren't right.

S.: There's never enough time for things in your homelife, like homework and so on. More than anything it's just the lack of time.

D.: There weren't any disadvantages, although I've had some very difficult times over the course of my career, but they've always helped me to progress and achieve something else, to ... Nietzsche said, "What doesn't kill you makes you stronger". Even though it was difficult and complex, I always drew something positive from it. So, I can't think of any downsides. I'm very proud to have decided thirteen years ago, when my first child was born, that I'd never sacrifice my children for my career. I don't know how my kids are going to turn out, but the company could never have given me that time with them. I'm happy I made that choice, and I'm probably not as high up as I should be because of it, but that doesn't matter. Because I know why I did it and in the end it was what kept me going.

C.: That's true, sometimes I realize that I am on the road a lot at the moment, and I'm very busy a lot of the time. Obviously, I have less time for myself and my private life. And that's a real shame. It's also true that I've sometimes let friends down. My children have grown up too fast and there have been a lot of special moments that I've missed because of not being there. But I'm still very close to them, I'm very close to my daughters. Being available means having time for things. And that's what I find most difficult. There just isn't time, no time for oneself, no time for one's private life. I think maybe when I retire, that's something I'll really appreciate. But at the same time, I don't know whether – I'm afraid I'll miss the other stuff.

M.: I think women who don't work nowadays are either women who don't earn enough, whose work doesn't bring enough in and maybe they have three kids and can't afford a nanny. For them it's less stressful to not work or just to have a part-time job. I think there are probably lots of women in that situation. I think there are still also women who are really well-off and don't need to work. I happen to know quite a lot about it because I belong to a network where there are some women like that. So, it does still happen. But there are less of them than there are women in middle management who have a job but it's not a very important one. Those are the two extremes, I think. And I also think these days in most young couples both of them work, because twenty to thirty-year-old both want to have an interesting job. Staying at home is not an option for them.

The French woman – a respected Jill-of-all-trades

All over the globe, the image of the French woman is one which is admired and talked about and onto whom the world projects its ideal image of womanhood. She embodies the stereotypical Parisian woman – independent, professionally successful, beautiful and feminine. According to the stereotype, French women are ambitious managers, fashion-conscious and sexy. Seen from the outside, they represent the cliché of the superwoman who is has it all: career, love life, looks and family.

To be a real woman, the French woman must be capable of performing in every area of life and, if you believe what is written on the subject, capable of playing all her parts better than women anywhere else in the world. The older generation of French feminists hold on to the ideals they fought for and are resentful of younger women who voice their problems and the burdens they bear. French women increasingly see themselves as being trapped by the double burdens of being a good mother and having a career – trapped by the demands of changing ideals and by the contradictions of their own lives. They have been led to understand that they can do everything, experience everything, have everything – but the reality is often brutally different. The yardstick for women in France is to have a career, a perfect love life and two or three children. In the last 40 years, French women have fought for access to all areas of life previously reserved for men. However, most French men are failing to keep up with this trend and do not take on their share of the domestic tasks. Instead, they fight to defend their supremacy. It is this aforementioned division of responsibilities, in the most personal areas of life, that constitutes the greatest burden on French women. They have not yet achieved an equal distribution of parental responsibilities. Some women fight this battle either with or against their husbands, but also against themselves – because some of them in fact fear losing the upper hand at home.

The findings on how women in high corporate roles are viewed in French society are mixed. On the one hand, the women state that it is normal for a woman in France to work full-time, and that if she does that well, it is viewed in a positive light. Women in top management positions who have made it are admired and celebrated as role models for other women.

Women nevertheless report various stereotypes as being associated with women in high positions. These include *"she behaves like a man"* (a bad thing!), *"there's got to be something wrong with a woman like that"* and that these types of women only get the jobs they do because they are protégées. It is further assumed that women leaders probably either have psychological problems or else have not found a man or cannot have children. In short, there must be something wrong with these women.

Women are judged in the French press not only on the basis of their performance, but above all on their appearance and their clothing. As to the image of women leaders in society, it is repeatedly claimed that it is down to the women themselves whether or not they are successful. The interviewed women pass from the image question to the question of why there are still fewer women at the top than men. The answer is the same. Many women prefer security and like to stay in their comfort zone but will not admit this to others or to themselves. Very many women, according to the older French women, do not actually aspire to high management positions.

> M.: Women don't want to sacrifice their entire lives for their careers. But until they have the social clout to change this, I'm going to keep going on about the issue of work ethics. The ethic has changed. Work isn't the main objective anymore. It's just one of a number of goals women have in their lives. But that doesn't make it a bad thing. And nowadays, professions like medicine and law that have become feminized are devalued. They're devalued because women don't want to work the way men do any more. I think that's pretty shrewd, but it's not recognized as being the intelligent thing to do. Because our country's political model hasn't caught up with the new values. I love our president. Emmanuel Macron is a fantastic president, but we have a president who works twenty-four hours a day. And he has ministers who work twenty-four hours a day. Whereas in the North, in Northern Europe, there's a minister who's on paternity leave. And until we have that kind of model in France, the old values will remain. But women don't want the old values anymore.

As has already been identified, from a social point of view, French women in leadership positions need be successful on all fronts: at work, as lovers, as mothers and as housewives. The pressure to fulfil all of these roles at the same time is high. It is striking that domestic and child-rearing responsibilities, in most cases, are still primarily the preserve of women. In most cases, these tasks rest solely on the shoulders of the women, who then attempt to delegate them as much as they possibly can. In French society, equality has been achieved with the help of state regulation. However, as far as the demands placed on top female managers are concerned, childcare provision remains patchy in spite of the regulations. Women can and should work full-time. But they are still expected to be responsible for managing the household and the childcare. The pressure to look good is high – higher than in some of the other countries in the survey – because of the stereotype of the ever-attractive French woman. This applies to women in top management positions just as much as it does to other women.

> Ag.: I'm not at all sure they value women as much as they do men. Whenever there's an interview with a woman, a politician or a businesswoman, the journalist always starts by saying: Mrs. XY was wearing a dress by so and so, and so on. They'd never say that about a man. So as far as society is concerned, with a woman it's not just about her intelligence. We judge her appearance. Every article about female top managers talks about her physique, her clothing and so on and I find it completely unbearable.

> M.: I think if you look back through French history, women have always worked a lot. But it didn't used to be obvious like it is now. And the ones who didn't work still had their role in society. French women have always done something or other, they've always been involved. Poor women worked alongside their husbands. And rich women had a special social role, they held salons and gave big dinners and receptions. They had their social role. These days, I don't think anyone criticizes a woman for working. French society doesn't criticize a woman for working. Because it's in our DNA. What's difficult nowadays though is that a 40-year-old working woman is still in the role of the mother, she's still got responsibility for her family and for the house but men are only just starting to pull their weight. I think that women have completely entered the world of work, but men are still only on the threshold of taking a full part in domestic life. In the last twenty years we've seen some changes, you do see men on the street carrying babies and looking after their children. But there still aren't many who take paternity leave or become really involved in bringing up their children. So, there's still one area of life that doesn't get shared equally, and French women who work experience a lot of pressure to be the perfect mother, the perfect high level executive and the perfect woman. They have to be perfect at everything. It's just not possible.

> L.: I think things are moving in the right direction. For example, at a recent meeting I met a woman who's at the top of the XY group. Wow. She projected a pretty positive image. Because if she's moving in those very political sorts of circles, that also means she has a big personality, the sort of disposition and so on that you need to if you want to achieve a place in those circles.

> Al.: For her to accomplish all that in her life, if she manages to have both, career and kids. In France we say how fantastic, how impressive, well done. Really amazing. But then you have these two different perspectives on things. There are people saying, "Yes, but she's abandoned her children", "Yes, but she's really well-off, she has the money to pay for nannies and daycare", "Yes, but …" I think people often judge you for something that should actually be the most natural thing in the world."

> D.: There's this syndrome, some women are called "lonelies", which means that women who've got to the top are surrounded by men and are really lonely. I think the clichés about women like that are still pretty negative because men say, "Oh yeah, she's only here because she's a woman." And about a lot of women people say they neglect their family. Women who've reached the top are always being judged. Even if she's really intelligent, really good at her job and the ideal person for the position, she still gets judged far more than a man does, I think. Recently we were discussing the shortlist for a CFO job. There were three candidates: one woman and two men. And someone said to me, "Well, obviously she's extremely ambitious, she's really assertive, she's done everything she possibly can to get this job." I don't think anyone has ever said that about a male candidate.

Is.: Image? I think there've been a lot of remarkable women who've opened doors, like Simone Veil, she was the politician who legalized abortion in France. It must have been in the eighties I think... She opened doors that were well and truly closed. I think there are a few women, like Christine Lagarde, who are well known in the US and who are driving things forward. There have been women writers, like George Sand, who also opened doors. Before them, there were scientists like Marie Curie. I think there's a tradition of strong women in French, going right back to Joan of Arc. In France there's always been this tradition of the strong woman. Female writers, female poets, female artists. There aren't very many women CEOs out there today. In the CAC 40, the forty largest French companies, there's only one woman, Isabelle Kocher at Engie. All the rest are men. But there are female astronauts, Claudie Haigneré, she's the woman who's spent the most time in space. There are lots of examples of women who have been successful despite the gender gaps in their fields.

M.: Twenty years ago, the picture was different, I think. Twenty years ago, I think successful women were women who were like men. But I think it's changed now. A successful woman doesn't have to look like a man anymore. I don't think there's a solution. I think there are two main expectations. There are women who resemble men, and I don't think that's a good idea. It's just what society expects. A lot of the female politicians we've had have had to look like men in order to survive. I don't think women want that these days, we don't want that anymore. But at the same time, people who see it differently aren't willing to accept that if a woman doesn't want to look like a man, she's going to look like a woman. And people don't like that either.

Ag.: It's because there's always this feeling of not being validated. That's the never-ending problem. Women have a hard time because they think that they're worth less than a man and that they're maybe not in the right job and that maybe other people might be right about that. They have doubts, the whole time. There's always a degree of doubt. About themselves, about their abilities and so on, because they've been having this done to them for centuries and they've been being told that they're inferior. And this is still the story they're hearing to an extent. It's a psychological thing. It's something that's really deeply rooted in our minds. But it doesn't have any basis in reality.

5 Japanese female executives: Beating the system

The numbers show that there are hardly any top female managers in Japan. Their career paths are exceptional, in a work system in which women in management continue to appear temporarily and as assistants. And yet there are Japanese women who have made it into high management positions in multinational and domestic corporations.

External factors affecting Japanese women's careers

For many years, Japan was the world's second largest economic power after the USA. At the same time, it was one of the top countries when it came to the under-representation of women in management. Japan is also one of the most complex countries in the world. Much of what at first glance appears to be straightforward is in reality ambiguous or even enigmatic. This is particularly true of the role of women in Japanese society. Here, traditional behavior is juxtaposed with modern expectations and ambitions.

Bringing up the rear – but setting new targets for women's rights

The question of why there are so few women in top management positions in Japan preoccupies many scientists and feminists. Although the number of well-educated Japanese women has risen steadily in recent years, Japan is at the bottom of the table of economic nations when it comes to women in leadership positions. There are hardly any women in Japan's economic elite or in politics. In a 2017 study by the World Economic Forum, Japan ranked a lowly 114th out of 144 countries. The study evaluated access to professional careers, politics, education and health. In the economy and in education Japan has made only slight progress in recent years. The wage differential between men and women has narrowed somewhat; more and more women are attaining a higher level of education. In the area of political involvement, the proportion of women amounts to less than 10 percent. In the category "Women in Parliament" Japan ranks a mere 129th. Politics in Japan is a decidedly male affair. Women rarely attain a ministerial post, and the job of Head of Government will probably remain out of reach for a considerable time to come. Two examples of the very few women in Japanese politics are the former foreign minister Makiko Tanaka, who only held the post for a brief period, and the former refugee commissioner Sadako Ogata.

Yet Japan's women are leaders in many areas. Not only do they have the highest life expectancy, they are also still the world's best in terms of literacy and basic education. When it comes to fully integrating women into economic and political processes, however, Japan regularly falls short in international comparisons. In 2014, Japanese Prime Minister Abe launched a series of countermeasures, so-called "Womenomics", with a target of 30 percent of managers being female by the year 2020. The Prime Minister argued that greater participation by women in all areas of business and politics was necessary for the country's future economic growth. According to Lewis (2015) in the *Financial Times*, Japan had the potential to increase its gross domestic product by up to 15 percent if women became more integrated into the workforce. The economic argument, the low birth rate and the ageing population have, after years of inaction, led to a gradual rethink in politics and economics. As is the case with voluntary quota agreements in other nations, the aim is for women in Japan to be represented in all areas of public, political and economic decision-making. In so doing, the government is recognizing the potential of women, because as Abe himself has noted, women are "the most under-utilized resource in the country". However, many observers pointed out the absence of further, more precise measures and a lack of implementation. According to Mollmann in Quartz, the Equal Opportunities Office *Danjo Kyodo Sankakukyoku* announced at the end of 2015 that a target of 7 percent of women in senior management positions by the year 2021 would be more realistic. In 2017, the data reported on Japan by the international survey of Thornton was 7 percent, followed in the ranking by Argentina with 15 percent.

The role of Japanese women in society – the shift from power to subjugation

Until the beginning of the Muromachi period in the fourteenth century, Japanese society centered around women. Up until that time, according to Iwao (1992), the culture and politics of the country were shaped by a variety of goddesses and a succession of empresses. *Amaterasu-ō-mi-kami* ("Great illustrious goddess shining in the sky") is the most important deity in the Shinto religion. She personifies sun and light and is considered the founder of the Japanese imperial house. It was believed at that time that women possessed the supernatural ability to communicate with gods, a power that men did not possess. Between the third and eighth centuries in particular, Japan often had female rulers, including six empresses. For a long time, Japanese women had considerable freedom and worked on the same terms as men. They dominated literature until the twelfth century and had the right to inherit. They had access to education and could choose their lovers freely but discreetly. Until the eleventh century, since society was women-centered, it was common at all social levels for the husband to live with his wife's family after marriage, or to live separately from her and be allowed to visit her only on certain nights. This female supremacy continued for a considerable period of time among ordinary people such as farmers, fishermen and traders in the rural areas, in which about 80 percent of the Japanese population lived at that time. The lives of higher ranking women, on the other hand – mainly those belonging to the aristocracy – were increasingly determined by Confucianism, in which the lives of women were subject to the three duties of obedience and to a set of feminine virtues. The duties of obedience were, depending on the woman's circumstances: obedience to her father, to her husband and to her son. The feminine virtues were chastity, the appropriate use of language, diligence and modesty. With the increased influence of Confucianism, women in Japan started to live with their husbands' families and more and more arranged marriages occurred. Eventually, in many cases, marriage became a pragmatic question in which economic considerations were paramount.

Kaibara (2010) and Reischauer (2020) describe how in the Edo period, from the seventeenth to the middle of the nineteenth century, women became entirely subordinate to men. They had few remaining rights and had charge of the household and of the work in the rice fields. In the Meiji period up until 1912, women continued to lose out in terms of power, and levels of social and labor market equality were low. Japanese society was dominated by men. In legal and ideological terms, during the Meiji period a hierarchical, traditional family structure emerged, in which each member took on a specific role dictated by age and gender, and this characterized the family in Japan until 1945 and beyond. The education of women was focused on their role as housewives and mothers. According to Iwao (1992), the traditional idea of womanhood was for a long period shaped by the concept of the *ryōsai kenbo* ("good wife and wise mother"). The women of the pre-war generation, those born around 1935, accepted this ideal and concentrated on housework and bringing up their children. They supported their husbands, who were the breadwinners. They were brought up according to these values and with the awareness that men were deemed superior.

After the Second World War, the new 1947 constitution redefined women's rights, placing special emphasis on gender equality. Female suffrage had not been granted until 1945. The women of the first generation born after the Second World War were guaranteed access to education and brought up in the belief that equal rights were a necessity. Nevertheless, despite new legislation and attempts to enforce equal rights, the traditional image of women was firmly entrenched in Japanese society and they were still expected to take on the role of the traditional housewife. For an increasing number of women, however, this was not enough and they sought work outside the home.

The feminist movement in Japan originated in the late nineteenth century. One of its significant early successes was the right to political participation in the early 1920s. After the Second World War, the proportion of working women was the highest of all industrialized countries. Laws such as the Gender Equality Act and the 1947 constitution now allowed women to work in typically male professions such as medicine, politics and law. In 1991, a maternity leave bill was introduced, allowing women to take a one-year break. In the generations that followed, the image of women steadily changed. The new Japanese constitution, which was based on the US legal system, placed greater emphasis on equal rights for women. Over time, they have become more independent and self-confident, but are still responsible for the family and household, such that it was, and still is, difficult to reconcile paid work with family life.

How the rest of the world perceives Japanese women

Prejudices and clichés still dominate the image of the Japanese woman around the world. The most common images are Madame Butterfly and Geisha girls. Japanese politeness, admired by foreigners, is influenced by the aesthetics and manners of Japanese women all over the country and is particularly evident in the service sector. In contrast, Japanese men are macho, according to stereotypical perceptions of Japanese society as being male-oriented. Over the course of its modernization process, Japan has adopted Western role models and ways of life like no other Asian country. Nevertheless, behind the globalized, Westernized facades are concealed Japanese identities and Japanese traditions. This is especially true of gender roles in everyday life. Even though the Japanese image of women is constantly changing, it is fair to say that certain clichés remain. According to these clichés, Japanese women are capable, obedient, petite, sweet, and exceptionally pleasant and gentle. There are some marked gender differences in Japanese speech. The word *onnarashi*, which is usually translated as *"womanly"* or *"feminine"*, refers to the behavior and speaking style typically expected of a Japanese woman. It is also known as "women's words" or "women's language". A few of the characteristics of Japanese female speech are a high pitched voice, more frequent use of courtesy forms and the use of "typically female" words.

Japanese traditions in professional life reduce opportunities for women

A number of researchers such as Kaminski (1984), Yuasa (2005) and Terri (1999) have investigated vertical gender segregation in Japanese companies, which in management is largely the function of an age-based hierarchy. The researchers see the explanation as lying in company traditions such as life-long employment without career breaks and age-related promotions. Women continue to occupy the lower ranks in Japan companies – the *kakaricho* – in which, by 2011, there had been only a modest increase in numbers to 15 percent. Women are also poorly represented in middle management, *bucho*, where the numbers of women are negligible.

These low percentages are attributed to the traditional working pattern, where a husband has a secure, lifelong company position and his wife supports him at home. This tradition legitimizes the limited career opportunities for women, who are restricted in companies to assistant roles. More than anything else, the tax system favors this conventional role allocation: if a woman earns less than her husband, she is entitled to a state pension for which she does not have to pay contributions and her husband is entitled to a tax rebate. Men whose wives are not in employment receive additional allowances on top of their salary.

Japan's system of lifelong work incentivizes those who have served the company the longest with no interruptions. Women are generally disadvantaged in this respect as it is assumed that they will not meet these requirements, due to marriage and motherhood. The chances of promotion for women in Japan are poor compared to those of men. It is only after about 20 years working in a business that they have a real chance of promotion to managerial positions explains Ziegler (1999), in her work about Japanese female leaders. Many cannot take advantage of this opportunity because after the birth of their first child, many women disappear from professional life for several years. Some return to the labor market at around 40 years of age, but even then only part-time, and this precludes promotions and high pay. The female professional world may thus be described as being "M-shaped". Among young adults, the proportion of female employees is high, because in terms of educational attainment they are often at par with their male counterparts; at the end of their 20s, the age at which many women have children, the slope of the curve drops rapidly, and it is only in their mid-40s, when women return to the labor market, that the slope rises again. For many women, the balance between work and family life is difficult to achieve. The long working hours, after-hours meetings (which typically take place in bars) and the system of internal job rotation, according to which employees are transferred to a new department or location approximately once every three years, are incompatible with family life. There are hardly any female role models in executive positions that women can be guided by. Because of the prevailing traditions, the majority of Japanese women decide against a career in management. This explains why, in 2014, only 11.9 percent of middle managers and 2.6 percent of board members in Japan were women, according to Aoki in the *Japan Times* (2015). The international Grant Thornton survey for 2017 estimated that women made up 7 percent of senior managers in Japan. This means that according to the available research, Japan ranked as lowest of the five nations covered in this book in terms of number of women in senior management positions.

The Japanese researcher Kumiko Nemeto (2016) describes how recruitment, salary and promotion policies in Japanese companies exclude the bulk of women and permit only a few to rise to the top. The Japanese employment system offers men, but not women, financial security. Gender inequality and prejudice against women are deeply rooted in a corporate culture shaped by a system of lifelong employment. Long working hours and stereotyping with respect to recruitment, promotion and pay, hampered the government's historical 2014 target. Japanese women receive on average about 27 percent less remuneration than men for the same job. In recent years in Japan, however, the Women Corporate Directors (WCD) initiative has become established. This supports women in leadership positions and aims to bring about a cultural change in women's equality both in Japan and internationally.

Motherhood and careers in Japan

Although the image of the strong, independent woman – which the media made popular in the 1990s – means that marriage is no longer as important in Japan as it once was, it is still an important topic in Japanese society. The image of womanhood in Japan still involves getting married and becoming a mother. The importance of motherhood is evident in the efforts many women make to become mothers, and Japanese has a word for the various efforts women make to become pregnant: *Ninkatsu*. Women often give up their jobs in preparation for pregnancy.

The typical career/life path for the average Japanese woman is as follows. After a good general education, she commences working, marries a professional man in her 20s, has children and then looks after her children, her husband and the household. Sixty percent of Japanese women who become mothers withdraw from working life after the birth of the first child, seven out of ten of mothers take a ten-year career break, on average. From this point on, their primary role in society is to look after their husband and children. The man on the other hand goes to work to provide for the family. It is fairly unusual for both partners to work if they have children. For the most part, after bringing up their children, Japanese women go back to work part-time. The social status of a housewife is determined by her husband's position and by how successful her children are at school. Returning to professional life after a long career break is difficult to accomplish, and as a result most women remain at home after starting a family. Women marry on average around 28 years of age. Once they are past marriageable age, many women devote themselves to their hobbies or their careers instead. According to Tokyocherie, women who are still unmarried and childless after the age of 30 are considered to be *Makeinu* – "loser dogs".

In the professional world, traditional attitudes towards the roles of mothers and fathers still prevail. The Japanese tax and social security system offers financial incentives to single-income households. If a wife has a low income, her husband receives tax breaks and she is entitled to a non-contributory state pension. In many companies it is also common practice for a man with a wife who is not in employment to receive a wage bonus.

It remains to be discussed whether the term "weaker sex" is appropriate when describing Japanese women, despite the distribution of roles as outlined here. Market researchers have found that in Japan, the woman's opinion is the decisive factor in many important purchasing decisions. It is also common in the urban middle classes for the husband to hand over his entire salary to his wife at the end of the month and to receive pocket money from her. Among Japanese couples it is traditionally assumed that the wife has the decision-making power in the household. Although women always show respect for their husbands when dealing with third parties, it is the former who often have the last word in important decisions. A survey from 2012 shows that 51.6 percent of respondents in Japan were in favor of the conventional distribution of roles. In Japan, as in other Asian countries, the family has high priority. Because of the distribution of roles, men take little or no part in domestic duties. Women in Japan spend on average three and a half hours a day on household chores, while men spend only eight minutes. Men's long working hours and extended commutes also favor this division of labor within the family. To this day, many women in Japan have no option but to choose between a career and the desire to have children. In Japanese corporate culture, there is little acceptance when it comes to combining the two. Returning to professional life after a long career break is difficult and often only possible on a part-time basis. In addition, primarily due to the long working day and prevailing expectations, women are under considerable pressure to act as sole carers for older family members. Since the educational success of Japanese children depends primarily on the reputation of the school they attend, the need to move to a new school often stands in the way of a job relocation. Women therefore often remain behind when their husbands relocate. There are state and private childcare facilities, but these are expensive and scarce. Waiting lists for childcare places are long, especially in the cities. As a result, only a third of Japanese mothers with young children work. Female executives in this country are still a minor sensation and the exception to the rule.

Japanese women – escaping from tradition

The number of women at Japanese universities has increased steadily in recent years. In 1990, only 15 percent of female school graduates went on to university. Today, that figure has more than doubled. However, the proportion of male school graduates who go on to university is still significantly higher, at 48 percent. The proportion of women in the working population has risen steadily to over 40 percent. The proportion of women in the 30 to 45 age group is markedly higher, indicating that more and more women either do not marry at all or remain in employment after marriage. Not only are Japanese women marrying later and later, an increasing number remain unmarried. The term "parasitic single", which was coined to describe this group, is a condemnation of women who choose to shun traditional female roles in favor of an independent lifestyle. In recent years, a break from tradition has also been observed among middle-aged women. More and more are deciding to get divorced when their husbands reach retirement age. Since partners often live parallel lives while the husband is working, many marriages cease to function when he retires. One way for women to pursue a career despite all the barriers associated with the traditional business environment is through self-employment, and this option is being taken on by an increasing number of women. These businesses tend often to be small cafés or bookshops; they also serve as a source of self-fulfilment.

Japanese women in senior management – career paths and strategies

The Japanese women interviewed for this study were all between 49 and 56 years of age and, with the exception of one divorced woman, were all married. Most have two children. At the time of the interview they were working for Japanese or multinational corporations in Tokyo or Osaka in strategically important positions such as president or Head of a business unit. Some were responsible for up to 650 employees in their area of responsibility. The majority of women have Japanese university degrees; two also have an MBA from the USA. All of the women speak fluent Business English. They have broad management experience in areas such as consulting, e-business, HR, sales, marketing, corporate strategy and corporate leadership. The Japanese women represent the smallest group in the Global Women Career Lab.

Career paths of Japanese women

In the career paths of Japanese women, we find Japanese companies alongside multinationals. Only a few of the women interviewed have worked exclusively for Japanese companies. The majority specifically chose foreign multinationals, both when starting out and when looking to advance their careers. Three types of career paths dominate in the Japanese group: careers with foreign companies involving changes of company and country, careers with purely Japanese companies involving few moves, and moves from foreign companies to senior management positions within Japanese companies in later career phases.

The Japanese female executives change companies on average three times. Careers typically start in international companies or consulting firms. The conscious decision to develop one's management career is described as a key factor in their success. In addition, there is very clear, pronounced career orientation, which distinguishes them very markedly from the overwhelming majority of Japanese women. All the women interviewed were determined to progress as far as possible in management and tend to look for key positions in which they have influence and decision-making power. All women, with one exception, have worked abroad, some in the early stages of their career following an MBA, others later while working for their second company. Foreign assignments included the USA, Germany and Sweden.

Decisions to change jobs were primarily determined by the women's own career orientation and it was the desire to progress that determined the change. But geographical considerations also played a role, especially while their children were still very young. The pursuit of a senior position right up to that of president or managing director is an important decision-making criterion for the women when changing job function or company. These women want to be movers and shakers and to act as role models within Japan. They are aware that at the moment, they are still the exception to the rule so are looking to act as role models by way of encouraging other women. All of the executive women interviewed are committed to the advancement of women in their companies as well as in chambers of commerce and professional associations. A high degree of solidarity with other women in Japan is evident from the accounts. At the same time, these women recognize the limitations of their female colleagues, and recognize these limitations are not solely the result of the system.

The Japanese women's career strategies can be summarized as follows:
1. Awareness of one's career orientation; determining what one wants to achieve in life
2. Selecting a company at the start of one's career in which women have opportunities for advancement
3. A cosmopolitan attitude and foreign experience, which are important factors in Japan when competing for positions in multinational companies
4. Choosing a husband who will support one's career unconditionally
5. Learning to present oneself correctly and to "market" one's strengths

The first of these, while not a career strategy in the strict sense, is very important to Japanese women as the management system, in Japanese companies in particular, does not make any provision for women's careers. Being aware of one's career orientation is the key aspect of the Japanese women's success. Because they are choosing a path that is not intended for women, they are exceptions to the rule in the Japanese management culture. Their decision to take this path disrupts the traditional system and positions them successfully on the career ladder. The first question that women all over the world ask themselves is: what will be my main role in life? For the Japanese executive women, professional advancement is their clear objective and a source of inner satisfaction and personal growth.

They deliberately choose companies, mostly multinationals, in which they have identified greater opportunities for women. The Japanese companies listed on some of the women's resumes were also chosen with this in mind.

> M2: Most important is actually the, what is it called, ambition. You have to be ambitious. Then you have to have some professional anchor regardless of male or female. You really believe in your professional skill set or experience, which makes you believe that you can be definitely successful. Maybe when I worked for more than 20 years after going to XY, I realized that I want to be the head sometime. I would like to be the head of the organization. That's why I chose this job as a president.

> M1: I think I had a very good sponsor at that time and XY (company name) was trying to really globalize their organization, and I think they thought it very easily that moving a Japanese to Europe and bringing a European to Japan would accelerate that opportunity to really enhance globalization for the organization. I think that I was the first Asian in the office and it was a very unique experience for me. It was my first time in Europe as well.

> M2: First choice of XY to AB was because I wanted to stay in Osaka, and I wanted to take executive position and there was no more executive position at my level for XY in Osaka, so I moved

to AB. Then AB to TA I wanted to come back to consumer business, and I also wanted to be the head of the company. That's when I moved.

K: I know some people worry about it a lot and they become more externally differenced. Because I'm doing this because of my internal passion and not so much about the pay or the title or how other people perceive me, but more for the intrinsic value, that adds to my strengths. That's doing things that are right, as opposed to how other people see me or evaluate me.

A: When I started to also look at different foreign affiliated companies, that was much more interesting because they were much more focused on hiring for the position and looking at the individual versus the gender, and I think XY (company name)was also, from that standpoint, very advanced from that standpoint as well. I did enter the supply chain, product supply when I entered, I was the first woman to join the purchasing area and it was told that females could not do purchasing at that time. There were some senior executives that also felt that way, but I think a handful of managers that believed in my capability really pushed forward and offered me the position to become the first there in XY. Surprisingly it was a Japanese who supported me.

M3: Honestly speaking working for three different companies, especially if you are a young female, I think working at the environment where you can be successful is better. If I go back to 20's, I would rather work for XY than other companies because you really need a system and boss' support especially at your junior level, so choose the right company.

Career preconditions for Japanese women

Internal independence from the evaluation by others and a very clear career orientation are prerequisites for the rise of the top Japanese managers. An iron will to pursue one's own professional goals in an environment that women in top management actually do not know is the basis for their success. What distinguishes them in leadership is that the promotion and motivation of their employees is a priority for them.

The Japanese women leaders' starting points: Ambitious mothers

The women describe their mothers as the driving force behind their careers, whether they were traditional housewives or whether they were employed. Typically, their mothers were headmistresses or teachers. Mothers who pursued their own careers were criticized for doing so by their husbands, their mothers-in-law and even by their paternal aunts. The daughters witnessed the way in which their mothers were subject to these restrictions and in effect joined them in rebelling against the limitations imposed by family. Mothers who were housewives had in reality wanted to pursue a career but were prevented from doing so by their husbands or mothers-in-law. They educated their daughters to believe that a woman can achieve anything. The interviewees' fathers were often critical of their daughters' career ambitions and inwardly disapproved of them, while at the same time tolerating them. Mothers were consequently these women's closest advisors, particularly when it came to launching a career and choosing the right company. In almost all cases, the mothers advised them to begin their career in a company that offered opportunities to women. As a result, the women were more likely to choose employment by multinational companies and only in rare cases, purely Japanese companies.

> M1: I think my father basically because of the fact that he himself was a medical doctor, but also my mother she also had a degree, which was very unusual during her years, and she was always saying that females should also have a career. I think that's very important because a lot of times here in the society, as you know as well, many people say you should be a good mother, a good housewife and I think that's very different from many people that instead of encouraging me to become a housewife and a good housewife, they were encouraging me to be a good professional.

> M2: My mother is a typical Japanese housewife. The only probably difference she had was, she actually really wanted to pursue her career. She has been the almost like a strongest supporter of my career. Whenever I wanted to do something, she was behind myself to support me. My father, on the contrary, is also conventional Japanese male who wanted female to stay at home. The difference of my father was he never forced it. He was a really kind and nice person. Even when he actually wanted me to stay at home, he never objected any of my decisions.

> Y: I actually self-selected to work for a foreign company fresh out of college. I'm trying to explain, I deliberately did not select Japanese company because I know I wanted to build a career, and also my mother was telling me that if you want to work and if you want to build a career, don't go and work for Japanese companies. You got to go to a foreign company. I didn't know much about it, but I just followed my mother's words. That's all. All my career straight out of college I self-selected to work for non-Japanese company because I had wanted to build a career. That's the reason why I didn't go to a Japanese company.

Japanese women's career motivations, skills and strengths

The Japanese women describe their professional foundations and keen ambitions very vividly. The confidence in their professional ability is what underlies their strength. They are independent of the judgments of others. Their inner enthusiasm remains unaffected by hierarchical thinking and the way in which others see them. These factors are the driving force and strength behind these Japanese women leaders. Another aspect of their inner drive is the desire to do something meaningful for others and to encourage and support fellow employees and other talented women, in particular. The women seek out specific industries based on the prospect they give more opportunities to make a difference. Other motivating factors are the quest for intellectual challenges and the opportunity to make things happen. Challenges are viewed as both an incentive and a driving force. These Japanese women do not acknowledge limitations on what they can achieve. The management system in Japan, as described earlier, does not represent a limitation as far as they are concerned.

They conquer the system by actively embracing the fact that they are unique, seeking opportunities, freeing themselves mentally from tradition and consciously working towards their objectives. They take a responsible attitude towards their unique role and use it to effect social change for the benefit of other women professionals. All of the Japanese women interviewed have the declared goal of empowering other women in Japan and enabling them to follow in their footsteps. A career, for them, is not just a means to satisfy their own personal ambitions, but rather is part of the wider social context.

> M2: I think the most important decision I made in my life was when I had my first child, I decided to pursue my professional career without compromise. I asked support to everybody around me including my husband, my mother, my boss, my co-workers. That was the biggest decision I made. After that actually joining a Japanese company or changing the job. That's not as difficult or as important when I look back. As a determination that you have to be a professional and you want to go up in the corporate ladder. That motivation and choice needs to come from women herself. I would like to be the head of the organization. That's what I chose this job as a president. It was very clear to me maybe when I worked for more than 20 years after going to XY (Swedish company), I realized that I want to be the head sometime.

> K.: Well, I thought I could lead this team or the organization better, why does he do it that way, I don't think it's good, we should do it differently. I looked at my boss and thought I could do it better, I could run the department better. Money is secondary to me.

> S: It's a good question because I don't think of myself as an ambitious person. I never had a desire to become a CEO or a president, or those titles, or the pay. It doesn't really motivate me at all. My parents, they're teachers, they're a little bit anti– they're Christians, they had the values I guess, some are anti-business, anti-money kind of people, so it was more about the value and the culture and the people, and an interest in those things that always drove me. I never had any desire to become a president or a CEO or get promoted faster than any of my peers. That has never been my motivation. I'm not sure if I– I never really thought about wanting to be the GM, but I welcome the challenge. [chuckles] I like challenge and I like working with people. If I can have any positive influence to at larger organization, that would be a joy for me, that could be rewarding. The next thing that my current sponsor or my current supervisor who is a female reporting to the CEO is that GM outside Japan, somewhere, and I have no idea when that comes up.

> Y: Success is to tell many female staff to be promoted is wonderful. I had females, I had the women's career forum with 100 workers, and I invited role models from other company first and ask role models to speak their career stories and the young female workers in Teijin listen to it and they think about, to be promoted is not bad, so don't quit. Yes, I will not quit. I want to continue to work and before that, they saw that a TV executive is very very special but after they listen to the role models, they thought that, oh it's not so special. It might occur in my life. If we can continue to take careers one by one. It is that someday I can be that executive.

> Y: I was very much fascinated by the internet and technology. When I was in Silicon Valley, I really enjoyed the aspect and technology changing the world, changing the culture of Japan. So those things really drove me, but also, after some point, I felt that it was a little bit empty. This new technology just seemed superficial, and I really came to realization that I really want to do something that has intrinsic value, with changing lives of the people. Do something that really matters to people. That's when I made a transition to the healthcare industry. That was 17 years ago, and I never regretted that decision. I never want to go back to those industries. So just the value and the impact that you can bring to the patient, to the lives of the people, is

driving me, but for me to get ahead, it's more about the people and kind of creating a culture. That's what's driving me.

Y: I want to fight with the discrimination maybe. I'm very interested in gender. I want to change the society for my daughter. I want to change the system, change the way of thinking of people.

M1: Perhaps. (laughs) I think it is really my curiosity that is driving me, that continues to keep me in the workforce. It is also wanting to do something back for the society. I really do appreciate my sponsors, my mentors in the past that have led me to really believe that I could do things beyond and that is why I would also like to give that opportunity to others. That is why I also do a lot of mentoring within the company and beyond the company. I think those are my motivations and I do believe that since I am still in the working area that I can also provide additional support from that standpoint.

Business skills such as negotiating, the ability to say "no" and a professional, self-confident appearance are among the Japanese women's strengths. Some of these are qualities not normally attributed to women in Japanese culture. Many of the descriptions of strengths relate to the women's leadership skills. The Japanese female executives see themselves as a source of motivation and encouragement for other employees. Unlike their male colleagues, they do not exclude any of their team members and are accessible, and responsive to employees' needs. Other strengths mentioned are technical business know-how, decision-making and negotiating skills. International experience is also considered an advantage, although the intercultural component was not evaluated in detail here. Intercultural aspects were not explicitly mentioned by the women as a career component, but by the time they finish their education, most of them have already demonstrated an openness towards foreign cultures. When competing with others, these Japanese women want to be out in front. They want to be the best but at the same time they do not often compete, because their primary concern is the organization. Other successful senior managers see the women as a source of motivation and as a learning resource.

> K: I never felt or I never really thought of competition. I don't feel like I'm competing with somebody else to a certain position. That's because I'm not driven by a title or a position, and that's not the source of my motivation. So sometimes I very much care about the pulse of the organization and the people's engagement level. When those reports come out and somebody is doing better than me, and of course, I wanted the best or the most engaging inspiring organization. I just go out and ask what they do to be so successful. That tell me I'm probably more of an internal reference person.

As is the case with the majority of the study participants in the other countries, vision is cited as a weakness by the Japanese women. The women describe themselves as practical in their approach rather than visionary. In contrast, one strength that their careers clearly demonstrate is an aptitude for, and a curiosity about, innovation. One woman describes how she had to learn to be bolder in challenging situations, such as during company restructures.

M1: I probably would say that, in general, I probably would lack it. I probably would say that I am somewhat supporting the visionary necessity with passion.

M2: Some people are really good at being more visionary. Visionary. I tend to be practical. I'm always inspired and impressed by the people who are visionary and long term focused.

K: Probably a middle, not where I should be. I have thoughts and I have a vision but at the same time, having a P&L responsibility I can't. So, I need to change, I always need to change while delivering today. That's the hard piece. Of course, there are certain directions we need to head, but at the same time, today's business, I know that it's produced by the current local champions and local contributors. They need to be on board but that is sometimes– so people who are delivering today may not be the people we need in our future. I just need to balance those things.

K: I still feel, contrary to what I just said, I'm not bold enough. Actually here, some of the things that I learnt at MBA and in my first job at the Silicon Valley startup, I had to unlearn after I worked for XY (company name) building my career within XY in the sales organization and other organization. For me to get accepted and then be successful, I had to learn how to be unthreatening in the sales organization and others, as a middle management. I'm not sure if I'm answering your question in the right way, but I feel I need to unlearn those things and to be bolder, and I see other people being more bold approaches and taking more of a revolutionary approach, not the evolutionary. So, I need to be more bold. Yes, knowing that people are not going to like it, but it's still right for the business. I try and do that, but more in a softer approach, maybe taking a longer time than I should.

S: It's a good question. I think just being studied in the abroad, especially in the MBA, and also my second job before working at Lilly was I worked in Silicon Valley, in a U.S. based company, so I really learnt the need to self-promote myself and sell myself, because that's not what I was taught when I was growing up. In Japan, it seemed more virtuous to be accepted by society, you want to be– especially women, you are not really taught or encouraged to sell yourself. Also negotiate, one thing I learnt in my business school and also in my job in the U.S., I learned how to negotiate, I learnt how to say no, so all these things, probably, I have more than the typical Japanese woman.

The Japanese women's leadership style: Supporting and motivating employees

The Japanese style of leadership is known for its emphasis on exchange of ideas and teamwork, in contrast to the American approach, which focuses on individualism and autonomy. The founder of Sony, Morita Akio, described the way of Japanese way of thinking about leadership as: *"A company will get nowhere if all the thinking is left to its managers."* This illustrates the core principle which underlies Japanese leadership in the field of science. The *Ringi Seido* method entails the collective involvement of all employees and consequently, consensus is paramount in decision-making. The associated extra time required is readily accepted. Nevertheless, hierarchies in Japanese companies are pronounced. Since many of the women interviewed work for US companies, they experience a management style at company headquarters that differs significantly from the Japanese one they are used to. The management style of the Japanese women interviewed varies and is a mixture of the highly cooperative and the occasionally authoritarian. A large number of accounts give detailed information about this inclusive style of leadership, according to which all employees participate in decision-making. However, the use of authority is just as necessary for Japanese women in multinational companies when it comes to driving decisions and initiatives forward. Moreover, according to the women surveyed, Japanese employees feel a need for confident, strong leaders that they can follow. Especially for female bosses, this assertive aspect of leadership is necessary for them to be able to hold their own as women in their teams. Although they tend by nature to lead in the standard inclusive Japanese management style and are very approachable as far as their employees are concerned, the women for this very reason also make conscious use of authority. They actively work on their leadership style and make use of professional coaches.

One woman describes how she pays more attention these days to maintaining her social contacts, in particular with her male colleagues – something that she used to do less of early on in her career because of the need to combine her career with her role as a mother. She also made use of professional coaching to achieve a balance between the inclusive and paternalistic styles of leadership. Other women describe themselves as too inclusive and see disadvantages in terms of the time it takes to implement decisions. Similarly, there are women who initially led in a rather hierarchical way with little room for interpersonal interaction but who are in the process of rethinking their style and developing it in the other direction. As an example, one president of a pharmaceutical company has used executive coaching to achieve a shift in her own style from rather authoritarian to more cooperative.

The Japanese interviewees see the advantages of women over men as lying in their excellent communication skills and their feminine approach to challenges. Women are better at dealing with difficult situations, partly because their career paths are by their very nature characterized by numerous challenges. In difficult situations, they are able to accomplish more, because men tend to be emotionally weaker in such conditions. According to the interviewees, Japanese women are better listeners than their male colleagues and so make fewer mistakes. Women tend to support and promote all employees equally. Men, on the other hand, tend only to support, and foster the advancement of, one or two of their closest confidants. The support and promotion of employees in general features prominently in the accounts. For Japanese senior female managers, the issue of how to support employees even during periods of restructuring or cost-cutting is a crucial part of their job. Promotion and motivation are closely linked.

> K: I try and explain that this is how the decision's made. It doesn't matter to them, so I really think about other ways to really motivate and engage them because that's always not going to work, so I just try and make sure that they have something that they look forward to that makes them come to work every day excited. It could be the promotion opportunity, even though my organization is shrinking, I can get creative to find a promotion opportunity, so for me, I'm proud that even though my organization is shrinking and I'm getting promoted to next level actually we don't have any less opportunity than the other business unit because we export talents

to other business units. To headquarter functions through my personal connections. I get every opportunity for any innovation activity, so in terms of adapting of new channels, the internet and all these things by the salespeople, I encourage them. Our product may be old, but we have a new innovative approach, so you are getting trained to be the sales force of the future, so I try and find these other things. That they feel that they are growing, and they are getting developed, don't give up, and I'm making sure that they feel that they are growing and they are being developed. Those things I do.

M2: I'm in a position where I'm wanting to grow my subordinate in order to replace me one day. In that sense, I think my motivation right now is to get the next generation up to speed and quickly, [laughs] that's something that I'm working on. Am I competitive to take another job? I think so because of the fundamental skills.

H: So far like Japan, it's quite volatile. They do want a strong leader who knows what they're doing and who looks confident. I know that I need to be that confident leader that the people would want to follow. It's actually not come so natural to me, so I try and that's something that I'm working on.

As a leader, I make sure that I have people who tell me their true minds at each layer. I try and have the relationship with every layer. I also have people, and I had that report so these are the regional sales directors. They also tell me what they think freely. Also, I have several people in the district sales manager level and even with level people who know me as a person and who feel comfortable speaking their minds and they tell me from their perspective. Having those kinds of firsthand allies or contacts in every layer, I think helps me make the right decision and I think that's one of my strengths.

M1: I try to work with people who have different strengths. Knowing yourself, knowing your weakness, rather than trying to strength my weakness, I try to find somebody who are good at those weakness. In the past, I was much more sales-driven and not necessarily inclusive. Now, I try to be more inclusive and discussion-based, or group-based, decision-making, and project delivery.

Japanese women are good communicators and make better use of this strength in leadership than do their male colleagues. Employees are consequently willing to be led by them. An additional strength is their readiness to encourage employee development and, unlike many men, they do this independent of any personal advantage. Particularly in times of restructuring and cost-cutting, Japanese women see this as one of their key management responsibilities.

S.: Not necessarily a stereotype, but I find that some women tend to have better communication skills. One thing I learned was that, especially at managerial or executive level, just like me, many female leaders and managers had to go through difficult phases and assert themselves. And that made them more likeable or more deeply thinking. You can help organizations at deeper levels. Men tend to be emotionally weaker because they haven't faced difficulties like many women.

Y.: More generally, I think that when I look at female leaders, female sales managers, female district sales managers in my organization, female leaders are generally good at developing people. Of course, there are many, many male managers who are very good at developing their people, but they tend to choose one or two people from the 10 people they have on their team and only develop those. Imagine, like their right hand. I think women develop them all. The low performers, middle performers too, but men only develop a few people and they pre-chew everything for the others.

Conflict management: Taking the long view

The Japanese women leaders take the long view when dealing with conflict and describe how they focus on what is best for the organization. They do not regard the emotional aspect of a conflict as being particularly problematic but instead simply see it as part of the day-to-day running of a company. Conflicts are welcomed as being both natural and necessary. When conflict arises out of restructuring or staff reductions, the women provide employees with detailed, clear information and try to find solutions that take into account the interests of both the employee and the organization. Fulfilling their employees' desire for strong leadership but, despite this, leading in an inclusive manner, is a balancing act that the Japanese interviewees perform daily. This becomes particularly important during a restructuring process. The head of one large business unit describes encountering repeated areas of conflict during a streamlining process. Her strengths, she says, lie in finding new ways to support employees during such circumstances, acting in a transparent manner and involving and motivating them. Contacts at company headquarters are used strategically in such cases. Another woman describes how she listens carefully to employees and involves as many people as possible when devising solutions to problems. The women make no mention of specific conflicts with competitors or colleagues. They strive to see the conflict in rational terms, to step out of the situation and to look for productive solutions that the majority of those affected are able to accept.

> M1: Conflicts. I believe– For instance, since I needed to deal with external folks many times throughout my career, the conflicts that I needed to face I think if I were a male, I would not have necessarily had to face that. I think from that standpoint I did feel disadvantage being a female sometimes. I think it's more from how seriously they were able to take me because being a woman, I think sometimes it was downplayed the authority that I would have or the decision-making capabilities that I would have. That was not what XY (Company name) wouldn't look at. It was more of what the suppliers would be looking at. I think the encouragement that I did get from my manager was helpful to overcome some of that in terms of they would flat out go that, "Don't she is the manager? She's the decision-maker, so deal with her." (laughs) I think the support was very important there.

> M2: What I do is actually involving other people into that conflict. Especially conflict at the workplace. I try to deal with it not personally, because it's at the end of the day business. I try get advice from other people. I try to get other people to help me in solving conflict.

> K: I don't think about competition much. Conflict, the day to day conflict I have, I'm trying to think, I can't really think of that. Conflict, I get unreasonable challenge from the top about the top line and the cost. I just think, you know what? What's really right for the company and sometimes what's right is different for short term versus long term. I try and think what is right for the patient for one, but also for, if I think about some of the people decisions or other trade off decisions, what's best five years, looking back five years or to think about

what's right to do for employees in the 20s or 30s, the young ones in my organization. I try and make decisions. That's to the benefit in five years from now, those are the things I think about.

Factors behind successful female executives in Japan

Japanese women in top management also benefit from mentoring and coaching to get into the male-dominated circles of power. They work specifically for their employees and care strongly about promoting them. Husbands are their greatest supporters.

Choosing the right husband

All of the Japanese women have husbands whose attitudes towards their partners' careers are described as unusually positive for Japan. The husbands are all willing to support the decisions necessary for the advancement of their partner's careers and are fully committed to the effect of such decisions on themselves and on how family life is organized. This also covers periods of commuting, for example between the economic hubs of Osaka and Tokyo, and temporary separations while a wife is working abroad. The Japanese women's husbands are thus very different from the majority of Japanese men who continue as main breadwinners and want to see their wives in the traditional homemaker role or else as the person who supports them in their own professional life. The women also talk about the husbands of successful female colleagues who are similarly supportive of their wives. One or two of the husbands are foreigners who have decided to live in Japan. There is one description of an American husband who is a university professor and who encouraged his wife to do an MBA in the US before pursuing a career in Japan. The president of another Japanese corporation has a husband who provides his wife with a great deal of support because his own mother was also career oriented. But in some cases, the women described husbands who became an obstacle to their careers; this can result in the wife filing for divorce.

> K: Definitely one thing is my spouse, being non-Japanese. Also, it's not so much about the nationality. I've seen– my direct report, my national sales director is actually a female. She has a huge responsibility. She has over 600 sales rep reporting in to her, but she is also a mother, she has a family. So, it's not that the nationality of the– Her husband is Japanese, so nationality doesn't matter, but I think the spouse, if they are supportive of their wives in building a career, it just makes a huge difference, and the support of the spouse and the spouse's family. Sometimes those expectations of your spouse not stepping up to do their part to raising children, to do the household chores, and sometimes the mother of the spouse can be a barrier, so these things are quite important. Both in my case and also my national sales director's case, I think we are fortunate, we picked the right spouse. (laughs) He encouraged me. At the time, he was working for XY and he was going to end his assignment in Japan, he got stationed back to Silicon Valley, so that's why we went. Partially to be with him, but also, because now I have an American husband, I felt like I need to really have a skill so that I can work anywhere

in the world. So that was the initial motivation for me to get an MBA. Also, he always encouraged me to get an MBA and really pursue and realize my potential. He has been very encouraging and supporting that I build a career.

M.: He also is really the supporter. I think he is a unique Japanese male. He wanted me to work. He doesn't like housewife. He always said housewives are staying at home bothering, always complain and his mother was also a working female so he wanted me to work and potentially, equally important, he doesn't care the fact that I am work which also I think is quite unique. He does not do most of the housework. If I'm at home, he doesn't do anything but he is really good at taking care of my kids. He doesn't do anything like preparing food or he doesn't actually prepare food. He doesn't do a lot of housework, but he likes to care my kids. When forced he can do housework at the minimum level.

Y: When my daughter was young, he didn't cooperate with me. After I changed my career to company XY, my position was higher than his. Many of Japanese men can't keep the upright if their wife more than him.

Japanese female executives are quick to share access to sponsoring, networking and coaching opportunities with their female co-workers

The Japanese women's mentors tend to be foreign CEOs of multinational companies (male or female) or women in senior positions in Japanese corporations. The women do not talk much about mentors in the true sense of the word but instead make reference to the concept of sponsorship. Various sponsors ensure the visibility of the women when it comes to career opportunities and also provide support and advice concerning the changes required when preparing to move up to the next level. One's boss is of crucial importance to one's career development in Japan and can also be a major stumbling block if, for example, he is not supportive of women, because without him no progress is possible within this strictly hierarchical system. A very useful result of mentoring which was reported was that it enabled the women to develop a holistic understanding of the field of business and of the international organization they worked for. Japanese female executives do not report specifically about mentoring relationships like in China, where not only the mentee but also the mentor benefits from the mentoring relationship. This may be due to the fact that Japan has been a developed, industrialized nation for much longer and the influence of foreigners is even today less strong than, for example, in China.

By their own admission, none of the women have done enough networking, due to time constraints. However, many occasions are cited in which the women have promoted themselves. They actively volunteer within their company to participate in one-off projects, such as initiatives for the advancement of women, in which they act as role models. Due to their unusual positions, the women quickly become well-known within their professional environments and are nominated for high-profile external positions, for example, in a chamber of commerce or in professional associations. Especially in Osaka, the country's second largest economic center, women in management positions are still so rare that whenever there is a need for a senior female manager, the same names crop up. Japanese women are thus in a position to take advantage of their status as unique role models. Another question is how the women manage to gain access to foreign networks in the multinational corporations they work for and to position themselves skillfully within them. Here, once again, the support of an executive coach is often used to help them identify their own strategy, and this then leads to success.

> S: The biggest support used to actually come from the boss. Your boss is very important, but sometimes your boss may not be the best supporter and in those cases, I think that females definitely should and need to have a network. That's what I learned from XY (US company), even when there was a strong male leader, there was a very strong recognition that without networking support females cannot be successful. It were always senior females who tried to support other females.
>
> K: I have had mentors, rather than giving a real advice, I think they really function as a sponsor. They spoke about me and they have been instrumental. They pull me into the challenging positions that allowed me to develop as a leader.
>
> M2: Yes. The two of us moved to the US. Initially, we were supposed to be split between Minnesota and Cincinnati. I was telling my sponsor, "I'll be based out of Cincinnati, my husband will be based out of Minnesota, and we'll just meet each other on the weekends." My sponsor said, "Why would you do that? There is similar opportunities for your husband to work here in Cincinnati." He went off to find a research lab that had what my husband could possibly work at through his connections. He was able to establish that connection through so that my husband was able to work in Cincinnati. I think he went far beyond what a normal sponsor would do. [laughs] I had mentors for different things and including becoming another type of mentor or having even a male mentor, female mentors, other organization mentors and I think I was lucky to have different mentors throughout my journey.
>
> Y: If I had a mentor? My former boss, my first boss in Teijin was a female. First diversity manager and I was assistant manager for two years in Teijin. After she was moved, transferred to another department, she was mentor to me. Sometimes, she gave me very good advice. As a diversity manager, sometimes first I did not communicate not so good. She said to me, "If you say so, though other people will misunderstand you. You should better say it like that."
>
> M1: In XY because I started from a junior level, I was automatically enrolled into those networking systems. I think that, especially in XY (Company name). where diversity was known as a check on positivity, there wasn't a lot of actually negative image around diversity being supportive of women, preference-driven, females promoted not because of their skills or result, but because they are women. I actually experienced a lot of difficulty being in center of discussion, because males have their own network, transfer network to discuss and decide things, and they did not want me to be involved. In XY-Japan because I was the most senior female, I started a senior female networking to include everybody in AstraZeneca Japan to start working together, and that's something I have to do in Takeda because there is to existing networking and I'm the most senior female.
>
> A: I think I can only recall my mentors after I joined in the German organization. I established the first woman's network for the product supply when I came back from Germany. Initially, I did not believe in the necessity of networking, but at that time, the sponsor, another female sponsor that I had really strongly pushed me for that. Through that experience, I also started to understand the importance of mentoring and the power of mentoring. I think that was how it was established for me. I think it is an opportunity for women to really see other women, because in

many of the situations, especially in product supply, it would be the only one in the operation line or it would be the only one in the logistics area. It gave an opportunity to really understand how other women are working through challenges and as well through the different challenges we would organize different training sessions started off even from training about sexual harassment.

H: I tried to get in by finding several individuals who actually could let me in. I also got the executive coaching support to get advice on how I can actually be in the center. That was really helpful. That relates to my executive coach. Company helped me to have executive coach. He really helped me to get into the circle. He did interview to my direct reports, subordinates, and boss. He identified the opportunities and challenges I was facing in that system. For example, some of the advice he gave me– People had image that I tried to cut the meetings, I tried to leave the office as soon as possible, I tried not to be in non-business situations. He actually advised me that in reality in the male world, many males go smoking together, go drinking together, you have to provide some room for colleagues or direct reports to talk to you in non-business situations, and I did it.

Barriers to women's careers in Japan

The main barriers to women's careers in Japanese top management are traditional role expectations, a traditional male oriented career system and the associated socialization of women. Barriers that prevent most Japanese women from even imagining a management career, let alone reaching top positions in Japan's business world.

Traditional roles persist despite government measures

The Japanese female executives have a poor opinion of equal opportunities with regards to top management positions. On a scale from one to ten they award marks of between one and three. The ratings were given by women who have spent most of their careers in international companies, but also by some who hold top positions in Japanese companies; the ratings refer largely to opportunities for women in Japanese companies. The women say that it depends on the particular industry or corporate culture, and that a slight positive trend can be observed. But in general, they arrive at conclusions in line with the published figure of 7 percent for the proportion of women in senior management positions in Japan. Only two women award a considerably more positive rating – to US companies, which despite the Japanese context, score eight out of ten.

The reasons for the mostly negative ratings may be traced back largely to the demands that Japanese society places on women. Although the legal framework, maternity rights and childcare services for working women have improved steadily, careers for women in senior management remain rare in Japan. Despite Prime Minister Abe's targets for promoting more women to senior positions, societal and family demands on women, which are primarily related to motherhood and childrearing, remain entrenched.

To embark on a career, a Japanese woman requires a sense of independence and an ability to break out of the established social order.

> M1: I have been out of school for more than 25 years, it has changed significantly. It's heading in the right direction and I think from a policy perspective, there are a lot of new policies and systems in society. There's more support for going on a maternity leave, going on a leave for taking care of the elderly. It has always been in place, but also the time, you can take longer leave now and you can also take leaves for the reason of taking care of the elderly. So that's been placed. Another thing is, I think that Prime Minister Abe is putting a lot of investment and pressure to increase the kindergarten and childcare facilities, that there's actually enough. There has been progress, but still the overall expectation from the society, both inside the professional community, as well as more of a private, like family expectations, how females are expected to take on some roles inside a household or in communities like schools, still there's so much burden on the female. That is not going away, but at the same time, we are expected to work. Prime Minister Abe's saying that the women should join the workforce which is wonderful. That side, change is happening, but at the same time, still a lot more expectation or the burden outside of work. All these family care and the schools' community activities are seen as a role that the female should play.

The traditional career model, socialization of women and the glass ceiling

The respondents' responses confirm the interconnections described earlier between the specific societal demands placed on mothers and the unique Japanese employment model, which make it extremely difficult for women to even consider a career at management level. Three main barriers, mainly in relation to Japanese companies, prevent women from advancing and simultaneously facilitate men's careers. First, very long working hours and after work drinking rites in excess of those required in Europe and China in average. Working late into the evening, which is very difficult to combine with motherhood, is a fundamental prerequisite for advancement to top management positions. Uninterrupted, lifelong careers with the same employer remain the norm and make it impossible for women to take advantage of statutory maternity leave. In Japan, promotions continue to be based largely on seniority, whereby only managers with many years' uninterrupted professional experience can move up through the company. Career advancement with selection based on achievement, which would give women a more realistic chance, is only found in a few highly Westernized companies. Only in these can women in Japan incorporate maternity leave into their careers.

> K: I think a tough position and I think many women, because of different reasons, and some competing priorities in their lives, raising children, when their peers are taking a sales management role, they just can't, because they have to take care of the family and the children. They miss out of that. When we select the leadership, we look for people who have gone through some tough times, and these women have not had a chance to– They're untested. They've

been sometimes protected too much. Being protected or just stayed out, they didn't take that route. They're just not so competitive when we want to pick a leader.

M2: I think in reality, even when there is a support, the suffering of male in Japan is always much higher than female. Also, still coming back to my first point, many work place demanded workers to stay longer, to work longer. That forced men to stay at work longer, which forced their housewives to stay at home longer. It's almost like a society's bad system, which makes it difficult for male to take more burden at home. That will automatically ask each family to decide which person can stay longer at home, and always lower salary worker, that's female take that role.

The second barrier originates in the women themselves. Since female role models are almost completely absent in Japanese society, most women do not consider aspiring to a career at management level; they cannot even imagine themselves in these types of professional roles. In addition, Japanese women are deterred by the very tough road to advancement that women in this country still face. The third barrier is the glass ceiling, which applies at all management levels. Men select other men for management positions and have deep-rooted preconceptions as to stereotypical roles, in which female managers do not appear. The glass ceiling in Japan thus starts far below the level of the corporate hierarchy. It would appear to be located somewhere just above the position of assistant. This means that the whole of lower management is separated off by a glass ceiling and is difficult for women to access. Taking one's first career steps in a Japanese company is a real challenge for women. The conventional structure is firmly established and is almost impossible to penetrate. It is currently much easier for women in Japan to instead begin their careers in multinational companies. Transferring into a Japanese company is possible at a later stage, even at the highest levels of the hierarchy. Beyond a given senior management level, women in Japan are no longer perceived as women but solely as executives. This applies to the highest-level position in a company and, in some cases, to the level directly below it.

M2: It sit everywhere in assignment or promotion selecting system because all those systems are run by current managers who have been the males. Glass ceiling, it exists in male mind. I don't think they recognize it as a bias but there is an invisible bias in their mind. They don't know female manager. At the entry level, actually there are quite a few cases where female students are better in interviewing, doing better in academic grades. At the entry level, I think females do not have any difficulty now.

K: That's a good question. I know that when I speak with my colleagues in the U.S., they experience the exact same thing, so I'm not sure if that's a Japanese thing. I think we all feel that at work you see other men spending probably two or three more hours because they don't have to do the household thing. Then when you go home, you compare yourself with other mothers, either without work or with part-time jobs, and you could be spending more time. Whether business or private, you always feel that you're not doing enough, so that's a constant feeling. I don't think that's very special to Japan.

Although there is agreement among the women in their assessments of the ongoing lack of equal opportunities in Japan, there is nevertheless some variation in their opinions. According to one president of a Japanese pharmaceutical company, all the management positions up to two levels below the CEO were held by men. She herself is an exception. However, the director of a large business unit reports that she herself has never experienced a glass ceiling. The decisive element in this experience, however, is that she works for an international company rather than a conventional Japanese one. She says that up to 25 percent of the women in her company are national sales directors or heads of business units. She herself is currently being considered for a leadership position. The second obstacle, the fact that women in Japan are not career oriented, might instead be the actual problem. In the view of the interviewees, many Japanese women opt not to choose a path to senior management because it strikes them as too difficult.

Because of the aforementioned obstacles, women in Japanese companies are still concentrated in more junior, supporting roles. The obstacles can only be overcome by the women themselves and even then, only by those who have the determination to succeed in overcoming the system. The Japanese interviewees are role models in particular when it comes to demonstrating that a Japanese management career *is* possible for women, even at the highest levels.

> M2: Now, I can't move to Japanese company. It is admirable being a president. People treat me as a president. People don't treat me as a woman. Actually, before TA, I worked for another global company, AZ. That was much less globalized than PX. Honestly speaking, I had a lot of difficulty being a woman in AZ because I was not necessary at a top-level. Nor at the top level, people must take it for okay, it doesn't matter whether I am male or female. I am selected to be the head.

> K.: I think that's possibly because I self-selected into a company, that I don't have to worry about those things. I do think many of the female employees, even in a company like XY, they are more in kind of support functions and not really the mainstream business. At the same time, I think if women have the right aspiration and are willing to do what it takes, you can pursue a career in more of the mainstream, pass to the GM. It's just that women seem to self-select out of those paths. Passing to a GM level needs to experience some tough times like a sales function. I think many women, because of different reasons, and some competing priorities in their lives, raising children, when their peers are taking a sales management role, they just can't, because they have to take care of the family and the children. They miss out of that. When we select the leadership, we look for people who have gone through some tough times, and these women have not had a chance to– They're untested. They've been sometimes protected too much. Being protected or just stayed out, they didn't take that route. They're just not so competitive when we want to pick a leader.

> S.: When I entered the working area, it was in 1991, it's just right after the equal rights for females after '89 and we still saw many companies still struggling with really entering the female into the workforce. With that, I think and being even offered by Japanese companies, but when asking, "What am I going to do?" They would start off by saying, "Well, initially we'll have you serve tea and you'll do this." And I'm going, "Really?" [laughs] That was not that exciting for me.

> Y: In Japanese company, the employment system is so-called lifetime employment, and most of the male workers works is very long about from their graduating from university to 60 years old,

in these days, 65 and they think that when they became 36 or 37 they will be Assistant Manager or Manager. When they become 45 or 50 half of them become a general manager, and they think it is natural. For female, there was so little role models especially in Teijin, female general managers are very very few. Before 2000, no general manager. Around 2002 or 2003 there is the first general manager in Teijin. It's very special case. She was graduated from university. She worked for Teijin and she was in intellectual property division. She studies so hard and she had license for, I don't know that what called. Yes, a special license, like attorney at law, like lawyers. In science field that lawyer. It is very difficult the special license. She was the first female general manager and also the first executive of Teijin. She was not married and no children.

H.: That law prohibited the discrimination on the surface. Before that the company said that they only wanted male for the professional career path, not female, but after the law, they can't say it.

M1: Even though the Prime Minister Abe is encouraging females to get into the workforce, you do still see even salary difference of what females can bring home versus males bring home. I see that a lot of talented women are not able to use their talent. I think that it's really a missed opportunity. I think it's both. I also sometimes go into the college based on my friends' requests to also go and talk to females right now who are in college. I'm sometimes surprised to hear that they want to grow up and become a housewife. I'm going, "What was is that I really worked on up to now?" I was in ACCJ was leading the woman in business companies to really make a change in the society, then I'm hearing this and I'm going, "What went wrong?" (laughs) I think it's partially because what they're seeing is that females are needing to struggle more because of the fact that they're working professionally, but they're also being expected to do– I think what they're seeing, and this is the comment that I got from the students was, that they see women they are professional they're still taking on a lot of the household burdens and not really getting the support from their husbands and all.

M2: I myself represent female to go up in the professional ladder or company ladders. In reality, minus one, all my direct reports are male. Below that minus two, also I'd say, 95 percent male. It's really a male dominant society. It's not unique to XY It was also same in my previous company that was AB Japan (company name). Quite a few female employees and a few examples of female managers but representation is really bad. I would say three barriers. One which is famous, Japan has been known for long working hours and the lifetime employment. That system itself is supporting male to become more successful in career because every employee if they want to go up in a company that are forced to work long hours which is a difficult choice for many females. Lifetime employment requires you to work consistently which is also another barrier for females who could have a chance to take let's say, maternity leaves. That was the first one. The second one is, I think it's the reverse side. Because of that, females really don't have role models who supported them to become successful. That works as a vicious cycle. Because of no role model, many females never think of becoming managers. That's the second one. First one is society related. Second one is more mentality related. Third one I would say is a glass ceiling. Many of the systems of selecting managers or choosing the assignments are basically done by male managers who are used to the environment. I see a lot of cases where there is unspoken or unknown bias within their mind of not selecting females even when there is a good candidate.

K: Yes. That's one, and especially, you see women in more of a supporting functions, like corporate affairs or compliance, but I think for the roles that really have a P&L responsibility, you need to have a sales experience or sales leadership experience, which is not an easy path for most women. It requires some tough experience.

Japanese top women managers- Motherhood versus a career

The interviewees from Japan actively considered the options open to them and made a clear choice in favor of a career. They have opted to free themselves from the demands society makes in terms of motherhood, have actively addressed their preference for a career and decided to put it first. The Japanese female executives interviewed have an average of two children. They relate how they deliberately chose foreign companies with shorter working hours and performance-based promotions in order to be able to achieve their career goals at the same time as being mothers. The care of small children was actively supported by their husbands, although in many cases it was necessary to fight hard to get this support. Neighborhood and other organizations were also used for afternoon care. It is striking how flexible these Japanese women are when it comes to organizing family life and how self-confident they are when it comes to dealings with their partners. They assert their career needs and negotiate for a high level of commitment on the part of their husbands in the bringing up of their children. According to their accounts, however, housework is rarely performed by spouses. The Japanese women remark that their partners' input is inadequate but accept this with a smile.

When it comes to child-rearing, Japanese society requires women to play a prominent role in certain socially defined events, all the way from infancy to high school graduation. The visible presence of the mother often determines the success of the children. Some traditional schools require the involvement and presence of the mother during the application process as well as in ongoing school activities. Husbands, and above all mothers-in-law, consequently urge women to remain in their traditional role. Even university educated women in senior management positions, for example, have to adapt to these prescribed rules if they want their children to be accepted into certain schools. For example, one senior manager describes how, when attending a morning coffee session, she concealed what she does for a living so as not to jeopardize her children's chances of getting a place at a particular school which has a good reputation. She had to apply creative methods to take part in these meetups but still carry out her leadership role.

As in all countries, some of the women interviewed express feelings of guilt, but they put these feelings aside for the sake of their career. Other women express no feelings of guilt and are very clear about the direction they are taking. However, motherhood has at times influenced the career decisions of all the Japanese women in top management functions. Companies and locations were chosen according to whether they were compatible with their children's needs. As the children grow older, the need to make decisions of this nature diminishes. As with the Chinese women, the Japanese women describe accepting overseas transfers partly to give their children this experience. Some women described how, when their children were still young, they used a coach to help them work out ways of coping with the burdens they faced at that time.

Y: In past if you want to continue to work, you can't be married. We can't be mommy and we can't have a child. I think it's my generation is the borderline because 1985 in Japan the job equality law was enacted. When I had a baby my mother and my mother-in-law said that it's better to quit the job. It's not good for baby to go nursery school, but I thought that it might be but I don't want to quit my job. I didn't know why then, but I didn't want to quit my job. It was a very good nursery. Only in home and young baby, it's not good for my health. My mental health. Every day, me and baby. I can't be–

M1: I had my first in the US, and that was a good opportunity to also understand– I had my first role model also in the US, because up to then I did not really see how a woman could really practically work and have a family. My first boss in the US was a female. She was a very well balanced, but a very successful woman. She was able to show me the way in terms of how to really balance, utilizing daycare and all. Also, I think by really pushing- putting the pressure off of myself to be okay about asking for help, asking for babysitters, or asking for cleaning help. I had my second back in Japan. They're a year and a half apart. They're very close, both were in diapers and all, but I chose cleaning support, as well as some babysitting support, as well as my parents were very close to where I lived as well. That was also a key support. My father is still working, and I would not say my father was much of a support, but my mother was.

K: That's a good question. I know that when I speak with my colleagues in the U.S., they experience the exact same thing, so I'm not sure if that's a Japanese thing. I think we all feel that at work you see other men spending probably two or three more hours because they don't have to do the household thing. Then when you go home, you compare yourself with other mothers, either without work or with part-time jobs, and you could be spending more time. Whether business or private, you always feel that you're not doing enough, so that's a constant feeling. I don't think that's very special to Japan.

H: I think it's always a challenge to manage time, so I always wish I could spend more time with my family. Especially with my children. There's always a sense of guilt that I spend so much time at work, even after I go home, emails and teleconference. That I could be spending more time with my kids, so I think that's the biggest thing.

Professional mobility, both within and beyond Japan, is described as being especially challenging for mothers. The Japanese women report that it is virtually impossible to move within Japan – for example from Osaka to Tokyo – if you have small children, because childcare cannot be transferred. The women consequently align their careers to the geographical needs of their children. Overseas postings are also described as challenging, given changing from the traditional Japanese educational system to an international school, for example, was perceived as being very difficult for the children. One woman reports that her son was unable to cope with the switch to an international school in Sweden. She solved the challenge by living separately from her husband and son, who went back to Japan. Similar situations also occur within Japan, where the woman needed to work in a different city to where her children had gone to school.

M1: That was a difficult decision but very good decision when I look back. This time, I decided to work in Tokyo by myself, so my family stays in Osaka and I basically commute every week from Osaka to Tokyo. That was also a difficult decision, I wouldn't have done it when kids are smaller.

I felt it's okay, now, as kids are bigger. My advice is for this type of difficult decisions, you try to manage it in the right time.

Obstacles and advantages: Female senior executives in Japan are the rare exception

The first word that comes to mind, when asking about the typical image of senior female executives in Japanese society, is *"exception"*. This in essence sums up the image that Japanese society has of the interviewees. Next come descriptions such as *"aggressive"*, *"different"*, *"communicative"* and *"lucky"*. Terms such as *"intimidating"* and *"threatening"* also come up but are then rejected. All descriptions clearly illustrate the hurdles that women have to overcome if they want to pursue a career at management level in Japan. They also illustrate the extent to which women in Japan need to be unaffected by the opinions of others if they want to advance in their careers. But this image of uniqueness also illustrates the opportunities that women in Japan can even today exploit as exceptions in the management world. Female executives are increasingly being judged positively in the public debate. They are acting as role models for other women, and as representatives of the Japanese political moves to use women's potential for the benefit of the country's economy. The strength of the senior women executives interviewed lies in the fact that they have a powerful sense of independence, are very determined and possess the ability to use the situation to their own strategic advantage.

> M2: I think people think of me as exception. It relates to the first point I raised. When my case became real because the first company I joined was XY which did not have this long working requirement or managers bias in selecting people. I grew up in a very special environment that made me as an exception. Image? I think aggressive, different, vocal and lucky.
>
> K: I never felt that I'm being viewed as a threat or scary. I feel I'm viewed from society, positively, because they need role models, or so some people think– I think that society needs more role models like us. So, I never had any bad experience. I think usually just being framed positively.
>
> Y: Society thinks that female staff is suitable for assistant. They are suitable for small works, tiny works

The women also experienced challenges in their roles when working abroad. It is in middle management that the women feel the challenges most powerfully. Individual Japanese women felt exposed in Europe, thrust into the spotlight by foreign managers and, more or less unintentionally, drawn into discussions about quotas for women that were being conducted at corporate headquarters. They describe how some of the foreign men reacted to their exceptional status by forming alliances, rejecting them and excluding them from networks. With the help of executive coaching, the solution found was to break down the perception that they were only there because of a quota and to actively engage in the men's networks.

M2: I think that, especially in Company XY (Multinational), where diversity was known as a check on positivity, there wasn't a lot of actually negative image around diversity being supportive of women, preference-driven, females were promoted not because of their skills or result, but because they are women. I actually experienced a lot of difficulty being in center of discussion, because males have their own network, transfer network to discuss and decide things, and they did not want me to be involved. I tried to get in by finding several individuals who actually could let me in. I also got the executive coaching support to get advice on how I can actually be in the center. That was really helpful.

6 German women: Shaping strategists in the middle of men's clubs and motherhood stereotypes

Successful German women are now shaping and strategizing their careers, despite men's clubs and cultural expectations about motherhood. In order to better understand opportunities for women leaders in Germany within the context of the country's cultural heritage as well as within a global context, it is worth taking a look at its past. The results of the current research may then be placed against the background of their social context. The historical socio-cultural influence on German women can be summed up with the words "housewives and mothers".

Socio-cultural preconditions for women's careers in Germany – shaped by both East and West

Socio-cultural influence lasted well beyond the mid-twentieth century and may still be felt today. As in many other societies, German society was patriarchal and women were frequently deemed neither independent nor capable of making decisions. Women in Germany were for a long time not permitted to work without the consent of their husbands or fathers, were not in control of their own money and had no legal rights with regards to their children. A woman's primary role was that of housewife. Job-related exceptions to this were, other than agriculture, menial writing tasks and needlework. But of course, there were women who, despite the prevailing climate, campaigned for women's rights, and in 1865 the first major German women's union was founded. The focus at that time was on educational rights for girls and women. Women were given the vote in the year 1918, 26 years earlier than in France. In 1920 women gained the right to qualify as university lecturers and this period also saw the first female German government minister. During the First World War, as everywhere in Europe, women were called upon to do work that had until then been reserved for men. During the National Socialist era, women were primarily seen as being there to assist their husbands and the rights that the women's movements had fought for were effectively reversed. Women were supposed to concentrate exclusively on their roles as mothers and to bear as many children as possible. On the birth of her fifth child, for example, a woman received a special award, the Mother's Cross, on the occasion of the annual Women's Day. Because of the prevailing high unemployment rate, they were forbidden to work during this era, and were forced out of all professions and universities. The holding of high office, which until then had still been in its infancy, became impossible for women and receded out of their consciousness. Established women's movements were brought into alignment with Nazi women's organizations. The latter had over six million members and their aim was to mold girls and women according to National Socialist ideals. Propaganda was used to firmly establish in the minds of both men and women that the primary roles of the German woman was that of housewife and mother.

After the Second World War, the role of women in Germany grew in two very different directions. In West Germany, with its system of traditional gender roles in which women were primarily seen as mothers, and in East Germany, where the emphasis was on employment for women. Both paths had major implications for gender equality. This fundamental difference in the roles of women in a divided Germany continues to exist to this day and has been attested in several studies. Many Germans are nevertheless either unaware of it, or only partially so, because the topic has lagged behind other political issues in the media coverage of social matters. In West Germany, in particular, an appreciation of the potential advantages of East German gender equality policies, which were reflected for example in childcare provision, was very late in coming.

West Germany: "Raven mothers", housewife marriages and homemakers

In western parts of Germany, traditional role models were maintained well into the 1990s. Despite the introduction of the first Equal Rights Act in 1949, the legal framework was anything other than adequate to the task of dismantling the traditional model. It was not until 1957 that the so-called "obedience paragraph" was abolished and in 1958 the Equality Act was incorporated into the constitution. This was the first time that husbands had been denied the ultimate right to make decisions on all marital matters. The so-called "housewife's marriage", in which the husband bore the main responsibility as breadwinner, was abolished in 1977 with the reform of the laws relating to marriage and family. Also characteristic of the position of women in West Germany were other regulations that prevented them from working full-time and which were only gradually abolished. According to Berghahn (2011), husbands could terminate their wife's employment until 1958. Until 1956, teachers had to leave the civil service in accordance with the celibacy of teachers. It was not until 1962 that women in West Germany were allowed to open their own bank account and only in 1965 were they permitted to sign an employment contract without their husband's consent. In the 1980s, under the motto "Mom is irreplaceable", socio-political and church efforts continued to promote the traditional image of womanhood. Even up to the present day, in parts of Germany the so-called 'Three Ks' of "*Kinder, Küche, Kirche*" (children, kitchen, church) continues to shape the public understanding of the role of women, even though there have been considerable improvements and advancements in gender equality. For many people, both men and women, this cultural heritage is still relevant whenever efforts to bring more women into leadership positions are discussed. Especially in western Germany, where most of society has clung for many years to the idea of the traditional family. It allows for a clear division of labor, and in most marriages, childrearing and housework were, and still are, the woman's responsibility. Socio-cultural paradigms and ideals still accord mothers the main role in the raising of children. In western Germany, it is traditionally thought that newborns and toddlers are best cared for at home by their mothers. Society's view, that the primary role of mothers is to raise children, has deep roots. Women who decide to invest more time in career progression still run the risk of being labeled "uncaring mothers". The judgment might come from outside, but is also very much internalized by most women. The term used in German for an uncaring mother, *"Rabenmutter"* or *"raven mother"*, is derived from the fact that ravens push their chicks out of the nest, leaving them to their own devices – and possible death. The negative image of the *"latchkey kid"*, which for many years was used to refer to children of working mothers who had to fend for themselves in the afternoons, fits with this. This same awareness continues to have an impact on the attitudes of many of the men and women brought up in West German society, even when they decide, as is increasingly the case, to have their children taken care of outside the home. State-run and private care for infants and school children is viewed with suspicion by German parents socialized in the west. Homemaking is valued and motherhood desirable; these social attitudes towards the role of women have prevailed over a long period. The growing self-confidence of women in Germany with regards to career planning is thus countered by a deep-rooted image of the mother as the principal figure in a child's life. In western Germany, the introduction of new career structures geared towards women has been slow in coming. While many men and women are nowadays aware of the existence of women in management positions, many also feel ambivalent towards them.

East Germany – full-time working women and outsourced childcare

In eastern Germany – the former German Democratic Republic, or GDR – the state invested a great deal of effort in ensuring gender equality. Authors such as Böhme (1982), Gerhard (2010) and Hille (1985) have examined the distinguishing features of the lives of working women in eastern Germany and have compared them to those in the western part. Society in the east was organized primarily around the gainful employment of both men and women. An additional aim of women's employment, other than making use of their labor, was to achieve gender equality. Policies relating to gender and family were geared towards promoting a work-life balance for women. If one looks at the 1949 GDR constitution, one finds that it not only enshrined the equality of men and women but that even at this early date, it laid down additional legislation with regard to equal pay and the reconcilability of work and family life. Women's needs were given priority. The state created a system for the care of infants and children, adapted to the needs of working women. As a result, 90 percent of women in the GDR were in full-time employment. Studies carried out immediately after reunification show that in the former GDR, the employment rate for women -- 91 percent – was similar to that for men and that childcare provision was extensive. Various sources note that this was one of the highest percentages in the world. The former GDR thus developed more rapidly and progressed further in the area of gender equality than did the former Federal Republic in the west. Critics argue that although the GDR's social welfare policies helped women to reconcile family and work, it did not enable them to reconcile family and *career* because the father's role in the family was not accorded the same importance as that of the mother. According to a 2019 report by the German Federal Ministry of Family Affairs, despite being equally qualified and having equal professional experience, hardly any top management positions were held by women. Other sources reported, however, that women did hold high ranking positions, for example, as judges or medics working in research. Academic opinion is currently divided as to whether women in the GDR experienced real equality of opportunity. In the minds of the citizens of the former GDR, however, it was the norm for women to work full-time in all sectors of the economy and to earn equal salaries. The image of the bad mother that predominated in the western part of the country was replaced in the GDR by the government's promotion of images of the active working woman. What remains unclear is the extent to which the values which dated from their shared past with the west played a role in East Germany's attitudes on the role of women.

Germany as a whole: Traditional western German values, only slowly giving way to learnings from the east

With Germany's reunification in 1990, the Federal Republic of Germany's (FRG) constitutional, legal and social framework was adopted throughout Germany. The ending of the period of separation brought together two different political and economic systems and two sets of people who had different experiences and ideas about family and society, equality and gender rights. In East Germany in 1989, before reunification, 91 percent of women of working age were in employment. In West Germany, on the other hand, the employment rate for women was much lower, at 51 percent. In the first few years after reunification, the changes that took place in eastern Germany were rapid and profound, altering almost all areas of society. In comparison, the changes in western Germany were less dramatic. The direction and speed of cultural, social and technological change were only slightly impacted by the "reunification factor". Society in the western regions of the country remained essentially unchanged. In the upheavals in East Germany following reunification, a number of institutions that had promoted equality were dismantled or discontinued so that objectively viewed, the first years of German unification were a step backwards in eastern Germany in terms of equality between women and men.

In comparing the two German states at the time of reunification, Vogel (2000) argues that it is possible to speak of a western German "lag" in terms of gender equality relative to the former GDR. The reason for this lag lay in the fact that in the former GDR, women's employment and childcare provision were already the norm, whereas in western Germany these important elements were only introduced many years later. To this day, even the new federal states have not yet returned to the level that they were at during the time of the GDR. The employment rate for women in Germany has risen steadily since 1989, but is still well below that in the GDR shortly before the Wall came down. In the reunified Germany, the pay gap for women in 2014 was 23 percent, with only very slight improvements having occurred. Women in both western and eastern Germany still have a significantly lower probability than men of attaining management positions, even though there are no longer any significant differences between the genders in terms of education and qualifications. According to a Federal Ministry for Family Affairs report from 2019, the proportion of women in management positions in eastern Germany is now slightly higher than in almost all of the regions of western Germany. The difference is in the order of 5 percent. Since the 1990s, it has become common for mothers in Germany to work part-time. Differences between eastern and western Germany in terms of attitudes to gender roles and women's employment remain, despite reunification. The majority of Germans who grew up in the GDR, and who were 16 years of age or older at the time of reunification, state that in the GDR women worked full-time to about the same extent as men, that women and men had the same opportunities to reach senior management positions and shared housework and child-rearing tasks equally. Opinions were taken from the Delta Equality Survey of 2015. People from western Germany do not share the same opinions and coincide with eastern Germans only in their perceptions of the extent to which East German women were involved in professional activities.

During the period of reunification, there was no widespread public debate as to the advantages of the GDR childcare system for women who were active in the labor market, as other issues dominated. From an equality perspective, it can be seen that the progress made by, and the advantages of, the former East German system were not adopted by the newly reunited Germany. For a long time, there was no public discussion on the subject. As a result, a large proportion of the population whose views were shaped by the former Federal Republic are either unaware of the differences in the circumstances of women in the former GDR, or else are somewhat critical of them.

Combining motherhood and a career

The differing childcare provision, the higher proportion of women in employment in the GDR compared to West Germany, and the self-image, identities and employment aspirations of women in the GDR have had long-term effects right up to the present day. In eastern Germany, only a quarter of mothers with small children feel the need to justify their wish to work full-time. In western Germany on the other hand, the situation is reversed and almost 70 percent of women with children say they feel this pressure. Following German reunification, employment rates for mothers with pre-school children have been higher in eastern Germany than in the west of the country. Among women with children under three years of age, 61 percent in the east versus 50 percent in the west are in employment. Among women with children between the ages of six and ten, 81 percent of east German women are in employment compared to 76 percent of women in the west. According to a study by McKinsey (2002), there are still marked differences between east and west in the provision of childcare. In the new federal states, children of working parents generally attend one of the childcare facilities that were established during GDR times. In western Germany, there is no equivalent comprehensive state childcare provision, so informal networks and private childcare play a greater role. The care of infants up to the age of two is also markedly different. In the west, around 30 percent of young children are looked after outside the home, while in the east the figure is more than 55 percent, depending on the source. Notwithstanding an increase in the number of daycare places for under threes and a legal entitlement to a place, there will still be a shortage of over 200,000 places in 2020, mainly in western Germany.

Once a child starts school, parents in western Germany experience even greater problems than during the nursery school years. Parental involvement, such as taking part in activities at nursery or school and the supervision of homework, is frequently taken as expected. According to a study by Borchard (2008) for the Konrad Adenauer Foundation KAS, mothers, especially among the middle classes, tend to take on a sort of assistant teacher role as a way of supporting children in coping with the demands placed on them by schools. This reinforces the role of the mother as the person responsible for activities within the home and that of the father as the breadwinner. In Germany as a whole, despite the increase in the number of crèches and the introduction of a family allowance, society still often expects mothers to spend a large part of their time with their children.

Women in top management positions in Germany

Despite having a female chancellor, Germany ranks only average in international comparisons of the proportions of women in politics. The proportion of women in the Bundestag is 30 percent. It is surely remarkable that a woman from the east of the country, Angela Merkel, has been governing Germany as Chancellor since 2005. She is one of the most powerful and influential politicians in the world today. According to the Inter-Parliamentary Union (2019), the IPU, Germany ranks 46th out of 190 countries in terms of its proportion of women in politics. Looking at the German labor market, a general picture emerges: more and more women are working but they still prefer to work part-time, especially if they are mothers. The reasons for this are complex and, according to Holst (2013), may be found in the interplay between cultural influences, family and tax policies, and a continued under provision of childcare services when viewed in terms of the needs of working women.

When considering the issue of women in management positions, it is important to recognize that German women operate in a society in which part-time work continues to be the norm for mothers. In Germany, around 45 percent of employees are women and, according to Eurostat, the employment rate for women was 71.5 percent in 2017. Although the employment rate is higher than in neighboring France, 47 percent of women in Germany work part-time. The proportion of women working part-time has increased by over 10 percent since the year 1973, and as such, it has become an increasingly female mode of working.

According to a Grant Thornton (2017) international study, women in senior management positions in Germany account for only 18 percent of the total. Data also compiled by Ankersen and Berg (2018) of the Allbright Foundation confirmed this picture. The situation in Germany is thus closer to that of Japan (7 percent) than that of France (31 percent) or China (38 percent) and is very far from that of Russian (47 percent). In comparison, the global average for the proportion of women in management positions is 26 percent, with the USA coming in at 22 percent. The aforementioned international study has been conducted for a number of years and looks, among other things, at changes in the participation of women in senior management. In the second management tier, i.e. middle management, there are considerably more women in Germany, the percentage standing at around 41 percent. In micro-enterprises with nine employees or fewer, Germany has the largest proportion of women in senior management positions, at around 25 percent. However, even in companies with up to only 50 employees, the proportion of women in top management positions declines rapidly.

The gender pay gap is an expression of the unequal treatment of women in a given labor market. According to the Global Gender Pay Index for 2018, Germany ranked 13th, with a 22 percent pay gap for women compared to men, just behind France, which ranked 12th. Germany's Institute for Economic Research attributes two-thirds of the gap to discriminatory practices. And adding salt to the wound, according to the 2019 Report of the Federal Ministry for Family Affairs and Women, women have little or no access to networks of decision-makers.

Who are the German women executives interviewed?

The German interviewees are between 35 and 62 years of age, with most of them being in their mid to late 40s. The majority are married and have one or two children. As with all of the women in the survey, the German interviewees' educational level is high. With two exceptions, Germany's top female managers have a German university degree equivalent internationally to an MBA. The two exceptions either underwent an apprenticeship or have an Advanced Technical College Certificate, which corresponds internationally to a bachelor's degree. The spectrum of qualifications ranges from business studies and law to mathematics and engineering. Six women subsequently obtained master's degrees abroad. One participant has a doctorate in law and, unusually, holds a license to practice law in the US. Another woman, who received only commercial training, became a university professor via an alternative route, i.e. without an academic degree.

In addition to women executive and supervisory board members, the interview group also includes managing directors, human resources directors and chief of marketing. The interviewees thus represent a good cross-section of senior management. At the time of the survey, the women were working for DAX-listed companies, large corporations and, in a few cases, medium-sized businesses. Only two of the women work for non-German companies, one of them abroad. Around half of the women have worked in two or three companies, but some have changed companies between five and eight times in the course of their careers. Only one woman has remained with the same DAX-listed company for the whole of her professional life. With only two exceptions, the women all gained professional experience abroad, mostly in one or two countries. The front-runners in terms of foreign postings are two women who have spent time in three or four countries. The majority of the women have worked in European countries, although some have had foreign placements the USA, China, Taiwan, Hong Kong or Japan.

How the German women executives perceive equal opportunities in their country

The German women were asked to rate their experiences of equal opportunities in senior management in Germany on a scale from zero to ten, where zero stands for complete lack of equality and ten for complete equality. Some women also rated other countries in which they had worked during their careers.

German women give their home country an average score of five. This means that, in the opinion of the top female managers interviewed, Germany is only halfway along the road to equality. Put another way, Germany, as a leading economic nation, is still fairly mediocre with regards to the situation of women in senior management. China was rated seven or eight by the three German women who also worked there. The highest score, given by two of the women, went to Sweden with ten points. France twice received a score of seven or eight, the US scored eight, and Japan came in last with four to five points, with the interviewee adding that equal opportunities there were on a par with Germany.

The German women leaders base their score of five out of ten for Germany on the pressure and harsh judgment meted out by society on women who want to concentrate on their careers. Society is still not ready for women in leadership positions, especially if they are mothers. This means that German women not only have to assert themselves in the workplace, but also in their families, in friendship groups and in society as a whole. It is not yet a given that women will strive to obtain a top management role. In addition, a lack of self-confidence among German women, in comparison with women from a number of other nations, is cited as another reason for the poor score.

M1.: In Germany you don't have to look far. Women, no matter what they do, are never seen in a positive light. So, I'd like to back that up. The way I always describe it is: Women who don't have children are randy women's libbers. Women who decide to work part-time, well, they probably have to because their husbands don't earn enough. Or because they want to find themselves. Women who work full-time and have children, well obviously they're the typical bad mother types and are only interested in themselves. I had a mentee who demonstrated this really clearly to me. She said: "My husband is proud of me actually. And because I've got my PhD now and because I want to go and work abroad." And she really WANTS to go abroad. But her mother-in-law's always telling her son: "You don't need her to go out to work. She does too much, you should..." So, it doesn't matter whether it's in the family or in the surrounding environment, there are very few positive messages that signal to women: "If you want to have a career, if you want to take the plunge, if you want to work, that's fantastic. It's the right thing to do, and it's great. The traditional ways of thinking are so entrenched that they act like roadblocks or barriers, and that discourages women, instead of people coming up to you and saying, "Wow, you've got fighting spirit. You can do it, you can totally do it." In my opinion, there's far too little of that in Germany. There's too much criticism, too many prejudices, old ways of thinking that don't make it easy for women to decide wholeheartedly to pursue a career.

B.: Yeah. I'd say it's a different kind of self-confidence. You just do have to be stronger than other people. I have the feeling, and I'm not talking about Germany now, I'm talking about my company. What I've seen in my company. Women often feel small. I can't do this and I can't do that. I have the feeling that in Lithuania women were more confident, regardless what job they did. It always felt that way. Here you have to support women and encourage them.

J.: And I think there's still a big difference in Germany. And I'd even say that I have the feeling that it's getting more socially acceptable to make flippant remarks if a woman has technical expertise or works in IT, for example, it's socially acceptable to make fun of them. It's happening more than it did. There's a distinction made. And what I also notice is that it's normal for Chinese women to pursue careers. And their family don't stand in their way. Of course, you do have to manage your time, but there's nothing standing in your way.

H.: The five out of ten I gave means I think that where there's a will, there's a way. You can do it. The bar is high, but it's not so high as to be impossible. But I do believe that the general state of affairs, the hurdles you have to overcome, the prevailing images, are still really firmly rooted and the environment we live in is still pretty backward. And then there are all these issues, like men taking parental leave, that's still criticized. The available childcare options are still relatively poor in my view. What also makes me give it a five is the stereotypes that are really prominent in my male colleagues' minds.

E.: Yes, Germany is definitely in the dark ages as far as gender rights and gender equality are concerned, in my opinion. But on the plus side, at least women don't have FGM done to them and they aren't kept hidden in chadors or whatever. Because that's illegal. If you look at the number of women in executive and board positions, we are right down at around 10 percent. If you look at how wealth is distributed, it's probably about 80:20. If you look at the gender pay gap, it's about 21 percent and it isn't budging. And if you look at who works full-time and who works part-time, the ratio's around 90:10. And if you look at how work is defined. In fact, work is still very strongly associated with collective agreements, even though it's no longer covered by them. So the images of what work is like are things like: full-time, unionized, male, hard-working, steel, that sort of thing. That's the general view and that's how pay is structured. So all the people who wipe people's bottoms and care for them and are really poorly paid, they're all women. And women are still in this same situation where what they do for a living is not properly valued, because they're not the ones who are feeding the family. Men see themselves as the breadwinners and that is how they are seen by others too. So unemployment feels a lot more threatening for men than for women, because women always have other options. But then again, men don't have the freedom to shape their own lives.

B.: I'll start with the countries which are top. With the countries I know something about. With Asia. No, Sweden. I've worked extensively in Sweden. Sweden is probably a ten. Or nine. Nine or ten. Scandinavia is somewhere near the top. What they brought in there, which in my view was the shrewdest move of any, was that they brought in equal parental leave, in principle at least. Both men and women can, as a general rule, work fewer hours for as long as the child needs a bit more looking after for whatever reason, and this means that both fathers and mothers can work reduced hours. And fathers have actually taken this up. I had a team in Sweden and this man, a peer really, did come up to me one day and said: "I need to spend more time looking after my children. I'm cutting back to four days a week." So women and men were treated exactly the same. It didn't matter who they hired. Because both men and women could come along at any time and say: "I'm going to cut my hours back." This ensured absolutely equal employment terms. And as I said, both men and women took advantage of it. I would probably put France at about a six. In France, they mainly have state-funded schemes, where the children are in school all day and mothers don't work on Wednesday afternoons. That's pretty widespread. And I think that there, women are generally accepted. The disadvantage in France is that women have to be incredibly sexy. I think it's really exhausting being a French woman.

German women's career strategies

The German women's career paths reflect a broad range of approaches. Half of the women have changed companies several times and have between five and seven companies on their CV. At the beginning of their careers, the women who have changed companies typically had an extended period of five to seven years in one or two companies. After that they repeatedly move companies after shorter periods of time, on average after two to three years. Almost half of the women have had careers in only two companies. Three of these women have returned to their original company after a position in another company and used the move to advance up corporate ladder. One example of this approach is a woman from HR who switched to a prestigious recruitment agency and subsequently rose to the top of her original organization – a DAX-listed company. Three of the women used a period of self-employment as an interim career move. The youngest woman in the group has so far spent her entire career in a DAX-listed company, including two overseas posts. The oldest woman in the group started out self-employed and then went to work for a large corporation and remained there for the remainder of her professional life. Only one of the women has had the experience of working for state-owned companies. The overwhelming majority of the women work for German companies. Only three of the women have had the experience of working in foreign companies, two of them on several occasions. For most of the female top managers surveyed here, experience abroad was acquired by means of an internal transfer; only three of them took up a position abroad as a result of changing companies. The women's career paths thus cover a wide range of profiles, some women remaining predominantly with one company while others switched between companies.

The primary reason cited for changing jobs is the desire for professional advancement, which was only possible by changing companies. Some women report that they were offered dummy leadership roles because male colleagues did not trust them with genuine leadership responsibility. For some of them, changing companies allowed them to leapfrog as many as three levels of the company hierarchy. For another subset of women, company restructuring or the closure of business units was what led to the decision to change jobs. Having foreseen that staying in the company would lead to career stagnation, they decided to take action and seek new opportunities. Some of the women actively decided to take breaks of up to six months or sought short interim solutions as consultants.

The German women's career strategies can be summarized as follows:
1. Seek opportunities for advancement
2. Seek out environments where women are welcome in leadership positions
3. Communicate career aspirations
4. Get out of your own comfort zone and head up large projects
5. Gain experience abroad for short periods
6. Gain a broad range of expertise, even if you are a specialist
7. Develop and make use of both company-internal and external networks

German women generally need an initial start-up period so that they can develop their career strategies. Many stay in their first position or company for a longer period than women in other countries. It seems as if the women needed to find an initial impetus in order for their future path to become clear. So clarity about their career goals took some time for the German interviewees. When asked what has been the main factor driving their career forward the answer is not staying too long in a company where, due to the corporate culture or the boss's attitude, women do not stand a chance. Going to companies where women are welcome in management positions is a strategy that the women have adopted after long periods in discriminatory environments. Whereas they might have remained and been relatively well protected in middle management, it is only by breaking out of the middle levels that their careers progress. For some women, it means changing companies after long spells at the second or third levels of management. In the case of one woman, for example, this meant deliberately choosing to continue her career outside of Germany. The career path of the specialist is in stark contrast to that of the generalist, who builds a broad skill base in a series of sales and management positions in various parts of the company. Personnel managers are the most common example of this. They acquire the broadest possible experience within their specialist area in order to become eligible for top positions.

For the majority of the women, overseas posts are both desirable and necessary. Taking a job abroad with a German company is a good way to gain international experience, as is the traditional expat route of relocating from company headquarters to an overseas subsidiary. In the latter case, however, challenges arise in terms of returning to the parent company and reintegrating with the family. Nevertheless, for most of the women, the temporary experience abroad led directly to an increase in their expertise. For most of them, however, it did not immediately translate into the next step on the career ladder. Aspects playing a central role in many of the women's careers were overcoming their fear of stepping out of their comfort zone and actively taking on major new projects. This might include, for example, building up new business areas, negotiating for major projects or restructuring business units.

B.: Well, I think one factor was understanding that the circumstances have to be right. Telling myself much more deliberately to look for a new job right NOW. Looking for companies where it's feasible. As I said, that was my big insight after my time at XY. There, women never amounted to anything. Saying to yourself when you're in that situation that you need to be much more selective in your choice of company. Well, my boss at AB, he was gender-blind. Or maybe he just didn't care. He only cared about us delivering results. I'd say this was definitely a major breakthrough. It's not just about being a woman. We do have a particular way of doing things. And every company has a particular culture. And then I realized that people usually promote people who are similar to themselves. So, of course, that means I almost never get promoted. Because, of course, I'm not like anyone else no matter where I go. And then you say to yourself, OK, choose companies where performance matters most. For example, I can't join a company that is, in my view, highly political. CD, for example, is very influenced by French culture. Although that's improved somewhat in recent years. But if you're not French there, then you get nowhere. And you have to sort through the companies more carefully as well. And say, "You would fit in there. You wouldn't fit in there." When it comes to switching companies, make your selection criteria much more explicit.

M1.: There's this quote: "If the task doesn't frighten me, then the task is too small." It was some African president or other I think, who said it. The first woman president. Nigeria or somewhere. It really spoke to me. I can see myself saying, "She's a funny one." That was on my first day at the XY newspaper. I was quite scared. But I can deal with that. I know my fear's trying to protect me and is giving me signals, but I also know that I can't allow it to stop me. I can't let it stop me from taking the next step. I think a lot of people stop at the point where they feel fear or insecurity. But I never do. I've never done that.

C.: So this one time, I started at XY, in I. (country), in 2002. I always knew I wanted to go abroad and so I just applied for a job in I. and so then there I was. Even if it was a long time ago, it was important. I did a lot of operative stuff there in the beginning. XY was still really small then. And so I got promoted very quickly. Which nowadays wouldn't happen. At 29, I was already the executive director and responsible for 1,000 employees. And because I was given both management and specialist responsibility so quickly, I think that impressed people. Then I moved, I went to O. (country). And in O. I was managing director again, for a regional company. But then I was quickly given responsibility for sales for the whole of the country. And for me that was another important position, because I think I came to see lots of things that I'd learned in I. in a completely different way. And I think I stepped on a few toes there. I think that I made myself a bit more noticeable because I did that. And then I was offered the job as CEO in L. (country). And I think I got it because I think my superiors saw how quickly I adjust to new situations and I have the courage to address issues and to implement things. And I think I've always done a really good job taking employees with me. So somehow, I always managed to get the whole team behind me, that's how we were able to push things forward together as a team. And in L. it was a completely new situation for me all over again. I started there with

30 employees. I'd never had so few employees in the whole course of my career. And I had to build up a completely new purchasing team, a real estate team, really build up everything from scratch, just like with a start-up. I had to completely immerse myself in a new culture. And then suddenly Mrs. XY arrived, after a sales career. She said, "You seem to have a good rapport with the employees. You get ideas across well. How would you like to restructure our HR department?" And so then I became Chief Human Resources Officer. It sounds easy, but it was a long road.

M.2: You really have to have the courage to take certain steps, dare to go abroad. Both at university and also when you're working. And you have to be in the right place at the right time, early on I was part of a team that launched a new product, and the product was really successful. So I was there from the word go, you might say, and as the product became successful, I became more successful too, if I can put it that way. Because I got first-hand experience, but of course, I had good luck as well. Because, I mean, that's just the way it is, you either work on a product which is successful or on a product which isn't successful. And then of course you get management responsibility very quickly. In S. (country) I'd already arrived at a point where I couldn't progress any further. I wouldn't have got any further up the ladder, because the next step would have been CEO, if you looked at the organigram, traditionally speaking. And of course, that wasn't going to happen. So we thought about it, and then we decided to go back to Germany for the time being.

E.: Each of my foreign postings had different facets. And they didn't build on each other, they broadened my horizons instead. I noticed in my first posting that there were seven levels to the hierarchy and that I wouldn't be able to reach the top in that company until I was about 150. And I didn't want that. I wanted to get there faster than that. So I left that company when the time was right. At XY I definitely had a number of decisive experiences. One was that I ended up in the business administration department, which was a kind of elite training ground at the time. And as a result, you also got a solid grounding in business administration. That was one of the things. The second was: I had a boss who enjoyed having me around and so was inclined to promote me. And the third thing was that shortly before I was going to leave XY, which was after about six years, I was given the opportunity to help build up a new business area within XY. So, my thirst for adventure was nourished there. And that's where I learned the international bit of the business and the Anglo-Saxon bit as well. And the pan-European bit. So those were some of the postings I had. Then I went to AB. Maybe the most significant thing there was that it was the first time I had been in such a local setting and I couldn't quite settle in there. But that was also a learning experience. But I also led big projects, really big projects. One of them was negotiating a major contract over a long period of time for over 300 million Euros. If I look back, that was over 15 years ago, I'm surprised at how much responsibility I was given. And the other thing I did was to carry out a major restructuring of a telecommunications company, which I had never done before. And that was also very much a learning experience.

H.: Well, my idea was actually to do another assignment in the Asia-Pacific region. I think that would have been great. And then I would have come back at a higher level. On the other hand, I think people, not just my boss, but also me, underestimated how much I loved my freedom even in those days. And it was like a straitjacket that I got forced into and I couldn't perform well like that, I couldn't develop to the same extent anymore. And I think that's something you have to be very sensitive to when you bring people back. And I think it goes both ways. I've seen it when we've had to bring people back from other countries, and then there were no jobs for them. You have to pay attention to things like: What did were they doing before and can they be re-integrated to the same degree? I was definitely spoiled.

German female top managers' career prerequisites

German women who make it into top management have had the benefit of a first-class education. They use the first few years of their careers to decide whether they want to try to reach the top. They are masters at shaping change processes within companies. This includes the ability to lead transformation processes and the desire to shape and establish new organizations.

German women's backgrounds: fathers as role models, mothers as promoters

Various studies exist in the literature as to whether, and to what extent, a person's origins have an influence on their career path. The findings demonstrate a clear link to the cultural and social conditions of the country to which the research pertains. "Origins" usually refers to structural variations within the family, such as the parents' occupations and their socioeconomic status. "Family of origin" refers here to the family into which a person is born. One of the few studies that addresses this topic, by the German sociologist Michael Hartmann (2002), yielded findings that are not entirely consistent with the image of the modern and accessible career with the notion of equality of opportunity. His research shows that the chances of achieving a position of leadership in Germany are 50 percent higher for children from white-collar families and 100 percent higher for children from privileged backgrounds than they are for children from blue-collar or middle-class families. In Germany, social background appears to have a direct influence on the choosing of elites. The study shows that the German business elite, i.e. the top managers of major German corporations, have for decades come from the same social grouping. More than four-fifths of them, almost always men, come from the well-to-do middle, and upper middle, classes. Although, according to the research in this area to date, only a small proportion of the inequality of career opportunities has been linked to social background, Hartmann (2002) and Resch (2014) have both found that differences in the choice of occupation and in the career paths themselves are influenced by family background. Children identify strongly with their parents with regard to profession. According to Schellhorn (2014), there is evidence that a mother's profession particularly influences a daughter's career choice, and that mothers influence their career decisions more than fathers. For German women, but not for men, there is a negative correlation between the level of education of their parents and their own satisfaction with their professional development. The higher the level of education of the father, the more dissatisfied a woman is with her own professional development, and the more distressed she is about reaching the "glass ceiling" and experiencing the incompatibility of work and family.

The majority of the German women interviewed for this book have university-educated fathers who have held senior management positions. Fathers who did not study at all also managed to work their way up to senior positions. Only a small percentage of the mothers are university graduates. With two exceptions, all of the mothers were housewives and only two of them, one from the former GDR, regularly worked full-time. Those mothers with qualifications are either teachers or have a medical occupation. One woman had self-employed parents and describes their constant struggle to save the company from insolvency. When asked about their role models when they were young, all but three of the women name their fathers. Their fathers worked hard and were thus often absent. During the few hours they spent at home, the women obtained an interesting insight into their work and at the same time learned the value of discipline and commitment to one's work. These women wished to earn their fathers' respect. There are indications that some of the women took on the role of the son their parents never had. The two women who name their mothers as role models come from east German families. All of the mothers, whether they were at home or whether they were employed, were performance-oriented and encouraged or demanded excellence from their children. In the women's accounts of childhood, it is also striking that independence was encouraged from an early age.

> S.: Well, as I said, my father's an engineer, an electrical engineer, he had to work his way up, he wasn't born into it. First, he trained as a technical draughtsman, then he went to further education classes, graduated from high school and then studied and did his doctorate abroad, and ultimately worked his way up to a very high position in a chemical company, so he had executive responsibility, as well. And my mother, she followed the traditional German pattern. She did work until she had me and my brother, she had us quite late, in her late 30s, but she had always done temporary jobs of one kind or another, because she hadn't had any formal training, and then when my brother and I were born she finally stopped work and never went back.

> C.: Yes, my mother always worked. But, you know, that was normal in the Eastern Bloc. She worked full-time as a teacher. And my father helped her around the house. I always had the impression that they shared the household tasks.

> K.: My father was a diplomat, we moved a lot. Afghanistan, India, Mali, Geneva, Brussels, Paris. My mother's a pharmacist. Whenever we were in Germany, she worked and when we were abroad, she liked to try and get jobs in medical organizations. But mostly she took care of us. My grandmother was one of the first women in Germany to study economics and later, when she got married, she was the one who drew up the statistics on my grandfather's estate. That's left its mark on me.

> M2: Yes, he was only there very rarely, but my mother was always there, she was the one who brought us up really strictly and my father was the one who was kind and relaxed. My mother wasn't always like that. He was the one who wore the trousers. When my father was there, it was nice, but he was very rarely there. And on weekends, when I was young, he did all the on-call shifts at the hospital and there were always a lot of patients. When I used to notice that he was worn out, I felt sorry for him, I think. Then he had to sleep a lot because he'd worked through the night, and the idea that he was helping bring children into the world was exciting, I used to pretend I was doing that a lot when I was playing. So he was my role model, I think.

> S.: And the other thing that definitely influenced me was that my father always told me it's important to take care of the financial side of things. Money isn't everything, but it makes life easier. And having a good education is the best way to earn good money. And I think that was an-

other thing that influenced me and made me say to myself: A good education is important, and this decision to study engineering is also important, because as he explained: "Look, sure, you can study psychology or business, but if you really want to have a successful career and earn good money and have financial security, then you're probably better off with an engineering degree."

The German women's management competencies

When asked about their strengths and skills, the German women respond in detail. They have first-rate foreign language skills. In addition to English, they have basic or business fluency in two to five other languages. One of the main areas of emphasis is the high level of expert knowledge among the German women. They are notable for their superior level of expertise and the detailed knowledge of their business area and markets. Their knowledge is underpinned by their qualifications and practical experience, for example in sales or other specialized areas such as IT or digitalization. Analytical skills and systems knowledge are mentioned just as often as expertise, generally. The women describe their affinity for numbers and their ability to deal with complex issues. They use this ability to undertake strategic shaping and planning. Visionary ability and innovation skills are mentioned by some of the women when talking about change management. They are characterized by their ability to facilitate continuous change processes through motivating and supporting their employees. Excellent communication and negotiation skills, along with persuasive power, are also abilities repeatedly mentioned.

> E.: One thing is, I'm pretty good at analysis. I understand facts, situations and connections fast. That helps. I can familiarize myself with topics that might at first sight seem difficult. And I can deliver whatever it takes to make a good impression. So that's a kind of hygiene factor. Incidentally, that's not the case with men. They can get away with doing less. That's honestly true. But then again, it's also true that there's not much that really upsets me. And that helps too. So that means that in situations where other people might think: "I don't know what to do", I can say to myself: "It's not really all that much of a problem". And that helps enormously, because there's often a lot of nonsense that goes on. And then, and I think this is really what distinguishes me, I have a kind of visionary power, I can see how things will turn out. And also, I've a feeling for the direction I want to go in. Not necessarily in my personal life, but in my job and in my business role. And also, I can transmit information and communicate it to others.

> C.: I'd say what I'm also good at, which is probably something my superiors have also observed, is an affinity for numbers, strategic thinking, an entrepreneurial mindset and the ability to really think outside the box. I don't have this silo mentality. Also, because I've worked in so many different areas, I know the company really well and I'm not your typical HR executive who can only see things through an HR lens. I know exactly what it means to sell in a branch store. For example, when I was in O. (country) I still carried on doing that once a month, simply in order to be at the coalface. I think that's really important. I'm very approachable. I'm not just some person sitting on the board somewhere. I'm also very close to my employees in the position I'm in now. We work together on things. I've always worked like that. You can't do anything all by yourself. Maybe sometimes I force the pace a bit to motivate people. But in the end,

it's me and my team in it together. And I probably have a knack for picking the right people to support me in the right areas. Because I also know which things I'm less good at. And so it's important to find the people who will balance that out.

S.: OK, my strengths, so there's the fact that you need to able to take people with you. I'm really good at that. I think that's an important aspect of success, too. Leadership pure and simple. Being able to persuade others. And of course, communication. Getting things across really clearly. And something I learnt later on is to speak in statements and send out appeals. That's definitely part of it. And I think I have that ability.

The German women's cross-cultural experiences are considered by some to be important for advancement, but only occasionally can particular skills be identified in the accounts which are clearly related to having a global mindset. The accounts are more concerned with recognizing and understanding differences and less with the ability to adapt and move between cultures. One of the women, who has spent many years in several countries as a result of her career, reflects that she does not see her strength as lying in her cross-cultural skills. In her case, concentrating on her German strengths has helped her career. Another woman is very frank about the fact that her focus is on the local market. She has never lived abroad and her work depends more on local knowledge and being able to speak German. Only four of the women commented on cross-cultural skills and even than only briefly. It is certainly the case that the German women are frontrunners in terms of foreign languages and foreign assignments. However, there are no accounts that suggest that they are strong in the area of adaptation and moving between cultures.

M1.: Well, I've seen it with my own eyes, I've never really managed to leave XY (region in Germany). Today, it's taken for granted in DAX companies, it's assumed that everyone'll complete at least two international assignments before they can progress to a management position. In other words, as is standard these days, everyone who wants a leadership position here has to get some international experience. Communication is a very German affair. I have to have a good command of German, I have to be able to network and I have to have my contacts here on site. And, if you've done international projects, then it will always have been with agencies. Sure, they have to be managed, but then you have teams too. So for me it wasn't a big deal to build on my skills in this area as far as I could. In any case, I would have had zero chance in marketing either here or anywhere else. I just don't have the profile you need for that these days, or that you would have needed even in the past, to work in marketing. I don't have the experience or any of the other things you need to have. It's a very niche area, definitely. And one which allows you to move up through the company with little or no international experience.

M2.: It was obviously very important for my career and made all the difference. Both the fact that I can practice law in America and the fact that I'm genuinely interested in China, which is very different from Hong Kong. To be able to understand both cultures and to approach them with an open mind. And I've found it incredibly enriching, and I'm different from many other German bosses who are on assignment in Hong Kong and who can't connect with the people because they aren't interested in the country and don't really want to understand the culture. In leadership, it's extremely important to embrace a country's culture and learn how people interact with each other. I can't just go over there with my German management style, I have to think about how to go about it, out of respect for the people over there, and deal with them differently. How I give feedback and things like that. But even then, I'd never do things like that just for the sake of my career, just so I can tick a box and say, "I've just been in China, or somewhere even more exotic, for a year". That just doesn't work. I really believe that only people who really enjoy being abroad should go. I know of people who say: I'm doing this right now, I hate China, but I think it's going to be great for my career, I just need to do it. They suffer for the whole year. That's not going to be good for either side.

C.: Yes, I think that's really important. Here we're always talking about diversity. But then again we also have really different cultures. And that makes a huge difference. And I notice when I'm in other countries that they can see I've been to other countries. I think maybe I have a different way of connecting with people. It makes you more open. And I also just know how to do certain things, I think. And there are just different ways of doing things depending whether I'm meeting with my colleagues or external partners in the US, or whether I'm in Eastern Europe, in Poland, for example, negotiating a deal. And then there are some schemes and processes which we run internationally from here. So we do also have some processes which are global in nature. You have to think about it hard, what does this mean to a Spaniard and what does it mean to a Finn? Is it doable? At what point do we need to make sure that this is something that gets determined at local level, because the cultural differences are just too big. That's a skill that I very much encourage people in the company to develop. And in top management, all the people have been abroad. They've all seen things from a different angle.

German women's career orientation: Start slow before aiming high

K.: "Men are more likely to consider exactly what it is they want. Women often don't have the courage. You have to strong-arm them to do it."

The German women's aspirations to reach the highest possible leadership position develop over time and only later on in their careers. When starting out, German women are primarily interested in gaining plenty of experience and in attaining a good, solid corporate position. Part of this includes gaining experience abroad. They recount how, once they reached a certain point in their careers, and sometimes only after several years, something clicked and their somewhat cautious career planning became more strategic. Many of the women were given encouragement by superiors and describe how they were asked by them to take on their first management position. The aspiration to achieve senior roles changes with greater self-confidence and a sense of achievement. The women describe how they became more self-confident over time. These accounts are in line with Fietze's (2011) findings on the correlation between personality and career success in German women. What all German women have in common is that, despite their socio-cultural heritage, they place emphasis on their professional careers and accept that their role as a mother is not a key consideration. This is a distinctive feature of the group in view of the continuing cultural influences within the country. The German interviewees also stand out in that over the course of their marriage or partnership they become the more career-oriented partner.

B.: When I was with XY, I was in international marketing, of course. That's such a great job. I mean, there's no better job than marketing, let's say, beauty products. And flying all over the world and doing photo shoots. It's just a fantastic job. With really nice colleagues and everything. But then, of course, at some point you say to yourself, hold on, it can't go on like this. The discrimination against women was pretty high. And then at some point I said to myself, "I need to think about this whole thing a bit more clearly, how I want things to be from now on." And that's when I started thinking much more strategically. What positions, what moves, what do I need to do. And I think that's one, well, one of my recommendations for other women, plan your career much more strategically. In retrospect, I think I did marketing for eight years in various roles at XY. Of course, that was much too long if you think about it from a purely career point of view. Of course, it was a lot of fun, I went all over the world. I think I did career planning twice. Well, the first time, I definitely wanted to be a managing director. That was a very clear goal. That was, I think, the first time I did career planning. And then I did career planning again once I was a managing director, which I actually was three times. In three different companies. You learn that you can actually do considerably more than you thought you could. For me, that was decisive. I was in Spain during the crisis. And they were actually being very successful there. And then, of course, I thought about how it would have been if the environment had been different. With better market conditions. What would the outcome have been? And from then on I actually thought, well, maybe I could actually aim a lot higher. At XY (company), when we were having problems with the German business. That was actually how I negotiated the thing with my boss. When I was head of marketing for Europe, I said to him: "We're having problems in Germany. You have nobody to solve it for you. If you send me, I'll solve it. And in return, you make me managing director." That's the deal we made. I was there for six months again later on. So it's important to plan your career. You need to have a planning horizon too. You must really think about where you want to be at the end of it. And go for particular positions in a fairly targeted manner. I've just become a board member, for example. That was one of the goals I set myself. I talked to people about it for about a year, in conversations and the like. So I know a lot of people who knew I'd like to do it. But then of course nothing happens. That's certainly one thing about me. When I set myself a goal, I really make it my goal. I set things in motion. I'm very single-minded.

M1.: So after I suffered that setback, the plan was, as I've just explained, not to trust to chance anymore but to have a sense of direction instead. And to know in my own mind what I expected from my professional life. Which things do I like doing, what gives me joy? I decided to try and work out where my talents lay." And in that way I realized that I knew a lot about PR and marketing. That was what I was good at. Those were my underlying qualities, even if I didn't have the formal training. And I just felt that what I really enjoyed and even found easy, those were the things that should guide my career path. I thought it all over and sorted it out in my mind.

C.: Um, this is a bit embarrassing to say, but none of it was planned. Because I started in I. (country), got promoted incredibly fast and never thought in my life that I would end up in O. (country) and suddenly responsible for sales for the entire country. But now that I'm thinking about it, I think this is a typically female thing. I never allowed myself to believe I could do it. That means my bosses saw more in me than I did myself. Which is why I often hesitated. Sorry? You want me to launch an entire country project? I don't know anything about shopping. But by the time I got offered a position on the board of directors, I had become a lot more confident and said yes. If my boss thinks I'm up to it, then I'm up to it. It doesn't matter whether I've done it before. Over time I've gained self-confidence. But I never planned anything. So, if you'd asked me, was it my goal to get onto the board of directors? No, not in a million years.

M2.: Then a new CEO arrived and he met the first and second management tiers, and then there was a re-shuffle. I got along with him really well, shared the same values, and what I'm about to say I really mean: for once in my life I dared to speak my mind, and as a result I was with XY for almost seven years and after that I was really ready, I knew everything inside out and back to front. I built up my career there. I couldn't get any higher there, but I was ready for a new challenge. Then he said: Wait a while, not yet, it's too soon, I've made a mental note of it, I'll be getting to you soon. And so I waited. I didn't go up to him every week and ask him again and again and try to negotiate for a better job. And then after about nine months, he told me that the head of HR had left, and he wanted to have a more structured, ordered, systematic approach in that department. As a lawyer I'd be able to do that, he'd been observing how I worked, I was good with people.

Personality, conflict resolution and handling competition

The German women's descriptions of themselves were categorized using BIP, Hossiep's (2003) Business-focused Inventory of Personality, in order to identify which personality traits are relevant to a management career. The strengths and characteristics described by the BIP dimensions paint the following picture for German female top managers. The women rate themselves highest in the areas of performance motivation and desire to shape processes. Performance motivation is defined here as the constant improvement of one's performance and self-measurement against high targets. Desire to shape processes covers the ability to lead business transformation processes, the will to shape business direction and the establishment of new organizations. The BIP dimension that rates second is that of teamwork and sociability, which here means willingness to interact with people and the cultivation of relationships within the professional environment. The number of female managers with BIP dimensions in the leadership motivation category are fewer in number again.

> L.: Yes, I really like influencing strategy, overall strategy, that is. Not only recruiting people, I want to have a big influence on strategy as well. Shaping is very important to me. Of course, you can help shape any area you are in. But if you want to help shape the fate of a company as a whole, then you have to be the managing director, you need to be at the top. For me that came after ten years.

> H.: So I think people have seen that I can both (pause) transformation, and also establish a new organization with people and not lose those people in the process. And I also have a very goal-oriented focus on business. Which means I know the facts and figures and I know how to build up a business and how to transform one. And it was actually pretty clear to us, even with the company we bought, that we would have to transform it into an organization. Not only because we were incorporating it into the company, but because the company was being managed by the owner. And in any case, whether we bought it or not, it needed reorganization. It had simply reached its growth limit, its sales limit, and they couldn't keep running the company the way it had been run. During my time in Japan I had already shown I could successfully manage things post-merger. That I could bring the two companies together, and then I was lucky that my boss at the time had a lot of confidence in my abilities and believed I could do it. And so I jumped into the deep end.

German women deal openly with conflict and are not afraid of it. They speak about their willingness to go on the offensive, their ability to address problems directly and to tolerate strong emotions. This applies to employees and colleagues as well as to their superiors. One or two of the women mention that they are less good at dealing with conflict. Others say they employ a calm, rational approach. Less attention is given to competitive behavior than in the other countries. German women, too, prefer fair competition. Their accounts are generally more restrained, "calmer", than those of women from other countries covered in the survey. The German women explained that they initially thought over and evolved their competitive strategies, and don't jump straight in or take things for granted when they go into such situations.

> M.2: Yes, I'm someone who looks for conflict and who deals with conflict head on. I'm definitely someone who is able to live with and address conflict both from above and from below and who's happy to debate issues. And I'm also of the opinion that conflict isn't a bad thing; I think conflict's a word with very negative connotations. I always find that discussions help you to grow, because you hear different opinions and experience different perspectives. And then mostly you make progress. I think it's always about change and improvement. From that perspective, I don't see anything wrong with conflict, and yes, I'm definitely someone who looks for conflicts, but who also likes to solve them.

> C.: Hmm. I'd say I prefer compromise, but in the end I'll always fight. I need to walk away feeling like I'm the winner. Like my husband says, no matter what we do, I always have this need to get better and better and be the best. I don't mind making compromises, but I have to feel like I didn't leave with a less than ideal solution. But I do like doing it.

> S.: I've learned to address topics very openly, even really unpleasant ones. Because I just believe that if you don't, it'll just get worse. And you can address any topic respectfully, even the most unpleasant ones. And if you're honest in a conflict situation and simply say: "It's really hard for me to talk about this, but I feel such and such," then you open completely different doors. And I take a gentle tone. It works incredibly well. And since I've been doing that, I've been even more successful.

> M1: I start from the assumption that competition is the most normal thing in the world. Even in Ludo or whatever, only one person can win. Everything's about competition. And we have to be aware of the fact that we're constantly competing. Women against women, men against men, and so on. Competition happens every day. And you have to know whether you can handle it or not. Because competition requires energy. And you have to know when it's time to sit this one out, when you don't want to play. And I think you have to accept that elbowing is a necessary part of professional life. You have to accept it and you have to be aware of it. You have to like it. And you either decide to join in, or not. But you must never assume that just because you've got a particular job, you'll always be in that job and you'll always be the boss. If you are the boss, you're on the top rung so you don't face the same level of competition. But circumstances can change and you might find yourself in second or third position again. And then you have to think: Do I want to get back on top? Or don't I? It's a decision you have to make. Do I want to compete? How much do I want to compete? And, if I do compete, well than I'll be in the thick of it, and there'll be nothing left to decide. Then it'll be what it is, and I'll just have to get on with it.

> H.: The competition is fierce. I'd say I've always felt a strong need to draw level. But even than I sometimes realized that other people are actually much better in this or that area or else their production is better, but I really am very competitive. And I think you have to be. And you also

have to fight, but you have to do it openly and honestly and transparently, and not go behind people's backs. That makes me angry. Then I get nasty, I'm not having that.

Power is seen by the majority of German women as a means to shape the future. With few exceptions, the women tackle the notion of power head on and express themselves very thoughtfully on the subject. They weigh up the advantages and disadvantages that they associate with power. In a few cases, power is spontaneously equated with abuse of power and the latter is something they oppose. When it comes down to it, however, many of the women use power in order to shape the future in a targeted manner.

> M1: Power. It varies a lot between men and women. I'd say men tend to be afraid of losing power. To them, it's everything. It's linked to competition. I got this job at the top, I'm the CEO now. So there's nowhere else to go. And for men, losing that position of power is purely about competition, it's all about fear. Women aren't like that. Women are more afraid of gaining power. Because power is still characterized by domination, force, abuse of power. I admit that I want power. I know that if I have power, I can shape. I can have an impact on things. And for me, the power to shape is the opposite of powerlessness. I don't want to be controlled, I want to be in control and have influence. And that's something I've proven I can do. But a lot of women are afraid of power. They don't want to exercise power in a masculine way and manipulate or use or belittle others. I think men and women have a different understanding of what power is. And what gives me power? Men need prestige more than women do. I think that they need these, I was about to say signatures, that's not what I mean, what's the word? They need to have a crown, what do you say for that? Men need power, the big car, the big office, and so on. But women don't even ask whether they're going to get a big car or a big office. Women just say: What will my task be, what can I achieve, who will be on my team? Women are after purpose rather than prestige. Women and men just do define and understand power differently.

> H.: So in my own team, in my own surroundings, power isn't that big an issue for me. I do have to radiate it and have it, because I have to make the decisions. People have to believe, when I've made a decision, that the decision counts. That's how you wield power. But I find all these peer-to-peer workshops we have so funny. OK, well, let's play-act it then. I can do that too. I like doing it.

> E.: Well, for me it has multiple facets. One is that power comes from doing. I think you just have to get on and do things from time to time and then something will come out of it. And that can be fun too. Then of course there's this power that gets attributed to people when they have a title. My management title gives me the power to hire and fire. But I think that's really rather simplistic, because in reality being a manager is all about shaping. And finding the necessary freedom and scope to implement things. And finding a means to express yourself. The same way that artists do. For me, artists have power. Because they are completely autonomous and find ways of expressing themselves and I find that very powerful. Even though they don't have any power attributed to them. But they can influence others a huge amount through their pictures or films or plays or whatever. And I find that extraordinary. And then there are things where it's simply a matter of trying them out and seeing whether or not something powerful can emerge from them.

> K.: I have a problem with the word "power". It's like in McClelland's research. I'm more concerned with achievement and affiliations and less with power. But I have to use power in

order to be able to shape. A lot of women in my network say, quite openly, "I love power, I want it." And that's ok too.

The German female executives' leadership style

The leadership style of the German women may be described as democratic and team-oriented. They aspire to be role models, to be approachable, to support employees in their careers and to make decisions as part of a team. The idea of the "mother figure" is cited several times. The descriptions suggest that they subscribe to a transformational style of leadership. The women set an example through hard work and in this way motivate employees to follow them. In addition, great importance is attached to supporting others. Unlike women in other countries, they do not explicitly mention authoritarian leadership, or if they do, they talk about it in a "discreet" way. But when decisions are needed, German women accordingly make them. They also make decisions on the optimal composition of their teams and, if necessary, on the replacement of employees. Executive coaching is cited by many as a helpful tool for achieving success which has paid off especially well in the development of their own leadership style. Coaching as an aid to personal development is cited more frequently by the German women than by any other country group. This suggests a considered approach to their own strengths and weaknesses, and a desire to grow beyond their own personal limits.

> M2.: I had endless leadership coaching between the ages of 30 and 40, on what you can do and how. These days I would sum it up by saying, you shouldn't spend too much time on your weak points, instead you should build on the good. If I know exactly what my good points are and what my bad ones are, so as I can eradicate the bad ones, that leaves only so much energy and it's just not worth the last twenty percent. So I prefer to improve on the positive eighty percent. I try to be a role model, I'm not the sort of boss who just delegates. I get involved. I'm not distant, I'm approachable. I always have an open door. Sometimes too much for my own good, because it takes a lot out of you, but I'm a bit like a mother duck waddling on in front and the ducklings following on behind, or something like that. I think it's nice when people grow and of course then they can take more of the work off my hands, but I can see that they don't earn what I do, so I'm always toughest on myself. I let them go home to their families and then I do the rest myself in the evening, rather than the other way around. But they'll walk through fire for me too. So I set an example, and I think that because I'm naturally energetic I often give very direct feedback. I'm either delighted and thank them about ten times and they feel good because of that. Or I think Wow, that turned out great and that's genuinely what I think, but if something really goes badly or not very well, I say that just as directly, then I say it can't go on like this, we're never going to do that again, we got that wrong, we're going to have to do it differently in future. And when I have to say for the third time that things have to be different from now on, we've had this happen three times, I expect more commitment or a more proactive approach, you let that slip out of your hands, that's not acceptable. I stay calm, I think, but I make myself extremely clear. I do that when things go well and I do it when they go badly.
>
> H.: I'm very team-oriented, I'm not a big fan of hierarchies, even though I think we need them to be able to make decisions, but in my daily work it's important to me for us to work as a team. I

also know when I need to make decisions. And I put a lot of trust in people. But when I notice that things are getting critical, I get very involved, which is surprises people who are used to having a lot of freedom.

M1: My leadership style is to help others grow, to let people develop. To really be empathic and find out what makes people tick, what motivates a particular person. What is that individual's motivation? Everybody in a team has different motivating factors, has a different underlying philosophy, and so on. So when I've grasped what that person's personal driver is. What he needs. You can talk about it with him in a normal way, you don't have to look into a crystal ball. But I can try to work that out with them quite openly and tell them what I'd like. And then you have to work out how you can achieve that together. I've had some people who I've helped develop their way out of working for me and into a different job. Because they were at a dead end. They didn't even realize it themselves. I had the courage to say, "I recommend you take such and such a step. But you won't be able to do that here. Maybe look at moving to a different company. I'll do anything I can to support you. It's not about 'moving away', it's about 'moving on and up'. It's your decision: If you want to move on, I'm right behind you. We'll find the right solution. But if you say, 'No, I like this job. This is where I want to stay. It's good here', that's fine too." But sometimes you really have to wake people up a bit and show them that there are wider horizons. Get them to start thinking about it. XY (company) has one disadvantage. Simply put, it's the very thing I was looking for myself: it's safe. Nothing catastrophic is going to happen to you here, you're not suddenly going to be gone and in a financial hole. The hole always gets plugged somehow or other. Change does happen here. But XY is so solid as a company and that makes you a bit lazy. So you end up thinking, "Why should I leave my comfort zone? I've got it good here." That's why our turnover is so low. Everyone feels comfortable here. But it's not necessarily what moves a company forward. So you always have to shake your employees up a bit and see if you can get them out of their comfort zone in some way.

M2: Well, I'd say I'm definitely an accessible type of boss. I'm a friendly leader, I'm certainly not the hierarchical type of boss. But despite that I have gained a lot of respect from my team. I got the best feedback from my employees of anyone at XY.

Career-enhancing factors for women in German management

The majority of the German women in the study are married and, unlike in many of the other country groups, they mostly have children. Their husbands take second place for them after their careers. German female top managers are using networks more and more often and want to make even more targeted use of them. Most German female top managers regularly use executive coaching.

Spouses of German women in top management positions are supportive, ideal partners

M1.: "He looks at me with shining eyes and is happy about my successes. He's the best husband anyone could wish for."

L.: "I have a really great husband. He's always got my back."

Eighty percent of the German interviewees are married, one interviewee lives with a female partner and the rest are single. All of the women's partners see their own careers as secondary to those of the interviewees. The majority of partners have a university degree. Only a small proportion have not studied. The decision to give priority to the woman's career was made by the couples with an eye to their likely future earnings and career opportunities. The decision to scale down the spouse's career was triggered by one of two circumstances: first, the birth of a child, and second, a posting abroad or the acceptance of a job abroad. The women describe their partners in very positive terms. The interviewees emphasize in their accounts how much they appreciate the fact that their partners treat their careers as a second priority or have put their careers on hold and how much their partner has given up for them. This is mentioned numerous times and shows the extent to which partners' sacrifices are valued. Women managers around the world are consistent in this respect. Career women, unlike career men – who predominantly, and without considering the matter, live life according to traditional roles – regularly express the fact that they appreciate their partners. They know that their careers would have been difficult without their partners involvement. In addition, they appreciate not only the practical help, but above all the emotional support they receive from their partners.

> M1.: He's my safety valve, to all intents and purposes. He calls me at six every evening and pulls the plug and says, it's time to stop work now and go for a walk. And at the weekend we're going to do such and such and you're not going to prepare that lecture, you can forget it.

In the German group, for most of the couples the traditional roles are reversed. The women's partners take on the traditional female role in the family and forego a career in the conventional sense. The spouses adapt their professional activities to their partner's careers or else put them second. The spouses' lives tend to consist of multiple stints of self-employment due to changes of location, job changes without any prospect of promotion, part-time work or a doctorate coupled with childcare responsibilities. The majority of the women describe the role allocation as successful and positive for both partners and for the whole family. Statements such as *"My husband isn't career-oriented, he's reduced his working hours to 35"*, characterize, from the women's perspective, a clear decision on the part of their partners to take on a supporting role. In addition to the highly positive accounts of these arrangements, however, some disadvantages are also mentioned. Some of the women report that their partners are no longer able to pursue a conventional career due to the many career breaks and job changes, even once the children are older. Or that periods of self-employment that had only just begun had to be broken off again because of the need to change location with the interviewee's job. It can be assumed that in some cases this scenario causes conflict between partners. What is certain is that some of the women interviewed have a guilty conscience with regards to their partner.

Despite good career development, over the long term, some of the women do not find it easy to be the main breadwinner. The comments about this are mixed. On the one hand, they feel the pressure, and on the other hand, this same pressure is a good incentive to improve how they perform when negotiating pay increases. Sometimes the women report that they have not properly discussed with their partner the way in which the couples' careers are carved up, but that instead, the distribution of roles just came about at a certain point in the past. Some of the women regret the fact that their husbands have missed the boat in career terms. These narratives describe the women's ambivalence to their success as business executives and their deeply rooted notions about traditional roles.

> H.: Well, my husband and I found a good balance right from the beginning. It was clear from the outset that we would both work and that we both enjoyed our professions and so we would need to divide up the household duties evenly. And we managed to do that really well until we went to T. (country) because at that point the balance between him and me shifted. Because I had this assignment in T., which was really demanding, he took over a lot more of the work around the home, which was okay, because the boys were six and nine by then and at a stage when it was fantastic for them to have their father around.

> B.: Well, my husband worked for XY for a long time. They're a multinational. So you can do your job out of lots of different locations. We talked about it at one point and he sort of decided that my career was the better one or at least, the easier one. Or the more lucrative one. (Laughter.) It's fair to say that we put his career on hold. And in any case, he was with a company where he could work in different countries. For example, when we were in Spain, officially he was employed in England. He just negotiated with his boss to let him work from Spain. We went back to England because around that time XY decided that all employees had to return home. To their offices. And there we were in Spain. It wouldn't have worked for him. The timing was perfect. So we decided to go back to England. So that he could start turning up at the office again. And I got my next job.

> S.: So in a way the financial burden fell to me when we decided that I was going to be the main breadwinner. And in some respects that really did put a strain on me and put me under pressure, but I'm an optimistic, forward-looking person by nature, and so it motivated me to be financially successful and to be rewarded fairly for the work I do. And especially when I started a family and had children and was financially responsible not only for myself but for several people, that was really the point at which I gave a lot more thought to where I stood in terms of salary and what the other people I worked with were earning, and whether I was getting paid a fair amount. So that was one of my motivations to grow and be a bit more demanding in my dealings with my bosses. And when I moved to XY, I made sure that I didn't sell myself short, I got a big salary uplift.

Mentoring and coaching is essential for German female executives to rise

Mentoring is an important element for German women over the course of their careers. There are many accounts demonstrating this. A distinction may be made between whether the mentor relationship originated in a company training program or whether it developed independent of formal programs. Informal mentoring, not organized by the company, is characterized as being substantially more career-enhancing. Conventional mentoring intermingles with sponsoring, in which the mentor and sponsor are one and the same person; someone who actively contributes to the mentee's career planning. It is fair to say that each of the women interviewed has had several mentors during her career. Half of the women had female mentors who were also their bosses and who occupied the highest position in the company. These women deliberately chose other women as their mentors, but two of the women had male board members as mentors. Around 70 percent of all the women have taken part in formal company mentoring programs. The descriptions of their experiences are mixed, from very positive to rather subdued. A variety of mentors, who are described as being more like advisors, play an important role in the women's careers. Mentoring relationships in which mentees move with their mentors when they change companies do not exist in the German group. Nor is there any mention of mutually beneficial mentoring relationships in which the mentor also profits to a significant extent, in business terms, from the relationship with the mentee. Only one woman remarks that the mentor also needs to see an advantage in the relationship and that it was therefore not always easy to establish a relationship with a mentor. The relationships are characterized by the advising of the mentee by the more experienced person or else by the mentor encouraging her to take the next step up the career ladder.

When asked about other people who have supported them on their career paths, German women name headhunters and frequently also executive coaches, with whom they discuss challenges and work out possible solutions. Women who have held several positions abroad but had no mentor describe how they deliberately hired a professional coach to support them in their progress. Executive coaching is cited by German women as the most common means of obtaining support in career matters and in the development of their leadership skills. In this respect, German women are extremely pro-active and specifically search out the support they need from a professional coach.

> M1.: That was the first time in my life that someone believed in me, trusted me and did everything they could to help me develop. He came up with this narrative for me: "She doesn't have a degree, but she can do it and wants to do it," to act as a personal motivator to help me bridge that gap and to help me prove to myself again and again that I could do it. That, I think, is one of the key things. Not only for me, but I notice it in a lot of other women and also in the mentees I work with, who need precisely that: to be taken by the hand and led and to be told yet again: "You can do this."

> S.: Well, mentoring definitely helps. You do have to be careful though, especially in companies who try to force mentoring on you. I've experienced one case where I was assigned a mentor, that was at XY, which was a complete flop because the chemistry didn't work at all. So from my point of view, the most useful thing is when mentoring develops naturally out of a relationship and you have a lot of contact with that person and you get on well, and a mentoring relationship just develops out of it. In my opinion, the best way is when it's never directly referred to as mentoring, but where you just do it. The relationship I have with our CFO, for example, I don't know if I would call her a mentor or a sponsor, in any case I have the sort of relationship with her where I know I can turn to her about all sorts of issues whenever I feel I have need of a spar-

ring partner, and I know there's someone there who's willing to listen to me and who can count on me and who'll stand up for me when the going gets tough.

M3.: Pretty early on, I'd say. I think I got noticed by one or two really good, much older managers and teachers, and they helped me without me really realizing it at the time. For example, Professor XY, we had this visiting professor from America. An older man. He liked to spend the whole summer in Germany, but because he was a bit bored, he started asking students, including me, if they would drive him around M. and he would invite them to dinner in return. I liked doing it but some of the others would never have wanted to spend their weekends like that. Because I had so much respect for him... And, at the time I had no idea that he was really well-known in the US and had written several laws there. I loved having these intellectual conversations with him. It was like talking to my grandma about the Second World War or something. I used to like listening to her when I was a kid. I spent the summer talking to him about all the old chestnuts (anecdotes), and then when I was in the US, he invited me to New York and always – I only really understood this afterwards – organized really interesting things for me to do, where I met a lot of interesting people, like this German Supreme Court judge for example, and other illustrious people from the US. And that was such a wonderful gift and it just grew naturally out of the interesting conversations we had. He was an old man who loved supporting young people and he didn't have any offspring of his own. But I didn't even realize it was anything to do with that when I first met him and had my first meals with him. That wasn't the point of the thing. But in retrospect, he has influenced my life a lot, and I still think of him with gratitude. He opened a lot of doors for me in the US, right up to the embassy, and that meant that I could go back there whenever I wanted to. He got a lot of happiness out of opening doors for people. But he always said, "I can open the door but only you can go through. That sums it up quite well. You'll find mentors, but it's never because you've though, "I'm going to find a mentor." But if you're an intelligent young professional, you tend to attract people who want to help launch careers. Coming together naturally is so much more interesting than when it's in some program that this is your mentor and you're going to have lunch with them.

B.: Unfortunately, I don't personally have a mentor who helps me take this or that step. I have tried to organize a mentor once or twice. I find it really difficult. Because you also need to find someone who has an interest in you for some reason. There have been bosses who've helped me. Bosses want you to have a successful career. They can open your eyes to things or help you out. That's definitely true. But I see this is as being more like a sponsor in the conventional sense, not a mentor. I think these days there are quite a few people who offer mentoring. So you can get coaching from first-rate, experienced coaches. For me what has worked best is finding someone to help me with specific situations. I just sought advice and approached people who could help me with that specific situation. But I don't have a long-term mentor of any kind at the moment.

So.: When I was about to change company, after 18 years with XY, I wasn't used to having to negotiate salaries. And so I called three different people. Two of them were former bosses and one of them was a colleague who had switched companies. All three of them asked me completely different questions. One of them asked me mainly about what I wanted and in the end that helped me make the right decision. Another asked me really critical questions about the company and the position. And the third one gave me some extremely practical tips and probably helped me squeeze an extra 30,000 Euros a year out of the company.

Sa.: Not long before I went on maternity leave, we got this new CFO, a very successful woman. And I wasn't aware of this at the time, but I'm pretty sure now that I received a promotion at that time because this woman was on the board and pushed for me to get it. What I'm trying to say is that it makes an incredible difference whether there are women on the senior management team or not. Now that I'm in a position to have such a role myself, to an extent, I in turn promote and bring other women on. She was the first woman who was above me really and who could exert considerable influence in favor of women. I don't know if I'd ever have become a boss if she hadn't joined the company. Even if my boss thought I was good and so on, whether he would have actually taken the step of promoting me, I don't know.

B: Well, I mean, that's really tough. I mean, it's really not easy. In theory I think it really helped for me to work out what I wanted to achieve in my next move. That's what made me switch from XY to YZ back then and then become the head of Europe. The first thing I always say to myself is, "What experience do I still need to get?" In that case, for example, it was the fact that I had never run a production process before. At that point, I spoke to various personnel consultants that I use as a career advisors. I have two or three personnel consultants I really trust. Who I have discussions with about things like what is the normal career path, what would be most exciting and what would suit me. So my recommendation to women would be to find yourself a couple of people who can hold up a mirror, because that's what they do all day long: they bring companies and people together.

German female executives are learning networkers

In Germany, as in many other parts of the world, the first thing that women mention when talking about networking is men's associations and informal male networks. Men in Germany have a tradition of networks and connections that they use to support each other over the long term and in which private and professional interests are interwoven. These include student fraternities. The women also mention well-known all-male clubs where membership is by invitation only. Networks in Germany are often theme-based and associations and male student fraternities, especially, have a long tradition. Men – and increasingly also women – belong to clubs such as the golf club or Rotary or else the regional Marketing Club.

The subject of networks has only in recent years begun to play a greater role in women's thinking. The women in the survey are all networkers. Sixty percent of the women interviewed belong to a particular, well-known German network for women in leading management positions. They talk about the trends in professional networking that they see occurring and report that for them, the first tangible results of networking have begun to make themselves felt. Networking among women is still relatively new. In contrast to men, women have been slow to discover how to use networks effectively and how to have mutual solidarity. While men in Germany traditionally help each other to advance up the career ladder and secure positions for each other, this is still a new experience for women. Until now, women have seen networks as more of an extended contact database, but without using them in a targeted way for career advancement. Women enjoy sharing experiences, learning together and exchanging views regarding challenges. German women are still ambivalent about whether and to what extent one ought to use one's network to achieve career goals. This indicates that most of them are still learning how to use their networks in a targeted fashion for career advancement, as well as how to give back.

Two conditions need to be in place to enable women to use networks to support each other in their careers more than they do currently. First, they need to be in a position of power that allows them to appoint staff. Second, they need to be able to consciously give preference to talented women when filling positions. Only where women have the power to appoint candidates to positions can they draw on women from their networks. Traditionally, women in Germany have not been taught professional solidarity. In an environment that often discriminates against women, women's energies are more likely to be channeled into the struggle to make progress in a male-dominated world. The idea of give and take in relation to one's career has not yet been learned. There is no such thing as a set of established rules for the use of professional women's networks and what one should put into them. There is also a fear of disappointment, in case a woman network member breaks the rules in a game she has not yet learned how to play and where she takes out more than she puts in. Moreover, the fear of being considered a token or "quota" woman and fear of promoting a "quota woman" limits the ability of women to create truly strong networks. Some of the women report that they recognized the importance of effective networks during executive coaching sessions and that their coach has helped them develop strategies for extending their network in a meaningful way. Many women come to realize that they can "practice networking" and quickly realize the benefits of networking for career development. The interviewees are already all active networkers, consciously support other women and actively think about the advantages of having strong networks. They have already learnt the art of networking.

> M.: I think I've internalized it: networking, approaching people, building relationships. And I think that's a great strength I have. I have a friend who said to me last week, "I put so much in but I get nothing back." I put a lot in too, but I get so much back every day. I'm always amazed at the number of gifts I get. I feel so, well, how shall I put it? So happy, so blessed. I've never thought of it that way before. To be honest, I give because I like giving. Not because I'm hoping to get something out of it or because I expect anything. Maybe that's just how I'm made. I just reach out to people and find a source of inspiration in them. Everyone brings something or other to the table that I can't. And I have something to contribute too. It's like ping-pong. I put something in, I get something out, and so it goes on.

> L.: Very important, very, very important and on the subject of women. It's really important for women to do much more networking among themselves. It is starting to bear fruit, very, very slowly. But it's extremely important, because men have been doing it for decades. And when jobs become available, they just call each other. There are a lot of jobs where people are hired privately because they just know each other. Deal. And women can do the same. It all starts like I said. But we need to do it much more often, it's extremely important. It's equally as important as one's performance.

> J.: I think I'm actually a very good networker. I know how to connect with people, with different kinds of people. Not just people who are culturally different, but also people with different personalities. And that's really helped me. But I have to say that I only starting using it to my advantage after I had had one particularly good mentoring, or more of a coaching session, with a role model, a great manager, a woman who said: "Networking is important, but also getting something out of the network." And I've literally been networking for years now. I'm very

good at it. But I've always made sure that I find people who go together well when I've got some cool project on, or I've somehow found a way to bring people together. But I never used to get anything out of the network myself. After I did do it for the first time, all of a sudden my career took off really fast. And I'm noticing it at the moment too, I'm getting a lot more support and just yesterday I had a really great conversation with one of our board members who encouraged me and motivated me to continue pursuing the path I'm on. And that's something I didn't do before, harvesting benefits from my network. I always just thought that you had to contribute to it. I think it's a huge support and encouragement in a career.

M3.: For me it's the same as these women who get promoted, artificially projected through the glass ceiling. In my life the right people have always been there at the right time. This unnatural sort of networking, based on the idea, today I'm networking and that's why I'm going to this event or that and I've got this or that strategy and now I need to get to know such and such a person, that's not my thing at all. I go by gut feeling. But networking in the sense of attending events and lectures and finding people who I really like talking to and who really have something to offer, without always having my career in the back of my mind, and staying in touch with people, that I really love. I'd like to be able to say that Generation CEO has really helped me, but it's getting bigger and bigger and more and more anonymous. I'm a person who likes to connect with people and I don't like to see my network as some sort of institution. Either we click and I like meeting up with a person and we talk about more than just how we might be able to help each other, but I also like people to go jogging with or something, or just people to meet up privately with. It has to come naturally, it has to just flow. Instead of thinking, Wow, this woman is such and such and so I'll get out my business card. That wouldn't be me at all and I don't like it when other people do it, either.

S.: I lived outside Germany for fifteen years. When you come back to Germany after such a long time and become Chief Human Resources Officer, no one believes you when you say you don't really know anyone here. My whole working life, really. I went straight to I. after graduating. So I didn't have any sort of network here in Germany. I don't remember exactly who it was, whether it was Mr. XY, in any case, one of the first consultants who came here one day wanting to tell me about some system or other. And I asked him how it was here in Germany? If he were in my position, which network would he join? And I don't remember exactly who suggested it to me, but I sent an e-mail to XY and said, I heard about your network and I'd like to join. I got an e-mail back saying, Come and see me. And so then I had this long interview with him. I was thinking to myself, what's going on here? This particular network wasn't actually about meeting other women, it was about getting to know other HR people and other business people generally. But it was a really good decision. It's a really great network. And now I meet regularly meet up with a few of the XY members. It's extremely helpful.

B.: Yeah, I guess that's probably why it took me so long to get started. (Laughter.) I don't think I really had a role model. As you can see, that's what's occupying my thoughts at the moment. What did help, as I said, was that much later on someone gave me a good tip. As you know, I'm a member of Generation CEO, and of course you meet a lot of other women there. It's a brilliant network for getting advice and support and ideas and suggestions. There aren't that many role models for us to look to, women who've walked this road before. There are a few, and I really want to sing their praises again and again. Every woman who's built herself a career in Germany. But I think it was really helpful to be accepted into this network. And just to see other women in positions of huge responsibility. To swap ideas with them. About how to deal with difficult jobs and situations. It's a really great network for practical advice and assistance.

The appearance factor: Ranging from situationally androgynous to subtly feminine

The most prominent example of how external appearance affects a woman's image is certainly the German chancellor, who at a certain point and after much criticism and initial ridicule, consciously remodeled her appearance. The image she created as the "mother of the nation" says a great deal about the core values that contribute to the image of the successful German female executive. The accounts that the German women give as to the effects of external appearance are limited and occupy considerably less space than in the French and Russian interviews. Many of the women state that in the course of their careers they have consciously focused on their outward appearance and have sought advice on the right choice of clothes and hairstyle. The German women think that beauty can be an advantage in a career, but only if it is paired with competence and knowledge as to how to co-opt men in the pursuit of professional goals without simultaneously encountering problems. The most important elements here are charisma and presence. The women emphasize their femininity through clothing as circumstances dictate, and without crossing the line into the private domain. While the French and Russian career women repeatedly mention aiming for a decidedly feminine appearance and striving for a female business identity, the German women's responses do not suggest that external appearance is an issue for them. As long as it is mainly men who are making the decisions about whether to promote women, it seems that German women will continue to take a pragmatic approach. They have no issue with cultivating what might be termed a rather androgynous business style, and they vary their style according to circumstance. They mention masculine stereotypes with regards to a woman's appearance; for example that very feminine women with rather high voices tend not to be suitable for top management. Furthermore, they report discrimination against full-figured women. And women with a more masculine appearance are frowned upon as being too aggressive. They conclude that it is not possible to please men, who up until now have been the ones making the majority of the decisions about promotions. The German female executives in the study consciously think about their appearance, but it is not a core aspect of their identity as managers. They cultivate a business style but now and then add a little color or a subtly feminine touch when they want to stand out. In this way, they use their appearance to their advantage, to enable them to stand out from the colorless mass of male executives. However, they do not use the company as a showcase for their femininity; instead, a business look is adopted. Only once, when discussing outward appearances, does the issue of competition among women come up.

> E.: You have a definite advantage when you go somewhere. If I'm going to a conference, I put on a red jacket. That way, if you're sitting in the audience and you want to say something, you always get chosen. If you're just a man in a dark suit, you don't stand out and you don't get asked. But the women, people remember.

B.: Well, let's put it this way. You have to learn to live with what God's given you. If you're attractive, you have advantages and disadvantages. If you're attractive, you have the advantage of hearing colleagues say they like inviting you round. It's a feast for the eyes when she's in the room. Of course, you have to be able to handle that. To make sure that people don't overlook the fact that you're productive as well and bring something to the table. I think that's especially difficult when you're younger. That's when being attractive becomes a nuisance. On the other hand, it can open doors for you. I think it's just a question of how you handle it. Whether you're able to use it to your advantage in some way or other. And if you are attractive, congratulations. That's great. You'll have the men interested in you of course. You just have to make sure you redirect it in the right way, that it's not misplaced interest. Don't flirt too much. Because it can quickly get dangerous. You don't want to be in a situation where you have to slam the door in someone's face and say: "Keep your hands to yourself!" But I'm sure in some situations it can open doors for you.

H.: I think you have to find a good balance between staying feminine and looking business-like. Short skirts and plunging necklines are counterproductive, to put it bluntly. Which isn't to say that it can't be an advantage in some situations, but in moderation, of course. For example, when I'm going to be having a really important conversation, I'll always put on a skirt, because I'll score extra points for being womanly.

M1.: Here's an example: two female managers, same job, very high level, just below the board of directors, having a conversation with, let's say, a board member. And this board member says to me: We should choose Ms. A, she comes across completely differently. When she walks in, have a look at what they look like. One of them is a size 48, maybe, and the other one a size 38, small, blonde, petite. The other one's dark-haired and mommyish. And he was really trying to tell me that she didn't know how to do her job. Well, that's an exaggeration. But he was judging women on whether they're attractive or not. From his own personal perspective. And he was using that as a criterion. But they would never say it out loud or in front of a group.

M3.: And if you're too good-looking, you might have other problems. You might get competition from other women. Well, that's what I assume would happen. It's not a statement of fact.

H.: Well, I think that you have to be very clear about that. You have to radiate an aura of competence, you can't look insecure. I have to be able to ask things without worrying about whether it's a stupid question I'm about to ask. I have to have a certain self-confidence and I also have to radiate it, I have to be thinking: I'm going to go into that room and people are going to notice me. And if nobody notices me, then I need to have a think about what I'm going to change so that they do notice me.

The advantages of being a woman

For German women in top management positions, every difficult situation presents an opportunity. They are aware of their strengths in what continue to be difficult conditions for senior female managers in Germany; communicating with employees and finding solutions that benefit many members of staff at once. They are also turning their apparent disadvantages into advantages and skillfully using their unusual status.

M1.: I really do believe that some skills are a bit more pronounced in women than in men. In the book, I call them "The three new C's", not "Kinder, Küche, Kirche"("children, kitchen, church") but "consensus, communication and-" ...what was the third one? "...cooperation." I think those are three strengths that women are more likely to have. That doesn't mean that men don't have them. But women are more likely to be good at them, they are more likely to say "We need to find a consensus so that we can all move forward. We need to communicate so that the customer understands why we're making this product. And it's not about making money, it's about us delivering something that will benefit customers. And what is the benefit to the customer? Trying to get that across. What did we say again? Cooperation and consensus. Exactly.

B: There's just one more thing I wanted to say. Even as a woman, I think many people underestimate the fact that you do also have huge advantages. Nobody wants to admit that. As a woman, I think you have three or four advantages. They're just so cool. The first thing is, everyone tells you everything. I can't tell you how many male executives have told me things they'd never tell another man. So that means you get hold of information no one else does. That's the first thing. Second thing is, you're not perceived as being in competition with men. By the time they suddenly realize you're in charge, it's too late. Men completely underestimate women as competitors. It doesn't enter their heads. You're not even on their radar. Until you're suddenly sitting up there in the top job. That's definitely another advantage. The third, of course, is being a woman. If you know how to use it. Men often don't know how to treat you. That makes a lot of men insecure. Especially when anything needs negotiating. I'll never forget negotiating with my Spanish distributor... The negotiations were really tough. At one point, he said these were the first negotiations he'd had where people weren't yelling at each other. Because he couldn't yell at a woman. (Laughter.) So you do have advantages. You must never underestimate that. You also have the advantage that you can more easily walk up to a guy and ask for help.

German women executives – inhibiting career factors

Women in Germany still have to overcome a variety of hurdles if they want to move up to senior management. The glass ceiling still exists, regardless of whether it was put there by men or is only in women's minds. Socio-cultural stereotypes, such as that of the "unnatural mother" (*"Rabenmutter"*), persist to this day and present women with the challenge of developing their own, separate, female success stories. Although female role models do exist, they are still all too rare.

German women and the glass ceiling

What do German female managers think about the much-discussed phenomenon of the glass ceiling? The concept of the "glass ceiling" seeks to provide an answer to the question as to why, although women are represented worldwide in lower and middle management, only a few manage to climb to the very top levels. An invisible ceiling which is difficult to penetrate is offered as an explanation of the fact that women's paths are blocked, but not those of men. According to this view, the glass ceiling is one of the reasons that women are excluded from the circles of power. Expectations regarding stereotypical behavior, informal organizational structures, affiliations, networks and informal rites are further aspects of the glass ceiling that have been examined by a number of authors. According to studies by the American author Eagly (2007), for example, the existence of a glass ceiling is attested by around 92 percent of US female managers.

Without exception, the German women in this study, too, regard the existence of a glass ceiling as indisputable. They describe the evidence they see of it in their own companies. Due to outside pressures, however, there have recently been efforts made to attract more women to executive levels and, for example, to specifically promote women to HR or legal management positions. There are isolated comments in the accounts to the effect that in Germany in particular, the glass ceiling is deeply rooted in women's minds and that they do not have the self-confidence to assume top positions. Part of the problem is that German women accept the current situation and do not actively aspire to top jobs. Eagly (2007) discusses women's allusions to what they see as a "labyrinth" and that this demonstrates why it is still difficult for them to understand the rules of the game and to navigate their way through. Unlike men, women have to slip through a hole in the career labyrinth when no one is looking. The obstacles within the career labyrinth are judged to be on the whole greater for women than for men. The foremost reasons given for this are the traditional attitudes to motherhood. One approach to dealing with the career labyrinth and glass ceiling is to move to organizations where the opportunities for women are better. This in turn also indicates that where a glass ceiling exists, German women feel that attempting to penetrate it is virtually impossible. The corollary for corporate management is that at times when executives are scarce, suitably-qualified women can only be retained if there is transparency with regard to advancement opportunities for female managers and if equal opportunities are in place.

> M1.: You probably already know this example. I think the... Philharmonic or the Vienna, I don't know exactly which, everyone wears sneakers to auditions. So you can't see whether it's a woman or a man and there's a curtain in front of them, then they play and then people say who was best. And since they've been doing that there have been considerably more women in the orchestra than before. Because of the gender-neutrality. It's a shame you can't do that for every job. At least not as easily as you can with an orchestra. But we women don't get the chance to be considered in a gender-neutral way and to only be judged on merit.

> B.: Yes. I think it exists. I can see it in my company. At our level, and even at the lowest management level, we have almost a 50:50 male to female ratio. But at the next level up, general manager, we are always wondering why our fantastic female sales managers and team leaders don't move up to the next level. There's a lack of trust surrounding women because, Oh, she'll get married, then she'll probably start having kids, then she'll probably want to stay at home. So people make a lot of assumptions about what a woman will or won't do or whatever. I hear it said quite often: Well, who knows what'll happen afterwards. At the moment you say you want a career, but once you've had your baby, you might change your mind. So people are always waiting to see what happens afterwards. So I think this glass ceiling is really more about the fact that people don't trust a woman to want to do it.

H: I think they do exist. I guess the easiest way to break through them is to move company. And I'm genuinely convinced that quotas have the power to eventually dismantle the glass ceiling. We can eliminate it, we just have to focus all our attention on doing so. But I'm firmly convinced that glass ceilings still very much exist not only in large, traditional companies but also in medium-sized ones. But there's no malicious intent. Well, I don't want to allege malice in all cases, anyway. This caring attitude that some women display is often the reason why the ceiling exists. If you run up again it, you should leave the company as soon as possible, because otherwise it's yourself you're harming. I'd like it if we could get agreement on quotas at management level. Because I do believe that there are jobs where we just do have difficulty finding enough women, even when they are available. But I think we'll soon be in a position to list all the jobs we want to apply a quota to. But I wouldn't want to say: "We need a quota for every role."

Discrimination from male superiors and colleges

The German female executives report having had many experiences of discrimination. These are specifically directed by men against women and can be divided into the following categories: Discrimination on the grounds of pregnancy or potential pregnancy, discrimination on the grounds of female managerial competence, and general discrimination in the form of demeaning attitudes. Discrimination occurs not only in one-to-one conversations, but also in the presence of others. If the discrimination is carried out by someone with the power to make decisions about the woman's career, German women relatively quickly decide to change companies in order to be able to achieve their goals. One of the women, after several instances of discrimination, went so far as to permanently move her career abroad.

> M1.: If I haven't already, I can give you another example from the 2015 Annual General Meeting. A man goes up to the lectern, a shareholder, and says: "Women lack leadership skills and have no place in management. I'm sitting there thinking, "Are we on Candid Camera?" But no. The audience claps. There we are, three of us female board members sitting there on the podium, we're there to render account. And there's applause in the room because women have no leadership skills. I think, "Mr. XY, as chairman of the board, say something." But no, he say nothing. We went up to him afterwards and said, "Hello, Mr. XY. Why didn't you say anything just now?" And he says, "He didn't ask anything." Then a female colleague asked him: "If he had said, 'Foreigners don't have leadership qualities", would you have still said nothing?" Then he says: "Yes, I would, I would have said something then." We said: "Do you realize what you're doing? What this means is, there isn't a lobby for protecting women. But there's a lobby for protecting foreigners." To tell you the truth, I also thought, "The guy was right." And afterwards I thought to myself, "If he'd raised the matter, there would've been uproar."

> L.: Just talking about it, just asking the question is a sign that it exists. There's no other country in the world where people ask whether you have children. That's discrimination.

> B.: I can tell you a lot of stories. And I'm sure a lot of other women could too. So anyway, when I was at XY (company). The discrimination was huge. One person told me about an appraisal interview were the other person made remarks like "Your performance fluctuates, like when you have your period for example." Isn't that awful? And a colleague of mine was told: "You're capable of doing the job, but I only want a man on it." That was discrimination in its purest and most outspoken form. When I got married, I told no one. Because then everyone would have im-

mediately thought I was going to have children and that would have been my career over. But it didn't only happen at XY. It happened at YZ too. I was sitting with my boss. That was after I had quit college. He told me that evening that women don't really want careers. They just want to go on nice foreign trips. That was the conversation. And women who have careers, they're all harridans. Time and again you come up against these really powerful prejudices and even verbal put-downs. And later on, when I was managing director in Spain, I thought about returning to Germany. I had two or three job interviews in Germany, but they were all pretty brutal. (Laughter.)

Culture shapes women's careers: The "Bad moms" image

All over the world it is observed that women in higher management positions are more likely to remain single and childless because of the prospect of the double burden of work and family. In a 2012 study by Henn, it was found that 20 percent of all German female managers were single and 71 percent of the women surveyed were childless. In the present survey, the majority of German female top managers have between one and three children and only two are childless. When it comes to motherhood, then, this group deviates from the figures mentioned here.

There has been extensive research into the effects of motherhood on women's careers. The term "motherhood penalty" refers to discrimination against women with children, who often earn less than women with no children. The main issues are career breaks and other absences, loss of salary and unplanned career changes. Absences due to maternity leave have a particularly severe impact. In one study, 70 percent of the women surveyed stated that maternity leave had damaged their careers, and 30 percent of the women in the same study stated that, as a result, they had not taken their entire maternity leave allocation.

This portion of the interviews with German women managers contains a great many accounts. All the women interviewed here agree that pursuing a career when you have children is difficult for women in Germany. This only applies to women and not to men, for whom a family has a positive effect on their image as an executive. It is assumed that children will prevent a woman from fulfilling her managerial responsibilities, whereas a male executive is seen as more valuable to the company because he is a devoted and caring husband. The women see the reasons for this mainly in prejudices prevalent in both the professional and social spheres. The women without children are of the view that their career paths would have been much more difficult if they had had children. They also mention the prejudices against mothers and acknowledge that they exist. Only one of the women, who has spent the majority of her career abroad, feels that the degree of success of a career is primarily down to mothers themselves. The majority of the women, however, argue that the main problem lies in structural discrimination. Mothers in Germany are faced with a dilemma between their desire to advance their careers and the societal norms imposed on mothers, and these conflict with the pursuit of a conventional management career. Women with children report that the pace of their career slows. There are instances in this group of women who missed out on being promoted due to pregnancy, as well as instances where promotion was deferred. In only one case was a pregnant woman promoted and it was thanks to a female CFO that this promotion took place.

The idea that infants are best cared for at home by their mothers is, as previously mentioned, firmly entrenched in German culture. And as the women's responses make clear, this steadfast view is held not only by men, but also by the women themselves. The underlying thinking is that external influences – in other words external childcare – overly early in life are harmful to infants and toddlers. The presence of the mother in this early phase of childhood is thus indispensable. Sending a baby or toddler to childcare is still viewed by many Germans as disadvantageous to the child's welfare. In this way the mother effectively becomes a scapegoat if she decides to do otherwise. Full-time care by a father or by grandparents is the exception rather than the rule in Germany. According to the accounts, this mindset is more prevalent in rural areas than in the cities. The women's accounts reveal that alternative childcare arrangements for babies and children under the age of three, whether delivered through crèches or by grandparents, aunts, fathers or nannies, are rarely, if ever, considered by mothers, let alone by male decision-makers. And even if a woman were to choose one of these options, in the eyes of everyone else – men and women alike – the attempt would be doomed to failure. Because in Germany, so the argument goes, good childcare can only be provided by mothers. After all, so the thinking goes, the mother would inevitably feel guilty about using childcare and would as a result be unable to meet the demands of her management role. These opinions form a vicious circle of social conditioning from which women need to free themselves – which they need to dismantle, in other words – before they can pursue a high-level management career and be a mother at the same time.

> M1.: So looking back ten years maybe, I can remember women coming in and telling me they were pregnant. And they'd come in and they'd practically have tears in their eyes and you'd be thinking, "Oh my God, she's ill. Or something terrible's happened." They didn't come in and sit there and say, "Guess what, I'm pregnant!" It was almost like they felt like they had to apologize because they were afraid that it was going to be a handicap. And that they wouldn't be able to get the balance right. And perhaps that is how it used to be. But these days things are a bit more relaxed. And the reactions the women get from other people are, too. Although, of course, when a superior gets the news, the first thing they think is " Hmm, so how am I going to fill the gap? What's going to happen? And what about when she comes back?" And you have to have a couple of options available to you. I like it when companies provide guidelines so that neither a woman who announces she's pregnant, nor her manager, need to worry. But I don't think a woman should put herself through that. If I've decided to have children, I should be there for them during the first five or ten years when they're really small and they need their Mum. I should be thinking: "I can do the 14 hours days after they're past that stage." I think people always behave as though when women get pregnant, they're going to be gone for good. That they're not going to be around any longer. That's just not true though. We just have these phases in life where we have to take a step back. A woman's career just isn't straightforward. You have stages in life where you spend more time with your family and others where you spend more time at work. And just because you... for example, my colleague

has three kids and a job in senior management, and she copes with everything very well. It works for her because firstly she wants to do it, and also because her husband is supportive.

M3.: There's a clear distinction between how men see it and how women see it. Men tend to see us as bad mothers. They wouldn't say it to our faces, but they do behind closed doors. How she can possibly think it's ok, given she's got children and what a pity it is. I also notice that all the men my age who sit round the boardroom table with me inevitably have a wife who doesn't work and who stays home with the children or who gets some fulfilment by doing a job of some sort. But she's not expected to have a career. Which wouldn't be good anyway because then dinner wouldn't be on the table when he got home. That's why they inherently don't have much sympathy, maybe they have a bit more for me because I don't have children or anyone to neglect and I don't have to cook for anyone in the evenings and I can really concentrate on my job, as opposed to women who do the job in addition to having children to look after. People always say, "It's amazing how you manage to do it all." And how fantastic. But in reality they don't really understand. I envy women who've done both. But from the ones I know quite well, I can see that they've not all been made happy by having it all. There are some women who say quite openly, "I'm glad I don't have to be around my children all day, because I need to work for my own sake. They're quite content, but many of the women who've managed to have both are extremely dissatisfied or have the constant sense that they're not doing right by either one or the other. And women who've done it the other way, and there are so many women of my generation who stayed at home with their children or only worked part-time and gave up their careers and then just stayed busy to earn some money, whether as a judge or whatever, good jobs like that, and then if you haven't completely subordinated yourself to your children's needs, the cliché is often that you're a "bad mother". So women are their own worst enemies and men don't really respect them either.

M2.: And I think it's like... at a certain point a woman finds herself thinking about how much she's going to have to sacrifice to get ahead. An example, a classic scenario, the first time my company ever really disappointed me. While I was on maternity leave, I got an offer, which I thought was brilliant, the fact that I got a job offer, even though I was on maternity leave. I was asked to take over the management of a subsidiary. I felt honored too, and it was just wow. Even though I was on maternity leave and everything. I thought, it's amazing that they're still thinking about me and supporting me and stuff. In any case, I went for this assessment and got right through to the end of the process. But then the boss didn't want me. In the interview I was repeatedly and subtly asked about my private life. Never directly, just subtly the whole time. Then in the last round it escalated a bit, because I addressed the issue openly. Because time and time again the question arose as to how I'd manage everything from a practical point of view, whether I was aware of what I was getting into and that I'd be away from home a lot in the first few weeks and months. And they put a lot of pressure on me, which made me feel like I was being attacked. And there were just these five men over 50 there. There was this constant doubt as to whether I'd be able to do it. And I'm sure that they'd never have asked a man the same questions they asked me in that assessment. And so I did a bit of a rethink and thought, I've definitely worked hard for ten years, I've definitely put in more than enough hours, and whatever I can't do any longer now that I have a family, that'll just have to be the way it is. Maybe where I am now in my career is enough.

The women in the survey who have children made the decision to continue their careers almost without interruption and have accomplished a great deal. The executives who have small children organize childcare and household responsibilities primarily with the help of partners, nannies and cleaners. Grandparents help out for a few hours at a time and in emergencies and only rarely for entire days at a stretch. In contrast to other countries, the women surveyed here do not have access to full-time schooling including lunch and afternoon activities. One interviewee describes moving back to Germany from Belgium with two children as having been a nightmare, because the entire process of finding a good school, from the registration procedure to the scarcity of good afternoon care, did not allow career women to plan properly. The women view Germany as, ultimately, still operating on a half-day model when it comes to caring for pre-school and school-age children, and the quality of care is poor. Their responses reflect the heavy organizational burden that falls on mothers and the still prevalent image of the uncaring mother which plagues women in Germany. Their personal coping strategy is to choose a supportive partner and to develop an attitude of indifference to value judgments.

The image of German female top executives

The survey responses make it all too clear what kinds of public image German female top managers have to contend with. They are rarely positive. Negative epithets exist aplenty, however: token female, self-indulgent, tough customer, inconvenient. Very often, the idea of the "unnatural mother" (*"Rabenmutter"*) is used when thinking about mothers with careers. Motherhood abruptly alters the positive image that a German woman in a senior role has up until then enjoyed. Because in Germany, once a woman is a mother, she is no longer really suitable for management and is no longer seen in a positive light. The social conditioning regarding motherhood even prompts some of the women interviewed, often those who are not mothers themselves, to view the prospects for mothers in upper management as unfavorable. Germany lacks role models demonstrating that it is possible to do both.

The attributes usually associated with successful managers, such as assertiveness and goal-oriented thinking, acquire negative connotations in relation to women. This "think manager, think male" phenomenon has been extensively investigated by the American scientist Schein (1996). According to her research, rising to top management demands qualities that are more likely to be attributed to men. Such qualities are, however, not normally attributed to women. German women talk in emphatic terms about the way in which these qualities are, in women, viewed negatively.

> H.: Well, I guess it's not as bad as it used to be, you don't get called a bad mother so much these days. But on the one hand people admire the fact that you can do it all and that your family's still intact. And on the other hand it's still viewed very critically, along the lines of, well, the idea that you're a bad mother is forced on you rather. "They never see their families."

> M2.: The popular wisdom is that career women have deliberately decided not to have children in order to be able to do their jobs properly. This is negatively linked to "She needs to feel fulfilled." It has negative connotations, definitely. And the woman with kids: "Well, I guess she knows in

her own mind whether she wants to do that to herself or not." People wonder if she can do it all and if she's really capable of achieving a balance.

The women have marked, and contradictory, opinions about Germany's supervisory board quotas. At the time of writing, further quotas for German businesses are under discussion in the political arena. The stigma of being a "quota woman" has the effect that women do not feel appreciated for their performance. At the same time, they recognize the opportunities offered by quotas. They are critical of the perceived damage to their image that quotas for women entail. Just like the French women, the German women are ambivalent about the effect of quotas on whether they are viewed as being suitable for management roles.

> C.: Or else people say, oh, she's the quota woman. C is on the board now, I don't feel like I'm a quota woman, but I don't think I'd want to be one. I'm here because I do an excellent job. I think it's a pity that a quota system had to be introduced. We won't solve the actual problem that way. And it changes men's sensibility and awareness, and women's too. So that's why. I don't always want to be only saying negative things about men. I also think that a lot of women are just too, well... they never come out of their shells. And targets for the number of women you had to have would definitely help us.

Dealing with challenges: pull yourself together, press on and seek support

In difficult situations or when faced with defeat, the German women's strategy is to "grit your teeth, learn from the experience and move on". The German female top managers' outstanding capacity for dealing with challenges lies in the fact that they learn from their mistakes and defeats and that they persevere. And they do what is necessary to learn from these difficult situations and to do better next time. Again, the support of executive coaches is used in a variety of situations to work out solutions to challenges.

> M1.: I got 42 percent and the other candidate 58 percent. A respectable achievement, but I was deeply depressed at the time, because I felt I'd made such an effort and now this had happened. That was rather negative and irrational of me and I was ashamed because – for some reason I didn't feel able to tell anybody that it hadn't worked out. But after I'd put the disappointment behind me, I thought to myself, well, this was actually a very valuable experience. And I'll try again some other time.

> M3.: Don't let it stop you, don't let it drag you down, put it to one side, that's part of life and keep on carrying on. Because if you think too much about things, it'll only pull you down. I don't think I'm necessarily better at it these days, but I once got a good tip from some headhunter, my first exam, you've probably seen, there were reasons why, but it didn't go as well as I thought it would. And in retrospect I can say that for the first time in my life I learned humility and the importance of being happy. You can be totally prepared for something, you can know it forwards and backwards, and still sometimes not succeed. You can definitely do it until you do your exams, and I think later on it can happen too that you get handed a new CEO or you have a boss with whom you can't work, even though you worked really well with the previous three

bosses. When that happens you mustn't blame yourself. You have to move on. Don't let yourself be dragged down, I think that's always the challenge and every defeat tells you something new. And I think at the end of the day, it's the defeats that help you mature. At least, in my job, I see so many people who have suffered defeats, personal and professional, in their jobs, and they get back on the horse and keep functioning and having a positive attitude. So every defeat is also a lesson. You aren't human if you haven't had those sorts of experiences.

B.: People who are out-and-out achievers, either they don't really exist or they're a bit abnormal, they're not all that human. We only become truly human and a successful human at that, when we've learned how to cope with defeat and find the lesson in the defeat and motivate ourselves to keep going.

So.: I got promoted to an important position as head of the business unit. It came about because of a restructuring. I was quite simply the right candidate for the job. And so suddenly I was playing in the Champions League but I didn't know the fundamentals and nobody explained them to me. And I myself didn't recognize what the rules of the game were. So I don't want to lay the blame at anyone's door. But I suddenly went from the Premier league to the Champions League. At that point I made an error. It was the right recommendation, the right commercial recommendation. But the thing was, the board of directors had originally been responsible for setting up that plant. But I didn't know that. In other words, I was basically indirectly telling them, "That plant you set up isn't any good, it isn't doing well and it won't do well in the future." I still stand by that today. But there was I ignorantly mocking it. And I mean, some of the other senior managers had already seen the presentation and the proposal as well. And either they just didn't think about it, or – but I don't think they intentionally set a trap for me. I don't think that's what happened at all. But it was unpleasant. And then people were thinking, "She just can't see it." But that's not true at all. I could. I just misinterpreted what I needed to do at that moment. That was my actual contribution to the blunder. From a commercial point of view, my solution was the right one. It was just that I presented it poorly. I didn't even get to the end of the presentation, they were interrupting me and carpeting me in a really unpleasant way. And afterwards it was so awkward. I just didn't feel very comfortable in the Champions League. You know, when someone cuts you short in front of an audience and portrays you as incompetent, then you lose faith in yourself and it turns into a vicious circle. So every time I had to do a board presentation, I felt uncomfortable. I didn't do it very well and so on. And you know who helped me out of the vicious circle? A woman. I told her how dreadful I found it all and that I felt trapped. And then I heard on the grapevine, over the network, that the board was trying to remove me from the succession plan. And then I got some good tips from certain people and I thought: Okay, now I'm going to learn how to play in the Champions League. And especially with the support of this one woman who was head of HR at the time, she was the first person who said to me, "You need to treat yourself to some coaching." And she sent me to a coach who worked through a lot of issues with me. And then she sent me to another coach who trains people in presentation technique. Well, it wasn't that I didn't know how to present, but that's what I mean about playing at Champions League level, it's basically about making position statements, using the right vocabulary, isn't it?

Sa.: When you take your next career step, for example. Well, I just recently had this incident where I – we're in the process of reorganizing our segment – right from the start I was set to be given this really responsible role. He told me from the beginning that he wanted me to have that job. And my boss is close to the marketing manager. So my boss is always saying that he considers the issue of women in management to be very important and does things that show that he means it. The sales manager is so macho (laughs), a proper macho. And the two of them work well together. So what has happened now is that, after months of discussion, where I was supposed to be getting that job, my boss has suddenly changed his mind and the team that I was supposed to be in charge of, the department that has these six teams, he has spun off four of the teams and only wants to give me two. He's given me a hundred different reasons why and they're all far-fetched. The more I think about it and the more I analyze the signals I'm picking up, the more I'm coming to the conclusion that this other guy, this sales manager, has spent so long telling him that he can't trust me to do a good job and that he's making a big mistake, that eventually he's said, okay, he'll give me less responsibility.

M1.: Well, the cost of all this is – I'm really going for the jugular now. I don't only dedicate my working day to the job. I do weekends, fourteen hours days, I have to be always available, new things crop up that play on my mind. Flexibility, time, everything that I put into my work, I can't put into my hobbies, or into my marriage, or into my family or into my friends. I'm always the person who can't. In other words, I'm not free to make my own decisions. Instead I've decided that fourteen hours days are fun, they give me joy, I can make a difference, I want to do it and I'm going to do it. For mothers, of course, it's even more of a balancing act.

H.: I think I lost my way a bit. Well, there were certainly times when I was the only one that mattered. You have to deliberately make time for yourself. And sometimes I did feel guilty about the children. Sometimes I was out of the country when they were lying at home in bed with a temperature. Or when I had to comfort them over the phone about something. And when we came back from Asia we had some serious problems with my little boy, and that was an real low point. That was definitely the reason why the job no longer – why coming back was such a challenge. Our little boy had such enormous difficulties. We solved it by getting some coaching. At one point or other I said: "We'll go to all the seminars and we'll treat ourselves to all the coaching we can get." And that was the best solution we could ever have made and it worked out really well for us.

7 Russian women: Succeeding through intuition and forging opportunities

Some literature sources rank Russia among the top countries in terms of women's participation in senior business leadership. The executives interviewed evaluate the different political phases in the country from their experiences and give insights into their understanding of roles between female manager, mother and a "real woman".

Socio-cultural framework of women's careers in Russia

In order to be able to place the experiences of the Russian female executives in context, it is worth taking a short trip back into history to understand how the situation of women in this country has changed over time. From a historical perspective, it is clear that Russia has frequently played a pioneering role in terms of women's rights and employment opportunities. The world's first female diplomat, Aleksandra Kollontaj, and the first woman in space, Valentina Tereshkova, were both from Russia.

Women in the Soviet era, perestroika and today

For centuries, Russia was an imperial nation ruled by the Tsar. After a short period of parliamentarism and capitalism in Russia at the beginning of the twentieth century, the communist revolution occurred in October 1917, followed by civil war. In 1922, a treaty was concluded to establish the Union of Soviet Socialist Republics, USSR, and from 1922 to 1991 the Communist Party governed as a one-party state. The Communist Party created a centrally planned socialist economy and promoted gender equality. In the mid-1980s, however, the global context changed and the introduction of market elements into the Soviet economy began.

Women were given the vote immediately after the revolution of 1917. The Soviet Union was thus the first large European country to do this, well before other countries, where women's suffrage was in some instances not introduced until some 27 years later. A commitment to the equal role of women in Soviet society was declared in the first Soviet constitution, in 1918. The 1936 constitution guaranteed women the same political, economic and civil rights as men. From the beginning, measures for implementing these rights established a comprehensive network of childcare facilities, ranging from maternity homes and crèches to full-time schools. The organization and hours of the childcare provision were geared specifically towards the needs of women in full-time employment.

Historically, according to Ashwin (2002, 2005) and Rzhanitsyna (2000), the employment rate for Soviet women was the highest of any economy in the world. In the

Soviet Union, it was considered self-evident that a woman would work full-time. Women accounted for 51 percent of industrial and service-related employment in the early 1990s, compared with 1928, when it was only 24 percent. In agriculture, according to Goskomstat (2007), women accounted for 45 percent of the workforce at the end of the 1990s. In the public arena, the role of women was much more firmly established than in Western economies. Women worked as crane operators, car mechanics and even as miners. While there is some evidence of gender segregation in employment, with Russian women working mostly in public sector areas such as health and education, the representation of women in government and science was considerably higher than in the West, according to Standing (1994) and Kay (2001).

The high number of women in the fields of science, engineering and politics is one of the main arguments for the view that women were given equal status under Soviet communist rule. From 1937 onwards it became unofficial Communist Party policy to increase the number of women in positions of political leadership. As a result, women came to make up 30 percent of deputies to the Supreme Soviet of the Soviet Union and around 40 percent in local and regional soviets. According to Metcalfe et al. (2005), this high proportion was maintained until 1989, when quotas were abolished. A large number of women also entered scientific and technical training programs. The Moscow State University Academy of Sciences, for example, had equal numbers of men and women participating in scientific programs and at the same qualification level. When research centers for engineering and biological sciences were established, a substantial number of women were appointed. In the 1980s, 51 percent of all students at Russian universities were women. The proportion of women in the technical professions was high; 60 percent of all engineers were women, for instance. In the postwar period in particular, women were active in all areas of reconstruction, including in physically demanding jobs in the metal, cement and oil industries. Half of all construction and industrial workers were women. Despite excellent state childcare facilities, the USSR still had what gender researchers call the "working mother's contract". From a societal perspective, women had to bear the burden of job, children and household alone. Full-time housewives were an unknown phenomenon in socialist society. The state provided many family-friendly childcare options and offered women, but not men, reduced working hours. The basic assumption behind this was that women should be the ones looking after their families, and unaided. Various researchers have criticized the communist state for institutionalizing a gender hierarchy based on patriarchal values, thereby addressing the reality of the social and economic inequalities between the genders. However, the large numbers of women in science, engineering and politics is one of the main arguments in favor of the existence of gender equality in the Soviet era. In the USSR, the equality between women and men in employment, education and politics remained unchallenged in the public discourse until the late 1980s.

During the restructuring of the perestroika era in the 1990s, conditions deteriorated for women. The economy underwent a complete restructuring after the collapse of the Soviet Union in 1991. Overall economic production in Russia fell year on year from 1990 to 1996. In total, the gross national product declined by about 40 percent. It took until about 2007 to offset the drop in production. Russian society was severely affected by the upheavals of the so-called "transition phase". Many men were unable to withstand the pressure and succumbed to alcoholism – a national problem still widely discussed. The economic liberalization was accompanied by a deleterious effect on the positions of women in the labor market. There were mass dismissals, primarily of women, as these had previously been employed mainly in "light industries", which were the ones more seriously affected by the restructuring. In 1992, 78 percent of those registered as unemployed were women. In the redistribution of property and capital which occurred around that time, women stood virtually no chance against men and were left empty-handed.

The dissolution of the Soviet state was marked by a period of political consolidation of gender-specific roles. With perestroika, the value system changed and women came to be seen as a group requiring protection, and one whose first priority should be the family. The Russian Employment Minister during the transition phase, Gennadii Melikian, is quoted by Kay (2001) as saying: "*Why should we hire women while men are unemployed? It is better for men to go to work and for women to look after the children and do the housework.*" Gorbachev also argued in 1987 that women should be allowed to return to their "*exclusively female vocation*". In order to encourage gender differentiation, the human resources departments of governmental organizations promoted flexible working hours, working from home, reductions in working hours and generous leave for pregnancy, childbirth and the care of young or sick children. These support systems were aimed solely at women. Because of these welfare regulations, female workers consequently came to be classified as more costly than men. Under these regulations, certain types of work were officially forbidden to women. According to a list given under Article 253 of the Russian Labor Code, women are prohibited from working in a total of 456 professions, on the grounds of protection for women. Above all, however, the reduction in childcare provision led to a much greater double burden on working women than was the case during the Soviet era and to increased gender inequality within the family.

However, the transition to a market economy also offered women certain opportunities, as Sperling (1999) and Ardichvili (2001) described in their works. Many women took the initiative and set up small enterprises during this period, some of them even doing business with neighboring countries. Former women lecturers, factory workers and teachers showed that they had entrepreneurial flair and that they could adapt to the new era and seize opportunities. It is probable that the many important female entrepreneurs in Russia today are the result of this phase. Historically, overcoming the challenges of the perestroika period was nothing new for Russian women. During the country's numerous wars, women had always had to rely on themselves and had helped to rebuild the country on several occasions.

Shortly after the restructuring, in 1992, the proportion of 30–40-year-old women in the workforce was over 90 percent, almost as high as that of men. By comparison, during the 1990s, the same figure for the USA was 70 to 75 percent. We can therefore conclude that there was at this time equality between men and women. The overall economic activity of women in Russia remains high to this day. Most women continue to work to provide financial support for their families. Population figures published by Goskomstat (2019), the statistical office of the Russian Federation, show that there are fewer men than women in Russia. In 2015 the ratio was 44 percent men to 56 percent women. A surplus of 15 percent of women is forecast for 2050. Various causes are cited, such as the large number of wars, the high incarceration rate, the high male mortality rate due to alcoholism, and the impact of a low standard of living, mainly caused by the upheavals in the country. Russian men die on average 16 years earlier than those in Western Europe and 14 years earlier than Russian women. The country also has a very high divorce rate, forcing many women to become the main breadwinner. However, Colgan (2014) explains that depending on the information source, women earn on average 30 to 36 percent less than men. The highest pay differentials are to be found in the north of the country, where the mining companies are located. Women's educational attainment still exceeds that of men. There are more women with university degrees, with 144 women per 1000 population having a university degree versus 142 men. The number of Russian women attending business schools is growing at a disproportionate rate. Although the number of females outnumbers that of males, and women are more likely to use their right to vote, women in Russia continue to be underrepresented in top political positions. According to Krasilnikova (2013), this is due to the nature of the political system, in which the highest offices are appointed rather than determined by ballot. In 2011, there were 59 women in the lower house of parliament, or about 12 percent. There are fewer than ten women in the upper house. For a long time, there were no women in high government positions; since 2009 the Russian cabinet has had only three female ministers. The Finance Ministry, Ministry for Agriculture and the Health Ministry have all been headed by women. Among the governors, there is just one woman – from St. Petersburg. In contrast, women are well represented in junior and medium-rank state posts. According to the latest statistics from the Russian State Statistical Service, in 2011, no less than 70 percent of state employees were women. It is unlikely that the situation has changed significantly since then. The introduction of gender quotas has met with resistance. The majority of the population believes that introducing quotas would lead to vacancies being filled by the wives, mistresses and daughters of politicians and business people.

The proportion of Russian women in top management positions

According to the Women in Business Report by Grant Thornton (2019), the proportion of women in senior management in Russia in 2018 was 47 percent, which would make Russia the country with the highest proportion in the world. The same annual global survey found that 91 percent of Russian companies had at least one woman in top management, while this was the case in just 75 percent of companies in the UK, 79 percent in France and 75 percent in the US. A similar proportion was given in surveys conducted by PWC in 2012 as well as by the International Labor Organization, IOL, (2017), although the IOL placed Russia only 25th out of 80 countries. According to these surveys, women leaders mostly occupy CFO and HRD positions. According to PWC and the Russian Association of Managers, women accounted for 93 percent of chief accountants, 70 percent of HRDs and 47 percent of CFOs in 2010, but only 6 percent of company presidents. Historically, there have been numerous traditionally "male" and "female" professions in Russia, and the impact of this is being felt right up to the present day. According to the recruitment consultancy Hays Russia, men predominate in sectors such as construction, IT, energy, heavy industry, engineering, defence, metal industry, surgery, fishing and mining. Typically "female" sectors, on the other hand, are human resources, finance, statistics, accounting, education, sales, (tele-) communications, the arts, health, psychology and media. In Russia, female CEOs and board members are thus more likely to be found in specific industries such as banking, media, tourism, beauty, sports, health and education, whereas the oil, gas and metal industries are more likely to be in male hands. Russian expert Krone-Schmalz (1992) writes that *"women in Russia do not discuss equal rights, they take them – in business, at least. In no other country are there as many career women as in Russia."* According to Gvozdeva (2002), the Russian Academy of Sciences' Institute of Sociology has published a rather different picture of the situation regarding the number of women in top management positions. According to this report, only 20 percent of companies have women on the board of directors. For some sectors, however, a figure of 54 percent was given. Ward Howell (2014), though, estimates that the proportion of women CEOs in Russia in 2013 to be lower than in the USA. According to him, only 1 percent of CEO positions in the top 160 Russian companies are occupied by women, compared to 4.4 percent in the Fortune 500. Credit Suisse (2014) has published a figure of 8 percent of female CEOs in Russia compared to a global average of 12 percent. According to the Federal State Statistical Service, a large number of women occupy positions as specialists in senior and middle management. Although there are more men in the very top positions, the gap is nevertheless small. In 2009, of the 19 percent of senior management specialists in Russian companies, 23.8 percent were women and 14.7 percent men, and of the 7 percent of senior management positions, 8.7 percent were held by men and 5.3 percent by women. The figures thus by and large revealed significant female involvement in senior management, but as often is the case, and depending on the source chosen, the figures vary. Half of the women in employment in Russia are open to being self-employed. The growth in the number of start-ups initiated by women is 350 percent, compared to 65 percent for men. According to the "Opora Rossii" Association of Entrepreneurs' Initiative Committee for the Development of Female Entrepreneurship (2017), there are an estimated 5.6 million small and medium-sized enterprises in Russia, of which about 30 percent were owned by women in 1999.

The Russian interview participants – an introduction

The Russian executives for this book were recruited using a "snowball system" which was initiated by a Russian entrepreneur and subsequently expanded by the first group of interview participants.

The Russian research participants were individually interviewed in the autumn and winter of 2019. They averaged 40 years of age; the age range being between 31 to 50 years old. They thus tend to be younger than the French and German women; their age distribution was similar to that of the Chinese group. Forty percent of the women are single and without children. Half of the women have divorced and remarried. Sixty percent of the interviewees have one or two children aged between eight and 18 years.

The women are very well educated. All but one studied locally, at leading Russian universities. Russian university degrees take an average of six years to complete. One of the women received a doctorate in Russia. Only one woman reports on the opportunity she had to participate in an exchange program with a US university. One participant obtained an MBA which included a UK module. The qualifications obtained cover a range of disciplines such as engineering and economics, and a significant number are in literary studies. The majority of the Russian women speak English well or very well, meaning that, with only two exceptions, the interviews were conducted in English. A proportion of the women also speak French, German or Spanish.

At the time of the interviews, the Russian female executives were working in media, fashion, technology, IT and consulting, among other sectors. The companies were small or medium-sized, private or state-owned enterprises, or else multinational corporations. This fact differentiates the group from the other four, where the majority of women were working for multinational companies. Their positions include top tier management such as CEO or Country Manager, and second tier management such as HRD, VP, BD, Chief Editor or CFO. The areas of responsibility are either local or include responsibility for Eastern Europe. Overseas postings do not play a role in their career progression. Only one woman moved abroad – to the UK – as part of her career with a multinational corporation.

Equal opportunities: A U-shaped curve

The Russian women give very varied answers when asked how they see equal opportunities in Russia with respect to careers for women. Out of ten, the score responses range from zero to between eight and ten.

The variation is perceived as having historical and regional origins and also as differing between industries. Moscow, as a modern business hub, receives high scores of eight or nine for equal opportunities. The women, however, consider rural areas to have virtually no equal opportunities, with the situation for women in management being rated very poorly at two to three or in some cases even at zero, which however may be partly explained by the general lack of opportunities. In terms of the different sectors, banks, with a score of eight, are considered extremely female-friendly whereas the media industry, with a score of six, comes near the middle.

When asked about the country's equal opportunities history, the women describe a U-shaped curve. In the former Soviet Union, their mothers had had outstanding career opportunities in the framework of the state system at that time. In some cases, their mothers had better jobs than their fathers. Their main criticism is that the range of possibilities available in those days was very much restricted to professions such as teacher, doctor and engineer. Because of the economic system at that time, there were no management careers in today's sense. The women give the Soviet period a score of between eight and ten, but nevertheless view it very negatively because, from their personal perspective, the range of career opportunities was extremely limited. From the interviewees' point of view, the situation for women deteriorated drastically during the perestroika years of the 1990s. The time around the disintegration and opening-up of the Soviet Union, as well as the period immediately afterwards, are given an extremely low score of between one and two for gender equality. They remember the opening-up of the economy as a brutal time. In terms of equal opportunities, the 1990s are described as representing the low point of the U-shaped curve. In some families, the distribution of roles shifted during this period. Whereas previously mothers had been extremely successful, now it was fathers who took the lead in providing for the family and in career terms.

Currently the situation is improving year on year and occupies the upper part of the U-shaped curve. Increasing numbers of women are successfully attaining top management positions. The curve has been rising steadily and is now scoring in the five to eight out of ten range, depending on one's perspective. Scores below eight are largely attributable to pay gaps of between 30 and 40 percent. In addition, patriarchal structures still persist and as a result, men outnumber women in certain areas. When asked to comment on the statistic of 43 percent of women in leadership positions, as quoted in the Grant Thornton study, the women are equivocal or somewhat negative in their opinions. While the women feel that the opportunities for advancement are virtually limitless, at the same time they are aware of the predominating masculine norms.

> E.: I used to hate the Soviets as a young woman. You know, when you are young you often see black or white. Today I see that it was the Soviets who gave women equal rights. The right to vote and equal educational opportunities. Men and women should be the same. There was a report about young people who came to us from Spain in World War II and were trained at the best universities. The women should return to the stove when they return home. Can you imagine that? In Spain in the 1950s women had to be housewives. Nothing else was possible. It was very different with us. I learned that not everything is black or white. Although I welcome the opening of our country, it was the Soviets who laid the foundation for equality with us.

A.: What I heard from my mother, there was no difference in the Soviet Union. Today the discrimination is higher.

V.: I give seven for Moscow because the ten lacks the inner respect of men for women, there is sexism. For other regions two to three, there are religious reasons, women should stay at home there. In the Soviet Union? Not higher in my opinion, five, I think. They are glorified childhood memories where those value it higher. Do you know the well-known film "Moscow does not believe the tears" by Menshov from the 1980s. This agrees with me. Katharina, a CEO, does not mention Georgij's position there. She doesn't want to hurt his pride. When he finds out, he leaves her, hurt in his pride. Men were CEO and women were only deputy. The film shows that in society's eyes it is not good for a woman to earn more to become a CEO. There are also sentences in the language such as "a woman at the wheel is like a monkey without arms". Do you understand? Today it is better because perestroika has made women stronger. You got more chances. They are women who start-ups who started trading with Turkey. It's the women.

I.: On a certain top management level, I think there is sufficient flexibility and sufficient equality, and there are a lot of women in those positions. Once we take a step further to the position of CEO, where a really senior position in a very, very big company, which is also a slightly different scale from a small company or a private entity, then it becomes a bit more complicated. But I've seen a lot when some women end up in those positions, they're very smart. They're worth mentioning that, but they are connected either way. They have a husband, they have someone. There is a certain level of connection that these women have that actually pushes them forward. It's not like I'm coming from the street, right, so I have no connection, literally none. There is no one that's pushing me. It would be difficult for me to find a CEO position in Russia, in a media company without being connected to someone. This is why I gave it a four.

O.: I think there are a few factors contributing to that. Firstly, Russia is an extremely corrupted country, extremely corrupted. There are a lot of people who are officially a CEO or business owner brings out the wife who are put there in a position that if prosecution comes, it's like I don't own anything, let's say somebody in power being a local MP or something in [inaudible] he can't own a business. All the businesses are set up into the name of their wife, and a lot of that is happening. Obviously, also because the situation is quite tough, I think there are really, really brilliant Russian women who despite being forced and faced with what's happening, they're warriors.

M.: Women are afraid of power, if they want it is absolutely possible, that is why I gave only five, in our company we are five women, all bosses are women. Every year 10–15 percent more women.

The Russian participants: analysis of career paths

The Russian women's careers begin somewhat arbitrarily, but are nevertheless creative, flexible and multi-faceted. Examples of post-university first-time jobs are DJ-ing and working abroad as a tourist guide. One of the women worked as a nurse before studying. The women with careers in media started off as journalists or production assistants. Less than a third of them began their careers immediately after university as an office junior in a large company, as is standard for an international management career. These women started their careers while still at university, for example by acting as assistant to a CEO, in accounting or in the marketing department of a multinational company.

In entry-level positions, communication skills and a knowledge of English are often cited as being a major advantage. The ability to communicate in English across national borders is a competitive advantage that many of the women had at the start of their careers. Some individuals report having had a head start in IT and digitalization. A technical background is an advantage in medium-sized companies especially.

The Russian women's careers tend to reflect the following pattern:
1. English and IT skills provide a competitive advantage at the outset
2. Intuitive, flexible, trial and error
3. Learning from within a new system, seizing opportunities
4. Decisions to switch companies are values-based
5. Clearly career-oriented with the aim of advancement

Russian women's careers involve between one and six companies. The majority change companies two to four times. The length of stay in a given role is between one and four years. At the time of interview, the women were either working in multinational companies or else in state-owned or private enterprises. The analysis for Russia thus covers all forms of company. Almost all of the women have switched between state and either multinational or private companies. Sixty-five percent of the women deliberately chose to work in companies with a Western management culture, but there are also examples of switching between state-owned and Western companies. The women from multinational companies know little about the culture in domestic state-owned enterprises or have little experience of the differences between corporate cultures due to nationality. The younger women tend to experiment and learn by switching companies. Overall, in comparison with the top female managers from Europe, who started out in established economic systems, the Russian women's early career phases are characterized by the fact that they only learn relatively later on about management and corporate structure. The Russian women have had but few examples that they can call upon.

> Y.: It was only after 2000 that multinational companies really started to penetrate the Russian market. They then built factories, large offices and tried to attract many employees. Some of them came before, but it wasn't that much. The career opportunities for women are better in the multinational, as foreigners think that women work better and harder than our men. Now is the time when a lot of local start-ups are emerging. It seems to me that there are more men active here. And some colleagues are starting to switch to Russian companies to use their USP with the knowledge of the multinationals there. The Russian business atmosphere is less experienced and more emotional than in foreign companies. We are still lagging behind. There is also a trend towards an international career as an expat. I read that 40 % of young people would like to go. Most who go with international companies have no goal of coming back.

All but one of the women's careers are locally based, albeit with some Eastern European responsibility. Only one of the women, having worked in England for a multinational company, has pursued a career abroad in the classical sense. Two of the women surveyed have experience of working for themselves in small or medium-sized companies. The flexibility observable at the beginning continues throughout the course of the women's careers. It seems that, with few exceptions, Russian women tend to respond spontaneously to opportunities that present themselves, rather than working strategically towards a specific goal within a given corporate structure. Many of the descriptions point to a "trial and error" approach. However, and this is also true worldwide of all the female top managers, Russian woman are clear what they want from a career: to get ahead, to move up, eventually to become the boss.

> O.: My career is more about business development. Not so much about the later execution and perfection. Not a lot about product and creativity, but rather about business as a system. At some point, I think it was 2005 or so, they wanted me to move to London and take a position there. Because it was kind of weird that I did so much of the business from here. At the time, I met my future husband and refused because we were in a relationship for two months. Then two years later they offered to move again with the whole family. I agreed at the time and moved to London to do the same job for XY, the emerging markets. Ended in the position of sales and marketing director for emerging markets. So I knew the country relatively well, but as a tourist, not as the one who lives there with everyday things. When you set up your whole house and start over and deal with things like transportation and supplies where you live, everything is different. It takes all of your energy. I then did a horizontal move. I got the position of VP of global customer strategy. Instead of working with emerging markets, I switched to established markets where we had offices, e.g. B. Western Europe, North America, Canada, Japan, countries with more developed markets, and worked at customer level. I've worked with clients like Apple, Amazon and Walmart, the big ones. I tried to implement our way of working as well as the specific projects and the system structure. Then I switched to F. as VP of Business Development for Western Europe, which in turn was a new position. At the time, it was a very good move since XY is no longer doing very well.

Being better qualified and better at their jobs than their colleagues were important factors leading to advancement. Other secondary factors allowing women the chance of a promotion were also often mentioned, such as a new line manager or the pregnancy of a more senior colleague. These promotions happened either with the help of a sponsor or the company's owner. Having the confidence of the owner or of superiors is repeatedly mentioned as a main reason for being promoted. Among women whose careers are international, having visionary ability and the capability to build a business from scratch plays a major role in their advancement, whether in Russia or another Eastern European country. Switching companies is either opportunity-driven or – and this is a noticeable feature – dependent on the CEO or owner of the new company. If they share similar values, the women are open to moving companies. If not, the women actively look elsewhere. Not all of them move up when they change companies. A large proportion of women say that they wanted to advance with each step, but only in some cases is this reflected in their career path. As is the case with Chinese women, the Asian crisis at the end of the 1990s is occasionally mentioned as having been a significant external influence that led to unwelcome changes.

Challenges in the course of a career include market slumps, age at the point of an upcoming change, and dealing with family issues when living abroad as an expatriate. As regards the future, the Russian women wish to continue as CEO or else to progress to this level, or to become shareholders. Several women see themselves as becoming entrepreneurs in the future. This is supported by published data, according to which the majority of companies in Russia are founded by women. And there are also those among the female Russian CEOs who would like to pursue their childhood dream of becoming a researcher, highly respected and with a secure job, just like members of their family were during Soviet times.

> E.: When I finished the university, the profession of journalist was very popular in Russia, because it was like post-Soviet era. Journalism was very popular, and especially TV journalism. It was like you becoming the biggest star because everything was open. I worked for the first non-governmental company in Russia, NTV. It's a strange story of, "How can I get there?" Anyway, it wasn't very prestigious at the time to get to that company. I started as a correspondent. It was the start of my career. Then time was changing, and I understood that I am not a correspondent. Somehow, I found out that such kind of things like marketing. For us, everything was beginning because we didn't know anything about the structures of a company. The marketing, it was another word. We didn't know there's such kind of a word and what is it. For me, I was lucky because I went to a university in Nashville, Tennessee. It was 1994 and at the time when I– first time saw a– Not a computer. I had a computer because my father had his own company and we were kind of wealthy, but it was at the time.
>
> First time I saw what does it mean, internet, because I saw that the first time, it was 1994. Then when I started to go for XY, it was 1996. I do remember the day when our CEO of the company said, "Now, we got internet." I had the advantage that I already knew that and then initiated things for the broadcaster. I was in four companies, and among those four was one that I later returned to. It was a big company that I'm going back to. My fourth company is a holding company, as we call it here. It has multiple channels and was a company of XY Groups from Sweden. We were on NASDAQ. It was a really big international company. There were many small companies in this company, so I switched from one company to another in this area.
>
> O2.: I tried to find a job by specialty, by my diploma, electronic engineer. Near my house, near my home, there is some electronic factory. It's sort of style, a former Soviet Union. Mostly they work for military and now they begin to work– became private, but it's producing some electronics. They opened a new department also with the government's budgeting. I wanted to design some part of Russian Satellite system if you know XY? I am kind of open-minded and I could talk to partners, to American specialists, because this technology is not available in Russia so we work with Germans, with Slovenian with Americans. I even had some project and I became a business assistant department- deputy of department. Like I said, it was like three years. Later, I was disappointed because they didn't create, didn't design. It's, to be honest, they want to just to cut the budget and do some private things. It's very common in Russia, in this case, it's very true. I was fed with this too and I decided, it's a former Soviet Union factory, it feels, old people like around 60 years old. It's still the same mentality. The young generation mentality was different. It was always like some confrontational you need to prove– I was tired from this. I switched back to a tech company. They needed someone with my background who could communicate with Germans. Then I found an equal position at AB. It took me a year to do that. And then the crisis came and everyone was released. Then I worked for a Chinese company. I didn't

like that because they do things differently. Never did what they said. Now I'm back in an American company. I always found the positions with my CV or now via LinkedIn or was it found on Facebook.

I.: To be honest, I've never planned a move. All I wanted and still want was to be higher on the next step.

N.: I didn't plan anything, so I got the jobs, other people who wanted that didn't get the jobs. I used my chances well. I want to be the best.

O1: I just took over marketing fast with copywriting that and discussing the positioning. It was a bit of a personal win as well because I think my marketing director at the time was quite lazy, he was quite happy for me. I would just do everything, so he kept giving me more and I kept doing more. At some point, I think the bosses realized that who is the one actually doing everything, and I just got the position. I ran and partnered with a few people. Also, I'd been the key contact person for our XY offices based on– We were overseeing Russia. Then the financial crisis that happened at the end of 1998, which kind of made Sony to really rethink the plan. They were viewing Russia at the time as a big market, which they will eventually establish an office rather than have a distributor. Because the crisis really affected the economy and the business, I think they went back from the plan, but they still decided to keep somebody higher on the ground, and they offered me a job. That was end of 1999, which I've accepted. They made me a sales and marketing executive, just reporting to them about things that are going on and being that middle person between the Russian business and their own office. Then again, I just think I have a lot of ambition and I just can't stop. If I see the opportunity, for me, it's like almost impossible to say, "Okay. Yes, it's there but 6:00 PM I'm going home." I just don't work like that. We worked in Russia and then I saw, "Why am I not working in Ukraine? Shall I go to Ukraine?" I'm very proactive in those things, so I'm opening up with questions and offers.

Obviously, nobody tossed me to do that but essentially, I thought that meeting people in other- at Soviet Republic, which were independent countries at the time. A few years later, I found myself that I'm running the whole of Western Europe still being an executive city in Moscow. I traveled a lot. I went to all the Romanians and Bulgarians. It was really interesting. I love starting business from scratch, where you have nothing and you need a few people who potentially can work with you and you get the whole thing running.

Career prerequisites for the Russian women

The top Russian female executives describe themselves as innovative and visionary. Visionary being a management skill that many other women tend to attribute to men. Their career orientation is strong and coupled with very high motivation to rise. They cleverly use their advantages as women where others expect weaknesses.

Strong mothers as role models

The Russian women's parents are all, without exception, university graduates. Their professions are largely in the field of engineering, but there are also soldiers, diplomats, teachers, artists and the self-employed. Their grandparents were in full-time employment and some held senior management positions.

In most cases, both parents worked full-time. In only 20 percent of families did university-educated mothers have a mere supporting role in their husbands' careers. The women's mothers and grandmothers' in some cases had more important jobs than their fathers' and were the women's role models, being as they were strong women whose influence was formative. It is striking that 30 percent of the women lost their fathers at a young age. The Russian women were influenced mainly by strongly committed professional mothers. One woman describes how her father took his own life when she was five years old. Only in exceptional cases are fathers described as having been role models, primarily in cases where a mother gave up her career. These mothers regretted their decision and were unhappy with the situation.

> N.: My mother was an engineer and my father an engineer for the planes. They used to work– My father used to work as an engineer for the whole of his life but my mother, she gave up the government work in the '90s. It was a very hard period for our country where the people who need to get their salaries and they couldn't buy any food and it was a really difficult time for the country. My mother, again, by the way, my mother made a decision that she changed something and she started her own business. She started her own small sewing factory. Let me remember how many years she used to do the business, about 10 or 12 years. That time I was a student and unfortunately my father died and it made my mother's state and position there- I mean, she lost the support of the father and it was very difficult if you're to survive after this post. It was very difficult for her to continue with the same speed and the same success. It was a very difficult period for sure, and for the businesses the success logged down, and finally, she decided to close it because it was a very difficult period for her. She is a very strong woman. She decided to stay home and help me with my kid. It was not easy for her. She had been entrepreneur. I am just working for a company. But for her it was not easy to stay home with a young child.

> O.: Both of my parents are in academia. My father is a professor in psychology and he's still working for a university. He's always been a lecturer, a researcher. He wrote 30-something books on educational psychology, quite academic, not obviously of psychology. Same with my mom, she is psychologist/linguist. She's been studying psychology of learning languages. Obviously, she hasn't made a career because we are a traditional family where my mom basically helps my father's career and looks after children, but she's still teaching in the university also up until, I think, two years ago. They're both 75 now. I think my mom stopped working for a couple of years ago. My dad's still working for one of the universities. It really works for them, so I don't judge them in any way, a woman who is "Less ambition, not a natural leader, more of a traditional woman," she would see my mom's position as power because my mom doesn't have to work long hours. She can enjoy being taken care of and being bought nice stuff. She also does the work she likes but it doesn't pay well. In all her life, she never had to think about how my family is going to survive, who's going to provide for them because she's always, my dad would have that role. She made view all this as a powerful position. This is a comfortable position. I do not want to be like my mom. I am born with I guess, with that fire inside which can't be there. Choosing between the two, I saw this is my father who's charismatic. He's very charismatic, like when he speaks, he's been invited to speak a lot and he makes those decisions. he's loud and grand and everyone runs about him trying to please him and do something nice for him. This is where I want to be.

> V.: My father killed himself when I was five. I remember that he always said "you are special, you will be good at school". I remember that. My mother is a famous journalist in Russia, at the end of the 80s she was a member of parliament for Yeltsin. Do you know Yeltsin? She was his advisor for national politics. Then she was at the demonstrations. I was also there. There were thousands

of people there, like a stand-up show, I was talking too. My mother, she taught me how to love, she was a strong woman, it is difficult to get love from such a woman, but I made it, I had to fight for love. She was in prison for five days, after which she stopped politics. When she came back, I was never more scared in my life.

E.: My father like a lot of men in Russia, in Soviet Union, they couldn't find themselves because there's nothing to do for them in that kind of socialistic things. You need to become a communist party member and all that stuff, and he never did. He was free-minded guy, so he didn't have a big career during Soviet era. He was doing like most of the people after Soviet Union collapsed. As soon as its collapse, the next day where the market became free, he became a businessman and he saw soon, I guess, success. He did a lot of singing and main of the things that he did, it was a structure business, constructing. I can say that he worked as a deputy for one very wealthy oligarch, like you call it in Europe. I couldn't say his name. My father became his deputy from that sense. It's very interesting how it worked in my family. It's an interesting scene because during the Soviet era, my mom had a big position in art dealer's business. We can put it that way. She was very happy with the position in Soviet time. She couldn't find a sure way after Soviet Union collapse as a career leader. She was upset with that until she died. It was always here. She didn't find a career step anymore.

The Russian women's management skills – innovation and vision

As discussed in the introductory chapter, there is no universal set of attributes that go to make up a good senior manager, and nor is there one for a good female senior manager. Women in top positions need to demonstrate a broad range of competencies in order to achieve a position of leadership and then to be considered suited to the role once there. Like all the women in this study, the Russian women were asked what they see as their core competencies and which of them had been particularly valuable when climbing the ladder to their current positions. The answers were categorized according to Regnet's (2017) classification of management skills, which was based on a global IMB study. The Russians had no trouble naming their skills and strengths and were also open about their weaknesses. The accounts are to the point, succinct and without the detailed descriptions and superlatives, which, for example, the French and Chinese women gave. In most cases, one or two core skills are mentioned.

The Russians describe themselves as experts in terms of the breadth of their business expertise, which is derived from their experience in a variety of business areas. More than half of the women have always worked in the same sector, e.g. media, and have gained recognition in it thanks to their expertise. Their strength lies in their skills and expertise in their particular sector, and this is acknowledged by their customers, colleagues and superiors. One of the women refers to the fact that she has won several awards in the media sector and emphasizes her high profile in the industry. A specialist area is digitalization, where some of the women are well ahead of their peers. Several of the women mention their international exposure, particularly in terms of their multilingualism and related market experience in Eastern Europe. However, only the woman who lived as an expat in England gives detailed information on multiculturalism as one of her core skills.

A distinctive trait of the Russian women is that they build trust by doing business loyally and with integrity, and as a result are entrusted with senior positions. The Russian women are distinguished by their ability to communicate clearly, formulate corporate goals and to develop well-defined ideas and strategies. Although the Russians, like most of the women, tend to doubt their own capacity for vision, analysis suggests that they in fact excel in this area. In reality, a majority of women report this, plus the ability to innovate, as being their core skill.

> E.: I can clearly explain what I want to, because now during my life, I've worked with different people who were like my bosses. I know that I saw it's not easy to find a person who'll tell you clearly what he wants from you. Usually, I can speak clear the goal, and I can explain to the other people what is the goal. Even sometimes I hope that then I can explain how to get there, because I'm very concentrated on the goals. If I know what kind of goal, I can see it, and I can see clearly what to do, and I can clearly explain. For example, I had a great, great boss as a man, mostly men. The only problem with them was they said, "You're much more talented than me, much more gifted," but they didn't understand sometimes what they want. They were talented at times. Then sometimes it's better for them to write a novel and not lead people, for example. For me, I'm not like very popular person. No, I couldn't say that I love to be in public. No, it's not about me. I know some people who just have fun being in public and they got energy from the people. I'm not such kind of person, but anyway for me it was much easier to cooperate with people and to explain what to do because it happened. Because the mass they have great ideas, they have desires, but they don't want to do all the steps. I'm very open mind, I am very well educated. I do my research everything. What's new and that is why I change all my rest to digital when it just started. I want to see something you are not stuck in the last place, in the past. I hate when the people are talking about "do you remember how it was right then blah-blah-blah".

> N.: I think that I'm very nice but I'm very tough. I understand business from both sides from the front office and back office and very often people from front office can explain anything to their colleagues from back office. That's why I can allow myself to be more tough because I understand all the business processes in sales. Also, I have very, very good in serious technical education. I believe that the main quality of good CEO to make decision and take responsibility and I know that I can do it. Also, I can inspire the team and this is also the main quality for CEO.

> O.: England, specifically or UK culture is very, very different from Russian one. I think I recognized that quite early and I think I'm lucky to have that trade which actually why I went on to learn languages. My education is languages. I'm a linguist. I never studied business, never had any business education whatsoever. I absorb a lot. I'm very perceptive. I look outside and I still do it. I walk in the street, I see a certain person saying certain things in a certain accent and I quietly repeat it so if I'm learning, learning never stops. If I end up in an environment, people have different models. Some say, "Yes, I can see those English. They never say anything straight away. It's unclear what they do things. They just– whatever." They use their cultural biases for judgment. I'm naturally different. I second to that and I'm like, "How does that world work?" Well with him just saying that made an impact. Why did I just say that and I saw people kind of– What did I do wrong? I agree with subconsciously and consciously, every day I study reactions of people towards how I am. I read about that, I'll ask them, I approve, I verify and I change and I change and I change so I can fit. You could probably hear a pretty decent English accent which I worked on. I can speak with Russian accent, but I

don't have to. You can put them for me to sound like that, to behave like them, it doesn't hurt my Russian values, but I think it's important that fit there. If they see you as a stranger, they will never trust you totally, so they must see you as one of their own. But I think it's exotic and quirky, but genuinely want their own. I think my skills of adaptability to culture is quite high. It's very conscious one as well like I realized why I'm doing it.

I.: I think in the course of my work I have the ideas. I have a vision and a very clear understanding of where we are going. It is not negotiable. I would always ask people to come up with ideas they have. And asking questions. I think in terms of the vision – and that goes back to the transparency and visibility of what is happening. So we do it together. We actually prepare a lot of things together. We throw a few ideas around and discuss them.

A.: In order to be informed about innovations, new technologies not only in our industry, but in management in general, I often invite external experts. So as not to be focused on my own vision, but to get several different visions to combine and get a better picture of the future, but it is not my natural quality.

The ability to communicate also includes the ability to persuade and to bring one's ideas to fruition. The Russians describe their capacity for using their strong negotiating skills to pursue projects with energy and commitment. When so doing, they make use of their identity as a female leader and see their feminine approach as an asset when it comes to asserting themselves.

I.: Relentless. That's my inherited trait, I think. I learned that from my father. It's like an inside family joke simply because he's essentially relentless. He's being who massive health issues, and he still keeps going because getting literally drag himself out of that other place twice. I'm constantly hearing this from my colleague. Maybe he's just trying to give me a compliment, is that I know how to balance and be diplomatic, and this is gender-specific and it may be, it may not apply elsewhere, but they will share this whole thing that's important. They're like a health feminist or a gender equality driven as we are, is that there's still a certain level of balance where you have to remain a woman. By that, I mean, that I am not waiving an ax, and running around like crazy all the time. There has to be a certain level of levelness and calmness and self-composure. I would even say that being able to level yourself and be composed is one of them, and being diplomatic. Because a combination of straightforwardness and diplomacy can take you a long way. But I also like to think that this is a specific trait I can count on. (laughs) If we're talking about traits that are more business-specific, I'm analytical.

A.: Strengths, I think that I am rather energetic, I think that I think about myself that I have no enough energy. But as I can understand from surrounding, that everybody think that I have a lot of energy but it's not enough for me, [laughs] I would like to have even more. I think this factor plays sometimes the main role in my career, in some development. The next is that, I do not see borders, not even physical borders, no borders for development. I think that if you want to make something, to reach something in the business and the same in the private life. What else? Maybe I am rather direct and rather sincere, it's not always the advantage, sometimes it's a disadvantage.

From out of the many accounts a pattern emerges that women are perceived as more loyal and less susceptible to corruption, with the result that male CEOs tend to hire them as directors. Here Russian women have clear advantages over men, who are more likely to be accused of corrupt behavior and hierarchical squabbling. Moreover, women are generally rated better than their male colleagues in terms of their work discipline.

> A.: I think that only now I understand the position of my ex-owner because now, I am in the position of co-owner of the company and I can estimate my colleagues, my heads of the departments. Because for me, at that time, it was really a surprise. I was, "I'm so young." Really, I was not experienced in this. Yes, MBA. I had an MBA but I had to learn a lot to become CO. Now I understand that they chose, they were several of them, they chose me because they understood that my attitude to their business, like for myself, for my business. Really, it was true. I was absolutely devoted to their business. When I had problems, I was so emotional. I tried to solve these problems maybe with more energy than if it's my own business.

> An.: There is a joke between a headhunter specialist that you should always take single women with their child for the positions because they can work harder. They do a lot for the company to compare themselves not only with other women, but also with men.

Russian female executives: Career-oriented and flexible

The Russian women are highly career-oriented and motivated. Their main focus is their interest in their work, combined with a powerful desire to achieve and the considerable demands they place on themselves. The Russian women want to achieve things within the company, be decisions-makers and to initiate change. They reject routine and like variety in their work. This strong desire to achieve is something that the women describe as having been present since childhood. They compete with themselves in order to excel.

They are also driven to attain the freedom that comes from high positions. They do not want to be told what to do, but want to take the decisions and shape the future themselves.

When asked about work-life balance, the Russian women often argue that there is no such thing. Due to being so focused on their careers, the women choose their work over their personal lives. At the same time, they strive to fulfil both roles – the perfect wife and mother and the career woman – but privately it is the career that they see as more important. Their other role serves mainly to meet the demands of society.

> N.: To be honest, I have never planned my steps. I wanted and I want that each my next step should be higher. As a child I knew that I would be a top manager one day. I remember in the Soviet Union you got ahead when you became a party member. I remember when I was 12. I told my parents that I wanted to join the party. They were a little shocked and asked why. I told them I wanted to be a top manager. I wanted it to be better than my parents, yes, money was a driving force and the level of communication that would make it possible.

> A.: Everything is always very interesting for me and I want to be involved. It is interesting for me to test myself. I think that is my incentive to test myself, to see if I can or not. This is an advantage and at the same time it can also be a disadvantage. I do it everywhere, in family sports, it's my second husband. It is also a challenge. Really. I always have to challenge myself.

> E.: I didn't want to be powerful or anything. No no no. I just didn't want anyone to tell me what to do. Yes, that also has its disadvantages (grins). We know that everything has its origin. I love my job like crazy, really. I love being creative, working with these brilliant people, I love it. It's like looking for genius. This is the difference to men who always want to be the best. I want to work with the best people, often better than myself. I always say you do better than me. You will take my place at some point, that's the way it is and it's a good thing. I'm not afraid that someone is better than me. I love working with good people. I just know what I want for myself. It doesn't matter what others think about it.

> O1: I remember that period because I was three months pregnant. Also, when I moved, a month later, my boss has announced he's leaving. I would have probably left with him as well. He was moving to another company. It was almost like a crisis at my hand at work, because I was brought into a certain position and then the whole thing just collapsed, so I don't know what I'm doing anymore. I did the same thing as I did before, I basically went to my bosses in LA and then said, "This is my vision how this whole thing might work. This is the team I'd like to have. I'd like to have an opportunity to run this, please." They said, "Go ahead." I was six months pregnant. I hired the whole team, I trained them. For me, it was almost like setting up a new business because emerging markets is quite separate part of business, so it was running a certain way before. I felt really strong because I know those people, they're my people, I know how they think, what their challenges are. I felt very strong, I think we need to almost run it as a separate business with our vision, so I put like a vision and a mission statement.

All three areas – performance motivation, leadership motivation and the desire to shape processes – are highly pronounced among the Russian women. Their strongest characteristic is their flexibility. They are able to look beyond their own horizons and successfully solve unforeseen problems. They are keen to take on responsibility and seek power in order to gain the freedom to influence events. Emotional stability and resilience are two further categories of the Business-focused Inventory of Personality, BIP, which emerged from the interviews. The energy these women expend and the strain placed on them are extremely high; so high, in fact, that many women need career breaks because of threatened or actual burnout. Under these circumstances they tend to quit their jobs, take a break and then return to a position at the same level. A similar practice was observed among the Chinese women, but they use the breaks specifically for having children and often re-enter the workforce at a higher level.

> O1.: When I talk about my values that I actually have somewhere on my wall. Responsibility is power. For me it is almost like being proactive in taking responsibility for something and that gives you the power to make things happen. I actively take additional responsibility. Then my way forward was a series of things. As I did with global emerging countries for a while, so did 57 countries.

Another strength seen among the Russian women is the ability to develop individual strategies and to push through their own ideas and solutions, even in the face of opposition – and this in spite of major challenges, such as market shifts or the pressure to achieve results. The women describe the individual strategies they develop despite the enormous pressure to be innovative. They cite their private lives as a source of strength, and a further source is their own flexibility when responding to change, as well as their willingness to embrace change and to be able to continue operating under changed conditions.

> E.: Every day I see what we got for the previous day. To work like 20 or more years everyday with these ratings. It's like you go for the foreign market and you are absolutely naked. Every day you go naked to the foreign market and everybody is looking at you and giving you numbers and charges. Today you are like five, no yesterday it was like you are not very good, you were like two. It's every day if you are thinking if you got the best numbers you are thinking you know that now your bosses is going to call you, or the company owners are going to call and you got all these phone calls like it's yelling. When you have this every fucking day, it was difficult for me to find the way where to get strengths to survive and to fighting for new challenges because in the morning you get all that, what the people think about you. (chuckles) They are not very intelligent in their sentences because it's media business. After that, you are supposed to go to find these ideas, to find programs, to put people together all that stuff. You need to do all your routine, which is not a routine because you need to be a very creative person every day. It's not like you put in two plus two. You need to create, create, and create. The most difficult thing to find is strength inside yourself to these new ideas.

> O1.: Lots of things changes because the market started deteriorating shortly after 2007. It's still deteriorating. The whole film market is going down and down and down. I think from that age, you just manage with the decline. It's a tough space to be mentally because you used to be a very sexy business, which everyone desires to be in, and you end up being a business which has to fire people and manage the decline every year. Keeping heart in it and keeping that motivation is actually quite hard. I think I found my solace in looking into efficiency. If I can't keep opening businesses because it's not there is no budget anymore, it's about efficiency. I started looking at accumulating our processes about legal things, about licensing, about our sales systems, about reporting. Again, that's I think how I've taken over the role. I think about things, and then I start knocking on their doors and say, "I think we need a sales system. I think we don't have a customer P&L. Why we don't have a customer P&L? Can I have a budget to develop one?" I'm bringing it there sometimes because I feel strongly we need something. I was lucky to have really accepting bosses, even though they kept changing, but generally, I got my way through in most cases and were given that responsibility.

> O1.: It was quite depressing. Lots of changes. Top management change, the whole customer strategy stopped being important. It was again, focused on, I don't know, making money, something else. The old values have gone from the business. I think the last year there, I was feeling quite depressed about not being able to make decisions and not being able to do things which actually help businesses. It's just felt that everyone personally just manages their own personal career, and that's financially. That is all people think about. I just can't operate like that. I find it enormously depressing. Also, what I realized reporting into higher levels of corporate, is that the higher you move, the less impact you're actually able to make to the real business, the more detached you are from a real business. You almost start being viewed as somebody who just sits in the board meetings and produces enormous number of debts in the presentations, but actually never actually touches business, and I hate that. I'm quite hands-on and I love to be in business, and I really don't like to be very corporate about that. I remember feeling just fatigued with another three-hour meeting where everyone- it's all so political. I think that F. offering me that position was really timely and actually very helpful because unlike S., which is very, very corporate structure. F. is actually quite entrepreneurial culture. They're a lot free, they have lots of flexibility. Obviously, the politics exist everywhere, but they're quite not as prominent. I just

found it enormously rewarding working for them, because I just fell back into business. I started traveling again, running across Europe, setting up.

Russian women are dealing proactively with unwelcome conflict

Like many of the women interviewed around the world, Russian women respond to questions about their ability to deal with conflict by making it clear that they dislike conflict. It quickly becomes apparent, however, that they are not afraid of it and know their own strength in conflict situations. They go for a confrontational approach, learn from past conflicts and, depending on their objective and on the circumstances, have different coping strategies at their disposal.

> V.: I do not like conflicts, it is like playing chess. I play chess. (laughing) I just do not have many occasions for it.

> E.: Usually, I'm not happy with that because I am not a conflict person. Sometimes conflict, sometimes it helps to make a new level, it's true, but it's better to make it a healthy conflict because if I am thinking about the conflicts at work, usually nothing good could happen after that. It's better to work feeling that the conflict is coming. For me, it's better to for me, I hope that I usually can see that. If it is in my hands, I'm trying to avoid the fight and trying to find the way how to avoid the conflict. The best way, talking to the other side. I always was good in negotiation. I guess because on my experience on the conflicts usually it's like people don't understand what the other person meant. Not because they have to put a gun on your head. No, it's usually just deep misunderstanding.

> A.: To my mind, there are three types of conflicts that can be in my life. For example, the first one is the potential conflict with your client or with outside partner. It's very difficult to make conflict with me. Because with clients, with partners, I am rather professional and for partner to create a conflict with me, it's really a very complicated task. The second type of conflict is the conflict with your colleagues. But here, from the age of 27, I'm usually on top position. That's why conflict is almost impossible with me. [laughs] But the most possible conflict for me is of the third type, and it's the conflict with co-founders. It's from my sister and with my husband. Here, for sure, the risk and the danger of the conflict is the highest. They are in equal positions. There is possibility to have to have the conflict of interest and the family also. (laughs) Yes. If to analyze my conflict behavior, I think I attack very fast. [laughs] Go back and observe. (laughs). I am here to find the balance between this attack. Sometimes I need to bite. So, I need to aid the situation of discomfort. That's to show the problem. But then I go back, try to be calm in order to make myself available to solve this situation that I opened.

> N.: My behavior changed, of course, during class the 20 years. I have very interesting case. When I was CEO in XY (company name), I had conflict with IT director. We have absolutely different position, and our boss understood that he had to choose one position, mine or my colleague's. He chose my position and IT director had to leave company. – I am winner, but in two years, I reevaluate this situation. I hired him back the guy who was IT director in my team. Sorry, it doesn't matter what I did during the conflict. I know today I was wrong. He is a good professional as IT director, but my position in this conflict wasn't right and I could reevaluate this situation.

Leadership style in conflict with cultural norms

Management in Russia is characterized by a rather hierarchical, authoritarian leadership style based on guidelines and systems of reward and punishment. The Russian top women managers thus operate in an environment shaped by transactional, authoritarian leadership. As described at the beginning of the chapter, this leadership style is associated more with men than with women. The Russian female executives describe their style as team-oriented, inclusive and tailored to the needs of employees. They are highly team-oriented. They make decisions wherever and whenever it is in the best interests of the company and try to give employees as much freedom as possible. The interviewees often describe how important it is to select and keep the right team, and the key to this is trust. If trust is lacking, the women have no hesitation in taking the necessary steps and replacing specific team members.

> N.: I think sometimes I'm very gentle with people. Men are harder there. They said it should be ready by tomorrow and they don't care how the employee does it. With me, on the other hand, my employees can come to me and say: "Okay, Natalia. Yesterday it was a very bad day, my child was sick. I had to leave my office early blah, blah, blah." I often say then: "Okay So tomorrow. "A man will say," I don't care. You're fired, "so easy. I don't think that's a good thing.

> O1.: Friendly and inclusive. I was actually accused of that once when I had this team, which I had when I was pregnant, et cetera. We built such a great team and such a great business and then things changed and bosses changed and the new boss who came over. He said, "What you build here, all of this is family. This is not how it should be in the corporate." But we were, we're still friends and we work there's so much motivation there. I don't micromanage, I delegate quite easily. I tend to rather say, "You know what, I trust your judgment, go run with that. If it doesn't come back well, we'll deal with that. Just have a try." I give responsibility quite easily. I tried to be very unhierarchical. I hate the whole, who reports to who outside of actually that makes sense of business like somebody needs to know who makes the ultimate decision but the way you talk, we must be all equal. I would say yes, quite democratic, I guess and very warm like I share a lot. I was actually doing a speech from company culture and building my own company right now, and I said, "You have to walk the talk." It's important for me that women have work-life balance. Not just women, the parents especially, so I promote that. I say, count to three, I have to pick up my child from school, or whatever." I think you should be very aware that they are dependent on your judgment. They always view you as like, will she hate me if I do that, will she allow us to work from home on Fridays? Do I damage my career? You should be aware of the impact you have on their life. If you strongly believe this is the right thing to do, you should exemplify that. I also think, obviously different corporate structures are quite different, but still, even within the structure, you're never responsible for the whole company. Some women do and then they can. Even if you're responsible for a certain department or certain area or something, you can still promote that even if the culture is different.

> N.: I believe that the main factor of success is that it is not only my success. It is the success of team. I need to track the strongest team. I'm sure that each of my team should be stronger in their functional area than me and that's why I need to trust them and if I trust them, I can delegate a lot of things and I don't like micro-management. I know that a lot of members of my team can evaluate these points because it's very important for team that I trust them, I don't check them every minute. As I told you that people who are more professional in some functional area me and the team I need to see the total pitch, the total strength and usually I fully trust

my members of the team but if I see as the head of team that we need to change our direction because it's necessary for common purpose. I will be authoritative in this case.

V.: Russian style is usually hierarchical 95 percent in Russia we have a formal self and informal one, in Russian companies they are very formal, with dress and so, I am now dressed like friend. I chose a company with my culture , Russian TV channels is usually very hierarchical, people are still vertical managed , I chose another culture in the telecom market, it is different from TV market, it is a more free atmosphere, communicate the whole pictures, describe them their advantage and their role, transformational and democratic, I am a member of the team , give them right to do mistakes, in difficulties help them to go forward in small steps, I am with them

Na.: If there is no trust, then I can no longer work with the person. Because trust is trust. I then decide relatively quickly that I will not work with this person. I then change the person.

When it comes to professional challenges, developing one's own management style was the main theme. Here the focus is on how to make use of different management styles, as well as on developing one's assertiveness and own individual management style. This posed a challenge to several of the Russian women, especially with regard to promotions to CEO level. The issue was to determine how, as a woman, to respond to different types of employees and how to assert oneself as the boss.

M.: The team leadership is a challenge. The people in the company are very different, so they need different leadership, different feedback and different motivation. You have to take this into account when leading.

N.: If you take the next step, you have to change. Well, you can't keep the relationships going. It's impossible to stay on the same level, impossible. Well, people, when they come to the boss, they want to see the director. They want directions and goals. Second, they want to see the person, but first, they want to have a very clear logic of strategic instructions. they want to know if you are the person who understands what the company needs. It was really difficult, probably six months or more, and I needed a lot of support from my husband because of course I cried a lot in the evenings. I said, "they hate me. They don't want to follow my views." I had to prove that I can be the person who can lead them and the person where they go and get good advice

Advantages of being a woman

What is striking, time and again in the interviews, is the humor and relaxed way in which most Russian female executives deal with stereotypes and discrimination by men. They seek out the weaknesses that the men have as a result of these stereotypes and use them to their own advantage. They display self-confidence, shrewdness and strategic thinking.

A.: I would say that Russian women in the business, they are rather strong, powerful. Really, sometimes I think that they can be stronger than men. The general opinion is the opposite. I would compare it with the attitude to women drivers on the roads in Russia. If something happens and the driver is woman, the reaction, "Ah." Everybody understands it's because it's women. I think the same in business. There is such attitude and such reaction. "What you can do, it's woman." The power of women, I use from this side. I'm using usually this general attitude to the woman, for a woman in business. I can become stupid. It's a very good possibility- to play your own game. I'm a woman, I do not understand these figures, and to observe the reaction. When you are in negotiations, you play a role of such a stupid woman. Your opposite side, your opponent, he loses the attention, his level of attention becomes slower. You can receive your results faster and even bigger result that you decided before or your opponents expected. Because when our man they make negotiations with the beautiful women, they pay attention, not to the topic of the negotiations. I do not consider myself beautiful, but I know that I have friends, women who are very clever and who are beautiful really. When men speak to beautiful woman, they think naturally that they are not clever. They cannot combine cleverness with beauty, it's a different range. A woman can use this power.

Family versus Career

Due to the high proportion of women in management positions in Russia, can one conclude that they see their primary role is in holding the job? In line with social demands, Russian women should first support their partners and be a caring mother. The top female executives interviewed report how they combine the sometimes contradictory role expectations.

Russian husbands: Impediments or mentors

"*A woman should fear her husband*", quoted Boll-Pajevskaja (2009) from the sixteenth-century book of social rules in Russia, the *Domostroy*. It also says, "*A man should love his wife*". Despite the traditional notions about the distribution of roles, a number of authors maintain that "authoritarian or hierarchical relationships" no longer exist in modern Russian families. Family and marriage are of great importance in Russian culture. However, divorce rates in Russia are very high and are similar to those in Western Europe.

How do the Russian female executives describe their husbands and the influence they have on their careers? The research provides examples across the entire range of possible family circumstances. A small number of the women have been married for many years, some are divorced, about half of them have remarried and a quarter are single. The women's descriptions of their husbands range between two diametrically opposed poles. At one extreme we find the extremely supportive partner, who acts as mentor in his partner's career and offers a shoulder to lean on during crises. At the other is the traditional husband who offers no support in household chores or child-rearing, despite the fact that all but one of the women earn more than their husbands. This group of men also do not advance professionally, instead remaining below their partners' professional level.

> T.: The couples are still very traditional, my husband did never work really, I had 2 nannies, he never did anything, I had 2 nannies and one house helper, my husband is not progressive, he did nothing for 16 years, so I divorced. Often women stay in marriage because it is the easier way, the word marriage in Russian means " I am behind my husband", you see it is so traditional. The society forces you to stay in unhappy marriage, better not so good husband than no husband, as a divorced it is a kind of shame

Those women who describe themselves as happily married say that they take care not to play a dominant role at home, but instead slip back into the conventional role of mother and housewife, albeit with the support of a domestic helper. A study by Metcalfe and Afanassieva (2005) reports that Russian women generally go along with the traditional distribution of roles, expect no support from their husbands and even approve of the double burden. This applies both to childrearing and to the household. The unequal burden on women is blamed on the state and the lack of childcare provision, rather than on partners. The Russian women thus have no real expectation of gender equality within the family, whereby men do their share of the domestic chores. In this area of life, equality between the genders does not yet seem to have been achieved.

> N.: We try to share and my family is not my company. In the family, I am a wife and I am a mother. Even sometimes when the professional changes, of course, happened in myself. So sometimes I teach myself that I want to say, "Okay, please stop it and do as I'm waiting. You should do it like this." I try never to do it like this. Even sometimes I want to do it. I know that the family is the world where two persons that live together and they can hear each other, they will live happily and for a long time. If somebody will demand always something, it will influence their relationship badly. My husband has a job lower than mine. Quite often, our friends ask Alex, my husband, or me, "So who is the leader? Who's the head? Probably she is because she is a big boss," and he said no, and I said as well. We are equal parts of one unique something. When I was promoted to director level, again, I cried in the evening. [laughs] I still remember in the morning when I needed to go to the office, I cried on my husband's shoulder and said, "I don't want to go there because they all hate me, they don't want me because I'm a new person and with my new rules, new experience, they don't want to change." He said, "Come on, you are a director. Go and do your job.

> I.: The one thing I have had issues with previously in Russia was the ability of men to accept that I have a senior position, and very young, and I earn my own money, and I have no interest in them unless they are [unintelligible] and unless they also let me develop. Because I have had those issues actually, and already thinking through that. And I convey through different kind of relationships. This one is different, and in a great way. But in general, I would say that I have this issue. Hopefully, I will never have to think about this again, since I'm looking into a relationship that is very long to permanent.

Children: yet another thing to be managed

Of the female Russian top managers, 60 percent have one or two children aged between eight and 18 years. Forty percent of the women have no children. Whereas in

Soviet times the state offered an almost seamless childcare system tailored to the needs of working women, after the country's restructuring the provision of childcare has been steadily reduced. A large number of childcare facilities have closed on cost grounds. Crèche places are no longer guaranteed and nurseries are based on the prevailing Western model, where childcare provision does not start until the age of three. How do the female managers cope with balancing children and careers? As in China, grandmothers often help take care of small children in the first few years of life. If the women are already earning a good salary, domestic helps and nannies are additionally brought into play. The stress of having to reconcile the two is considerable, but the desire to continue with a career is greater. Most of the respondents have the attitude that they want to have a career and that children do not pose an obstacle to this, even though they represent an additional task to be managed.

> M.: I had a driver, a nanny and my mother (laughing) I had no problem with that.

> N1: I think that I can be proud of my career and of my family, both. I really believe that I'm the best wife and I'm the best mother. The family has never been on the second slide for me, never. I was only at three months on maternity leave. Because I started to work half a day. During nine months. Then fulltime. Three or four years he was at home, and then during two years, he went to kindergarten. I had a housekeeper and a driver then. With 6 he went to school.

> N2: So I was in this company when my daughter was just two. I stayed at home for two years. I was so emotionally connected to her. When I look back and think about whether I should have done something different? Yes, I would do it differently because the two years was not what I wanted. Do not get me wrong. My family is important to me. For example, I'm giving a big party just for our wedding day. With 40 guests. When I was thinking about going back to business, the problem was finding someone you could really trust. At that time, we had no childcare options. It was difficult to find someone to trust with your child. My mother did that when it was difficult for her too. I was really so emotional, I missed her so much and I just gave her a hug and tell her that I miss so much. Actually, she didn't pay attention. That time I understand that, okay, maybe I was missing her more than she was missing me. She was absolutely in the TV and she was watching something and she said, "Okay, come in. Yes, I'm very happy. Okay, go." For me, it was really difficult. I'm a very responsible person and I love business, I love doing business and when I started working, of course, I was hungry to solve that problems, to make some decisions. How to say? I'm trying to find the right word. When a person jumped into the water, how to say? I actually was overwhelmed of all the new things around me. Of course, that two years, I was very closed from their world, I was sitting at home, doing some home things, about the baby, about the home. It's awful. I was hungry and surrounded by women who were forced to be housewives. Unfortunately, there is not a big opportunity to do it differently because you're limited by financial. Of course, we had to do it our self, for our family, so I did it. Then my mother helped me. To tell the truth, if I have another child, I think it'll happen differently, absolutely. Of course, depends on many things.

> A.: Yes, I left the company. For me, pregnancy is a very difficult period, so the first pregnancy and the second, I spent almost all months in the hospital. That's why I was made to leave the company but then after the birth of a child, I did not work only for six months [laughs] and I think that my children, maybe they have no influence to my career absolutely. I can say that, they have no influence. To my mind, there are two different ways and it depends from

the internal personal concept, and these ways are opposite. One way is to devote yourself to children. Have more than three children to devote yourself, to devote to children and to husband but there is one condition that husband needs to earn enough money. Maybe this condition is not the main one. The main is the internal concept of a woman. If she considers that she needs to devote herself, she does it. The second opposite way is to make a career and children are not obstacle to this and you have time to do both things and to have three children for example, and to have a career and to be very active in a public position. Really, in my surrounding, there are women like these who are much more active than me and really, I don't know how many hours is their day. (laughs) Sometimes, for me, it's a secret because, (laughs) I have some friends who have, for example, four children and one of them is adopted, with some problem and then the job with the international career and everything (chuckles) is at level. I think that the secret is to be active and not be afraid to start something that you want. When you start you will find the time, but if you do not start, you will always believe you would not have time for both. You need to start and then we shall see.

O1.: Yes. I might have done that probably. I hardly remember few years where I had young children, like babies, because I breastfed them until one and a half, both of them. I breastfed through three years on the row, working full time, and traveling every week. I was cooking, I was spending all weekends with me, I had zero time for myself. I never had holidays outside of being with children. I think it's like it's in a date, I can't remember those years. I think I slept for four or five hours every night for a few years. I look badly and I think I recovered when I divorced, so those five years of both having children and working in building career, he was always like, I don't know, a crusade, like, "I'm just doing this. Whatever happens, I have to survive. I have to survive." Not really thinking about yourself, and how you feel, and what you want. I had a nanny at some point, so she would be there up until I come back. I think the challenge for me was that you wake up at 7:00 AM in the morning so you can, I don't know, feed your kids, spend some time with them. Then the nanny comes in at 8:30 a.m. You go to work, you're there till 5p.m., you rush back, you literally run back so that kids don't feel deprived. You pick them up from your nanny, you're with them up until they're in bed by whatever, 9 p.m. Then you keep on working, because I was not coping really well. You go to bed at midnight, and then they wake up every two hours or something because they're babies. You sleep like four or five hours, and then every morning you wake up and you keep on going. It's a robotic experience. You just keep on going. I'm quite high functional, so what I learned is that I actually can function quite well on very little sleep, bad food habits, and being multi-tasked to the point of breaking. I still function. I know a lot of people would fall into depression.

I.: It is difficult to find a balance between work and family. I think there is no balance. In my case, the work takes up a lot of space. And it was difficult to accept that. So I don't spend five hours with my daughter every day. It was difficult to accept. I love my job.

E.: They can manage it because they are strong. Some of them can, some of them not. They're usually very strong. People know than, that during six or seven years you couldn't call anymore. Because they're spending their time with their family. They have enough salaries and money to find people who support them, the people who are taking care of their kids, but usually they are working 24/7 and they are getting crazy. I know a lot of people like that, especially in our business, in the media. We are all crazy and we don't have a life. We have only our work because it's not possible to have a life. That is why most of us, and for example me, take some time off or change profession after seven years because it's not possible on the long run.

Factors holding back Russian women's careers

The much-described glass ceiling also exists in Russia. But not everywhere in the country. Stereotypical comparisons with male leadership behavior and male characteristics are viewed as good leadership by women themselves and perceived as weakness in themselves.

Russia also has a glass ceiling

For the majority of women, the presence of a glass ceiling is evident in politics and in CEO appointments, especially in large state-owned enterprises and in rural areas. The glass ceiling is perpetuated by men who feel unable to respect women in these positions and by women who are afraid of power. In certain areas, according to the accounts, there is either no glass ceiling or else it is not obvious. This is especially true in small and medium-sized enterprises. In multinational companies the glass ceiling depends on the culture at the head office.

> A.: I can guess that there is a glass ceiling in big corporations. In small and middle, I did not notice such glass ceilings.

> N.: It exists in Russia as well. Especially in some big companies. You will never see the ladies managing. For example, our famous XY (company name) or government companies, there are a lot of men bosses in every place. But in the private business, you can see quite often that the ladies are managing and this is our case, this is the case of my company.

> T.: Of course no women can be president of this company, I can think of only 2 ministers in high positions, so there is a glass ceiling in politics, no women responsible for large territories in Russia politics, only one example I think, on the business side I do not know, of course stakeholders must have an open mind to put a women on such a position so it depends, but with the influence of Western style of management women can be high, if it is a big manufacture in Siberia only men can be manager of this.

Stereotypical comparisons with male executives

Overall, the Russian women appraise those aspects of themselves that they see as weaknesses in a very frank and self-aware manner. As with the accounts of their skills, their answers are to the point. One weakness often mentioned is impatience. In addition, they say that they would like to be tougher and faster in their decision-making, in other words, to embrace and make use of the authoritarian aspects of leadership that they see in men. In some of the interviews, women expressed a prejudice against certain team members and an inability to trust. Certain stereotypical attitudes can be discerned in the women's perceptions of businesswomen as compared to businessmen. One example of this is that they consider women to be overly emotional but men to be tough, and they see the latter as being good for business.

This analysis result is in line with the few findings available from other researchers, such as Metcalfe and Afanassieva (2005), on Russian women in management.

> N1.: I think for men and women it's the same task, but for men sometimes they have the advantage that at the beginning everybody believe they can do. For women, sometimes depend on the environment they think, "Can she do? Can she not do?"
>
> N2: Of course, men are more strategic and certainly really smart, sometimes smarter than women. But women, when we make decisions, don't just do it fundamentally based on numbers, as men do in most cases. Women also do it based on feelings. I read an article about it and they say that if women also make decisions based on their soul and heart, it is very good for a healthy business. Because if there are only numbers and very dry decisions, it is not very good for the future, not very good for the atmosphere in the company. The woman is still a mother. Of course, I will never say that to my colleagues. I am a manager who never discusses and makes decisions without emotions. Never. Because I'm emotional to tell you the truth.
>
> I.: This is something I would like to have. I need this fearlessness to believe in things. Whether it will work or not. Also, fearlessness of speaking and reciting crowds. Even if I have no idea. … well he's a businessman. He's a great businessman, he knows his business very well, of course, otherwise he wouldn't be a president. He is fearless in seeing things, imagining things and asking questions. I can actually give him an answer like, "Hey, President, that's not possible. It just won't work." But he put the question back. I think the ability is great. It is this fearlessness.
>
> A.: What I am trying to explain is that the ladies due to all these things, they are more responsible and they work harder. They are hard workers. Of course, it is reflected in all the spheres of our life, in the family, in business. Even my boss, for example, the owner of the company, he said, "I was really stupid when I used to hire men as the CEO of the company because- well, there is not only the point of the sex, of course. But men and men, they always need to fight, need to understand who is the leader. When the combination is different, when there is a lady and a man, in my case, for example, my owner is a man and he's a very strong man, very powerful and very strong character. Having this position here, I have to be flexible. This is great about ladies. They're not straightforward as men, but at the same time, I am responsible. I can work for many hours and I will never say, "I am lazy, I'm tired. Please give me some water, some break, something." But men in our country.

Coaching by business psychologists

When asked about mentoring, networks and coaching, few answers are forthcoming. The Russian female executives mention sponsors who have recommended them for a higher position and owners who see the women as their "right hand man". There are no accounts of mentoring, in the sense of imparting knowledge and sharing experience. There is also very little to report on the subject of networking. None of the women mention executive coaching, a concept which is still new in Russia. On the other hand, many of the women receive regular support from "business psychologists", especially during periods of intense stress. The psychologist becomes a trusted advisor when weathering difficult career phases and personal problems. It is noteworthy that the Russian women mention "their psychologist" openly and matter-of-factly.

> Y.: When I was still working in the multinationals, I was like in a box. I was focused on the job. The others are also more concerned with reconciling long working hours and family. Some do a little targeted for job changes. Only now do I sometimes go to conferences. The people here are rather closed, not like in China with networks.

Russian female executives: identity and image

What is an ideal woman like, from the Russian perspective? Sociology research, traditional fairy tales and national customs can all help to answer this question. In Russian fairy tales, the main characters are often wise, skilled women, for example "Wassislissa the Wise", the main character in many of the stories. Russian authors tend to choose female protagonists characterized by strong values and who are central to the family and the raising of children. They are women who support their husbands.

Somewhere between manager, mother and "real woman"

In Russian, femaleness is very important. While in German, "Germany" is known as the "fatherland", in Russia the country is known as "mother Russia". Many Russian symbols are feminine and many scientists classify Russia as a "feminine" country, although there is no consensus here. There is dissent among scholars as to whether to classify the country as a patriarchy or as a country with some matriarchal traits. Although Russian women played an important role in history and culture, they often remained in the background. There is an old proverb which illustrates a belief that many Russians have: "behind every successful man, there is a wise woman". A traditional song conveys that "only a Russian woman can be a wife, a mother and a lover all at the same time".

> T.: They think of me with respect, I achieved all by my work, I am a role model for my subordinates, they would say "you are a mum, you are a leader, you are a successful woman".

> V.: In Russia the most important for women is to be married and have kids and then career on top, is good. But if you do not have a husband and a woman who only focus on career, this is not well seen here.

The Russian women's lifestyles changed after the restructuring of the economy and the growing consumerism that went with it, such that the traditional role models were likewise restructured. Boll-Palievskaya (2009) writes that Russian women seek to enhance their femininity for cultural reasons. Femininity in this context means maternal instinct, a caring attitude and a willingness to support a man with warmth and tact. In one study of Russian women, the interviewees speak of becoming "a real woman". Female managers see their primary roles as those of supporting their husbands, looking and acting feminine, and seeking ways of having a successful career within this framework of values. At the same time, researchers are currently observing the emergence among Russian women of a female professional identity, which is in turn is leading to greater career confidence. According to Chirikova (2002), Russian studies report that due to the institutionalization of gender roles Russian women tend not to feel qualified to take on leadership responsibilities. An interesting difference between Russian and Western literature lies in the former's focus on the capacity of women professionals to assume a female leadership identity. Metcalfe provides a substantive report on this, in connection with a more comprehensive analysis of leadership differences between men and women. Integral to female professionalism are a feminine style of dress, make-up and feminine behavior. These debates are in keeping with contemporary studies on gender and management which focus on aesthetics, health management and gender fluidity. This is also discussed in the chapter on French women. In both Russia and France, there is ongoing debate as to how best to achieve a female managerial style in which professionalism and femininity are combined.

Results from a study by Gvozdeva (2002) indicate that female managers frequently have stereotypical perceptions of management skills and qualities and a tendency to devalue feminine attributes. In order to gain access to employment opportunities, education and professional development programs, women have to actively consider the question of femininity and sexuality. The findings highlight the gender-specific nature of the economic transition, the conflicting organizational demands placed on women and the new market structures that are shaping the experiences and identities of women managers in Russia.

> N.: If she has a beautiful expensive car, a good position, most of the people will think, "She has a connection with the boss or with some man, some powerful man who had interest in her." 100%. Especially in my case, I heard so many times that I'm very attractive, of course. It's clear why. I never paid attention to that. I think it's stupid to pay attention, even to discuss it, but people say so. Another way is, if she's successful, she's- can I say, a bitch? I think you can understand what am I meaning. She's a bitch because she doesn't care for her family, for her children, for her husband. She's a crazy businesswoman. Probably she has problems with her head and with her nervous system.

> I.: So it's the prejudice is massive. I have to say that also given that I don't really talk about my personal life that much, with the exception of close friends. I've heard so many different rumors about myself. Some of them hilarious. I've literally, as you may imagine, given much work into my career path, and be where I am 33 years old. There were a lot of people who obviously think that I've slept with literally every single CEO of every company I work. This is the kind of prejudice that can happen here. Everyone that knows me personally, they obviously know that none of that is true. But the thing is that you can see the prejudice here. I think in Russia it's, I should say, a little more obvious than in the West. The one thing I have had issues with previously in Russia was the ability of men to accept that I have a senior position, and very young, and I earn my own money, and I have no interest in them unless they also let me develop. Because I have had those issues actually, and already thinking through that. And I convey through different kind of relationships. This one is different, and in a great way. But in general, I would say that I have this issue. Hopefully, I will never have to think about this again, since I'm looking into a relationship that is very long to permanent.

> E.: They only say that she puts all her energy to make a career. It's like a deep oriental thinking, because we are oriental country even in the European part. I am from an oriental family because at that time my grandmother was one of the big bosses in Moscow. My grandfather, her husband, was a worker. They couldn't even read. He didn't have an education. He couldn't read, but his wife was one of the biggest bosses in Moscow. She was like a CEO for the big factories. I do remember when I came as a child just to visit her, it's like a big, big factory, machines. My grandmother was like a director. When she was coming home, when her uneducated husband was waiting for her, she was preparing the dinner and, I don't know, the cooking, and all that stuff. Even now, I've never seen him work. At work, she was like– [roars]

> A.: About five years ago, I didn't want to work in a top management because a lot of women some were divorced, alone and not happy private life. For me, I don't want to be there in a top management. The women in top management, they have no choice. They just have to achieve their goals because there are problems in their private life, but then I meet some women who have three or more children and they are good in their family and happy with their partner, so husbands, as well as they happy at work and it changed my mind. It's not so many women that are happy in both areas. It's difficult to change the mind of me and also society. Just a moment. They are persistent, they are working a lot, they spend a lot of time at their job. Sometimes, they not only spend the evening at the office, they also work at night at home. They put their lives on achieving professional goals.

Russian female executives: beauty and career

"Beauty will redeem the world", wrote Dostoevsky. *"The expectation that a woman should be beautiful is a particularly Russian phenomenon. Beautiful women are worshipped and idolized in Russian society,"* writes Boll-Palievskaya (2009) in her book about Russian women. As previously mentioned, the demographics of the country mean that there is a surplus of women and so men are a scarce commodity. Nevertheless, a successful career does not free a Russian woman from the social expectation of being a wife first and foremost. According to Russian values, a woman's appearance is of great importance.

> N.: Natalia: I had one decision, one opinion about this. I will never change it. The appearance and it helps greatly. Just understand me in the appropriate way. When a person is really nice and attractive, it helps, because people are more open, they trust you more. It's really more comfortable to communicate with a person who is nice. Of course, during the first probably few minutes, but then, of course, you should show up your intelligence, your understanding, your profession, and everything. At that first period, it helps a lot.

> E.: I guess it's very important like everywhere. I've been in the States. I have some friends. They look different. [chuckles] You can be very good looking, you can be a not such a good looking, but in Russia, we are still like in the '80s compared to Europe or the States because we couldn't do our steps very fast. We're already doing them very fast, but it's not possible to make them so fast. I guess we can compare the States to rethink how the people behave, how the men behave to women and how the women are supposed to look like. It's close to that. It's better you to have a look, but it's not such a – for us, it's better if you have a wealthy or successful husband, so if you look like hell, you will make a career. (laughs) It's a little bit different.

A.: It's very important to be stylish person, to have very expensive things and details from Channel or Dolce & Gabbana or something, it's very important. Not so many people, especially women, can combine these things well. Professional stylists became more popular than before, here in Russia. People, sometimes even men, understand that they cannot combine things by themselves. They do need help for that to be a higher level, more respective, to have more money or something. That's why. It's important when you don't have your own good vision from your nature, you should have a stylist. It's important. It can be posture. They're calm and some ways of appearance. Manner of talking. It's also important for me how the person talk about everything. When you meet the person, in first 90 seconds, you can see just their appearance.

N.: One of the important things, because as I told you, women in Russia have to be the best in housekeeping, in baby teaching, and, of course, the queen of beauty. Yes, it's so-so because we have some stereotypes, if she is beautiful, she is not smart. Can it be that if she's too beautiful, it's not good for going in senior management, but if she's ugly, also not good?

T.: Women in Russia love to dress very much, they are often overdressed, when they have money they invest in brands and jewelry, women in power they all dress up well. they like it, in hierarchical companies you should demonstrate your position or your wealth. Of course, you can wear sneakers but Prada or LV. Rolex and Zara is possible as well, something must show that "she is ok", she is not a student. if you are a pretty woman, men will admire you, everyone likes beautiful people.

8 The ideal female executive: A résumé based on the global analysis

After evaluating all the data from the international research, along with the insights offered by the women top managers interviewed, the question arises as to what insights the Global Women Career Lab can offer to other women as they progress along their career paths. There are vocal calls worldwide for more female management role models who can offer women benchmarks against which they might measure their own performance and grow and improve. It is still often necessary for women to orientate themselves according to management criteria originating from research involving men – studies which, in the management literature, are regarded as setting the standard. In addition to the country-specific findings, the analysis allows conclusions to be drawn as to the characteristics which best describe the ideal international top female business executive. Is it possible to identify common features of successful women, over and above the differences that can be discerned in the country chapters?

What characterizes the ideal female top manager?

In what follows, a picture of the typical successful female corporate manager will be painted, for use as a reference point. It is important to note that these characteristics are to be found among all women in all countries. Only a few characteristics stand out as being unique to individual groups. This is to be expected, as all of these women have successfully advanced to the top echelons of corporate management in their respective areas. References to specific countries serve the purpose of deepening understanding rather than as a way of differentiating between the women.

It is hoped that women from all over the world will thus be provided with a framework for evaluating their own approaches and for developing the skills they need in order to become top managers.

The ideal female top manager pursues a management career unperturbed by her social environment and by prevailing norms. She is unaffected by the judgments of others.

As the Japanese women in the study have shown, a top management career is possible even in settings where there have previously been next to no women in top positions. The underlying quality that has enabled them to get this far is, among many other things, their independence from the stereotypes and demands made by society with respect to the prevailing image of womanhood. These include being unaffected by negative value judgments associated with strong women or by the role expectations surrounding motherhood or by stereotypes regarding how equipped a woman is to be a senior manager. All of the women in the Global Women Career Lab are undeterred by the notion "think manager – think male", according to which a successful leader is defined as having typically male characteristics, and instead have created their own "think manager – think female" definition with which they have successfully challenged the stereotype. They are very aware of prevailing social attitudes concerning successful women, but as far as they are concerned, the merits of their own image as a successful woman outweigh these. They acknowledge negative value judgments with good humor, but do not allow themselves to be put off by them. For many of them, being brought up by a strong mother has contributed to the fact that they do not accept having restrictions placed on them. In those places where women have grown up with more restrictive norms, such as in some parts of Germany, powerful women's networks actively discuss how to overcome the barriers faced by women in management.

It starts with an iron will: the ideal female executive is extremely career oriented and combines this with a powerful desire to pursue a management career and achieve personal advancement.

These female management role models are very evidently career oriented. This is reflected in all of the interviews in all of the five countries. Being anything other than a professional is out of the question for these successful women. And they want to be the brightest and best at their jobs. Any of the other possible expectations generally placed on women are subordinate to their primary role as manager. They are prepared to do whatever it takes to achieve a top management position. The women concentrate on strategically charting their own course within the constraints of today's corporate world with its established rules and power structures. A strong desire to pursue a management career is their alpha and omega and is arguably their main common denominator.

The ideal female manager, whether consciously or otherwise, has found the right spouse for her career plans. Almost all of the women in this study describe their spouse as being very supportive of their career. And the women appreciate this support and express their appreciation of it. All of the women interviewed are in agreement that having the right spouse is a very important factor in a woman's career. The stereotype of the "Shanghai Man" who does the household chores and is also frequently there for the children, does not apply in its entirety to all of the women's spouses, but in some cases this ideal is indeed attained. The women in the study accept that all spouses have their limitations and appreciate them for what they do. The majority of the women refer to the emotional support provided by their spouses, who offer support by taking a positive view of their partner's career and are good at giving advice. Many put their own career on hold or else do not aspire to have one. The ideal female manager is above all looking for a partner who will support her in her endeavors. In this study, a suitable partner is generally a husband with few or no career ambitions, or else one who has a positive attitude towards the complete reversal of the traditional roles.

Most of the role models interviewed here have children but remain in their primary role as leaders and do not aim for balance. For the women in the global survey, this is not a contradiction in terms. They define themselves first and foremost in terms of their management careers. For them, becoming a mother does not mean that they need to substantially change how they perform their primary role, that of business executive. Although many report temporary career slowdowns, they remain consistent in their objectives. This is not always easy, but for these women it is the only right way. None of the women see any need to be there for their children all or even most of the time and delegate a lot of the responsibility to others. They also agree that a good balance between the demands of a senior management position and those of being a mother who is almost always present is not really possible. The desire to achieve this seems unrealistic to many of them. The ideal female manager places the emphasis on lessening the burden of childcare and household chores and is more than happy to be completely relieved of them. Women who attempt to juggle, largely on their own, a top managerial job and both of these other tasks quickly reach the limits of what is feasible as well as of their own health. The ideal female manager proceeds very differently. A whole variety of solutions to the childcare question are described by the women. Many of these work very well, although not all are perfect. What the women have in common is that they have decided to use the available help, to invest in help or to organize their family structures in such a way that they receive sufficient and reliable support. Ideally, the female manager is almost entirely freed of both of the additional tasks and instead concentrates on spending quality time with her children.

The ideal female manager is highly motivated, aims to be a role model and shows solidarity with other women.

In the scientific categories of the BIP-Dimensions which categorizes personality factors linked with managerial success, all of the women surveyed scored highly in the areas of Performance Motivation, Leadership Motivation and Motivation to shape processes. Some countries show clustering in Performance Motivation, which refers to the achievement of top performance, and also in Motivation to Shape Processes, which refers to the responsible supervision of change processes in a company. The women's underlying motivation derives from the search for fulfilment through employment. Many would like to be role models, for other women and also for men. They measure themselves against their own personal benchmarks in terms of performance, leadership and behavior with the aim of becoming role models for employees and colleagues through their integrity and authenticity. Female role models are motivated primarily by values other than material ones. The women derive deep satisfaction from their responsibilities, stand up for their teams and support and encourage their employees. The ideal female manager shows a great deal of solidarity towards other women and has also benefited in turn from such solidarity. In places where there are already a large number of women in senior management, the descriptions of female superiors, supporters and mentors are many and varied. In many of the career paths described, women who have supported the executives interviewed play a special role. All the women studied during the research for this book have the desire to show solidarity towards other women. This was their main motivation for agreeing to lengthy, in-depth interviews, sometimes revealing highly personal topics, and for joining the Global Women Career Lab.

The successful female top manager engages actively and self-confidently with career planning, seeks opportunities and is unafraid of change.

Active career planning includes being clear about one's career goals. The majority of respondents give their goal as "Become the boss". To get as high up in the company hierarchy as possible, in order to be able to shape and to make a positive difference for employees. For many women, this goal is defined at an early stage, while others develop it in the course of their professional experience. They observe superiors, compare themselves to them and are certain that they can take on the same level of responsibility or more. This requires a fair degree of self-confidence. The majority of the women in the Global Women Career Lab have a high level of self-confidence, and when uncertainties arise along the way, the women seek targeted support, for example from their mentor coach. The female senior managers are flexible in their choice of company, work content and location. One of the strategies for success is to go where the opportunities are. Or, as the Russian women do, to actively seize the opportunities that lie ahead and to "jump on the career ladder". This also includes changing jobs when the glass ceiling (in most countries a given) cannot be penetrated. And these women have the ability to run the degree of risk that comes with change. They would in fact tend to regard remaining in a job too long as a greater risk, where there is nothing more to be gained. The majority of the women change company several times and demonstrate the classic characteristics of what is known in the literature as the "unbounded career". The desire for promotion and the search for new challenges is the primary motive for change.

The ideal female manager has a first-rate education and develops her management skills in a targeted manner.

The women in the study usually have two or more degrees from prestigious universities, are fluent in multiple foreign languages and list early experience abroad on their CVs. German and French women, in particular, have actively taken advantage of the opportunities offered by the broad range of choices available to them, and typically have already achieved many of the milestones associated with the ideal management resume early on in their careers. Many of them are multilingual and have obtained degrees abroad. French women in particular have taken advantage of the elite Grandes Écoles system and actively use it. Other women – such as the Russians – whose options are from the start more limited, work continuously on developing their skills. The top female managers have broad management expertise in various industries and sectors. They are also very aware of their weaknesses and address them without hesitation in order to develop and grow. Many of them work regularly with a qualified mentor coach to this end.

Early recognition of one's leadership style and the early assumption of leadership responsibility.

These female role models begin early on in their careers to reflect on their own particular female path to leadership and take on leadership responsibility at an early stage and in a targeted fashion. They concentrate on their female leadership strengths and deliberately use these to counterbalance or complement the skills which their male colleagues lack. Their leadership styles vary, but all of the women aspire primarily to lead in a transformational and democratic way. They know, however, that depending on the environment and the situation, a more transactive, authoritarian style of leadership, which scientific studies have generally attributed to men, can also be required. The ideal female executive has an awareness of the entire range of potential leadership approaches. For her, employee performance and development are central to leadership. The Japanese and Chinese women in particular offer numerous examples of this, and these provide food for thought regarding the strengths of the local management cultures.

Simply the best: The ideal female manager takes a positive, sporting attitude to competition and is not afraid of conflict.

Fair competition spurs these successful women on to top performance and gives them the opportunity to learn from others. For many of these women, the powerful desire to perform well is driven by a wish to excel and achieve outstanding results. If someone else performs better, the women use this as an opportunity to learn. Conflict, on the other hand, is not always so easy to resolve. The cultural aspects described earlier play a role here. Some of the women – for example the French – are fighting types who enter the fray head, while others tend to rely more on face-saving wait-and-see strategies. Within their respective cultural environments, the women tend to regard conflict in a positive light and actively engage in a variety of conflict resolution strategies.

Getting back on the horse – the women's response to challenges.

Top women managers take the many challenges they encounter over the course of their careers as an impetus for personal development. It is clear from the descriptions that the journey is not always an easy one. Women in top management are masters at dealing with challenges and the recommendations given above are the key to this success. They represent the core belief shared by all the women in this study: Giving up is not an option.

Lifelong learning – a core belief.

The female managers view personal development not as mandatory, but instead as an ongoing choice that does not end even once they have reached the top of the ladder. On the contrary. Curious and open-minded, they embrace current issues, methods and management theory. Many of them become coaches in an effort to provide better leadership for their employees. Topics such as digitalization, environmental protection, networks and agility in management are some of the themes they focus on. The promotion of diversity in companies is also an important topic.

The targeted, proactive use of mentors, networks and executive coaching are integral components of a successful career.

Receiving support from more than one mentor is essential for the career advancement of the women interviewed, and is usually not formally encouraged by the company, but is instead initiated proactively by the individual. The women benefit from their mentors' experience and networks of relationships and are aware of what they can offer their mentor in return. When it comes to mentoring women benefit from an increased level of trust compared to men, especially in those instances where foreign executives are operating in non-domestic markets. Successful female executives establish networks, often at an early stage and while they are still attending one of the elite universities. They go on to make use of these close contacts over the course of their careers. All of the women agree that they could do more in this regard. Above all, they should use the networks to further their own personal professional objectives, as they see the men doing. Up until now, women have networked primarily as a means of acquiring collective knowledge. The ideal female manager, however, does what the men do. She puts a lot of effort into her network, i.e. she supports and helps others in practical ways, and in return she uses the network to help her achieve her own objectives. The women have many observations to share about their relationships with their Executive Mentor Coaches, some of whom they have been consulting with for many years in order to overcome a range of challenges. Use of a coach is generally independent of a company and is regarded as a worthwhile and important element of personal development. For the ideal female manager, the mentor coach is thus a company-external, neutral partner who takes her out of her comfort zone and supports her in making the right career decisions.

9 Recommendations for the next generation of female executives

The top female managers in the five countries offer up a long list of recommendations for other women who aspire to reach the top. Much of the advice revolves around courage, determination, self-confidence and the will to succeed. Without these personality traits, none of the 110 women executives would have succeeded. An important message is to be authentic and true to oneself and to act with integrity. A prerequisite for this is that one must first know what one wants out of one's career. Many women around the world continue to find it difficult to follow their own path without experiencing feelings of guilt because of the cultural expectations placed of them. Because unlike men, they are expected to meet a different set of demands in terms of their role in life. Being without guilt means being inwardly free from the value judgments of others, going one's own way and expressing one's own opinions, especially with regard to one's role as a mother. Spouses are also very important. According to these women from around the world, the right choice of spouse has been a decisive factor in their careers. In addition to this, there are serious discussions to be had within the family at an early stage to ensure a woman with career ambitions has secured the support of her partner in order to be able to pursue her own career. The women's personal lives are thus of no small importance in the equation. Being visible and the effective, proactive use of mentoring and networks are other areas that the interviewees from the five countries identified as significant.

Finally, here are a selection of insightful recommendations from successful female executives:

> D. (France): The first is "Believe in yourself!" Because if you don't, things will be really difficult. And the second is… "Find a good partner."

> E. (France): Stop discriminating against yourself and complaining about "being a woman" and stop discriminating against other women. Women won't make things more equal by complaining about things not being equal. That's a somewhat radical point of view, but it's what I believe.

> C. (Germany): Be brave. Everyone fails from time to time. There's this saying: fall down, get up, straighten your crown, keep on walking. And don't take things personally, take things seriously. I know it's easier said than done. I think women do that quite often though, take things personally. And they take things home with them and get disappointed and upset. I think men are better than us at that. So don't take things personally and be yourself. Don't get caught up in power games. I believe it's important to be able to look yourself in the eye. Because I think that if you don't remain true to your own values and to yourself, you can't be successful. Only then can you really talk with enthusiasm about the things that matter to you. And not just talk about the things that you think the boss wants. Do things out of passion. In any case, I think you can only do a job well if you are really passionate about it and just really enjoy it. And then everything will work out and anything is possible.

> X. (China): My advice to young women: 1. Have an independent spirit. For me it has to do with my childhood, the fact that I had to cope on my own from an early age and had to take on re-

sponsibilities. 2. Courage 3. Boundless curiosity. That's something I have, because I'm never afraid of change. You have to be prepared to take the hits, like in the long jump, you have to practice a new jump over and over again, otherwise you end up stagnating.

B. (Germany): I'd say to young women in particular: "You have to put your hand up much more often and say I'm willing to do this or that. When I got one of my career breaks, when I became managing director, I went to my boss and said, "You're having a problem in Germany right now. I'll solve it for you and in return, you make me the CEO." They're not used to women putting themselves forward. And I got this really good tip from a woman at that time. She told me she went to one of her bosses and said: "You like earning your bonus. If you give me the job, I guarantee that my part of the business will work successful, so I guarantee you that my responsibility area of your bonus will be running well." And then I said, "Well, I'll take a bonus too if it works out." You just have to give things a go.

I. (France): Don't sell your soul, be yourself. That's really important. In other words, don't try to be like a man, don't try to be what you're not. It's really important... It's not about being successful, it's about being successful as a team, that's what the world's all about these days. I've had a lot of fun in my career because I've met some fantastic people, I've made a lot of friends, the people I've worked with. I've met a lot of people in my professional career who've become friends. And that's what makes life worthwhile.

H. (Germany): Well, I think you have to be very clear in your own mind about that. You need to radiate ability, you can't look insecure. You have to be able to ask questions without worrying about whether the question's silly or not. You need to radiate self-confidence, you need to be thinking all the time: I'm going to go in that room and people are going to notice I'm there. If nobody notices me enter the room, I need to think about what I'm going to change so that they do. So the first thing is to set yourself clear goals and the second thing is not to let anyone get the better of you. Obstacles are there to be overcome. It's extremely important to remember that. You need a good sounding board. You need people who can give you a hand and sometimes help you overcome a hurdle. And you need feedback, you can't live without it. And that's very important to me with mentees, too.

A. (France): I'm talking about having options, keeping an open mind about working elsewhere. I moved to Japan and then to China. Right now, Asia is where it's at. I'm going to stay in Asia. If Singapore ever goes into decline, I'll go wherever we need to go. So the first thing is, if you get stuck in Germany or somewhere, don't complain about it; move. You have to know what you want. The second thing is, you and your spouse have to be able to cooperate. I could never have done any of the things I've done if I hadn't had the husband I have. He goes to at least half of the parent evenings, he goes on at least half of the school trips, he goes on outings, he takes the children to at least half of their weekend activities. You need to find a partner who matches your expectations. If you know you want to work, find someone who respects that. I think, especially in Europe, some women want a man with a good job and a certain status. When they marry, they marry to get status.

M.C. (France): You have to have guts and you have to create your own opportunities. Which means being extremely resolute too. And of course, you have to do your job.

A. (France): You have to decide whether you're going to go on the offensive and accept people thinking you're a bitch, or whether you're going to let yourself be trampled underfoot. But if you decide to go on the offensive, then do it without hesitation. It's a personal choice. I don't think there's a one-size-fits-all solution. It's up to you to decide. But the most important thing is, it's really not good to think you're not good enough. And if you don't do something, you have to be honest with yourself and say, "I'm not doing that because I don't want to". But it's a big mistake to not do something because you think you can't. And you can change your image. People are quick to forget, so you can alter your image.

J. (China): It's important for top female executives to remember that you're a woman first and foremost. When I was working as a Chinese woman in Japan, I learned a lot about how Japanese people see the role of women. Sometimes I played up to it a bit. I would say, "I can't do that. Would you help me?" You can play-act from time to time, you don't always have to seem as strong as a man. It's perfectly okay to show that you're not a man. Maybe you're stronger on interpersonal skills, maybe you're stronger in how sensitive you are towards the people around you, the feel you have for things and so on. Sometimes it's okay to show weakness, then you can get people to help you. If a woman tries to show that she's as strong as a man, sometimes it actually makes things harder, it turns into a contest. Don't pick a fight with a member of the opposite sex, turn the fight into a compliment instead. Find your feminine strength. Be a woman.

D. (Russia): Well, we interact with so many people. We almost need some way of evaluating or analyzing who might be able to help us move forward. So ask yourself: "Who has the power?" If you feel like you can get along with them, then that's great, get in touch with them. Talk to them. Send them something. I've thought a lot about this. To be honest, I had to learn networking the hard way. I had to get to where the people with the power were, because I was in Russia, after all. I didn't want to moan about problems because I didn't want them to think I was weak. So when you want to have a discussion about an important business challenge, first you need to identify who the right person is to talk to. Pick out who the top people are.

B. (Germany): Well, organizations like Generation CEO. That isn't for everyone, of course. Then there's this European Women Association in Frankfurt. Find yourself a network, maybe the Baden-Baden Entrepreneurs' Talks. Establish your own little circle of advisors, a circle of confidants, your own personal company board of sorts. A sort of little company board of your own. Get people involved who can give you different types of advice. Think it through. What resources are at my disposal? Who do I know?

A. (France): It's a scientific fact that people like working with people who like them. People turn to people they know. Why is business full of men? Because men stick together and when they need someone for a job, they look for a man from within their own network. Women need to work on their relationships, including headhunters. Headhunters only know the people in their own network and they'll only recommend someone from within their own network. Women should help each other, support each other, teach each other, give each other opportunities, give each other visibility and so on. Every connection you make leads to another one. Networking.

D. (Russia): It's like starting to do the job you want before you get it. They have to be able to see you, it's all about being seen and believing you can do the job. They have to be able to see you. If there are several women who want to be the next director, start doing the work of the director before you've got the job. It gives people the feeling that you're responsible, you have a grand vision. Then when they're wondering, "Who are we going to hire for the job?", you've already done all the work. People trust you. They have to be thinking, "She's never stabbed anybody in the back and she's really helpful, and she's not just an employee. She's a fantastic partner. She can cooperate with the powerful men, as a partner she'll be respected in that job."

K. (Japan): I owe my current position to sponsoring, actually to networking. These people believed in me, they had confidence in me and pushed me forward and suggested me when an opportunity was being discussed. I wouldn't be where I am today without them. Then, find the right husband. I really think that's critical for women, it has been for me and I have seen it in the women around me as well. They all have the right partner who really supports them and who's happy to see them getting on in their careers. Not all men are like that in Japan. Then, you need to understand your own aspirations, your motivations, what is most important to you, because sometimes you just face so many challenges. When you ask yourself, "Why do I work? What do I want to leave behind, what mark do I want to leave behind?", you need to know the answer. You need to be able to remember that answer when things get tough and then it's easier to keep going when you've thought it through. It's especially important for Japanese women to be able to sell themselves and negotiate in terms of what they have to offer. It's just so important. Some women are hesitant because they don't like doing it. To be honest, I don't feel comfortable selling myself and negotiating on my own behalf, but if I think about who and what I represent, then I feel totally comfortable, not selling myself but selling my organization and my team. Negotiating on behalf of my organization is fine. I don't like doing it for myself, but when I think about my team, I feel much better about it. That's really important.

A. (China): Negotiate with your husband. Start a couple of years before you have children. Before you have a baby, if you want to continue your career the same as before, you need to spend plenty of time preparing your husband to accept the idea. For a couple of years beforehand.

D. (Russia): I've tried to summarize my recipe for a successful career. I think it's important to strike the right balance so people don't see you as a threat because you say the wrong thing at the wrong time or you're wearing the wrong facial expression. That upsets people. You have to be good at adapting. But at the same time, if you adapt too much, people will never see you as a leader. You have to gain the full confidence of the people making the decisions. My second point would be you have to have a sponsor or someone who thinks really highly of you. Choose people you think are great and who you get along with. You have to make yourself almost irreplaceable in their eyes. When they get promoted, they'll want you to join them. Because they trust you, to the extent that you'll take the blame when things go wrong. Because you take on their work even when you haven't been asked to. I might be a bit misogynistic, but I do also try to be realistic about what actually works. I don't think women should adopt this image of a ruthless leader like men do, because there are still men at the very top and they're going to keep trying to knock you off your pedestal if you do that. So for a woman it's better to be seen as non-threatening. I think it's important to keep the balance between being supportive, non-threatening, trustworthy and strong.

Mn. (China): Stamina. That's extremely important. I think that's the main advantage women have over men. Because when we keep on insisting on something, we win in the end. I think it is important to continue doing sport. If you have to work long hours. I think a healthy body goes hand in hand with good performance at work and at home. You really have to stick with it and keep doing it. (laughs) What else? Maybe being lazy. If you feel comfortable in a job, you run the risk of staying there too long and getting into a rut. In reality you need to be a bit more proactive than that. Get out of your comfort zone. See other things."

Ax. (France): One thing, women need to figure out is what they want in life. What do you really want? Another thing I would tell women is that you have to stop feeling guilty. We have to stop feeling guilty. When I have a function, my husband comes home and spends time with the kids. When he has a function, I do the same. We have to stop feeling guilty. I mean, you can't always be at home. It's not going to work. You really have to stop feeling guilty just because you're a woman. I think it stops women from achieving their full potential.

K. (Germany): The difference between a good employee and an excellent employee is passion. So do a job you're passionate about. Be unaffected by the judgements of others, because first and foremost you have to feel good about yourself. Stay curious, get out of your comfort zone and take on new challenges from time to time.

Annex

Acknowledgments

It is thanks to the inspiration and support of numerous top managers, female and male, that I have been able to add new countries to the endeavor I began in my previous book, *How Chinese Women Rise*. For this book, I started my journey in Shanghai, traveled on to Cologne, headed back to Japan and from there continued on to Russia, before I finally settled into a lasting home in Paris. Based on the many recommendations I received, I succeeded in interviewing a large number of women as the basis for this book and used the results to explore the careers of women all over the world.

My special thanks go to all the women in senior management positions who generously offered me their time, gave me their trust and took part in this unique international investigation. We were all united by one desire: to share our experiences with other women pursuing management careers and to stand with them in solidarity.

Gundula Fichtler was my constant advisor and fiercest critic. As a multi-reader of specialist books, she brought in her perspective and support and encouraged me more than once. Ian Lawrance from Australia has always been on my side to help with the English version of the book and assist me with various English language challenges. He edited the English book and was tremendously engaged. I received support during this project from Professors Gregory Wegman and Samuel Mercier of the University of Burgundy. Christine Hesse, CEO and branding expert from Hesse Design, gave the Global Women Career Lab a distinct identity. Weidong Xu, a former managing director and board member in Germany, opened doors and established contact with a large number of Chinese women living and working in Europe and also established contact with a wonderful network of German women in management positions. In France, Muriel de Saint Sauveur and Claudia Wiesner supported me generously in my recruitment efforts. They stand as representatives of the many other women in Germany and France who helped me likewise. I also thank Mari Nogami and Kaoru Kano in Japan, who already played a pivotal role in my workshops while I was in Kobe. Eugeny Zegna, an entrepreneur and coach from Moscow, who took part in one of my coaching certification seminars in Shanghai, enabled me to build a network in Russia and many of his contacts there and proved enormously supportive. Shelley Shen, HR Director and Diversity Head at PAM-LAN-Institute Saint-Gobain APAC, continues to help me build links with China.

Finally, I would like to thank my children, Lara and Luc, my husband Jean-Luc and indeed my entire family, for the interest and enormous patience they showed while I was researching and writing this book.

Author's note

During my time as executive in Europe, I had the opportunity to observe, guide and support many women during their careers. Some advanced quickly, many disappeared from the scene once their children arrived, and still others "got stuck" in middle management. Later, I coached numerous women from many different nations in the course of their careers and explored with them more deeply the issues that preoccupied the female managers more than they did my male clients. The themes are similar all over the world, and yet they differ according to nationality, environment and culture. In my work as an executive coach and trainer, I have repeatedly noticed the self-confidence and aplomb with which a subset of women, regardless of nationality, rise to very senior corporate positions. I grew curious. What makes these women different from their female colleagues? Did they have a secret strategy for getting ahead? It was then that the idea was born of taking a closer look at the global phenomenon of women in top management. An idea that I had been cogitating on, discarding and then returning to for many years suddenly crystallized in my mind while I was running a coaching certification course for executives in Shanghai. Thus I began investigating the careers of women in top management.

With the help of the network I had established through my work as an executive coach and trainer, I was able to do the very thing that would have been a major hurdle for many researchers: I established contact with a large number of remarkable female executives, in five distinctly different leading economies, who were willing to contribute to my research and take part in long, qualitative interviews. The book began with the question: what factors had made it possible for these women to work their way up to board level? It quickly became clear to me that rather than comparing the women in my study with their male counterparts, I wanted to focus on their unique career paths and the experiences they had gained in their respective environments. The focus should be on women's careers from the perspective of female role models who had made it to the top echelons of organizations.

This book is the result of five years of research involving more than 110 top women executives from five countries, with careers in over 500 companies and in more than 20 countries. They agreed to become involved in my "Global Women Career Lab", as I decided to call my international research group, and to take part in detailed, exploratory, qualitative interviews. I have gained an abundance of insights from these women's accounts and am eager to pass this knowledge on to other women around the world, as well as to the men and women who support women in their careers – be it in business, politics or the community. The interviewees have achieved what many women all over the world are still striving to accomplish: to rise to the top of a company. The aim of this book is to pass on my interview partners' experiences.

The insights that I have gained on the subject have been borne along on a wave of solidarity and an intense desire to learn and to succeed.

Methodology at a glance: The Global Women Career Lab

The Global Women Career Lab is a unique international research project carried out in five countries from 2014 until 2020, in which a total of 110 women in executive positions at multinational companies participated. To date, women in senior management positions from five countries – France, Germany, Russia, Japan and China – have participated. The career paths of these women involve more than 500 companies worldwide and work was undertaken in over 21 countries.

All interviews, analysis and interpretation were carried out by the author herself, there were no other people performing the interviews. The University of Burgundy in France supervised the project technically. Methodologically, the empirical research took a qualitative, explorative approach that was based on the conceptual framework; the reference model was presented at the beginning of the book. The approach to research took the form of a multiple case study. The data collection instrument comprised semi-structured, problem-centered interviews and the analysis was based on qualitative, reductive content analysis following the Mayring approach.

Table 2 summarizes the individual elements that make up the "blueprint" for this research:

Table 2: Methodology of the Global Women Career Lab.

Research questions	Theory-based
Conceptual framework	Developed from theory
Research methodology	Qualitative, conceptual framework-based, empirical, explorative
Research design	Multiple case studies
Data collection instrument	Semi-structured, problem-centered interviews (single person)
Sampling strategy	Theoretical sampling
Data collection process	How, where, transcription process
Analysis of data	Qualitative structured content analysis
Analysis of researcher's role	Open discussion about researcher's bias

The total number of interviewed women, 110, is big for a qualitative research project but does not allow generalizations to be made. Generalizations are not necessary for the purpose of the current research for this book as it does not aim to produce statistically representative results. However, quasi-statistical analyses were carried out in subcategories where it made sense to do so. Hence, it appears possible to relate the results to wider questions about the careers of female executives on the basis of the theoretical sampling process presented here. Moreover, this systematizing analysis is able to provide a meaningful contribution to current debate and provide stimulus for theory and practice going forward.

Participants in the research

Most of the 110 women selected for the Global Women Career Lab were between 45 and 55 years old, however, there are also some participants under 40 or over 60 years old. The youngest respondent was 32 years old and from China. The women over 60 came from China, Germany and France. This means that some representatives of Generation Y who have already achieved managerial positions are represented, as well as women who are close to retirement in China. The participants in the Global Women Career Lab represent a wide age range.

The companies in which the women work are primarily global businesses. In China, participants came from 26 multinational companies with headquarters in countries such as Germany, the USA and France. In Europe too, the participants came mainly from global companies. Four Chinese companies were also denoted as the employer. In Russia, state-owned companies as well as private and multinational companies were represented. It was important that the women chosen to take part in the research represented a broad range of sectors. Overall, the women worked in over 20 different sectors, with a focus on industry and service. The industry sector, for example, covered many different areas of business including automotive, pharmaceuticals, steel processing, household, food, consulting, fashion, travel, luxury goods, telecommunications, media and more.

The women for the lab were selected according to the definition of "female senior executive", which was formulated in advance. Theoretical sampling was used to ensure that the appropriate women were selected in keeping with the research questions to be covered. The sampling was driven by a separate definition of "women in top management". If you compare the different studies on women in management and statistics on how often women are represented in senior management positions, it is striking that there are internationally different interpretations of the term senior management and the underlying hierarchy levels. Some research on women in management concentrates on the highest position in a company, that is, the CEO, board member, president or general manager, as women are least represented in these roles worldwide. Other studies lack a specific definition of precisely what is meant by top or senior management. Furthermore, it needs to be understood whether multinational companies are taking a global or a local perspective, as this can result in completely different definitions of the term "senior management". It is also necessary to clarify whether a global or local view is assumed in multinational companies, which can lead to a completely different definition of the term senior management. Theoretical sampling in this study should ensure that the appropriate women were selected based on the research questions.

The following criteria were used in the selection.

First criterion: Only salaried women, and no women entrepreneurs, were considered for the research investigation. Some of these women had been temporarily self-employed during their careers. For this book, women in management were selected based on having broad decision-making power, having a high degree of responsibility for employees and/or budget, or operating at a high executive level in the company. Second criterion: The women's hierarchical position, as expressed in their job title. For the purposes of this study, "senior management" includes all local hierarchical levels from General Manager (GM) and President through to Senior Director. In HR terminology, this equates to Level 1, Level minus 1 and, in a few cases that conform to the underlying definition, Level minus 2. Accordingly, the following hierarchical titles were deemed to meet the selection criterion for the definition of "senior executive" used in this study: CEO, President, GM, Vice General Manager (VP-GM), Chief Financial Officer (CFO), Chief Operating Officer (COO), Vice-President (VP), Senior Director, Director. Women were interviewed regardless of whether they were responsible for a purely local role or held international responsibilities. Third and final criterion: The following areas were important for the selection of women: their freedom of decision making, the degree of influence on corporate strategy, personal responsibility, budget responsibility and the number of employees. This set of criteria primarily served to resolve the differences in the use of titles by different companies. With the exception of a few respondents, all women had employee responsibility at the time of the survey. The women without employee responsibilities held strategic functional roles, belonged to the management team of the company and/or held multiple executive responsibilities in the course of their careers.

Recruiting for the Global Women Career Lab

All participants for the Global Women Career Lab were recruited via professional contacts made by the author in the course of her work as executive coach and management trainer. Following the snowball principle, the participants in turn recommended other women. Contacts in China were identified via professional networks, including a board member at the German Chamber of Commerce and the owner of China's largest executive coaching provider. Most of the contacts in Germany came from a former Chinese managing director and supervisory board member who activated her network, which is aimed specifically at women who are aiming for board or supervisory board positions. In France, it was possible to set up a pyramid scheme in just three months, with different women opening doors as mentors to the study. The Japanese executives were also recruited from the author's former work contacts from her time as a management trainer in Japan. In Russia, the entry was made through a Russian entrepreneur, a participant of a coaching certification course which the author had led. In all five countries it was thanks to women and men in solidarity that these unique interviews could take place.

The success of the recruitment efforts can be attributed to several factors. One factor of definite importance was that the author was trusted by people she had met through her work as executive coach and management facilitator, which led to recommendations. Another related factor was the high quality of the recommendations made by people with good connections in Russia, France, China, Japan and Germany. These factors made contact and establishing a good working relationship easier. The framework of the doctorate made it easier to build trust when recruiting and in the important phase at the start of the interviews. Personality and "chemistry" certainly played a role as well. The fact that a woman with a corporate background was leading the research project and carrying out the interviews also made it easier to establish contact. A final, crucial factor was the women's solidarity, which made the large number of interviews possible.

Interviewing and method of analysis

All interviews were conducted by the author herself in the languages preferred by the participants, English, French or German, with interviews in English being the majority. The interviews had a length of two hours on average. The basis for each interview was the same open questionnaire, which was based on the model of the research, the FemCareer-Model. However, each interview was unique, as the open questionnaire allowed for the unique particularities of each woman and her career experience. Most of the interviews in China and France took place in the women's offices, almost in the normal work environment. The remaining interviews were conducted via Skype or telephone. From her work as an executive coach, the author was used to working using direct or indirect means of contact. It was possible to ensure that a trustful and open interview situation was achieved in both cases. The empirical study was methodically structured as a qualitative, empirical, exploratory study that built on the conceptual reference model already described, the "FemCareer-Model". The analysis of the data followed the qualitative content analysis methodology. For further details on the examination methodology, please refer to the original doctoral thesis of part one of the research. (Al-Sadik-Lowinski, 2017).

The research model: The FemCareer-Model

There are many determinants of women's careers and that these determinants can affect the success of a woman in her managerial career in a number of ways. For the Global Women Career Lab, it was necessary to find an approach that took as much account as possible of the topic's complexity, while also structuring the findings in a digestible and understandable form. The FemCareer-Model described in Figure 1 forms the "roadmap" for the reader and shows the perspective that is adopted in the book. The model does not claim to be complete and some of the determinants mentioned earlier are not considered here, or only to a minimal extent. The organizational perspective and associated influences are only examined in passing in this model, and only in cases where they emerge out of the women's descriptions. As a result, the following overview covering the influences on the careers of women in management in Russia, Germany, France, Japan and China is a selection based on the specific perspective of this model.

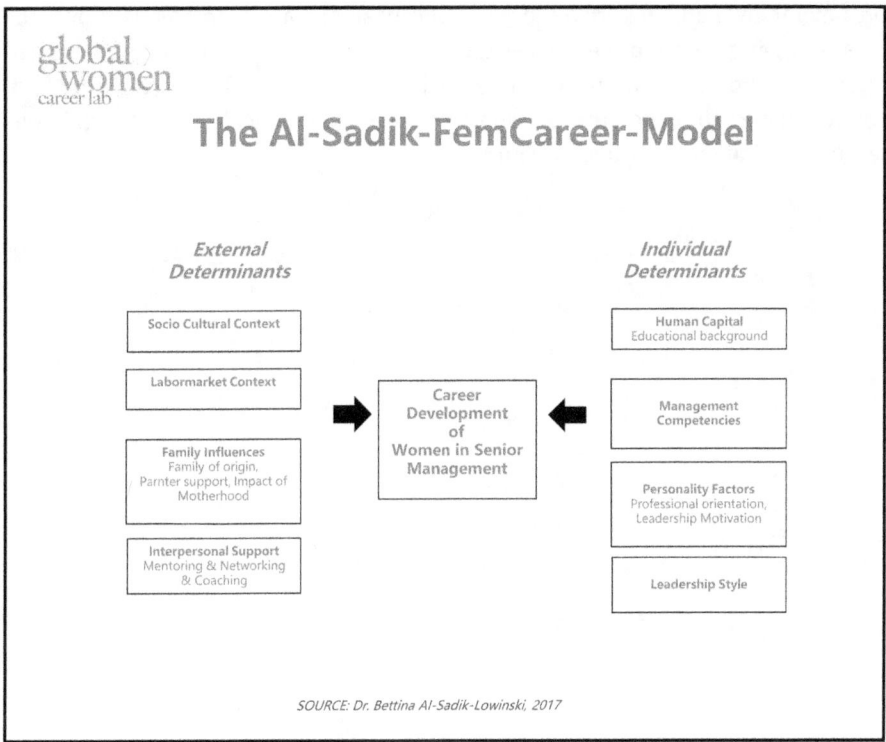

Figure 1: The FemCareer-Model.
(for citations: "Al-Sadik-Lowinski-FemCareer-Model", 2017)

The Female Career Model focuses on external determinants and individual influences on the careers of female senior executives that result in different career paths and plans. These paths and patterns are regarded as being tangibly affected – to a greater or lesser extent – by determinants. They have both descriptive and evaluative components.

The external influences are ones that impact on women's careers from the outside in the form of overarching conditions. They derive from the cultural traditions of society, the labor market situation, specific aspects of gender policy, familial situations and interpersonal support. Interpersonal support refers to personal support systems such as networks, mentors and supportive superiors. Taken together, these factors form the external framework within which the women's careers unfold.

The individual influences are made up of aspects that are specific to the participants, grounded in their personal backgrounds and personalities, and linked to their career paths. They include their educational backgrounds, particular skills, aspects of their personalities that are relevant to their careers and their specific leadership styles. Career paths are associated with individual assessments of career success, which can be expressed through various factors, such as individuals' personal level of satisfaction and the position they have achieved in an organization's hierarchy. Paths describe the particular positions a person has held over the course of their career and the choices they have made. The country context is essential to each "bin" of the territory of this model. The model is also informed by findings from the existing literature on women's careers and critical career determinants that are not limited to particular countries.

Bibliography

Adler, N. J., Izarelis, D.N. 1988. Women in management worldwide. New York: M. E. Sharpe.
Al-Sadik, B., 2017, More than half the sky? Descriptions and determinants of the career development of female Chinese senior executives working for multinational companies in China, Cuvillier.
Al-Sadik, B., 2018, How Chinese women rise, Cuvillier.
Ambafrance, Frankreich in Deutschland, Französische Botschaft in Berlin, https://de.ambafrance.org/Statistik-und-Fakten-zur-Gleichstellung-der-Frauen-in-Frankreich (Retrieved October 11, 2029).
Ankersen, W., Berg, C. 2018. Schlusslicht Deutschland, Allbright Stiftung.
Ardichvili, A., Gasparishivili, A., 2001. Human resource development in an industry in transition, Human Resource Development International, Vol. 4, No. 1, pp. 47–63.
Aoki, M., 2015, Japan drastically lowers its goal for female managers in government and private sector, Japan Times, https://www.japantimes.co.jp/news/2015/12/25/national/japan-drastically-lowers-its-goal-for-female-managers-in-government-and-private-sector/#.X0pXfS1XZBw (retrieved, February 13, 2020)
Arthur, M. B., Hall, D. & Lawrence, B. S. 1996. Handbook of career theory. (5th ed.). Melbourne: Cambridge University Press.
Arthur, M. B., Rousseau, D. M. 1996 and 2001. The boundaryless career. New York: Oxford University Press.
Ashwin, S., Yakubovich, V. 2005. Cherchez la Femme: Women as Supporting Actors in the Russian Labour Market, *European Sociological Review*, Vol. 21, No. 2, pp. 149–164.
Ashwin, S. 2002. The influence of the Soviet gender order on employment behaviour in contemporary Russia, Sociological Research, Vol. 41, No. 1, pp. 27–37.
Ashwin, S. and Lyktina, T. 2004, Men in crisis in Russia: the role of domestic marginalisation, Gender and Society, Vol. 18, pp. 189–206.
Ayman, R., Korabik, K. 2010. Leadership: Why Gender and Culture Matter, American Psychologist, Vol. 65, pp. 157–170.
Berghahn, S., 2011. Der Ritt auf der Schnecke, http://www.fu-berlin.de/sites/gpo/pol_sys/gleichstellung/Der_Ritt_auf_der_Schnecke/Ritt-Schnecke-Vollstaendig.pdf?1361541637 (Retrieved March 3, 2020).
Betz, N. E., Fitzgerald, L. F. 1987. The career psychology of women. Academic Press.
Blanchard, D. A., Warnecke, T., Button, L. S., Italiana, V., Demirbas, G., Auth, D., & Murphy, M. P. 2010. Women in China, between Confucius and the market. https://scholarship.rollins.edu/as_facpub/225 (retrieved April 15, 2016)
Black, J.S., Morrison, AJ.,. 2014. The global leadership challenge, Routledge, N.Y.
Böhme, I., Die da drüben, Kapitel 7 DDR, Rotbuch, 1982.
Bollinger, D. 1994 The four cornerstones and three pillars in the "House of Russia" Management System, Journal of Management development, Vol, 13, No. 2, pp. 49–55, MCB.
Boll-Paievskaya, D. 2009. Russische Frauen, Innen und Außenansichten. Books on Demand.
Borchard, M, Henry-Huthmacher, C., Merkle T., Konrad Adenauer Stiftung, KAS, Eltern unter Druck, 2008, https://www.kas.de/de/einzeltitel/-/content/eltern-unter-druck1 (Retrieved February 20, 2020).
Bourdieu, P. 1982. Die feinen Unterschiede, Kritik der gesellschaftlichen Urteilsfähigkeit. Frankfurt am Main, Suhrkamp, p. 164.
Bowen, C.-C., Wu, Y., Hwang, C. & Scherer, R. F. 2007. Holding up half of the sky? Attitudes toward women as managers in the people's republic of China, The International Journal of Human Resource Management, Vol. 18, pp. 268–283.

Budig, M. J., Misra, J., & Boeckmann, I. 2012. The motherhood penalty in cross-national perspective: The importance of work-family policies and cultural attitudes, Social Politics: International Studies in Gender, State & Society, Vol.19, No. 2, pp. 163–193.

Bundesministeriums für Familie, Senioren, Frauen und Jugend. 2019. 25 Jahre deutsche Einheit, Gleichstellung und Geschlechtergerechtigkeit in Ostdeutschland und Westdeutschland, https://www.bmfsfj.de/blob/93168/8018cef974d4ecaa075ab3f46051a479/25-jahre-deutsche-einheit-gleichstellung-und-geschlechtergerechtigkeit-in-ostdeutschland-und-westdeutschland-data.pdf (Retrieved March 11, 2020)

Burke, R. J. &McKeen, W. 1990. Mentoring in organizations: Implications for women, Journal of Business Ethics, Vol. 9, pp. 317–332.

Calla, C. 2019. Parität ist aus der französischen Politik nicht mehr wegzudenken, Helene Weber Kolleg, Frau Macht Politik, EAF, https://www.100-jahre-frauenwahlrecht.de/themendossiers/paritaet/frankreich-paritaet-in-der-politik/ (Retrieved March 3, 2020).

Catalyst. 2016: The world databank 2016: Labor force participation rate, female, estimated China 2014, http://www.catalyst.org/knowledge/women-workforce-china (Retrieved February 20, 2020).

Cattell, R. B. 1986. The 16 PF personality structure and Dr. Eysenck, Journal of Social Behavior and Personality, Vol. 1, No. 2, p. 153.

Caligiuri, P. M., Cascio, W. F. 1998. Can we send her there? Maximizing the success of Western women on global assignments, Journal of World Business, Vol. 33, No. 4, pp. 394–416.

Chen, C. C., Yu, K. C., & Miner, J. B. 1997. Motivation to manage: A study of women in Chinese state-owned enterprises, The Journal of Applied Behavioral Science, Vol. 33, No. 2, pp. 160–173.

Chen, F., Liu, G. & Mair, C. 2011. Intergenerational ties in context: Grandparents caring for grandchildren in China, Social Forces, Vol. 90, No. 2, pp. 571–594.

Cheung, F. M., Halpern, D. F. 2010. Women at the top: Powerful leaders define success as work and family in a culture of gender, American Psychologist, Vol. 65, pp. 182–193.

Chin, C. O., Gu, J., & Tubbs, S. L. 2001. Developing global leadership competencies. Journal of Leadership & Organizational Studies, Vol. 7, No. 44, pp. 20–31.

China Daily, September 13, 2013. Chinadaily.com.cn. Source: State Administration for Industry and Commerce (Retrieved February 12, 2017).

China Daily, Xinhuet, March 6, 2001. chinadaily.com.cn (Retrieved April 20, 2017).

Chirikova, A. E., Krichevaskai, O. N. 2002. The woman manager, Sociological Research, Vol. 41, No. 1, pp. 38–54.

Coler, R., & Giersberg, S. 2009. Das Paradies ist weiblich: eine faszinierende Reise ins Matriarchat, Berlin, Kiepenheuer.

Colgan, F., McKearney, A., & Bokovikova, E. 2014. Employment and diversity management in a Russian context. In: Klarsfeld, L., Booysen, A.E. & Ng, E., Handbook of Diversity Management, 2014, Business 2014

Cooke, F. L. 2012. Human resource management in China: New trends and practices. London, UK: Routledge.

Credit Suisse Research Institute. 2014. Table 1: Percentage of women on boards by country. The CS Gender 3000: Women in senior leadership: p. 8.

Davidson, M. L., Burke R. J. 2016. Women in Management Worldwide, www.taylorfrancis.com.

Devillard, S., Graven, W., Lawson, E., Paradise, R., & Sancier-Sultan, S. 2012, Women Matter 2012. Making the Break through. McKinsey & Company.

Du, X. 2016. Does Confucianism reduce board gender diversity? Firm-level evidence from China. Journal of Business Ethics, Vol. 136, No. 2, pp. 399–436.

Eagly, A., Carli, L. 2007. Through the labyrinth – the truth about how women become leaders. Boston, MA: Harvard Business School Press.

European Women on Boards, EWOB, Gender diversity index. 2019. https://europeanwomenonboards.eu/wp-content/uploads/2020/01/Gender-Equality-Index-Final-report-vDEF-ter.pdf (Retrieved February 18, 2020).

Farrell, D., Grant, A. 2005, China's looming talent shortage, McKinsey Quarterly, Vol. 5, pp. 70–79.

Fietze, S., Holst, E., & Tobsch, V. 2011. Germany's next top manager: Does personality explain the gender career gap? Management revue, pp. 240–273.

Fong, M. S. 1993. The role of women in rebuilding Russian economy, elibrary.worldbank.org.

Frank, E. J. 2001. Chinese students' perceptions of women in management: will it be easier? Women in Management Review, Vol. 16, pp. 316–324.

Fraser, N. 1992. Revaluing French feminism: critical essays on difference, agency and culture, in Fraser, N. and Bartky, S. (Eds), French Feminism, Indiana University Press, Bloomington, IN.

Funken C. 2015. "Der Wirtschaft gehen relevantes Erfahrungswissen und exzellente Kompetenzen verloren", in Welpe I., Brosi P., Ritzenhöfer L., Schwarzmüller T. (eds), Auswahl von Männern und Frauen als Führungskräfte. Springer Gabler, Wiesbaden.

Galetti, N., Wissmann, N. K. 2019. Französische Frauen in der Politik, Parität und Patriarch, Adenauer Stiftung.

Ganrose, C. S., 2007, Gender difference in career perception in the People's Republic of China. Career Development International, Vol. 12, pp. 9–27.

Ganrose, C. S. (Ed.). 2005. Employment of women in Chinese cultures: Half the sky. Cheltenham, UK and Northampton, MA: Edward Elgar.

Gerhard, U. 2010. Die staatlich institutionalisierte "Lösung" der Frauenfrage. Zur Geschichte der Geschlechterverhältnisse in der DDR, in Hartmut Kaelble u. a. (Hrsg.): Sozialgeschichte der DDR, Stuttgart 1994, pp. 383–403.

Gorbachow, M. 1987. Perestroika: New thinking for Our Country and the World. London: Collins Publishing.

Goskomstat, Statistikamt der Russischen Föderation, www.gks.ru/free_doc/2006/b06_13/04-01.htm; www.gks.ru/free_doc/2007/b07_11/05-01.htm; www.gks.ru/bgd/free/b07_00/IssWWW.exe/Stg/d06/80.htm; www.gks.ru/bgd/free/b07_00/IssWWW.exe/Stg/d100/8-0.htm (Retrieved October 10, 2019).

Gournay, Marie le Jars de, (1622) On the equality of men and women, in: Desmond, M. C., (2013) The equality of sexes. Three feminists of the seventheenth century, Oxford press, pp. 220 and in: Beitz, U., Neue Zürcher Zeitung, 2016, https://www.nzz.ch/feuilleton/marie-de-gournay-eine-intellektuelle-in-der-fruehen-neuzeit-ueber-die-schwierigkeit-klug-sein-zu-duerfen-ld.89935 (retrieved January 16, 2020)

Gunkel, M., Lusk, E. J., Wolff, B., & Fank, Li. 2007. Gender-specific effects at work: An empirical study of four countries, Gender, Work & Organization, Vol. 4, pp. 56–79.

Gvozdeva, E. S., Gerchikov, V. L. 2002, Sketches for a portrait of women managers, Sociological Research, Vol. 41, No. 1, pp. 55–68.

Halpern, D. F., Cheung, F. M. 2008. Women at the top: Powerful leaders tell us how to combine work and family. New York: Wiley Blackwell.

Harden, J. 2001 Mother Russia at work: gender divisions in the medical profession, European Journal of Women's Studies, Vol. 8, No. 2, pp. 181–99.

Hartmann M. 2002. Leistung oder Habitus? in Bittlingmayer U.H., Eickelpasch R., Kastner J., Rademacher C. (eds), Theorie als Kampf?. VS Verlag für Sozialwissenschaften, Wiesbaden.

Hassenkamp, M. 2019. Paritätsgesetz in Frankreich, Junge Frauen werden durch junge Frauen ersetzt, Spiegel, 8.03.2019, https://www.spiegel.de/politik/ausland/paritaet-ist-frankreich-ein-vorbild-fuer-deutschland-a-1256355.html (Retrieved April 24, 2020).

Hayes, C. 1998. World class learning, Black Enterprise, Vol. 28, No. 10, pp. 85–89.

Helwig, G. 1982. Frau und Familie in beiden deutschen Staaten, Wissenschaft und Politik. Köln.

Henn, M. 2012. Die Kunst des Aufstieges: Was Frauen in Führungspositionen kennzeichnet. Frankfurt/Main: Campus.

Herbert W. Hildebrandt, Jinyun Liu. 2006. Chinese women managers: A comparison with their U.S. and Asian counterparts, Human Resource Management, Vol. 27, No. 3, pp. 291–314.

Herve, F. 1995. Französische Frauen, Via Regia, Blätter für internationale kulturelle Kommunikation, H 24.

Hille, B. 1985. Familie und Sozialisation in der DDR. Springer

Hofstede, G. 1998. The cultural construction of gender,iIn G. Hofstede (Ed.), Masculinity and feminity: The taboo dimension of national culture, pp. 75–105. Thousand Oaks, CA: Sage.

Holst, E., Busch-Heizmann, A., & Wieber, A. 2001. Führungskräfte-Monitor 2015. Update, 2013.

Hossiep, R., Paschen, M. 2003. Das Bochumer Inventar zur berufsbezogenen Persönlichkeitsbeschreibung: BIP. Hogrefe, Verlag für Psychologie.

Hunt, C. M., Crozier, S. E. 2011. Women in Management in Russia, In: Davidson, M.J., Burke, R.J., 2011, Women in Management Worldwide, Gower

International Labour Organization, IOL 2017. Women in business and in management, Gaining momentum in Eastern Europe and Central Asia, Geneva, https://www.ilo.org/wcmsp5/groups/public/-ed_dialogue/-act_emp/documents/publication/wcms_624225.pdf (Retrieved March 12, 2020).

International Monetary Fund. 2015. World Economic outlook, www.imf.org/external/pubs/ft/weo/2015/02/ (Retrieved March 5, 2020).

Inter-Parliamentary Union, IPU, 2019, https://data.ipu.org/women-ranking?month=8&year=2019, (retrieved march 12, 2020)

Iwao, S., 1992, the Japanese women, Tradition image and changing reality, The Free Press

Judge, T. A., Piccolo, R. F. 2004. Transformational and transactional leadership: a meta-analytic test of their relative validity. Journal of applied psychology, Vol. 89, No. 5 p., 755.

Kaibara, E., 2010, Onna Daigaku, A Treasure Box of Women's Learning. Gardners Books

Kaminski, M., Paiz, J. 1984. Japanese women in management. Where are they? Human Resource Management, Wiley.

Kay, R. 2001, Liberation from emancipation? Changing discourses of women's employment in soviet and post-Soviet Russia, Journal of Communist Studies and Transition Politics, Vol. 18, pp. 51–71.

Kirchmeyer, C. 1998. Determinants of managerial career success: Evidence and explanation of male-female differences, Journal of Management, Vol. 24, pp. 673–692.

Korabik, K. 1994. Managerial women in the People's Republic of China: The long march continues, in N. J. Adler & D. N. Israeli (Eds.), Competitive frontiers: Women managers in the global economy, pp. 114–126. Cambridge, MA: Blackwell.

Krasilnikova, O. 2013. Fokus Russland: Gesellschaftliche Gleichstellung der Geschlechter ist eine Utopie: Interview mit Dr. Oxana Krasilnikova, Dozentin am Lehrstuhl für Politikwissenschaft der Kazan Federal University, Zur Situation von Frauen in Russland.

Krone-Schmalz, G. 1992. In Wahrheit sind wir stärker, Frauenalltag in der Sowjetunion, Fischer.

Lepine, I. 1992. Making their way in the organization: women managers in Quebec. Women in Management Review, Vol. 7, No. 3, pp. 17–21.

Lewis, L. 2015. Japan: Women in the workforce, Financial Times, https://www.ft.com/content/60729d68-20bb-11e5-aa5a-398b2169cf79 (Retrieved April 22, 2020).

Li, C. 2000. Confucianism and feminist concerns: Overcoming the Confucian "gender complex". Journal of Chinese Philosophy, Vol. 27, pp. 187–199.

Liang, Z., Zhondong, M. 2004. China's floating population: New evidence from the 2000 census. Population and Development Review, Vol 30, pp. 467–488.

Linz, S. J. 1996. Gender differences in the Russian labour market, Journal of Economic Issues, Vol. 30, No. 1, pp. 161–186.

Liu, Xiaolang. 2014. The situation of women in China and implications for female careers. Presentation at Salon Yongfu, German Consulate, Shanghai.

Lyness, K. S., Thompson, D. E.. 2000. Climbing the corporate ladder: Do female and male executives follow the same route? Journal of Applied Psychology, Vol. 85, pp. 86–101.

Mainiero, L. A., Sullivan, S. E. 2005. Kaleidoscope careers: An alternate explanation for the "opt-out" revolution. The Academy of Management Executive, Vol. 19, No. 1, pp. 106–123.

Mayrhofer, W., Meyer, M. & Steyrer, J. 2005, Macht? Erfolg? Reich? Glücklich? Einflussfaktoren auf Karrieren. Wien: Linde Verlag.

McClelland, D. C., Bovatzis, R. E. 1982. Leadership motive pattern and long-term success in management, Journal of Applied Psychology, Vol. 67, pp. 737–743.

McKinsey, Mai. 2002. Perspektive Deutschland- Auswertung zu Müttern und Kinderbetreuung.

McKinsey 2012. Women matter, https://www.mckinsey.com/~/media/McKinsey/Business%20Functions/Organization/Our%20Insights/Women%20matter/Women_matter_mar2012_english%20(1).ashx (Retrieved January 13, 2019).

Melamed, T. 1996. Career success: An assessment of a gender-specific model, Journal of Occupational and Organizational Psychology, Vol. 69, pp. 217–242.

Metcalfe, D., Afanassieva, M. 2005. The woman question? Gender and management in the Russian Federation, Women in Management, Vol. 20, pp. 429–445.

Metcalfe, B. D., Linstead, A. 2003. Gendering teamwork: rewriting the feminine, Gender Work and Organization, Vol. 19, No. 1, pp. 94–119.

Miner, J. B., Chen, C. & Yu, K. C. 1991. Theory testing under adverse conditions: Motivation to manage in the People's Republic of China. Journal of Applied Psychology, Vol. 76, pp. 343–349.

Mollman, S. 2015. Japan cuts its target for women in leadership positions from 30% to 7%, Quartz, https://qz.com/567026/japan-cut-its-target-for-women-in-leadership-positions-from-30-to-7/ (Retrieved April 22, 2020).

Monousava, G. 1996. Gender differentiation and industrial relations, in Clarke, S. (Ed.), Conflict and Change in the Russian Industrial Enterprise, Cheltenham: Edward Elgar.

Nemeto, K. 2016. Too few women at the top- the persistence of inequality in Japan, Cornell University Press

Neubrand, A. 2009. Frauen in Führungspositionen- Ein Vergleich zwischen Deutschland und Frankreich. Diplomica.

Noland, M., Moran, T. & Kotschwar, B. 2016. Is Gender Diversity Profitable? Evidence from a Global Survey, Petersen Institut for International Economy.

Opora rusii, https://mdz-moskau.eu/warum-russland-keine-frauenquote-braucht/ (Retrieved May 5, 2020).

O'Neill, D. A., Hopkins, M. M. 2013. Patterns and paradoxes in women's careers, in W. Patton (Ed.), Conceptualising women's working lives: Moving the boundaries of discourse, pp. 63–79. Rotterdam et al.: Sense Publishers.

Patterson V. 1997. Breaking the Glass-Ceiling: What's holding women back? Wall Street Journal, 14 December 1997.

Pizan, C. de, Le livre de la cité des dames, 1405, in Forhan, K. L. (2002) The Political Theory of Christine Pizan. Burlington, Ashgate.

PWC. 2013. Spotlight on Russia – Women leaders in Russian businesses https://pwc.blogs.com/gender_agenda/2013/08/spotlight-on-russia-women-leaders-in-russian-business.html (Retrieved March 22, 2020).

Powell, G. N. 2011, Women and men in management. (4th ed.). Los Angeles: Sage.

Puffe, S., Carthy, D. J., Naumov, A. I. 1997. Russian managers belief about work: Beyond the stereotypes, Journal of Business, Elsevier.

Ragins, B. R. 1997. Diversified, mentoring relationships in organizations: A power perspective. The Academy of Management Review, Vol. 22, pp. 482–521.

Rastetter, D., Cornils, D. 2012. Networking: aufstiegsförderliche Strategien für Frauen in Führungspositionen, Gruppendynamik und Organisationsberatung, Vol. 43, No. 1, pp. 43–60.

Regnet. R. 2017. Frauen ins Management - Chancen, Stolpersteine und Erfolgsfaktoren. Göttingen, Hogrefe

Reiners, F. 2008. Networking in Organisationen, in O. Neuberger (Ed.), Schriftenreihe Organisation & Personal, Bd. 19. München: Hampp Verlag.

Reischauer, E.O., 2020, Japan, Story of a Nation. McGraw-Hill Professionals

Resch, Katharina. 2014. Ungleiche Karrieren. Erklärungsansätze für den Einfluss der sozialen Herkunft auf Karrieren. Karriereverlaufe in Forschung und Entwicklung: Bedingungen und Perspektiven im Spannungsfeld von Organisation und Individuum: 34.

Reuter, S. 2003. Frankreich: Die vollzeitberufstätige Mutter als Auslaufmodell, Politik und Zeitgeschichte, Kapitel 4, Familienpolitische Maßnahmen im Dienst der Arbeitsmarktpolitik in den neunziger Jahren, Bundeszentrale für politische Bildung.

Rittner, M. 2001. Zivilgesellschaft und Gender-Politik in Russland, Frankfurt: Campus.

Rosner, J. B. 1990. Ways women lead: The command-and-control leadership style association with men is not the only way to succeed. Harvard Business Review, Vol. 68, No.6, pp. 119–125.

Rosinski, P. 2003. Coaching across cultures: New tools for leveraging national, corporate, and professional differences. London: Nicholas Brealey Publishing.

Rump J., Eilers, S. 2017. Auf dem Weg zur Arbeit 4.0, Heidelberg.

Rzhanitsyna, L. 2000. Working women in Russia at the end of the 90s, Problems of Economic Transition, Vol. 43, No. 7, pp. 68–86.

Sanchez-Schmidt, M. T. 2013. Au Coeur des femmes. Talia.

Sandberg, S. 2013. Lean in: Women, work, and the will to lead. Random House.

Schein, V. E., Mueller, R., Lituchy, T.& Liu, J. 1996. Think manager – Think male: A global phenomenon? Journal of Organizational Behavior, Vol. 17, pp. 33–41.

Schellhorn, H. 2014. Welche Auswirkungen hat die Erwerbstätigkeit von Müttern auf die Sozialisation ihrer Kinder.

Sickinger, C. 2005. Französische Familienpolitik – ein Vorbild für Deutschland?, Frankreichinfo 4/2005, Friedrich-Ebert-Stiftung.

Sperling, V. 1999. Organising Women in Contemporary Russia: Engendering Transition. Cambridge University Press, Cambridge.

Standing, G. 1994. The changing patterns of women in Russian industry, World Development, Vol. 22. No. 2, pp. 271–284.

Stanford, J. H., Oates, B.R. & Flores, D. 1995. Women's leadership styles: a heuristic analysis. Women in Management Review, Vol. 10, pp. 9–16.

Stockmann, N., Bonney, N., Sheng, X.W. 1995. Women's work in the east and West: The dual burden of Employment and Family Life, London: UCL Press Ltd.

Sturges, J. 1999. What it means to succeed: Personal conceptions of career success held by male and female managers at different ages, British Journal of Management, Vol. 10, pp. 239–252.

Süssmuth-Dyckerhoff, C., Wang, J. & Chen, J. 2012. Women matter: An Asian perspective – harnessing female talent to raise corporate performance. McKinsey.

Tagscherer, U. 1999. Mobilität und Karriere in der VR China – Chinesische Führungskräfte im Transformationsprozess. Heidelberger Geographische Arbeiten, Geographisches Institut der Universität Heidelberg. Heidelberg: Ruprecht-Karls-Universität Heidelberg.

Tan, J. 2008. Breaking the "bamboo curtain" and the "glass ceiling": the experience of women entrepreneurs in high-tech industries in an emerging market, Journal of Business Ethics, Vol. 80, No. 3, pp. 547–564.

Tatli, A., Vassiopoulou, J., & Özbilgin, M. 2013. An unrequited affinity between talent shortages and untapped female potential: The relevance of gender quotas for talent management in high growth potential economies of the Asia Pacific region, International Business Review, Vol. 22, pp. 539–553.

Temkina, A., Zdravomslova, E. 2003. Gender studies in post-soviet society: Western frames and cultural differences, Studies in East European Thought, Vol. 55, No. 1, pp. 51–61.

Terri R. Lituchy. 1999. Japanese Women in the Workplace, Restructuring Japanese Business for Growth, pp. 209–219,

Tharenou, P., Latimer, S. & Conroy, D. 1994. How do you make it to the top? An examination of influences on women's and men's managerial advancement. The Academy of Management Journal, Vol. 37, pp. 899–931.

The World Economic Forum. 2015.The global gender gap report 2015, pp. 140–141.

The World Economic Forum. 2017.The global gender gap report 2017.

Thornton, G. 2014. Women in Business: From classroom to boardroom. Grant Thornton International Business Report.

Thornton, G. 2015, 2017, 2018. Women in Business. Grant Thornton International Business Report.

Tucker, M. F., Bonial, R., Vanhove, A., & Kedharnath, U. 2014. Leading across cultures in the human age: an empirical investigation of intercultural competency among global leaders. SpringerPlus, 3.

United Nations. 2000. Convention on the Elimination of Discrimination Against Women: Russian Federation, Fifth Periodic Report, UN, Washington, DC.

Vogel, C. 2000. Einstellungen zur Frauenerwerbstätigkeit. Ein Vergleich von Westdeutschland, Ostdeutschland und Großbritannien. Potsdamer Beiträge zur Sozialforschung.

Wang, Z. 1997. Maoism, Feminism and the UN conference on women. Women's studies research in contemporary China, Journal of Women's history, Vol. 8, No. 4, pp. 126–153.

Ward Howell, Succession in Russian Businesses. 2014. https://www.wardhowell.com/upload/iblock/560/5602e844aa1b05281c2b68e7b1bfd726.pdf (Retrieved February 3, 2020).

Wegener, A., Lippert, I. 2004. Studie Familie und Arbeitswelt – Rahmenbedingungen und Unternehmensstrategien in Großbritannien, Frankreich und Dänemark, Memeto, S. 51–56 and 83–84

Whiston, S. C., Keller, B. K. 2004. The influences of the family of origin on career development a review and analysis, The Counseling Psychologist, Vol. 32, No. 4, pp. 493–568.

White, B. 1995. The career development of successful women, Women in Management Review, Vol.10, pp. 4–15.

Wiegel, M. 2018. Die kleinere Hälfte, https://www.faz.net/aktuell/politik/ausland/in-frankreich-wird-die-paritaet-von-frauen-bislang-maessig-in-parteien-umgesetzt-15890863.html (Retrieved April 24, 2020).

Women's Forum for the Economy and Society, 2019, Global Conference, Paris.

Worldbank. 2018. https://data.worldbank.org/indicator/SP.DYN.TFRT.IN?locations=EU (Retrieved March 28, 2020).

Yuan, L. 2013. Traditional Chinese Thinking on HRM Practices: Heritage and Transformation in China. Springer.

Yuasa, M. 2005. Japanese Women in Management: Getting Closer to 'Realities' in Japan, Asia Pacific Business Review, pp. 195–211.

Zahidi, S. & Ibarra, H. 2010. The corporate gender gap report 2010. Geneva: The World Economic Forum.

Ziegler, Y. 1999. Japanische Frauen in Führungspositionen: Untersuchung des Karriereweges und der Motivation zum Aufstieg bei 25 Karrierefrauen, Personalwirtschaftliche Schriften, Bd.16, Hampp, München.

Zeit. 2018. Frankreich fehlen die Babies, Nr. 8/2018, https://www.zeit.de/2018/08/geburtenrate-frankreich-weniger-kinder (Retrieved April 12, 2020).